LEMON-AID

1978-1979 Edition

LEMON-AID

1978-1979 Edition

Phil Edmonston

David McKay Company, Inc.
New York

Library of Congress Cataloging in Publication Data
Edmonston, Louis Philippe.
  Lemon-aid.
  1. Automobile purchasing. 2. Consumer education. I. Title.
TL162.E324   629.22′22   76-62542
ISBN 0-679-51176-8
ISBN 0-679-51177-6 (pbk)

10 9 8 7 6 5 4 3 2 1

MANUFACTURED IN THE UNITED STATES OF AMERICA

Contents

●

Introduction
   WE ARE BEING TAKEN FOR A RIDE!, xi

   I. *New Cars: Haggle or Be Had,* 1
   WHERE TO BUY, 2; SELECTING THE RIGHT CAR, 3; PAYING THE RIGHT PRICE, 8; SIGNING THE CONTRACT, 9; THE PSEUDOEXPERTS, 13; SAFETY-RELATED DEFECTS, 16; NO "NEW" CARS, 19; PRODUCT CRITICISM: General Motors, 19; Ford Motor Company, 23; American Motors, 28.

   II. *Used Cars: Dealers and Double-Dealers,* 37
   WHY BUY A USED CAR, 37; WHEN TO BUY, 40; WHERE TO BUY, 41; WHAT TO BUY, 43.

   III. *The Car Repair Jungle,* 47
   SPECIALISTS, 48; INDEPENDENT NONSPECIALIZED GARAGES, 48; GAS STATIONS, 49; AUTOMOBILE DEALERS, 50; DICTIONARY OF DIRTY TRICKS, 51; REPAIR RACKETS: SELF-DEFENSE, 61.

   IV. *Legal Rights and Wrongs,* 66
   MISREPRESENTATION, 66; MISLEADING ADVERTISING AS TO CAR QUALITY, 72; MISLEADING ADVERTISING AS TO GAS MILEAGE (DEALER), 72; MISLEADING ADVERTISING AS TO "SUGGESTED RETAIL PRICE," 73; MISLEADING ADVERTISING AS TO GAS MILEAGE (DEALER AND MANUFACTURER), 73; DEFECTIVE USED-CAR LEMONS, 73; ODOMETER TAMPERING, 74; SOLD "AS IS," 74; WORTHLESS GUARANTEE, 74; FAULTY MANUFACTURE, 74; UNSAFE NEW CARS, 81; EXPERT WITNESSES, 86; THE RUSTPROOFING RACKET, 93; RUST HUCKSTERS IN '79, 101; IS RUSTPROOFING WORTHWHILE?, 102; DEFECT INVESTIGATION, 107.

   V. *The Art of Complaining,* 120
   THE ART OF EFFECTIVE COMPLAINING, 123; HOW TO START A CONSUMER GROUP, 124; CONSUMER PRESSURE TACTICS, 125; SMALL-CLAIMS COURT, 132; LAWSUIT MATERIALS, 135; WHERE TO GO FOR HELP, 138.

VI. *"Secret" Auto Warranty Extensions,* 146

DEFECTIVE GM TRANSMISSIONS, 146; FORD SE-
CRET WARRANTY EXTENSIONS, 149; CHRYSLER
PAINT WARRANTY EXTENDED, 149; CHRYSLER
VIBRATIONS, 150; WHAT TO DO? WARRANTY
COMPENSATION GUIDELINES, 151; FORD USA: SE-
CRET RUST WARRANTY, 158; DEFECTIVE FORD
COMPONENTS, 159; FORD 1974 MODEL PROBLEM
DESCRIPTION, 161; VOLKSWAGEN WARRANTY EX-
TENSIONS, 163.

VII. *Used-Car Ratings,* 175

USED-CAR PRICE, 175; FREQUENCY OF REPAIRS,
176; BODY RUSTING, 177; GAS MILEAGE, 177; TECH-
NICAL DATA, 177; GENERAL MOTORS: AREAS OF
PREMATURE RUSTING, 178; FORD: AREAS OF PRE-
MATURE RUSTING, 180; AMERICAN MOTORS:
AREAS OF PREMATURE RUSTING, 181; CHRYSLER:
AREAS OF PREMATURE RUSTING, 182; MILEAGE/
PRICE TABLE, 184; THE GAS MILEAGE FAIRYTALE,
185; "LEMON" USED-CAR PROFILES, 187; CONSUM-
ER GROUPS BLAST VEGA, 187; VOLVO: A MONU-
MENTAL DECEPTION, 190; VOLVO SAFETY HAZ-
ARD, 197; BRITISH LEYLAND, 200; A LEMON IS
BORN, 215; SAFETY HAZARDS, 216; PERFORMANCE
DEFECTS, 221; "THINGS THAT GO 'BUMP' IN THE
DARK," 222; CHRYSLER'S ANTICONSUMER ATTI-
TUDE, 224; THE DIESEL DILEMMA, 229; THE VAN
INVASION, 232; THE FOUR-WHEEL-DRIVE REVO-
LUTION, 235.

1970 MODELS, 241:

General Motors, 242: [Chevy II Nova, 242; Chevrolet (Full-
sized), 242; Camaro, 243; Pontiac Tempest, 244; Pontiac
(Full-sized), 245; Pontiac Firebird, 245; Pontiac Grand Prix,
246; Buick (Full-sized), 247; Oldsmobile (Full-sized), 248];
Ford Motor Company, 248: [Ford Maverick, 248; Ford Mustang, 249; Ford (Full-sized), 250; Ford Fairlane, 251; Mercury
Cougar, 252]; Chrysler Corporation, 252: [Plymouth Valiant,
252; Dodge Dart, 253; Plymouth Belvedere, 254; Dodge (Full-
sized), 255; Chrysler (Full-sized), 255]; American Motors, 256;
[AMC Hornet, 256; AMC Gremlin, 257; Ambassador, 257]

1971 MODELS, 259:

General Motors, 260: [Chevelle, 260; Vega, 260; Chevy II
Nova, 261; Chevrolet (Full-sized), 262; Pontiac Ventura II,
263; Pontiac Le Mans, 263; Pontiac (Full-sized), 264; Buick
(Full-sized), 265; Oldsmobile (Full-sized), 265]; Ford Motor
Company, 266: [Ford Pinto/Bobcat, 266; Ford Maverick, 267;
Ford Mustang, 268; Ford Torino/Montego, 268; Ford (Full-
sized), 269]; Chrysler Corporation, 270: [Plymouth Valiant,

270; Dodge Dart, 271; Plymouth Satellite, 271; Dodge (Full-sized), 272; Plymouth Fury, 273]; American Motors, 273: [AMC Hornet, 273; AMC Gremlin, 274; Ambassador, 275]

1972 MODELS, 276:

General Motors, 277: [Vega, 277; Chevy II Nova, 277; Chevelle, 278; Chevrolet (Full-sized), 279; Pontiac Ventura II, 280; Pontiac Le Mans, 280; Pontiac (Full-sized), 281; Buick (Full-sized), 282; Oldsmobile Delta 88, 282]; Ford Motor Company, 283: [Ford Pinto/Bobcat, 283; Ford Maverick, 284; Ford Mustang, 285; Ford Torino/Montego, 285; Ford (Full-sized), 286]; Chrysler Corporation, 287: [Plymouth Valiant, 287; Dodge Dart, 288; Plymouth Satellite, 288; Dodge (Full-sized), 289; Plymouth Fury (Full-sized), 290;]; American Motors, 291: [AMC Hornet, 291; AMC Gremlin, 291; Ambassador, 292]

1973 MODELS, 293:

General Motors, 294: [Vega/Astre, 294; Chevy II Nova, 294; Chevelle, 295; Chevrolet (Full-sized), 296; Pontiac Ventura II, 297; Pontiac (Full-sized), 297; Le Mans/Tempest, 298; Buick (Full-sized), 299; Oldsmobile Delta 88, 300]; Ford Motor Company, 300: [Ford Pinto, 300; Ford Maverick, 301; Ford Mustang, 302; Ford Torino/Montego, 303; Ford (Full-sized), 303]; Chrysler Corporation, 304: [Plymouth Valiant, 304; Dodge Dart, 305; Plymouth Satellite, 306; Dodge (Full-sized), 306; Plymouth Fury, 307]; American Motors, 308: [AMC Hornet, 308; AMC Gremlin, 308; Ambassador, 309]

1974 MODELS, 311:

General Motors, 312: [Vega/Astre, 312; Nova/Chevy II, 312; Chevelle, 313; Chevrolet (Full-sized), 314; Ventura, 315; Le Mans/Tempest, 315; Pontiac (Full-sized), 316; Buick (Full-sized), 317; Oldsmobile (Full-sized), 317]; Ford Motor Company, 318: [Pinto/Bobcat, 318; Maverick/Comet, 319; Mustang II, 320; Torino/Fairlane/Montego, 321; Ford (Full-sized), 321]; Chrysler Corporation, 322: [Valiant, 322; Dart, 323; Satellite/Belvedere, 324; Polara/Monaco (Full-sized), 325; Fury 325]; American Motors, 326: [AMC Hornet, 326; AMC Gremlin, 327; Ambassador, 328]

1975 MODELS, 329:

General Motors, 330: [Vega/Astre, 330; Nova, 330; Chevelle, 331; Chevrolet (Full-sized), 332; Ventura, 333; Le Mans/Tempest, 333; Pontiac (Full-sized), 334; Buick (Full-sized), 335; Oldsmobile (Full-sized), 336]; Ford Motor Company, 336: [Pinto/Bobcat, 336; Maverick/Comet, 337; Mustang II, 338; Torino/Fairlane/Montego, 339; Ford (Full-sized), 339; Granada/Monarch, 340]; Chrysler Corporation, 341: [Valiant, 341; Dart, 342; Satellite/Fury, 343; Cordoba/Charger, 343; Monaco (Full-sized), 344]; American Motors, 345: [AMC Hornet, 345; AMC Gremlin, 346; Pacer, 346]

1976 MODELS, 348:

General Motors, 349: [Vega/Astre, 349; Nova/Concours, 349; Chevelle, 350; Chevrolet (Full-sized), 351; Ventura, 351; Le Mans, 352; Pontiac (Full-sized), 353; Buick (Full-sized), 353; Oldsmobile (Full-sized), 354]; Ford Motor Company, 355: [Pinto/Bobcat, 355; Maverick/Comet, 355; Mustang II, 356; Torino/Montego, 357; Granada/Monarch, 357]; Chrysler Corporation, 358: [Valiant/Dart, 358; Fury, 359; Cordoba/Charger, 359; Monaco (Full-sized), 360]; American Motors, 361: [AMC Hornet, 361; AMC Gremlin, 361; Pacer, 362]

1977 MODELS, 363:

General Motors, 364: [Vega/Astre, 364; Nova/Concours, 364; Chevelle, 365; Chevrolet (Full-sized), 366; Ventura, 366; Le Mans, 367; Pontiac (Full-sized), 368; Buick (Full-sized), 368; Oldsmobile (Full-sized), 369]; Ford Motor Company, 370: [Pinto/Bobcat, 370; Maverick/Comet, 370; Mustang II, 371; Torino/LTD II, 372; Granada/Monarch, 372]; Chrysler Corporation, 373: [Fury, 373; Volare/Aspen, 374; Cordoba/Charger, 374; Monaco (Full-sized), 375]; American Motors, 376: [AMC Hornet, 376; AMC Gremlin, 376; Pacer, 377]

1978 MODELS, 378:

General Motors, 379: [Chevette/Acadian, 379; Monza/Skyhawk/Starfire/Sunbird, 379; Nova/Skylark, 380; Omega/Phoenix, 381; Camaro/Firebird, 382; Oldsmobile Cutlass, 383; Oldsmobile 98, 383; Le Sabre, 384; Monte Carlo/Grand Prix, 385; Century/Regal/Le Mans, 386; Malibu, 386; Cadillac Seville, 387; Corvette, 388]; Ford Motor Company, 389: [Fairmont/Zephyr, 389; Pinto/Bobcat, 389; Mustang II, 390; Granada/Monarch, 391; LTD/Thunderbird, 391; Versailles, 392; Continental, 393]; Chrysler Corporation, 394: [Omni/Horizon, 394; Volare/Aspen, 394; Fury, 395; Le Baron/Diplomat, 396; Cordoba/Charger, 397; Monaco, 397]; American Motors Division, 398: [Gremlin/Spirit, 398; Concord, 399; Pacer, 399; AMX, 400]

FOREIGN USED CARS 1970 TO 1978, 402; DOMESTIC VS. IMPORT, 403; BRITISH IMPORTED CARS, 404; BRITISH LEYLAND, 405: [MG, 409; Rover, 410; Austin, 411; Jaguar, 412; Triumph, 413]; FRENCH IMPORTED CARS, 415: [Citroen, 418; Peugeot, 421; Renault, 425]; GERMAN IMPORTED CARS, 428: [BMW, 430; Capri, 434; Mercedes-Benz, 438; Opel, 443; Volkswagen, 447; Audi, 454; Porsche, 459]; ITALIAN IMPORTED CARS, 462: [Alfa Romeo, 464; Fiat, 469]; JAPANESE IMPORTED CARS, 473: [Colt, 475; Datsun, 481; Honda, 487; Mazda, 491; Subaru, 495; Toyota, 500]; SWEDISH IMPORTED CARS, 508: [Saab, 512; Volvo, 517].

Preface

●

Car models that are criticized in this book are rated mainly by the volume and severity of reports of consumer groups in the United States, Canada, and Europe; government tests; internal automobile company documents; and personal inspections by the author.

Consumer complaints, which form the core of the book, have been contributed by the Automobile Protection Association and the Washington Center for Auto Safety from the more than two hundred thousand complaints registered by these groups during the past five years.

It is not this book's purpose to single out any one particular automobile manufacturer or to disparage the automobile industry. It is understood that all car makers have some quality control problems. The car ratings only try to put defects into a model-by-model perspective so the new- or used-car buyer will be guided as to the *probability* of certain defects occurring.

These ratings are certainly not infallible. It is just as difficult to make a car model a lemon as it is to manufacture reliable models. This is why confirmation of any suspected defects by an independent mechanic is a prerequisite to the rating of individual cars.

Acknowledgments

●

With grateful thanks to the staff at the Washington Center for Auto Safety and Walter Dartland, Consumer Advocate for Dade County, Florida, I dedicate this book.

PHIL EDMONSTON

Montreal
October 1978

Introduction

●

We Are Being Taken for a Ride!

The automobile industry is founded upon fraud, deception, and a wholesale disregard for public safety.

Environmental protection is treated with contempt by an auto industry that intentionally misleads government Environmental Protection Agency inspectors, conspires to delay the development of pollution control devices, and then invents Rube Goldberg type emission control systems like the catalytic converter. This "better idea" from the auto industry catches fire, emits a rotten-egg smell into the car's interior, requires more expensive unleaded gasoline, *increases* gas consumption by as much as twenty-five percent, and *still* pollutes the atmosphere, unless the vehicle is perfectly tuned. In 1908, Henry Ford sold the Model T at an average retail price of $950 to more than 10,607 automobile enthusiasts. Eight years later, Ford reduced the price to $360 and sold the same Model T to more than 472,350 new-car buyers.

Early Model T owners had spread the word that when one bought a Model T, "what you saw was what you got" —and the car-buying public liked what it saw.

Somewhere during the past 60 years, the automobile industry has cast aside the precepts of simplicity in design, stringent quality control and reasonable prices that were symbolized by early auto-industry pioneers such as Ford. Not only has the industry forgotten its humble beginnings but it has actually begun to turn against its supporters with a vengeance that makes the shark in *JAWS* look like a pet goldfish.

Today, many new-car buyers view the automobile industry with hostility and distrust. Wary consumers have learned that what you see you may not get, and what you don't see may get you.

There's some official sympathy for that view.

The public is once again spreading the word, because it does not like what it sees. Among the things it sees:

—New cars selling for $5,000 may cost five times as much if they are rebuilt with new parts.

—Low-speed "fender bender" accidents no longer damage the fender, but may require the complete replacement of the bumper for $200 to $500, according to the Washington-based Insurance Institute for Highway Safety.

Within the last decade more than 70 million cars that could explode, catch fire, lose a wheel, or suddenly careen out of control have been recalled by the manufacturers. Even the recall letters arouse consumer suspicions that the auto industry is uncaring.

Ford, for instance, found that the rear wheels of its 1972 Montego and Torino models could fall off as a result of defective axle bearings. It promised to install plates that would provide an audible warning of trouble in the rear end. Consumer protests soon forced the manufacturer to change its attitude and correct the defect.

Another car manufacturer found that some of its 1975 models could suddenly catch fire if left idling. Volkswagen sent owners of its Scirocco and Rabbit models a letter that advised them not to leave their cars idling and to avoid "parking the vehicle near combustible objects." Nowhere was the fire danger mentioned, however. This model, too, was later recalled.

Even if a new car is not recalled, there is still no guarantee that it will be a reliable means of transportation. During the past three years consumer protection agencies have been flooded with complaints from new car owners. Many of these performance-related complaints show that new cars are far more defect prone than cars made five years ago. Complaints concerning premature rusting, paint flaking at high speeds, and defective automatic transmissions seem to lead the list of new-car defects.

The catalytic converter that is used on many new model cars has also served as a means by which the auto industry punishes society for making it clean up the air. Consumers owning catalytic-converter-equipped cars have complained that their cars have caught fire, the exhaust emits a rotten-egg odor, unleaded gasoline is often unavailable or outrageously priced, and the converter itself may cost as much as $200 to replace.

As if this was not enough, one study shows that the catalytic converter may lower gasoline mileage by as much as 20 percent.

Besides making cars that are overpriced and underengineered, the automobile industry has rapidly won a reputation of deceiving its customers in several ways. Some of the better known practices are:

—The warranty merry-go-round. Warranties are made to sell cars, not fix them. In 1972, the auto industry began to cut back its five-year/50,000-mile warranty because it was costing too much. Obviously, cars were not being made to last five years. Rather than manufacture a more durable car, the industry drafted a new one-year/12,000-mile warranty.

At the same time, the auto industry built up secret warranty slush funds that paid for warranty work carried out after the normal warranty period had expired. Ford paid more than $22 million repairing cars that were subject to premature rusting, defective valve-guide wear, slipping automatic transmissions, and excessive oil consumption.

These extended warranty programs were kept secret by the automobile industry. Most consumers benefiting from them were told that it was a "goodwill" gesture on the part of the manufacturer.

No one told the public that these programs were established to compensate owners for breakdowns and damages caused by defective body and mechanical components.

"Goodwill," indeed!

It has been estimated by one industry source that General Motors' true warranty cost averages only $25 to $35 the first year an average new car is guaranteed. Toyota owners get about $45 to $50 worth of free repairs during the same warranty period.

—Gasoline mileage. New-car mileage claims grow more suspicious with each new model year. Mileage figures are generally extrapolated from American Environmental Protection Agency tests. These tests take well-maintained cars and subject them to mileage runs that approximate ideal conditions. Few motorists drive their cars with so many advantages working in their favor. So, new-car mileage claims can have a margin of error of 20 percent.

—Odometer rollbacks. Tampering with new- and used-car odometers has become a tradition for some of the largest car dealers in the United States.

Consumers are fed up with defective cars and deceptive practices. They are fighting back.

One irate woman writes: "I never thought I'd be writing to tell you and your colleagues that I, one lone consumer who felt she had been shafted by a large corporation, won the battle with that corporation. My rusty and unsafe 1972 fastback was bought outright by the dealer . . . and I am $1,300 richer. Just a few months back that same dealership said they wouldn't give $64 for my car.

"I think my $1,300 check is proof of what a lot of persistence, a lot of letter writing and a little picketing can do . . . provided, of course, that the complaint is a valid one.

"A quiet customer gets shafted every time . . . particularly by car companies."

One truck driver got so angry with his car dealer that he parked his truck in the dealer's driveway until his car was repaired.

Issy Barr painted his truck with lemons and parked in front of the dealership. When the dealer got an injunction against the truck and its lemons, Barr protested by spending a night in jail. Finally Barr and the dealer came to an out-of-court settlement.

United States federal and state warranty legislation has given little help to automobile "lemon" owners. Even the recently-enacted Magnuson–Moss Warranty Act, which was trumpeted by federal officials as the solution for consumers owning vehicles with irreparable defects, is now considered to be practically worthless.

Federal Trade Commission Chairman Michael Pertschuk testified last March before the Senate Consumers Committee that until "consumers can sue to make an auto-maker buy back a 'lemon,' and be allowed to use that car until the lawsuit is settled, the Federal Trade Commission will continue to get more complaints about cars than anything else." With current legislation, consumers cannot sue in federal courts to make a car manufacturer repurchase a car needing frequent repairs unless the vehicle is covered by a "full warranty." Unfortunately, 98 percent of the car manufacturers give a "limited" warranty, and thereby effectively deny their customers the wider range of warranty rights that come with a full warranty. Because the state courts require dissatisfied owners to give up possession of their vehicles during a lawsuit, they are not much help either.

Since most consumers cannot afford to give up their cars during the several years litigation may entail, state courts offer little relief.

The state governments have beefed up their consumer-protection legislation and increased the powers of their small-claims courts. Still, in spite of federal and local consumer legislation, car owners remain relatively unprotected from the abuses of an automobile industry that has made motoring a nightmare.

This last year was a banner year for consumer fraud in the automobile industry. General Motors, the industry giant, began the year by pleading guilty to substituting thousands of motors in its 1977 Oldsmobile, Pontiac, and Buick models. This admission cost GM more than $40 million in the United States, while its Canadian victims are still systematically denied the same compensation.

And how about Ford's "better idea" in placing failure-prone fan blade assemblies in its cars and then refusing to recall these cars until one mechanic was killed and several injuries were reported from flying fan blades?

Ford's dangerous gas-tank design is another example of corporate insensitivity and irresponsibility. Early this year a California magazine and consumer advocate Ralph Nader made public secret Ford internal documents showing the 1971–1976 Pinto/Bobcat gas tank to be so dangerously designed that low-speed rear impacts would cause the gas tank to explode and flood the vehicle's interior with burning gasoline. Ford denied the charges and accused Nader of "publicity seeking."

Several months later, a California jury awarded $128 million to Richard Grimshaw, the 18-year-old victim of a fiery Pinto crash in which he was burned over 95 percent of his body and lost his nose, four fingers, and left ear. After getting this judgment reduced to $3.5 million and losing two other identical lawsuits, Ford threw in the towel and announced the recall of more than 1.5 million Pintos and about 35,000 Bobcats. This action came 8 years after *Automotive News* reported that the United States Army Engineer Corps had concluded that the "drop in" trunk fuel-tank design was "unsafe." It is estimated there will be hundreds of Pinto/Bobcat burn victims before these cars are repaired.

Similar hazardous fuel-tank designs have been used on other Ford models since the early 60s. So, even if the NHTSA-estimated average two-thirds of the affected 1.5 million Pinto/Bobcat owners fix their cars, one-third or 500,000 potentially mobile infernos could join Ford's other cars having the same gas-tank-design defect.

What incentive is there for Ford, or any other car manufacturer, to make safe and durable vehicles? Product liability lawsuits and recalls are all paid for by the government through corporate tax write-offs for recall campaigns and litigation expenses.

Obviously, the automobile industry needs to be made more socially responsible. However, more government legislation is *not* the answer. What we need most is to make the legislative remedies which already exist easily accessible to the average citizen. For example:

1. Small claims courts should have a maximum jurisdiction of $1,000, prohibit lawyers, and not allow appeals. Such a system has been quite successful in Québec.

2. Hold corporate executives personally responsible for fines or imprisonment where gross negligence or conspiracy has been proven. In the 60s several General Electric officials were sentenced to short exemplary jail terms for price-fixing. Their sentences sent shock waves throughout the industry.

3. Make greater use of treble and punitive class-action damage claims. If a car manufacturer realizes that a $10 million fraud may end up costing the company $30 million in damages, that fraud may never be committed. The same principle applies to the unsafe design of vehicles.

4. Prohibit corporate tax write-offs for litigation expenses where corporate liability is established.

5. Encourage the financing of grass-roots automobile consumer-advocacy groups through voluntary contributions solicited through annual driving-license renewals. This would be done in much the same way that political

contributions are made through annual income tax statements.

None of these measures require major legislative action. However, the adoption of these measures would go a long way in preventing the corporate fraud that so characterizes today's automobile industry.

Where is Henry Ford now, when we *really* need him?

Using Lemon-Aid

Let's face it. Anytime you deal with the auto industry you're going to get cheated. The purpose of *Lemon-Aid* is to keep the cheating down to a minimum.

Used cars are favored over new cars in the overall ratings. Generally, with a used car the investment is less, the car can be inspected by an independent mechanic (try that with a new car dealer), a private seller is less likely to be dishonest, and the car has been pre-dented, pre-rusted, and pre-scratched.

Most of the 1979 car ratings are extrapolations of the performance of these same car models last year. For example, if one car maker has a weak dealer network and slow parts delivery, a new model will merely add to this deficiency. Exceptions do occur, however, and they are noted in each year's edition of *Lemon-Aid.* This was the case with Volkswagen's failure-prone 1975 Rabbit. The company spent more than $5 million in retroactive compensation and corrective repairs within a year. By the 1977 model year, the Rabbit became an excellent new car choice.

Chrysler's Volare/Aspen models proved that just the reverse can happen. When these cars were first launched in 1976, they profited from the excellent reputation of the Valiant/Dart models that were discontinued. *Consumers Union* and *Lemon-Aid* were misled into thinking these cars were just copies of their excellent predecessors. Complaints are still pouring in from disgruntled Volare/Aspen owners.

Cars that are first introduced to the public are generally poor buys. Parts are rare, depreciation factors are unknown, servicing may be inadequate, and premature rusting may be a problem. For this reason they are seldom rated highly in *Lemon-Aid.*

Consumers Union and *Lemon-Aid* ratings often disagree. This can be explained partly by the larger number of consumer complaints *Lemon-Aid* studies and the greater emphasis put upon these complaints. Because of the haphazard assembly-line quality control measures found within the auto industry, the testing of one vehicle by an independent engineer is insufficient. This is *Consumers Union*'s method. Unless test results are analysed along with owner complaints, *CU* will continue to make errors like its "Best Buy" designation for the early Rabbit and Fiat models.

Some models may not be rated in *Lemon-Aid* either because it lacks information, or because a similar model, but with a different nameplate, has already been rated.

Prices quoted in *Lemon-Aid* are realistic, but may require some tough bargaining. And, it may be next to impossible to make a used-car dealer meet the *Lemon-Aid* listed price. Remember, too, that as you go west, car prices increase.

Finally, don't even trust *Lemon-Aid*. Get that used car inspected by an independent garage—before paying a penny.

LEMON-AID

1978-1979 Edition

CHAPTER I

New Cars: Haggle or Be Had

•

According to the United States Senate Subcommittee on Antitrust and Monopoly, which in 1969 held hearings into the high costs of car ownership, owning a car means that almost one-third of every dollar spent supporting the "infernal combustion machine" is used in purchasing repairs that are not necessary, or are not performed ("the sunshine treatment"—leave the car outdoors for the day and charge the motorist for repairs) competently or at all.

As if this litany of automobile-industry deficiencies were not sufficient, there is also a good chance that anyone who drives a car has been cheated at least once every day that the car is driven. Some examples:

Parking Rates: Would you believe that it can cost more to park your car than the money you earn per hour of work?

Insurance Rates: Some rather good cars from the 1970 vintage year can be bought for $500–1,000, yet for some drivers under 25 years of age, the price for insuring the same car may exceed its selling price.

Depreciation Rates: Would you invest in a stock that guaranteed you that it would be worth less than half its value after two years? Yet, this is what is bound to happen if you buy a new car (except for Corvettes and 4-wheel-drive cars).

Gasoline Prices: Forget about what the manufacturers advertise as being the gas mileage you *could* get with their car. Look at the asterisk that always follows the mileage statement. That asterisk means that you may not receive the gas mileage promised, and that whatever gas mileage you get will depend upon your driving habits, traffic, atmospheric conditions, the positions of the stars, and perhaps the weight of your mother-in-law. Don't be fooled by the advertisements that say that unleaded gasoline will result in a cleaner-burning engine and in more miles to the gallon. Actually, unleaded gas may be 3–5 cents more expensive, unavailable in some areas, and it may actually increase your gas consumption.

In the wheel-and-deal jungle of new-car shopping, practically everyone who has ever bought a new car has been at least partially cheated. For example, a dealer may refuse to sell a new car for anything less than a few dollars under the "sticker" price and then turn right around and sell the same car a few minutes later to somebody else for hundreds of dollars less. It all seems very mysterious and illogical to most consumers. Imagine walking into a major department store and bargaining over the sales price of a new stove in the same manner as is done by most new-car dealerships with new car purchasers. Chances are that the department store would throw you out.

But the automobile business is different; it is still a maverick industry where some honesty and full disclosure of essential consumer information has come only through very recent federal legislation in the United States. So, with inadequate legislation for protection, the average new-car buyer can only arm himself with solid facts, patience, and the suspicious nature of a Sherlock Holmes. This chapter will deal with the basic facts needed to buy a new car.

Where to Buy?

When buying a new car, the most important factor is to select a reliable dealer. Try to purchase the car from a franchised auto dealer, since this gives the protection of having somewhere else to complain to if there is no action on the dealership level.

Beware of automobile brokers who promise to sell a new car for less than the dealer's cost. Such a thing is impossible, although some legitimate companies, such as

Car-Puter, Inc., can sell certain new cars for about $125 over dealer cost, plus shipping.

A dealer's reliability can be checked out in a variety of ways. A few calls placed with the local consumer-protection agency or the clerk of the regional small-claims court will usually turn up some vehicles identified by the dealer nameplate on the rear trunk. If these customers have been treated fairly by their dealer, they will be glad to recommend him.

Generally, franchised new-car dealers located in small suburban and rural communities are less prone to engage in all the nefarious tricks of the trade found elsewhere. Prices may be lower, too, since overhead expenses are often much lower than in metropolitan areas. This may not be true, though, if the suburban or rural dealership has a low volume of sales and must make the maximum profit on each sale.

New-car dealers selling more than one make of car can present special problems. Overhead expenses can be quite high, and franchise cancellation by the manufacturer in favor of an exclusive franchise elsewhere is an ever-present threat. Parts availability may also be a problem, since a dealer with two separate franchises must split his parts inventory and may have an inadequate supply of replacement parts on hand.

Selecting the Right Car

The new 1978 car models are definitely smaller, lighter, and less economical than post-1971 models up to 1978. Prices, however, are generally $300 to $350 higher this year. Along with this price increase comes the disturbing realization that a deterioration of product quality has also become widespread.

Consumers are also spending more money for less car in 1978. The industry is committed to reducing the size of its cars to reduce gas consumption. As a result, its standard models are returning to the same size and weight they had in the early 1950s.

Criteria for Selection

Before visiting any dealerships, draw up a list showing those features most desired in the new car. This chart should prevent the salesman from loading down the car with useless and expensive optional equipment. Ideally, the following features should be stressed:

1. Vehicle should be in the compact- or intermediate-size category to allow for some fuel economy, comfort, and collision protection.
2. Parts should be easily available at reasonable cost.
3. The dealership network must be widespread, well trained, and experienced.
4. The vehicle should have a history of average or low depreciation with few exterior model changes each year.
5. Repairs should be easy to make at any independent service station.
6. Rusting should not have been a problem with previous models.
7. Eight-cylinder engines should be avoided unless the six-cylinder model is inadequate.

If a new car is purchased during the first few months of its official introduction, select the vehicle from those cars already in stock. This provides the opportunity to really examine the vehicle closely for transport damage and also to verify if all options are included. This verification should never be done on a rainy day or at night, since many mechanical flaws, such as oil leakage or premature rusting, may be missed. Usually, the dealer will sell the cars in stock for a bit less than those cars that have to be specially ordered. Also, if the vehicle is ordered, there is a good chance the factory will goof on at least 10 percent of the options that were ordered. Sometimes, too, the vehicle may not arrive for three to six months after ordering and any subsequent price increases (usually about 5 percent) will have to be paid by the purchaser.

New cars purchased late in the model year should be specially ordered from the factory so as to minimize premature rusting and insure that the car is as "new" as possible. Check the date of manufacture plate affixed to the door on the driver's side.

Catalytic Converters: Unsafe and Expensive

According to a recent publication of the Washington-based Center for Auto Safety, a number of American federal government agencies have expressed concern that catalytic converters may be a "potential fire hazard" and have issued reports warning employees against possible heat risks associated with such antipollution systems.

A bulletin from the U.S. General Services Administration reported that temperatures of certain converter-equipped exhaust systems were reaching 1,200 to 1,300 degrees, approximately twice that of exhaust systems on prior year models. The GSA added that a vehicle with a converter that is "driven or parked on a surface of easily combustible material, such as dry grass, could cause a fire."

The Air Force has put out a regulation prohibiting any vehicle with a converter from being driven within 50 feet of any aircraft or "other potentially hazardous area."

Earlier this year, the Insurance Institute for Highway Safety reported that a new 1975 Malibu purchased for a crash test caught fire "apparently as a result of overheating of the catalytic converter."

The National Highway Traffic Safety Administration has received about 1,000 complaints of heat-related incidents with the catalytic converter on post-1974 models, of which about 120 involved actual fires in the vehicle. The rest were incidents where the seats or carpeting were found charred or smoking. This number of complaints did not merit a formal investigation, according to one Department of Transport official. Nevertheless, the NHTSA has established a public file to gather data on catalytic converter-related hazards and is especially looking for incidents involving high-mileage vehicles (after 40,000 or 50,000 miles), such as police cars.

Canada has reported at least one death in a vehicle fire caused by a catalytic converter. Quebec Coroner Hermann Mathieu ruled that the catalytic converter caused a 1975 Pontiac Grand Prix to catch fire and kill its sleeping occupant (MAT-39-1976 E, Police 271-090676-001, September 29, 1976). Coroner Mathieu recommended that *all* vehicles equipped with catalytic converters be recalled by their manufacturers for correction. He also recommended that police agencies that may require prolonged idling of their vehicles' motors be warned of the safety hazard.

Automobile manufacturers are aware of this fire hazard and caution owners not to let their cars idle over long

5

periods of time and to insure that their cars are properly tuned. Unfortunately, these suggestions are impractical because:

1. Cars caught in traffic jams will be idling over a long period of time, but cannot be turned off, since that would slow traffic flow even more.

2. Who can guarantee that dealers, garages, or gas stations will tune up cars properly? Is not a car in flames too high a price to pay for a poor tune-up?

Although everyone agrees that automotive pollution must be reduced, the use of the catalytic-converter pollution-control system appears to be needlessly hazardous and problem prone. Other car makers, such as Honda and Chrysler, have reduced car pollutants without using catalytic converters.

Motorists wishing to save money by cutting down gasoline consumption would also be wise to steer clear of catalytic-converter-equipped new or used cars. Government reports have confirmed many drivers' complaints that the catalytic converter can reduce gas mileage by as much as 20 percent.

Vehicles equipped with catalytic converters may also cause problems because they require that only expensive unleaded gasoline be used. And, as if that were not enough, John Moran, a U.S. Environmental Protection Agency spokesman, has admitted that a recent $3.5 million study shows that the converters will give off .05 grams of sulfuric acid per mile in a fine mist, and, thereby, could create another serious health hazard.

Tires

Tire selection is also a very important part of new-car buying. Be suspicious of the factory-installed tires that are standard with each new car. Consumers have complained that some car manufacturers install tires that are no more than oversized rubber bands that may not last more than the first 5,000 miles. Consider paying the extra money for radial tires, since they should make up their extra cost through a longer tread life—generally between 20,000 to 30,000 miles more than regular tires —increased gas economy, and better high-speed performance. Before leaving the dealership, make sure there is a spare tire in the trunk that has not been used. Check the tread wear by inserting a quarter in the tread of the spare and comparing the depth of penetration with the tread on the remaining four tires. Please read page 17 before buying radial tires, however.

The Perimeter of Protection

With the introduction in 1927 of front and rear bumpers, side running boards, and simple fenders, a protective perimeter was formed to protect the car and its occupants. These basic parts did not readily relay damage from impacts to the adjacent area of the auto body and frame. Since then, however, the auto body proper has crept constantly outward toward the protective perimeter, and either diminished what protection there was or done away with it entirely. The designers are creative enough to meet this challenge, but it has not been in the manufacturers' interest to cut down on the high profits realized from repairs to cars that are easily damaged.

Now we come to the art of dangerous designing. If an automobile engineer set out intentionally to design an automobile with built-in factors that would contribute to accident involvement and expensive repairs, here is what he would do, in nine simple steps:

1. Give a large, expensive expanse of glass but neglect to give wipers large enough to clean a safe portion of the glass in hazardous conditions.

2. Place all lights at such low levels on the car body that they are easily damaged by minor accidents and easily obscured by road dirt and spray.

3. Put the headlights in cavelike recesses, so at night, or when there is limited visibility, they cannot be seen from the side by other drivers. This will aid in snow collection around the lights and force the car owner to pay for side running lights also.

4. Complicate the headlight problem by installing concealing covers that are expensive to repair and can freeze closed in winter.

5. Put rearview outside mirrors far enough away from the driver so that his field of vision is reduced, and no adjustment can be made from the driver's seat without expensive remote-control options.

6. "Protect" the car with ornamental bumpers that only absorb 1 percent of the impact.

7. Give minimal or no protection to side-door panels,

so that they are easily chipped when the door is opened or when another car touches them.

8. Construct "hidden" windshield wipers that get frozen into their cavelike compartments in winter, and get stuck up by leaves and other foreign matter in fall.

9. Construct "hidden" gas tanks that form part of the rear trunk compartment and may act as a "bomb" in rear-end collisions.

Paying the Right Price

Don't place too much confidence in suggested retail prices. The federal government forces car dealers to display the suggested price on a sticker that is affixed to the window of new cars. However, no matter where you buy a car, remember that if the sticker says you pay $3,500, you can begin at that figure and reduce it, by bargaining, at least several hundreds of dollars.

Most new-car salesmen are reluctant to give you the information on the amount of profit each car brings. It will be easy to find the dealer's profit, though, if you remember that the following percentages will apply to 1979 models

Luxury (fully equipped) Models	29 percent above cost
Standard	27 percent above cost
Compact	20 percent above cost
Subcompact	12 to 15 percent above cost

In purchasing a compact, for example, the sticker price may be $5,000 complete. Count on one-fifth, or about $1,000, going to the dealer. With this information, it should not be too difficult to arrive at a fair price that makes both parties happy.

Before going to the dealer, be sure to find out how much insurance and financing charges would cost from an independent agency. Many times the dealer gets a special kickback when he has the customer insure or finance his car through the dealership.

Customers who are on guard against paying too much for a new car often fall prey to the habit of selling their trade-in for too little. So, consult one of the many used-car guides that give used-car values before agreeing to any trade-in deals.

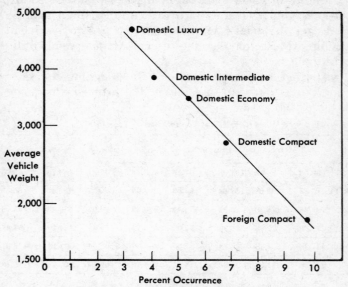

**PERCENT OF ACCIDENT-INVOLVED VEHICLES
IN WHICH THE
MOST SERIOUS INJURY WAS FATAL OR SERIOUS**

Average Vehicle Weight

- Domestic Luxury
- Domestic Intermediate
- Domestic Economy
- Domestic Compact
- Foreign Compact

Percent Occurrence

Source: New York State Highway Department Study Conducted for Dot

Usually these books are difficult to acquire, and car dealers seldom turn them loose. Some banks and insurance companies, though, keep copies on hand and allow consumers quick access to them.

New-car prices are lowest during the first three months of winter. And, if the weather has been especially bad, prices will be even lower. It's best to visit the dealership late at night, since the salesmen will be more flexible in negotiating prices and more prone to be worn down by the slightest sales resistance.

Try to visit the dealership near the end of the month. During this period the salesmen must achieve their monthly quotas to be eligible for special sales bonuses. Even if there are no bonuses, most salesmen will want the extra sale posted just to show the boss a better monthly performance.

Signing the Contract

If there ever is a single most important rule with contracts, it should be never to sign a contract lacking all details or one that is blank. Check the contract to see

9

if the financing is being done by the company you have chosen, and for the monthly payments agreed upon. If the salesman offers to meet your demands, pencils your demands into the contract, then says he will get the boss's approval *after* you sign, you had better be careful. Get the approval *before* signing the contract.

Another rule to remember before signing the sales contract is never to take any verbal promises from the

What It Will Cost You to Finance Your Car

$	12 Months		18 Months		24 Months		30 Months	
1,000	**69.08**	89.09	**101.96**	61.22	**135.44**	47.31	**169.70**	38.99
1,500	**103.68**	133.64	**152.94**	91.83	**203.28**	70.97	**254.40**	58.48
2,000	**138.28**	178.19	**203.92**	122.44	**270.88**	94.62	**339.40**	77.98
2,500	**172.76**	222.73	**254.90**	153.05	**338.72**	118.28	**424.10**	97.47
3,000	**207.36**	267.28	**305.88**	183.66	**406.56**	141.94	**509.10**	116.97
3,500	**241.96**	311.83	**356.86**	214.27	**474.16**	165.59	**593.80**	136.46
4,000	**276.44**	356.37	**407.84**	244.88	**542.00**	189.25	**678.50**	155.95
4,500	**311.04**	400.92	**458.82**	275.49	**609.60**	212.90	**763.50**	175.45
5,000	**345.64**	445.47	**509.98**	306.11	**677.44**	236.56	**848.20**	194.94
6,000	**414.72**	534.56	**611.76**	367.32	**813.12**	283.88	**1018.20**	233.94
7,500	**518.40**	668.20	**764.70**	459.15	**1016.16**	354.84	**1272.30**	292.41

$	36 Months		42 Months		48 Months		60 Months	
1,000	**204.56**	33.46	**239.84**	29.52	**275.84**	26.58	**350.00**	22.50
1,500	**306.84**	50.19	**359.76**	44.28	**413.76**	39.87	**525.00**	33.75
2,000	**408.76**	66.91	**479.68**	59.04	**551.68**	53.16	**700.00**	45.00
2,500	**511.40**	83.65	**599.60**	73.80	**689.60**	66.45	**875.00**	56.25
3,000	**613.32**	100.37	**719.52**	88.56	**828.00**	79.75	**1050.00**	67.50
3,500	**715.60**	117.10	**839.44**	103.32	**965.44**	93.03	**1225.00**	78.75
4,000	**817.88**	133.83	**959.36**	118.08	**1103.84**	106.33	**1400.00**	90.00
4,500	**920.16**	150.56	**1079.28**	132.84	**1241.28**	119.61	**1575.00**	101.25
5,000	**1022.08**	167.28	**1199.62**	147.61	**1379.68**	132.91	**1750.00**	112.50
6,000	**1226.64**	200.74	**1439.04**	177.12	**1656.00**	159.50	**2100.00**	135.00
7,500	**1533.48**	250.93	**1798.80**	221.40	**2069.28**	199.36	**2625.00**	168.75

Cost of borrowing shown in boldface figures
Monthly Payment shown in lightface
Interest calculated at 12½ percent per annum

10

salesman concerning the car. This is especially true of your car's trade-in value. Many salesmen may quote a fantastic price for Old Nellie, but after signing, you may discover that "the boss refused to approve" the salesman's high quote for the car. Is the contract invalid after a trick like this? Very seldom. Any agency using this trick will have all the legal right to enforce the contract signed. Read the entire contract and force the salesman to list, completely, in the contract all the obligations of both parties.

Perhaps it would be best to make clear at this point that not all new-car dealers are crooks or shady operators. Many new-car dealers are active, respected members of the business and social community. The salesmen working for them have been working successfully for many years. Practically every salesman has had extensive training in the correct sales techniques to apply with most customers and legitimate sales techniques are good for the industry. But, since the auto industry is founded upon fraud, it is very difficult for honest men to be competitive.

A line must be drawn against those sales tricks that just waltz on the borderline of fraud. For your assistance, here is a list of the most popular and objectionable sales tricks used by most new-car dealers:

1. Highballing—The dealer quotes a low price no other dealer can match, then, after you sign, he "discovers" he has made a "mistake."

2. Easy Credit—Credit is never "easy." If the payments are small, the interest is high, or else you have a big last payment.

3. Selling Below Cost—No dealer will sell below cost. He can always sell to a used-car dealer for a $25 to $50 profit.

4. Buy at Once—Don't let the salesman convince you that you must buy right away. Always compare several dealers' prices.

5. No Cash Deals—If the dealer is pushing credit that is not needed, chances are he is aiming at making a double profit: one on the car sale, the other on the financing charges.

6. Bait-and-Switch Advertising—This trick is used to advertise a phony deal to lure customers into the showroom so they can be sold on the regular car models.

7. Miscellaneous—Stay away from salesmen who slip a note under the wiper blade of your car quoting an irresistible price for your car. Many times these salesmen act as private parties just to fool you into trusting them. This type also loves to make use of such phrases as "wholesale," "demonstrator," or "repossessed." Demand proof for every important claim made.

Dealers' After-Sale Service

Make	Quality of Service	Adequacy of Repairs	Avail- ability of Repairs	Fairness of Charge	Courtesy of Dealer
AMC	A	A	—	+ +	A
Audi	A	A	—	A	+
BMW	+ +	+ +	—	—	+ +
Buick	+	A	A	—	A
Cadillac	+ +	A	A	A	A
Chevrolet	—	—	A	—	—
Chrysler	—	—	—	—	A
Citroen	A	A	—	—	—
Datsun	A	—	—	—	A
Dodge	—	—	A	—	A
Fiat	—	—	—	—	—
Ford	A	A	A	—	A
GMC	A	A	A	A	A
Honda	+	+	A	+	+
International	—	—	—	A	A
Jeep	—	—	—	A	+
Lincoln	A	A	+	A	A
Mazda	—	—	—	—	A
Mercedes-Benz	—	—	A	—	A
Mercury	A	A	A	—	A
Oldsmobile	A	—	+	—	—
Opel	—	—	—	A	A
Peugeot	—	—	—	—	—
Plymouth	—	—	—	—	—
Pontiac	A	A	A	A	A
Porsche	+ +	+	A	A	A
Renault	—	A	+	A	A
Toyota	A	A	A	—	A
Volkswagen	+ +	+ +	+	+ +	+ +
Volvo	—	—	A	—	—
British Leyland*	—	—	—	—	—

*British Leyland products included the Austin, Rover, Triumph, MG, Jaguar.

+ + Much better than average
+ Better than average
A Average
— Worse than average
— Much worse than average

The Pseudoexperts

Consumers looking for objective, useful information to help them choose a new or used car will find that with few exceptions, the automobile industry has a strangle-hold on the media.

Car Columnists

Take car columnists, for example. Many major newspapers across North America offer their readers information of special appeal to automobile enthusiasts by employing an automobile columnist. Theoretically, this idea is a good one, and the stated purpose of informing the motoring public is to be encouraged.

However, in practice, many North American car columnists do nothing more than rewrite and publish the constant stream of biased and misleading press releases emanating from the automobile industry. Very little investigative reporting is carried out, because that type of public-interest journalism does not sell advertising, takes considerable effort, and will result in the drying up of information sources within the industry.

It is important to note that car columnists do not carry much respect within their own profession. They generally rank a little below travel columnists and barely above the daily horoscope in importance. One of the few times a car columnist is noticed is usually around late September or in the spring, when new models are being introduced and newspaper publishers fall over themselves trying to get a piece of the advertising pie.

Automotive executives find car columnists useful for giving the automobile industry a respectable image and for defending the industry from attacks by public-interest consumer groups. In this context the columnists do their jobs well.

For example, what automobile columnists have criticized GM for its failure to provide Vega owners with adequate compensation to cover constant motor and fender replacements on its 1971 to 1974 models? Or, why did *Automotive News* run a front-page story quoting GM executives who admitted that the 350- and 400-series automatic transmissions were defect prone and would be guaranteed for 50,000 miles, and then refused to follow up on the story when GM officials later denied the claims and consumers were forced to seek compensation in small-claims courts? The Ford Motor Company has been particularly adept at using the press to "stonewall" inquiries and mislead the American public. Henry Ford II recently summed up his own personal opinion of the public's right to be informed in the following dispatch from the Associated Press:

FORD'S IDEA: "KEEP QUIET"

"Never complain, never explain," Ford Motor Co. chairman Henry Ford II says of his weekend arrest and subsequent fine for drunken driving in California.

With that short comment, the auto chief chuckled and headed for an industry banquet last night in Detroit where he received a 30-second standing ovation from nearly 3,000 beginners.

Ford was charged in Santa Barbara, Calif., with drunken driving after his arrest in a car Saturday night with a companion, Kathleen Duross, a shapely, 35-year-old Detroit model and interior decorator.

Municipal court judge Arnold Gowann's sentence was a fine of $375, the amount Ford posted as bond after his arrest, a suspended 35-day jail sentence and two years probation.

This policy of stonewalling public inquiries has been used often by the Ford Motor Company in the cover-up of its premature-rusting problems with its 1969 to 1973 models. In the political context, investigative reporting would blow open Ford's rust cover-up, but in the automotive trade journals and among most car columnists the dictum "never complain, never explain" is the golden rule.

Car columnists are also great moochers. They are given all the latest new models to test drive and continue to get these free cars as long as their reports are favorable. It's not surprising to see car columnists quickly learning the art of superlative description for mediocre models and becoming masters of the understatement when describing "lemons."

Travel junkets are another fringe benefit most automobile columnists receive from the industry. Although many of the more reputable national newspapers have made rules prohibiting industry-paid junket traveling, most newspapers still allow the practice. This is one reason why the major automobile manufacturers often choose exotic vacation spots to wine and dine the car columnists at the annual press preview of new models.

Published Car Tests

A lot of popular car magazines and so-called car experts make use of some pretty effective gimmicks, like the "Car of the Year" ploy, or extensive articles describing the driving advantages and disadvantages of the new cars marketed each year. These reports are usually written around September or October of each year so as to coincide with the lucrative advertising that most companies place in their favorite journals. Actually, these supposedly independent car tests are a lot of baloney.

Automobile testing done by most popular car magazines is carried out over a period of a week. The car is supplied by the manufacturer and tuned to just the right specifications. Of course, the dealer's servicing of the vehicle will be impeccable. Finally, the manufacturer will probably load the car with an assortment of expensive options to compensate for any of the vehicle's obvious faults.

With this rigged test, the car maker cannot lose. And if the tester wants other free courtesy cars to test, the published report had better gloss over the more obvious vehicle defects and treat in the superlative some of the car's more mediocre features. Also, if the magazine or newspaper receives advertising from the manufacturer, any criticism that gets through the driver's own self-censorship will be muted by the editor. Another very important reason for discounting these tests is that they cannot predict a car's vulnerability to rust.

The "Car of the Year"

This has been used so often that it has started to get out of hand. Recently, *Motor Trend* decided to choose ten cars of the year as a special bonus to its subscribers. Even the automobile industry's trade paper, *Automotive News,* had to step in with an editorial blasting the whole concept of choosing a car of the year. In essence, the criticism of the practice centered on the fact that different drivers have different needs and appreciate cars on a purely subjective basis. Therefore, every car ever produced could be the car of the year for somebody.

Once again *Motor Trend* has used its car-of-the-year award that is so well-appreciated by its advertising manager and the auto industry alike. In fact, judging from *Motor Trend*'s previous car-of-the-year awards, one can almost *expect* the car of the year to be more of a "lemon of the year." Let's take 1978 as an example. *Motor Trend* designated the 1978 Omni/Horizon as "car of the year;" unfortunately, this award was made before the car was delivered to the public, according to the June 1978 issue of *Automotive News.*

Consumers Union, also stupefied by *Motor Trend*'s award to Chrysler, had the following scathing comment for *Motor Trend*'s "car of the year:"

> Most years, the commercial backscratching that sometimes passes for journalism, or even for product testing can be ignored; it's just a drop in the ocean of flackery. But sometimes, as this year, those who take such flackery seriously risk paying with more than their dollars.

Still, what do you expect from the magazine that gave the "car of the year" award to General Motors' ill-fated Vega/Astre?

In conclusion, the best place to look for new- and used-car ratings is in the April edition of *Consumer Reports,* or in *Lemon-Aid.*

Safety-Related Defects

Since 1966, more than 70 million automobiles have been recalled by the federal government for the correction of safety-related mechanical defects. Statistics show that most recall campaigns only succeed in reaching about 70 percent of those vehicles needing correction. Therefore, it is a safe bet that many of the used cars offered for sale, both privately and by dealers, are potential time bombs if their hazardous defects have not been repaired.

Once a car is recalled, the manufacturer is obliged to repair that vehicle regardless of the number of prior owners, or mileage, or time in service. Anyone wishing to check out whether or not a used car has been recalled should write to the National Highway Traffic Safety Administration, Department of Transportation, Washington, D.C.

Remember, automobile repairs are expensive enough without paying for repairs that are the manufacturer's responsibility.

Radial-Tire Alert

Radial tires are a good investment for new-car buyers expecting to keep their car a minimum of five years with an annual mileage of 10,000 or more. Nevertheless, some radial tires presently on the market may be hazardous and should be checked carefully before being put into service. The best method of verifying the safety and reliability of a brand of radial tire is to contact the National Highway Traffic Safety Administration, a division of the Department of Transport, Washington, D.C. (800-424-9393, toll-free)

Because of their proved incidence of tread separation and defective construction, certain Firestone, Goodyear, and Uniroyal radial tires should be carefully examined before being driven at high speeds. In many tire tests carried out by both private and public agencies, Michelin tires have performed exceptionally well. However, these tires may be especially vulnerable to sidewall damage from impacts with curbs, median dividers, and the like. According to two well-known product liability lawyers, Arnold Portner and Harry Phils, ". . . all 170 million car tires put into use in the United States each year are defective." Both lawyers have charged that tires lack safety features in their design, lack inflation pressure monitoring devices and fail to give adequate warnings and instructions as to their use.

All the tires on a car should be the same size and construction. Mixing different sizes and types of tires (bias ply, bias belted, and radial) can make the vehicle dangerously unstable, particularly at high speeds.

Tire pressures should be checked at least once a month and during extreme fluctuations in weather temperatures. Inflation pressure should be measured when

I—TIRE OWNER COMPLAINTS

*NHTSA Radial Tire Survey

Tire Company	% Number of Complaints	Survey Cards
Firestone	46.4%	41,441
Goodrich	33%	4,842
Goodyear	32.3%	24,420
Uniroyal	32.2%	10,049
General	25.6%	4,500
Michelin	1.7%	1,901

*Carried out in 1978 by the National Highway Traffic Safety Administration, Washington, D.C.

II—TIRE FAILURE COMPLAINTS

*NHTSA Tire Failure Reports on File

Tire company	Failures per 1,000 tires sold
Firestone 500 (Radial and non-radial)	8.8
Goodrich	2.3
Goodyear	2.2
Uniroyal	1.9
Michelin	1.1
General	0.75

*1978 study by the National Highway Traffic Safety Administration, Washington, D.C.

the tires are cold. An accurate pocket tire pressure gauge used first thing in the morning before setting out will indicate if adjustment is necessary.

Additional pressure, as specified in the vehicle owner's manual (usually four pounds), is essential for full-load and high-speed driving. Incorrect tire pressure will adversely affect the handling of a car and can lead to increased tire wear and possible premature tire failure.

Tires should be checked regularly for road wear and damage. Insufficient tread depth is both illegal and highly dangerous, since it greatly reduces the tire's grip in wet or slippery conditions. Uneven tread wear indicates that repairs or adjustments to the car's suspension system may be necessary.

Vibration or shaking is usually an indication of a tire problem. Wheels should be balanced and tires examined for damage, including tread separation, cracks, or bulges in the side wall, and losses of chunks of rubber from the tread. If damage is suspected, tires should be replaced or examined by an independent expert. Don't take defective tires back to the manufacturer. They may never be seen again.

The most demanding situation for tires is holiday driving, often at full load or for long distances at high speeds in hot weather. Tires should be checked carefully before setting out, and during the trip.

If a tire manufacturer refuses to replace for free a defective tire or disclaims responsibility for damages caused by the tire, contact a clerk of the nearest small-claims court or hire a lawyer. This will often bring about a settlement out of court.

No "New" Cars

There is no guarantee a vehicle is really "new," since the dealer may have disconnected the odometer and used the car for several thousand miles as a "demonstrator" for his customers' or staff's private use. Even if the car has not been used, it may have been left outdoors for a considerable length of time. New cars left outdoors often deteriorate as rapidly as a used car driven on a daily basis. In fact, most new-car dealers have to keep their cars running periodically to prevent the rusting of internal mechanical components. Nevertheless, rust will attack any new car that is left outside for more than a few weeks. Often gas lines will be clogged by particulates formed by the rusting of the gas-tank interior. This can lead to complicated motor problems. Rustproofing a car that is more than six months old is a waste of money.

General Motors

This year, General Motors continues downsizing its vehicle line (actually giving less car for more money) to include its E-body luxury cars like the Cadillac Eldorado, Buick Riviera, and Oldsmobile Toronado. With wheelbases of only 114 inches, compared to the Eldorado's '78 wheelbase of 126.3 inches, General Motors expects to trim these models by about 1,200 pounds each. Length has been shortened too, by about 20 inches, thus giving the Eldorado an overall length of 204 inches, compared to last year's 224 inches.

All these cars now use front-wheel drive and share an independent suspension system. A fuel injected 350-cubic-inch or an optional 350 diesel motor have replaced last year's 425 V-8 motor in the Eldorado. Toronado owners will have to be content with the 350 V-8 gasoline or diesel motor instead of the traditional 403 V-8 power-plant. Buick Riviera customers stand to lose the most from GM's motor switching. The 350 V-8 has been replaced by a turbo-charged 231 V-6 motor that has already generated scores of complaints from owners unhappy with the V-6's excessive vibrations.

GM's Chevette subcompact offers little that is new except for a few minor grille and headlight changes. Odds are the Chevette and Acadian will meet the same fate as the discontinued Vega/Astre subcompact if sales are not maintained.

There have been few changes made on the X-body Phoenix Skylark, Omega, and Nova compact models apart from the grilles and the addition of rectangular headlights. The Omega model, though, does have a new front and rear end.

This year, motor changes are the big news at GM. For example, Malibu and Monte Carlo owners can, for the first time, order the optional 267 V8, and Buick's 231 V-6 has been replaced by Chevy's 200 V-6 as the standard powerplant for the Monte Carlo.

Sports cars in the Camaro/Corvette model lines have only undergone slight cosmetic changes. Firebird, however, has kept its 400 V-8 optional engine for a limited period; but this engine, too, is destined for extinction by 1980.

Pontiac's Le Mans, Bonneville, Catalina, Sunbird, and Grand Prix models are now sharing a new 301 V-8 motor and a minor facelift. Apart from that, little is new.

Engine noise has been a major problem with all of GM's 1975–1978 model powerplants, and the problem appears to affect all car makers using unleaded gasoline in their engines. This problem is expected to carry over into the 1979 model year.

Robert Pease, supervising inspector for Massachusetts' Office of Consumer Affairs, has confirmed that his office has been deluged with motorist complaints about excessive engine knocking in recent model cars.

Pease believes that the engine-knocking problem is caused by unleaded gasoline containing too little octane. Most unleaded fuel has an octane rating of 91, which is about 3 points less than the octane rating for regular gas and almost 8 points below that of premium leaded fuel.

During the past 3 years, the octane rating of regular and premium leaded gasoline has dropped from 95 to 94 octane (regular leaded) and 100 to 99 octane (regular premium). Industry spokesmen blame this lowering of the octane rating on Environmental Protection Agency pressure to reduce the lead content in gasoline.

So far, no engine damage has been linked to the knocking problem. Motorists are advised to use premium unleaded mixed with regular unleaded gasoline to cure the engine-knocking problem. The mixture can be varied until the engine knocking ceases.

GM Warranty Performance

This year's warranty remains basically the same as that given with the 1978 models. GM's warranty performance has declined, however, to the point where warranty repairs are often rare and minor. According to one study published in *Automotive News,* General Motors only expected to spend $35–$50 per car for warranty repairs in 1978. When one considers *Consumers Union*'s finding that the average new car, when delivered to the customer, has about 25 major and minor defects, it is easy to see why General Motors' warranty pay-out is far from generous.

Thousands of GM customers have complained this year about the excessive paint peeling on their new cars. It seems that all GM models are affected by this paint defect that first appears on the trunk, roof, and hood of the car. In the past, this type of complaint was promptly taken care of, free of charge, by GM during the first couple of years of ownership. However, since 1973, the paint peeling and subsequent premature rusting has become so widespread (particularly on the Oldsmobile Cutlass and Buick Century models) that General Motors has cut back on its former "goodwill" policy of free repainting for the affected cars.

Now, instead of receiving some compensation, car owners are given bizarre rationalizations for the paint and rust problems by GM factory representatives, who blame the problem upon "environmental pollution," salt, poor owner-maintenance, stone chipping, windshield-washer fluid, or, if all else fails, on excessive "bird droppings." Owners refusing to accept these excuses have had their cars examined by independent body shops and have found that the paint was too thin, that body design encouraged chipping and premature rusting (especially along door bottoms and wheel wells), and that the metal was not adequately prepared with a sufficient amount of primer to make for satisfactory paint adhesion. With this independent proof, hundreds of General Motors customers have won up to $1,000 in damages, without a lawyer, before United States and Canadian small claims courts.

So much for "bird droppings."

Apart from refusing a great number of paint and rust claims, General Motors also continued to have trouble with the warranty on its original-equipment Goodyear radial tires. Angry GM customers have been passed back and forth between the two companies in much the same way as Ford dealers passed on Firestone radial-tire complaints. This warranty merry-go-round will probably continue well into the 1979 model year, and the only way to stop it is by filing a small claims lawsuit against both GM and Goodyear.

Owners have also criticized GM's refusal to honor warranty claims relating to inadequate ventilation, trunk water leaks, cracking dashboards, diesel motor flaws, inadequate "mini" spare-tire performance, failure-prone 200 series transmissions, defective windshield antennas, and overheating catalytic converters that cause fires and give the vehicle a unique "rotten egg" smell. All of these defects seem to make GM's new cars a "Mock of Excellence," rather than GM's heavily promoted "Mark of Excellence."

Because of car owners' general dissatisfaction with the standard 1-year/12,000-mile warranty, General Motors, along with hundreds of independent firms, is now selling supplementary 3-year warranties for about $200.

This extended warranty concept is a masochist's dream-come-true. It locks you into the dealer's service bays for three years, a deductible fee is sometimes charged, and the dealer can still refuse warranty repairs, alleging that you "spun the wheels on sand" in the summer, "spun the wheels in the snow" in the winter, "abused the vehicle," or were "negligent" in some way.

And, of course, this warranty will not pay related financial losses such as towing charges, taxi bills and car rentals, loss of time, and the general inconvenience of being without a car for several days to several weeks. Imagine paying $200 for all of this supplementary warranty non-coverage. Yes, Virginia, P. T. Barnum lives . . . in Detroit.

One final word about extended warranties. A lot of companies are jumping into the business with every product imaginable. Rustproofers, paint protectors, drive-train specialists, and oil companies are all selling their own brand of security. Nevertheless, if any of their guarantees contain restrictive clauses similar to those already noted, remember Hans Christian Andersen's "Emperor's New Clothes"—and save your money.

Ford Motor Company

Ford has been slow to downsize its models this year. The Mustang and Capri have been radically transformed along the lines of the Zephyr and Fairmont models, with a weight reduction of only a few hundred pounds and an increase in overall length to 179.1 inches. The Capri is no longer imported from Germany.

Most of Ford's downsizing has been concentrated upon the full-sized Marquis and the LTD models, while weight has been trimmed by about 600 pounds, and overall length has shrunk from 224.1 inches to 209.1 inches with Ford, and 229 inches to 212 inches for the Mercury models.

Unfortunately, Ford has followed GM's initiative and only offers a mini spare tire in many of its '79 models. Owners report that the mini tire wears out quickly, cannot be replaced easily, and fits in a special storage compartment too small for the regular-sized spare tire. As a result of these inadequacies, many new car buyers are demanding a regular-sized spare tire before accepting delivery of their new car. The Firestone company (criticized along with Goodyear and Uniroyal for allegedly making failure-prone radial tires) knew years ago that the introduction of the mini spare tire would result in considerable public dissatisfaction; but, as the following quote shows, Firestone's vice-president saw it as a great opportunity to squeeze out extra profits for his company:

Smaller tire, bigger market. Firestone executive vice president Mario Di Federico answers critics who claim Tempa-Spare will reduce tire sales. (Tempa-Spare is a temporary spare tire, 40% lighter and 17% smaller in diameter than conventional tires. The company expects it to be offered on some 1977 cars.) "Now, buyers get five conventional tires with a new car," Di Federico says. "With Tempa-Spare, they'll have to buy that fifth tire in the replacement market, where our profits are greater." (*Industrial Newsletter,* July 12, 1976)

Ford has also cut down its V-8 "muscle" motors of the 460 and 400 variety. For '79, the 460 engine is being phased out and only the full-sized Lincolns use the V-8 400-cubic-inch motor. Even the 351 V-8 has become optional, while the 302 V-E is retained by Ford as its standard engine for the LTD and Marquis models.

Ford Warranty Performance

During the past three years, Ford has been the target of angry customers, who have been victimized by the premature rusting of Ford's 1969–1974 models. This criticism has led Ford to be more responsive to consumer complaints dealing with performance-related defects. For example, Ford recently admitted to Canadian officials that it did have a secret rust-compensation warranty extension covering models up to three years after purchase. With pressure from the Canadian Automobile Protection Association, Ford of Canada agreed to give back $3 million in retroactive rust compensation to Canadian owners of 1971–1974 rusty Fords. The company also agreed to offer a free 3-year rust-protection warranty beginning with its 1977 models, without increasing the price of its new models more than other car makers who do not offer the rust protection warranty.

Of course, Ford's consciousness-raising for customer performance-related complaints has only come about as a result of its losing a considerable amount of sales to General Motors and Chrysler a few years ago. Now that Ford has regained its sales position, sustained and organized consumer pressure may once again be necessary to get Ford to admit the existence of hundreds of other secret warranty extensions, called "policy extensions,"

"Special Adjustment Bulletins," etc. Already, two major lawsuits have been filed against Ford, demanding that these secret warranty extensions be disclosed to the public.

Walter Dartland, the dynamic and tenacious Consumer Advocate for Dade County, Florida, has filed a $750 million class-action suit on behalf of Florida residents victimized by Ford's prematurely corroded automobiles. Dartland feels that Ford should give Americans retroactive compensation for rusty cars similar to that recently given to Canadian Ford owners.

Minnesota's Attorney General, Warren Spannaus, and the state's consumer services director, Tobey Lopakko, have also filed suit against Ford for its refusal to disclose publicly scores of secret warranty extensions covering defective components in the following motors:

- 2.3-liter engines (1974–1976 Mustang, Pinto, and 1975–1976 Bobcat, Capri).
- 250-cubic-inch engines (1975–1976 Monarch, Granada, Comet and Maverick).
- 400-cubic-inch Windsor engines (1974–1977 cars and trucks).
- 351-cubic-inch Cleveland engines (1974–1977 cars and trucks).
- 360–390 FE truck engines (1974–1976 trucks and M 450–500 motor homes).

So, although Ford has improved slightly in the way it responds to customer complaints, it still has a long way to go before its warranty-response record is satisfactory.

Ford's handling of safety-related complaints can only be described as abominable. The company has lied to reporters and government officials, and it conspired with its attorneys so that key court documents were not produced even though they were subpoenaed. Ford's "stonewalling" customer complaints over the unsafe design of its trunk gasoline-tank assembly; flying fan blades; and automatic transmissions which unexpectedly slip from "park" to "reverse" while the motor is idle, indicates just how little the company cares about safe automobile design.

Chrysler

Chrysler has had a terrible sales year. Chrysler Chairman, John Riccardo, has already announced record-breaking 1978 first-quarter losses after taxes of $120 million and end-of-the-year figures will probably show overall losses to be also about $120 million.

The company has had to slow down its downsizing program due to a shortage of capital.

For 1979, Chrysler has few new offerings. Some models like the St. Regis, Newport, and New Yorker share a smaller wheel base of 118.5 inches and use the stretched version of the (Cordoba/Magnum) B-body platform. Mechanical components are similar to 1978 models, despite Chrysler's advertising hype to the contrary. This means that traditional mechanical problems of loose suspension, defective brakes, failure-prone transmission and differentials, and water leaking into the interior, will persist.

Fury, Monaco, and Charger models have been dropped for the 1979 model year. Chrysler is replacing them with the St. Regis, Newport, and New Yorker models using the basic stalling-prone 225 slant-six and 318 V8 engines. This downsizing will reduce the weight of these models from 3,800 to about 3,600 pounds. The rest of Chrysler's models have undergone minor styling modifications, with the 360 V8 becoming Chrysler's biggest passenger-car engine.

Rust protection by Chrysler is still only good for one year in America, while Canadians are given a 3-year rust-protection warranty.

Chrysler Warranty Performance

Chrysler has the worst warranty performance record in the entire domestic and foreign automobile industry. Its small customer-relations staff is arrogant, incompetent, and totally insensitive to customer pleas for a fair hearing of their complaints.

Perhaps, if Chrysler's anticonsumer attitude was just limited to a few staff members, the situation could be easily corrected. But reports from thousands of angry customers throughout the United States and Canada indicate that the customer-relations staff is following a hard-line warranty policy dictated by Chrysler's executive officers.

This corporate-inspired refusal to honor justified warranty claims has earned Chrysler the "Crocodile Corporation of the Year" award from the American Gray Panthers, a militant senior-citizen organization. The group says many of its members were victimized by Chrysler's failure-prone Volare/Aspen models. The Washington-based Center for Auto Safety and the Canadian Automobile Protection Association, both nonprofit, public-interest consumer groups, have repeatedly blasted Chrysler for turning a deaf ear to consumer complaints.

For 1979, Chrysler has made no major changes in its warranty policy guidelines. This, combined with the company's poor sales record, means that there will be even less money in the warranty kitty than ever before.

Owners have already reported that chronic stalling problems have turned their dream car into a daily nightmare, with the ever-present fear that another vehicle will ram into their stalled car. Reports of transmission and differential breakdowns are legion. In fact, some owners question whether Chrysler has invented a timer that causes the failure just after the warranty expires.

Water leaking into the passenger compartment, defective Goodyear and Uniroyal radial tires, excessive suspension vibrations, inadequate brakes, and premature rusting are the major items complained about by Chrysler owners.

With a minimum of corporate "goodwill" on Chrysler's part, most of these problems can easily be corrected, and Chrysler may once again earn rather than lose money. Chrysler's arrogant and insensitive anti-consumer attitude was clearly expressed by a company spokeman who said—after learning that Volare/Aspen front hood latches had failed, thereby causing the front hood to open while the vehicle is traveling at high speed —"well, at least it'll keep the driver from falling asleep." If Chrysler maintains this attitude, it will continue in its sales decline, and by 1980, the company will be lucky if it's selling Tupperware.

Chrysler Omni/Horizon

This model is more of a "Lost Horizon," than the revolutionary car touted by Chrysler. Both the Omni and its twin, the Horizon, are totally unacceptable and potentially dangerous new cars.

Several accidents due to faulty steering have been reported and *Consumers Union* testing shows these models to have "inferior emergency handling" characteristics. Owners have also reported parts and service to be inadequate. All these problems, combined with Chrysler's poor warranty record, have already hurt Omni/Horizon sales and have caused the cars to depreciate rapidly during the first years of ownership.

American Motors

Last year was a disaster for American Motors. Sales slipped to a near record low and only by its announced merger with France's Renault auto company did American Motors buy time to strengthen its sales position. Unfortunately, American Motors does not have the capital to spend on bringing out new models or refine the rather lackluster image of its older models. And refinements are necessary, since none of AMC's passenger cars last year kept pace with '77 sales. Even the Concord (a Hornet in disguise) was a sales disappointment.

This year's Gremlin model has switched to the Spirit namplate and has modified headlights, windows, and grilles. While the VW 121 four-cylinder is still the base engine, the Pontiac 151 will soon replace it. Also, new this year is the optional 304 V-8 being offered with the Spirit (Gremlin) GT coupe.

All the rest of the models have been left relatively unchanged apart from minor grille and headlight modifications. The Matador coupe, wagon, and sedan have been discontinued.

American Motors Warranty Performance

For years, American Motors has had the best warranty performance track record among all the domestic automobile manufacturers. This year is no different. But it's not because AMC is so good, it's just because the other car makers are so bad. American Motors is just the best of a bad lot.

Tricks of the Trade: Psychological Warfare

Car dealers will use almost any psychological trick to get a contract signed. The best way to combat this psychological trickery is to be aware of the many sales techniques employed.

The following confidential sales literature is used by Ford to train its new car salesmen in the art of selling cars. Study the literature carefully since knowledge of sales techniques is the best defense in resisting them.

"Controlling and Closing the Sale" (Excerpts)

Critical Instructions

First of all, do you understand what a closing question is? Let me define it. A closing question is any question you ask the answer to which confirms the fact that he's bought. What is your complete name? What is your mailing address? These are closing questions, aren't they? Now here is the critical instruction whenever you ask a closing question, SHUT UP—SHUT UP. The first man who talks, loses. And this is true. When you ask that closing question, you shut up.

You see, if you shut up, only one of two things can happen . . . (1) he goes along with you or (2) he gives you a reason for not going along. As a salesman, you can cash either one, can't you? But what happens to you? There's three seconds of silence and you get jittery. Now you got to add something, and now you open your big, fat mouth and he's off the hook. You talk about PRESSURE. There is no pressure you will ever exert that will remotely approach the pressure of silence. But I submit these two words. "SHUT UP" are the most important words you will ever learn as closers.

Basic Close

This is the most fundamental of all closing devices. It's called the "order blank" close. In order to use the order blank close, it's a very simple process. You ask a man a question, the answer to which you fill out on your order blank. You don't say, "Well, should we go ahead? You simply ask him a question and fill out the answer on your order blank. You assume that he's bought, all you do is to fill out the form. What do you do when you get to the bottom of this thing? You've got the whole thing now filled out. What do you do when you get to the bottom? Not sign it. What's wrong with the word "sign"? What have you been told about signing things? You've been told, "Read it, be careful, be beware" haven't you? All your life you've heard people say, "Don't sign anything." Now, the great salesmen today do it very simply. They just swing it around, hand the pen to the man and say, "Would you okay this for me, please." This is strange. They won't sign it but they will okay it.

Alternates of Choice

Now they're all kinds of alternates of choice. You always get a choice of buying this or buying that or buying this way or buying that way. What are some other alternates of choice? Cash or credit card, excellent. You prefer a deluxe or standard? Give them the colors. Which do you prefer the white or the gray? Stick shift or automatic? Standard or ethyl? Excellent alternates of choice. Always start them out with this phrase, Which do you Prefer.

Puppy Dog

Puppy dog. You know how you sell a puppy dog. Very simple. Let someone have it overnight. This is the way you sell a puppy dog. Now many products are sold this way. I met a few months back a fantastic guy who sold more color televisions than any color television dealer in the United States of America. He did a lot of good advertising that was designed to generate people walking into his place of business. When they came in they always stopped to look at a color television set and he walked up to them and he said, "I imagine you've been wondering whether your family could live with one of those things or not, haven't you?" I'll send it out and let you take a look at it. What is your address? Two weeks maximum a guy come walking into the store and he'd say, "How do I go about buying that darn thing?" Why? All the kids in the neighborhood had been in, hadn't they? They'd had all their friends in, haven't they? Could they now say they sent it back? This is puppy dog selling.

Ben Franklin Balance Sheet

You use this on the prospect who is just indecisive, you can't really jell him. You start with what we call a story close and it goes this way. "As you know, sir, we Americans have long considered Benjamin Franklin one of our wisest men. Whenever old Ben found himself in a situation such as you're in today, he felt pretty much as you do about it. Here's what old Ben used to do. He would take a sheet of plain white paper. Now you take a sheet of plain white paper. And he would draw a line down the middle. And on this side he wrote YES, pointing to the Left-Hand Column, and on this side he wrote NO. And then here, pointing to YES, he would list all of the reasons favoring his decision; and here, pointing to NO, the reasons against it. When he was through, he simply counted the columns and his decision was made for him. Why don't we try it and see what happens? Now you swing the paper around, put it in front of him, hand him your pen and say, "Let's see how many reasons we can think of favoring your decision today." And then when you get to the "NO" area, you just say, "Well, let's see how many reasons you can think of against it" and then YOU SHUT UP.

You start him on the "YESSES" and he can't switch fast enough to know to think of more than 4. And then all you do OUT LOUD is to start counting YESSES, 1, 2, 3, 4, 5, on this side, let's see how many we got on this side 1, 2, 3, well, the answer is pretty obvious, isn't it, Sir? By the way, what was your correct mailing address? This is a dandy but you need the Ben Franklin validation to make it work.

Summary Question

Summary Questions: Now this is what we call a "NEGATIVE YES" close. By this I mean in this close we allow him to say "NO" but every time he says "NO" he means "YES." Now, you always start in this way: Just to clarify my thinking, Sir, what is it that isn't quite clear to you. Is it the integrity of (and here you name your Company) "No" he says. "Is it my personal integrity?" "No" You see his "No" means "Yes" doesn't it. And now you start summarizing all the facets of your presentation one question at a time, by asking him, "is it this," "is it that," and the last thing you get to, by the way, is money. That's way down here. Now each you "is it" and he says, "NO" you've got a "Yes" haven't you?

Call Back
Call Back: The guy says to you, "I want to think it over. I want to sleep on it." And you say, "Well alright." Then you go and a week or so later you come back and you walk up to the door and you'll punch the door bell or you'll walk into his office and the first word you say, "well, did you think it over?" and he says "Yes, No." When you walk in to see this person that you had to call back on for a decision, you start out by saying, "I'm very sorry, but the last time I was here there was something I forgot to tell you. I think it is important" . . . now tell him SOMETHING NEW, I don't care what it is. And after you have told him something new, you go on by saying, "Let me just review briefly the things we talked about last time." . . . and now you GIVE HIM THE WHOLE PRESENTATION ALL OVER AGAIN. I mean it, the **whole** presentation. The only differences being that this time you occasionally say, "As you remember," "You will recall," "We said that," "We agreed that," but give him the **whole** presentation and go into a normal closing sequence and don't ever ask him if he thought it over.

Lost Sale
Lost Sale: This is the close to be used when you lost it. This is to be used when everything else you've tried has failed. Pack up and as you get to the door, stop, hesitate, turn around (this is still old stuff) then you say, "Pardon me, sir. I wonder if you would help me for a moment?" "Before I go on," this is part of the close, "may I apologize to you for being so inept a salesman? You see, if I had been able to make you feel the way I feel about, for example, this home, you would have owned it now. Your children would be planning to play in this backyard. But, your children aren't going to have this yard to

play in. And I WANT YOU TO KNOW THAT I KNOW THAT IT'S ALL MY FAULT AND I'M TRULY SORRY.

"As you can see, I have to make my living this way. Just so I don't make the same mistake again, would you mind telling me what I did that was wrong?"

What will I tell this boy, and he'll say, "Ah, didn't I cover that?" "Ah" and he was right back in again. This is Old Hat except the apology. Let me ask you something. Did you ever apologize for not making a sale? But, if when you apologize to them, for being so inept a salesman, if you mean it, **and you should mean it,** if you apologize with sincerity you will find this Lost Sale Close gets you sales.

Secondary Question
Secondary Question: A great, good friend of mine who was once a salesman of mine selling an intangible business service. When he was ready to close, he would say to a man, "As I see it, Sir, the only decision you have to make today is this. Do you want this for the two- or three-year term? By the way, do you want to use your pen or mine?" What did he do? Sure, there is an alternate of choice there but that wasn't a simple alternate of choice, was it? Here's what he did. He posed the MAJOR question. "As I see it, Sir, the only decision you have to make today is this. Do you want this for the two- or three-year term? But, he didn't give the man a chance to decide. He immediately followed it with a MINOR decision, "By the way, do you want to use your pen or mine?" You realize that when the man made the minor decision, the major decision was carried. Now this is Secondary Question Closing.

Sharp Angle
Sharp Angle: This you save for that situation when someone says to you about your product, "Can it do this? Can it do that? Will it do this for me? Will it do that for me?" And you now Sharp Angle him by saying, "DO YOU WANT IT IF IT DOES?" Now remember you must be able to do it. Instead of your simply telling him, "Why sure it will do that." You've sharp angled him. "Do you want it if it

does?" Now, when he agrees that he wants it if it does, you have your sale made upon proof, haven't you? But if you simply go ahead and prove that it does, you have no confirmation and no sale. This is Sharp Angle.

Closing on a Final Objection

Closing on a Final Objection: Now, let me set the scene for you. Normally, when you reach for your first close, a man seldom says "NO." Normally, he gives you an objection. Isn't that right? What do you do? You answer the objection. Does this get you a close? All it does is pop another objection. Now you get involved in this death knell of salesman. Can he think up more objections than you can answer or can you answer more than he can think of, and as fast as you kill one, he pops another. Now I'm going to give you a formula first and then I'll go back and explain the formula.

Step 1. Hear him out. Step 2. Sell him his objection. Step 3. Confirm the objection. Step 4. Question it. Step 5. Answer it. Step 6. Confirm the answer. Step 7. Close. Now let me tell you how it's done. First of all, as I said, hear him out. After you have listened to his objection, you now sell it to him and here's how you sell him his objection. You expand it and you look defeated . . . you've got to look licked. "Well, as I understand it, Sir, you feel that the gas mileage on this car just isn't good enough to save you the amount of money that you think you have to save on the operation of an automobile." Now, what have I done. I've looked defeated. He said "I don't get enough gas mileage on this car," and I expanded it. I looked a little licked and now I confirm it. "Now, that's the only thing standing between us. I mean if it wasn't for this darn gas mileage thing, you would go along with me today. Is that right?" If he says, "Yes," he's dead, isn't he? So he says, "Yes that's right. If it wasn't for that sure I'd go along."

Now, what's the next thing you do? You question it. You confirmed it by getting him to agree this was the only thing standing between you. You question it by saying, (and again you take the blame) "Just to

34

clarify my thinking, Sir, why do you feel this is so impossible in terms of mileage?" and now you SHUT UP. Why should you ask him about this objection he just gave you? Here's what happens. When he tries to explain this to you, one of these things happen: (1) He does explain and now he's hooked on it even further, isn't he? Of course, I'm assuming you're going to answer the objection. If you can't, you are in real trouble. (1) He actually re-explains it and hooks himself on it harder. Or, (2) in the process of trying to explain it, he pops the real objection or (3) and in the process of explaining it, it looks stupid even to him. It didn't even make sense to him anymore. But he's told me this is the only thing in the way, hasn't he? Where does he go from here? Well, let's assume he reconfirms himself to this objection. Now, what do you do? Answer him. After you've answered it you can confirm it by saying, "Now, that completely settles that, doesn't it, Sir? By the way, what was your correct mailing address?" Where does he go? Will you tell me? He has told you this is the only thing standing between you and in many cases he has told you very enthusiastically if you looked licked enough. You enough of an actor to make this work? If you are, it's worth money.

I'll Think It Over
So now let's go on to the next one. The greatest single problem you have in selling, I'LL THINK IT OVER. "Tell you what, I'm just not the kind of person who makes snap judgments. I just can't make a decision right now but let us think it over." You say to him, "That's fine, Sir. Obviously you wouldn't take your time thinking this over unless you were real interested, would you? I'm sure you're not telling me this just to get rid of me. So may I assume that you will give it very careful consideration." See, he thinks you're going to let him go. So he agrees all the way. Yeh, he's going to give very careful consideration. Just to clarify my thinking, Sir, what phase of this program is it that you want to think over? Is it the integrity of (name your firm)? What are we doing to him? We're Summary Closing him. Remember that Summary Close? Now

what's going to happen to him? You're going to say, "Is it this?" "No" "Is it that?" "No" "Is it that?" "No." All of a sudden he's going to realize what's happening. He's going to say, "Yeh, that's it." Well, now what have you got? You got a Final Objection. Now close on the Final Objection and you tell me where he goes. You see the problem with I'll think it over is a very simple problem. There's nothing to get your teeth into. What you have to do is to take I'll think it over and reduce it to a specific objection. Now in this I'll think it over close that I just gave you there is one point where if you stop for a breath, you'll blow the whole thing. Can any of you find that point? "He's got it." "What phase of the program is it, Sir, that you want to think over? Is it . . ." You see if you say, "What phase of the program is it, Sir, that you want to think over?" He says, "The whole thing" and you're dead. You've got to get in that first "is it" without stopping for breath. But once you get in that first "is it" you start really moving in on him. Now, that's I'll Think It Over.

Question Closing
Did you have anyone for example say to you, "Can I get it in green?" And what do you say? "Yeh, you can get it in green." Question Closing—demands you say, "Do you want it in green?" Now if he says, "Yes" he's bought. "Could I get 30 days delivery?" The smart salesman says, "Do you want 30 days delivery?" Now when he says "Yes," he's bought. You offer a quantity discount? "You want a quantity discount?" "Yes" He's bought.

CHAPTER II

Used Cars: Dealers and Double-Dealers

●

Why Buy a Used Car?

A good used car should cost approximately $2,000, be no more than two to four years old, and give economical, reliable performance for at least three years.

The type of car referred to above is really not difficult to find. Depreciation is the primary factor for the low price of a two- to four-year-old used car. Look at the following example of a typical new-car purchase order and you will notice the enormous amount of money wasted when buying a new car.

New-Car Expenses

Example 1:
  $4,000 Purchase price
  $ 320 Sales tax
  $ 730 Interest 16.8 percent (over 36 months
       on $3,000)
  $ 125 Rustproofing
  $5,175 Total cost

There are only two reasons for buying a new car: the manufacturer's guarantee and the prestige of possessing a new car. Unfortunately, these two reasons do not stand up under close scrutiny.

Worthless Guarantees

New-car guarantees seem to be intended to sell cars, not service them. In testimony before the United States Senate Subcommittee on Antitrust and Monopoly, auto industry spokesmen have repeatedly admitted that warranty work is refused by dealers because manufacturers fail to pay adequately for warranty repairs.

In one well-documented case presented before the Subcommittee, General Motors actually sent a confidential memo to all its dealers advising them to discourage warranty repairs unless the defects were safety-related.

Any consumer still not convinced that auto warranties are worthless should speak with any Vega or Astre owner. General Motors did nothing about the Vega and Astre's engine failures and front fender rusting until three years after the vehicles were purchased. Even now, owners are frequently turned away by dealers who refuse to fix these cars under warranty.

Warranty Madness

Most consumers are reluctant to buy a used car, no matter how cheap it is, because they are afraid of buying a defective model that is not backed up by the manufacturer's warranty. Well, unfortunately, the strength of the new-car warranty seems to be a myth, if new-car dealers and warranty specialists are to be believed.

According to warranty processors working for the new car companies, the toughest company for getting warranty claims accepted is General Motors, the car industry giant. In fact, these specialists state that General Motors' Oldsmobile Division pays an average of $25–30 for warranty repairs for each Oldsmobile covered by GM's one-year warranty. Chevrolet Division shows a small increase with a $25–35 per-unit average warranty cost. These warranty payments contrast with Toyota's computed average warranty cost of $45–50 per vehicle.

It seems hardly worth the two-year depreciation rate of 50 percent on most new cars if one's primary reason for buying a new car is to benefit from the automobile manufacturer's warranty.

Relating to Reality

Although automobile manufacturers refuse to divulge the cost of warranty service per unit, many car dealers privately complain that they are catching, as one dealer put it, "holy hell from the factory service reps for being too liberal, and losing customers because the manufacturers give customers the impression that the warranty will fix everything." The credibility of warranties in the car industry has dropped so low that dealers have been forced to fight back. The American-based National Automobile Dealers Association (NADA) has actually served its sternest warning on the car manufacturers in a recent speech by the NADA's President John Pohanka, who accused the car makers of destroying dealership service morale through abusive warranty practices. Pohanka, himself a car dealer, made the following charges against car manufacturers:

1. Fears and threats are part of the daily routine in warranty administration.
2. Warranty compensation is given out only as a cost-control measure, rather than as an assurance the customer is satisfied.
3. Dealer service managers are drowning in a sea of warranty bureaucracy.
4. Warranty labor- and parts-compensation formulas to dealers are inadequate.

Pohanka did not accept any of the responsibility for the present warranty madness on behalf of franchised new-car dealers, preferring instead to blast the car makers. However, confidential documents leaked from Ford's quality-control meetings show that most of the inadequate dealer warranty servicing is caused by poor diagnostic procedures by dealership service personnel, negligence, and incompetent dealer mechanics. Only about 25 percent of the warranty problems were caused by owners, Ford concluded.

A used-car purchase can be very profitable. The following example shows why.

Example 2:

$2,000 Purchase price*
$ 160 Sales tax
$ 244 Interest 16.1 percent (over 36 months
            on $1,000)
$2,404 Total cost

Example 3:

$5,175 New car
$2,404 Used car (two years later)
$2,771 Total savings

It is evident that the average car buyer can save more than 50 percent by switching from a new car to a used car two years older. Of course, annual repairs will be necessary, but that would also be the case with a new car. So, even by adding $200 to $400 a year for repairs, considerable savings will still be realized.

Although used-car prices are directly affected by the mileage a car has traveled, the importance of mileage in determining a used car's quality is overrated. Most car dealers figure 15,000 miles per year as average mileage for used cars, or a total life expectancy of only 100,000 miles for the car, before major repairs make selling the car unprofitable for the dealer.

When to Buy

The best time to buy a used car is in the winter, around January and February. It is also a good idea to visit the dealership just before closing. Since the dealer has very few customers this time of year, prices are very low. Also, when a customer arrives late at night, the dealer will want to make that one last sale to put him over the top of his quota if the day has been good. If the day has been terrible, with few customers coming in, the used cars failing to start, and snow covering most of the cars, the dealer will accept the lowest reasonable price just to encourage his salesmen to come back the next morning.

If no privately owned cars are available, the next place

*The $2,000 selling price is based upon a two-year-old vehicle that sold for $4,000 when new (see Example 1). Approximate mileage is 30,000 miles. Condition is average.

to look is the franchised new-car dealership. Many used cars are taken in as trade on a new car, so there is a constant turnover of used cars available. Generally, a good new-car dealership will not sell unsafe or poor-quality used cars, preferring to sell these cars at whole-sale prices at different automobile auctions.

Where to Buy

The most reliable and inexpensive used cars are sold by private owners, through newspaper classified ads. Prices are lower because the car's owner does not sell used cars as an occupation and does not expect to make a profit on the transaction.

Used Rental Cars

If there are no good used cars available from private owners, then the next best deal might be the purchase of a used car from one of the major car rental firms. National rental companies such as Hertz (Ford), Avis (Chrysler), and National (General Motors) offer used cars in most of the major cities throughout the United States.

Rental cars that are being unloaded upon the used car market usually have seen about two years service and registered about 20,000 miles yearly, depending upon whether they have been rented or leased. The cars are generally well-maintained, sell for about 10 percent more than the listed wholesale price, and are sold with a strong guarantee. Many of the car lots selling used rental cars will also provide buyers with a complete history of a car's use and allow an independent inspection of the car's mechanical components by a qualified mechanic of the buyer's choice.

There are a few risks, however, in buying used rental cars from the major rental companies. Since the car has been driven by as many as 100 drivers, it is possible that the car has been used by many inexperienced, immature, and abusive drivers. Drivers of this sort can cause the strongest car to quickly fall into disrepair.

It is also quite possible to get cheated by rental companies selling used cars. And bigness bears no relation to honesty, either. For example, Hertz recently admitted cheating customers in the selling and repairing of some of its used cars in its Alexandria, Virginia, outlet after the Washington-based Center for Auto Safety exposed the practice. A Hertz spokesman in New York assured the consumer group that steps would be taken to prevent other customers from getting falsified information about cars that had been in crashes, or that had not been repaired properly. Hertz also promised to verify that all cars' service records were accurate.

Nevertheless, no matter who sells a rental car, an independent mechanical examination should be performed before purchase.

Used-car buyers in the mood to buy a used rental car may call the following toll-free telephone numbers for the location of a lot selling used rental cars in their vicinity:

Hertz	800–654–3131
Avis	800–331–1212
National	800–328–4567
Budget	800–229–9650

If a used car is defective, and a limited guarantee has been given to the customer, the new-car dealer has at least the garage facilities to honor whatever warranty was given. Just as with new cars, though, there is no guarantee that the warranty will be applied. However, a dealer without repair facilities cannot under any condition honor his warranty.

Buying a used car from a franchised new-car dealer can cost from $200 to $500 more than the same car bought from a private individual. For a good used car that has been completely reconditioned, though, this profit is not excessive.

Probably the worst place to buy a used car is at a corner used-car lot. These places often specialize in inflated finance charges, rolling back odometers, and selling police cars and taxis as "executive" cars. These dealers have to deal in "junk" cars because their operating capital is insufficient to invest in good cars. There are some small used-car lots that are an exception and do not sell junk; however, these are rare.

Repossessed cars are not a bargain either. Often, finance companies or investment companies will offer repossessed cars for sale at prices even lower than those prices demanded by private owners. Unfortunately, repossessed cars are rarely well-maintained and have often been abused.

A final word should be said about used-car dealers selling cars from their homes. First of all, this practice contravenes numerous zoning regulations, and is, therefore, illegal. Also these "Gypsy" dealers buy many of the cars they sell from automobile auctions where the quality is poor. Finally, it is not a good idea to buy a used car from these dealers, because one can never be sure that the car is not stolen or is not still owned by a finance company.

What to Buy

Four-Door Sedan

This is probably the most reliable used-car model available. There is usually plenty of rear seat room, less road noise and body rattles, and a cheaper list price than other models. Also, the addition of side pillars increases the chances of surviving a rollover accident.

Two-Door Sedan

This model has all the advantages of the four-door sedan, except that the rear-seat passengers have less room to enter or leave the car.

Four-Door Hardtop

This model costs more than the other used-car models, but it has a more streamlined appearance because of the absence of side pillars. As a result, road noise and dirt enter the interior more easily. This model is very popular because of its appearance, but chassis durability is not very great, with squeaks and rattles a common complaint.

Two-Door Hardtop

This model has essentially the same characteristics as the four-door hardtop, but offers less back-seat space than other models. It is usually priced higher than the sedan.

Convertible

Any salesman selling a convertible in the Northeastern United States automatically receives the P. T. Barnum award for salesmanship. Any consumer buying a used convertible should have his head examined. Because of extreme climatic conditions, the use of salt for road de-icing, and the lack of rollover protection provided by convertibles, the purchase of a used convertible is not a good idea.

Convertibles are also expensive to maintain, particularly if the top needs replacing. It is also very uncomfortable to sit in seats heated by the direct rays of the sun. In fact, it is possible to be burned by some vinyl seats heated in this manner.

Station Wagons

If passenger and cargo space are prime considerations, a used station wagon is the answer. Station wagons still command high prices on the used-car market, though, so don't expect to pay less than $2,000.

One of the most serious disadvantages of a station wagon is the difficulty in keeping the interior heated in the winter. Exterior road noise is also a frequent problem because the interior has a tendency to echo normal road noise with added resonance. Rear doors are also very rust-prone.

To the insurance underwriter, cars more than five years old are not good risks. It is difficult to get comprehensive (material-damage) coverage on such cars unless the car has been insured by the same company all along, or unless an inspection has shown that the car has been kept in exceptionally good condition.

Things are even worse for liability coverage. Companies are afraid to insure these cars because of the high risks they present. It is well known that cars over five years old have many hidden defects (which don't necessarily show in most state and private vehicle inspections), such as defective steering linkage, worn wheel bearings, bad wiring, worn shock absorbers, and brake system leaks. Defects such as these endanger the lives of drivers, passengers, and the public in general.

When buying a used car, try to find the name and address of the previous owner. Since he no longer has an interest in the car, you may find out many of the defects that even the dealer does not know. Don't depend too much on the odometer reading. It is possible that a car driven 30,000 miles will be in better mechanical shape than another driven only 10,000 miles.

In choosing a used car, keep in mind that a recent, medium-priced car is a better buy than an older, more luxurious model. With an average-sized family, the best buy is a recent compact, intermediate, or low-priced full-sized car. The four-door sedan is the best body style because other styles tend to fall prey to drafts, rattles, knocks, and noises as they get older. Be careful of used convertibles, since tops are expensive and hard to find for used cars.

Used-Car Buyer Examination

1. Make sure the doors close tightly and windows operate smoothly.

2. Check tire wear for balancing, aligning, steering, or frame problems.

3. Road test the car for gear shifting and power. Watch for black exhaust.

4. Check car underside for frame damage from an accident.

5. Look to see if the clutch or brake pedals are too old or too new for the mileage.

6. The car mats will also tell you how hard the car has been used.

7. Test the car's headlights at night to find their effectiveness.

8. Watch for small holes on the roof that may have held a taxi sign.

9. Check for rust. Tap all metal surfaces for solidity.

10. Don't fall for a "private" car sale. Many dealers pose as private parties.

11. Check the motor for leaks.

12. Let the car stand idle for a few hours and look underneath it for leaks.

13. Listen for engine noises at idle and full throttle.

14. Compare the car's serial number with the motor serial number.

15. Push down on one end and see whether the car comes up quickly or inches up. If it comes up quickly, the shocks need replacing.

In conclusion, when buying a used car, don't expect to get new-car performance. If the car was that good, it would have been sold long before you arrived on the scene.

CHAPTER III

The Car Repair Jungle

●

Car repairs will cost the average motorist from $250 to $400 a year. And, if the estimates of a United States Senate subcommittee are correct, at least one-third of every repair dollar spent will have been unnecessary. In fact, the United States Subcommittee on Antitrust and Monopoly concluded in 1969 that repair gyps cost the American public more than $9 billion annually.

Not long ago, Paul King, a journalist with the *Toronto Star,* decided to inspect fifteen local car repair establishments to determine whether a simple two-dollar repair could be easily diagnosed and carried out for little more than the two dollars estimated.

King took the car—gimmicked with a faulty spark-plug wire that contained only the rubber covering—to car dealers, gas stations, franchised car-repair centers, and independent garages. Only six garages correctly diagnosed the problem and correctly repaired the car. Nine other garages performed unneeded repairs, did unauthorized work, or failed to diagnose the problem. And in one place charged more than a hundred dollars after fixing things that were not defective.

Obviously, the average motorist gets about the same low quality of car repair service as this investigative journalist. Nevertheless, not all car-repair agencies are so incompetent. Some garages have a reputation for honesty and competence among the motoring public, despite the general trend in the opposite direction. Based upon experiences of consumer groups, such as the

Automobile Protection Association, and various newspaper action-line columnists, some of the following repair agencies offer repair services that may range from excellent to criminal:

Specialists

The mass-marketing of specialized repair centers has been so successful that even new car dealers are referring their customers to places like Firestone, Mister Muffler, and Sears for specialized repairs. These repairs can be performed more quickly, at less cost, and with a longer guarantee by these businesses than by other car-repair agencies. Also, mechanics may be far more experienced in trouble-shooting just one mechanical component of a vehicle than the average dealer or independent garage mechanic who may need to know a little bit of everything. Parts supply is also more comprehensive for transmissions or mufflers, for example, than other nonspecialized repair agencies.

Specialized repair agencies have gotten a black eye from the actions of a few transmission repair firms like the Aamco and Cottman transmission franchises that appeared to be overzealous in selling rebuilt transmissions. Aamco's actions resulted in that company signing a consent order in the late 1960s with the U.S. Federal Trade Commission where the parent company pledged to hire ex-FBI men, among other retired law enforcement officers, to monitor the honesty of local Aamco franchises.

Overall, specialized repairs should be done by franchised repair agencies. They are the best place to begin comparing prices and guarantees.

Independent Nonspecialized Garages

These are usually small repair shops where the quality of repairs is easily controlled, overhead expenses are minimal, and repair costs relatively inexpensive. Diagnostic skills are well developed by mechanics, who take the time to fix defective parts rather than replace them. Many of these garages are one-man operations, or family-run businesses with only a few employees. With the closing of gas stations resulting from the proliferation of self-service gasoline retail outlets, more independent garages are being established by former gasoline station owners.

Since most independent garages are labor-oriented rather than parts-oriented, customers seldom complain of repair overcharges. The most frequently heard complaint, however, is that the independent garage mechanics often take longer to repair a car than other repair agencies. Considering that the extra time is taken to fix the car correctly the *first* time it is repaired, this problem does not appear to be very serious.

So, when nonspecialized mechanical repairs are required, look for an independent garage to give out the most competent and honest service.

Gas Stations

Gas station owners are caught in a vicious circle. They receive an inadequate profit from the sale of gasoline and, therefore, find it difficult to purchase diagnostic machines or hire competent mechanics; and yet, the public has to rely more often on the corner gas station for repairs because it is open when others are closed. Oil companies have not helped the situation much either by opening up self-service stations across the street from their own dealers, giving inadequate franchise training and keeping gasoline profits low for the dealer.

It is not surprising that car repairs done by many gas station mechanics are poorly carried out. Gas station franchises have to cut corners to make a decent profit, so they cannot hire the best mechanics, carry an adequate supply of replacement parts, or give the most solid guarantee. Some skilled mechanics may even have to be taken off a repair job in order to pump gas during rush hour.

Of course, oil company franchisers in Canada are concerned over the numerous consumer complaints lodged against their gas station leasees. The Alberta Royal Commission on the Retail Marketing of Petroleum Products (also called the MacKenzie Commission) concluded in the late 1960s that the average gas station leasee was exploited and abused by the oil companies through a monopolistic "cartel" established by the petroleum industry. Following that, Imperial Oil (Esso) took out full-page newspaper ads declaring, "We're not crooks." The

Royal Commission thought otherwise, but unfortunately, the federal government has still failed to act against oil company marketing practices that tend to make suckers of us all.

Until real reforms are made in the retail marketing of petroleum products through gas stations, the wise consumer should first go to other repair agencies, where the probability of honest, competent repairs is greatest. Tourists especially should be on the look-out for car repair gyps practiced by dishonest gas stations in other provinces and in the southern United States.

Florida Consumer Affairs Director Jane Robinson has warned northern tourists to be wary of the "mechanic pirates" at gas stations located along Florida's interstate highways who sell unneeded repairs. Dishonest mechanics have been known to splash oil underneath cars and then convince owners that costly motor or transmission work is necessary. Another favorite ruse is to puncture tires or shake the front wheels violently in order to sell ball joints.

Out-of-state vacationers wishing to protect themselves from gas station crooks are urged to:

- Make a second check of suggested repairs at an independent garage
- Never leave a car untended at interstate service stations
- Call police if threatened or crooked practices are suspected
- Continually complain to oil companies and public officials if fraud is suspected. Remember, although oil companies often plead they are not responsible for repairs, their commercial messages usually say the opposite, and a reasonable case for corporate responsibility can easily be pleaded.

Automobile Dealers

Car dealers' main objectives are to sell cars, credit, insurance, and parts. Repairs are viewed by most dealers as a means whereby lagging profits in the sale of new and used cars can be boosted. Public confidence in dealer repairs has slipped so badly during the last decade that more than half of the new-car owners switch to independent garages as soon as the manufacturers' new-car warranty has terminated.

Dealerships have a high overhead, are parts oriented, and often give "commissions" to their customer service advisers based upon the amount of parts and labor the customer can be convinced to purchase. Skilled mechanics can be found at some of the larger new-car dealerships, but dealers often prefer to hire lesser-skilled help who are more competent at replacing a part than at diagnosing the problem and repairing just one small defect in the part assembly.

Obviously, car dealers are the last place one should look to for honest and competent repairs.

A Dictionary of Dirty Tricks

Although some repair agencies are better than others in offering honest and competent work to their customers, almost all garages in business engage in some "dirty tricks" that cheat customers. This car-repair fraud is said to be prevalent because garages are forced to cheat their customers just to stay competitive. Consumers have the best chance of not being cheated by frequenting small, neighborhood garages, and by keeping in mind some of the following rackets regularly employed by the automobile-repair industry:

1. Shop supplies—This is an arbitrary surtax placed on a repair bill by the garage owner. The amount of the tax is calculated either upon the parts or labor portion of the bill. Charges may run from a low of 3 to a high of 25 percent. Although this gimmick is widely used by dealers, many gas stations and independent garages have begun to employ this trick too. Dealers have defended this practice by saying that it pays for many of the "hidden" expenses of car repairs for which dealers often fail to charge their customers. Restroom soap and tissue, rags, solvent, and miscellaneous nuts and bolts are also supposedly covered by the "shop supplies" repair surtax. Dealers have not disclosed, however, why they do not simply add on the cost of these miscellaneous items and increase the hourly rate. At least, the average customer would know that a $25 labor charge and a $25 part will result in a bill for $50 and not $50 plus a few extra dollars for nonspecified items.

Never pay a bill that charges for "shop supplies."

2. Worthless guarantees—Be wary of garages that offer only partial guarantees on their repairs. These guarantees are usually for only a few months and limit liability to a certain percentage of the total bill. The clincher in this type of con is that the garage requires the customer to have his guaranteed corrective repairs done at the *same* garage that botched up the job in the first place. When the car is brought in, the garage owner is free to charge any boosted repair price the traffic will bear, while still claiming to fix the car "under guarantee."

3. Ambulance chasers—Ever wonder how it was possible for two trucks to arrive at the scene of an accident so quickly? Well, police have wondered the same thing, and out of their curiosity has come the realization that many tow truck operators illegally moniter police emergency-radio broadcasts so they can be the first to prey upon distraught accident victims. The customer is usually asked to sign a form that many motorists are led to believe is only a towing-authorization form. Then when they come to claim the car, they are told that work has started on the car, since the repair-authorization form has already been signed at the accident site. If work has not been started, the garage owner will often demand that a certain percentage of the estimated bill for repairs be paid before the car will be released to another garage. Thus, if the collision repairs are estimated to cost $2,000, the garage can charge 10 percent or $200 as a penalty to the owner for not leaving the car to be repaired.

Don't ever sign any authorization forms proffered by friendly tow-truck operators.

4. Unauthorized repairs—This trick is used by mechanics who specialize in motor and transmission work. A low price is quoted for a specific repair and then more defective components are found that require more extensive repairs. A specific dollar amount written into the repair order will help crim this racket. Asking for the old parts will also be a good bluff in this situation.

5. Boosting—Garages normally get about 35 percent profit on the price of parts and almost 50 percent profit from the hourly labor rate. If the repair charges exceed these guidelines, ask for an independent verification of the charges by another garage.

6. Phantom parts—Some garages will charge for parts that were never replaced, or for new parts when old or reconditioned parts were really used. This practice is frequently found in body shops where a used door or other major body component is substituted for the new part that was agreed upon. Insurance companies will check out any shops suspected of using this gimmick on their policyholders.

7. Sunshine treatment—When a mechanic does nothing to your car except park it all day outside, this is called the "sunshine treatment." This trick was originally discovered by investigators working for the United States Senate Subcommittee on Antitrust and Monopoly, looking into the car repair industry in the late 60s. The modern variation of this trick is for the mechanic to park the car all day inside the garage and hope that the change of temperature will temporarily fix what is wrong.

8. Flat-rate fantasy—Flat-rate manuals or guides are published by car manufacturers and independent publishers to indicate the number of hours a particular repair should require. Although all the flat rate guides are unrealistic, those published by the car makers appear to be the most conservative in the time they allot for most repairs. Independent publishers of flat-rate manuals are often more liberal in time allowance because they like to use the extra time that is indicated as a selling tool for the guides. Garages like to justify unrealistic repair bills by pointing out the alloted time in the flat-rate manuals as proof that the repair was done at a reasonable cost.

9. Repair specials—Heavily advertised by oil companies and car dealers alike, these repair discounts are just gimmicks used to get customers into the garage. Consumers can tell whether a special is really "special" by examining the small print of the advertising to determine what cars or parts are not covered and exactly what work is going to be performed. The most common special discounts are offered for transmission inspections, tuneups, summer and winter inspections, and tire replacements.

10. Diagnostic clinics—During the last decade, oil companies have invested heavily into the development and promotion of automobile diagnostic clinics. The clinic idea was a sound one, but the oil companies' salary bonus, given to clinic technicians for the amount of parts and labor sold clinic customers, was a dirty trick that exploited motorists. Recently, a lot of unfavorable publicity concerning Esso's diagnostic clinics has apparently forced that company to re-assess its clinic marketing strategy.

Until the oil companies decide to operate diagnostic clinics that do not offer repairs, motorists would be best to search out some of the clinics run by the automobile associations.

11. Overzealous Repair Salesmen—The marketing of some specialized car repairs has become so sophisticated that the average customer will rarely leave the professional repair salesman's garage without purchasing unneeded repairs. The Cottman Transmission Company has even developed selling transmission repairs into an art, according to the following confidential Cottman documents:

To: ALL CANADIAN AND BUFFALO CENTERS

From: James W. _____   October 8, 1974
        Operations Department

Re: Items Discussed and Agreed Upon at the Meeting Held at the Constellation on Saturday, January 19, 1974

Attending:

Mike Bobor	Bob Biggar
Frank Zicari	Frank D'Amico
Jack Colquhoun	Bill Holt
Ed Copp	Bob Rostance
Paul Mathewson	Bob Dawson
Jim Davidson	Richard Ostroff
Leo Kervin	Charles Nicholson
Richard Berke	Ken Jomes
Ken Gaffney	Roger Pasquarella

Gentlemen:

I enjoyed seeing you all again during our recent series of meetings in Toronto. Your enthusiasm and participation was most encouraging. Now the most important thing is to implement the procedures and concepts that we discussed and attain *RESULTS.* Meetings can be beneficial; however, results and *profitability* are the *only* things that count.

Please find attached the summary sheet of the goals that we established for ourselves. Keep these figures handy and refer to them often. If you are not approaching these figures, in reality, evaluate why you are not and discipline yourself to concentrate on your specific problem areas. In any case, when you identify any area of your operation that is causing you difficulty, call Frank D'Amico immediately.

The following items were discussed at the meeting:

1. Initial Contact (Track 10)
   A. Adhere strictly to *Service Track* (10).
   B. Make definite appointment times with every customer so that *he feels more obligated to keep* his appointment.
   C. Record the customer's phone number and call him back if he does not show.
   D. It is in your best interests to record all leads for specific follow up purposes and to provide *accurate* data for a meaningful evaluation of your proficiency in this area. You have nothing to lose by conscientiously recording leads, as is expected, and everything to gain.
      NOTE: If you are unable to work anything out with the customer and it appears that a put-back is imminent, call Frank D'Amico to assist you with the sale. The Buffalo centers call one another for this double teaming effort, likewise you may utilize nearby Cottman centers for this assistance. The fact that another party is showing concern for the customer can many times save a sale.
   E. Even after the customer has agreed upon this 90-day overhaul, you must *still drive on to* sell the difference for the Lifetime, always closing on benefits. The Lifetime is in the customer's best interest.

4. Attitude About Saturday
   If you are determined that Saturdays will just be a non-productive clean-up day, this will be the result. You should psyche yourselves into turning Saturdays into highly productive days. When a car is retained on Saturday morning, you should strive to get that car sold and *delivered* that day.
   A. The customer wants his car for the weekend.
   B. Determine at retention:
      1. Does the customer have a credit card that you accept (Charge X, Empire Card, Master Charge, etc.)?

2. Is there an available stock unit ready to install, either at your center or a nearby Cottman center?

C. *Sell the customer on the premise that the Lifetime can be ready today because we have a unit in stock,* or we can *overhaul your transmission* with the 90-day and have it ready for you on Monday.

5. Attitude

Your attitude is the one critical factor that will make your center successful. You must believe that you are the most qualified person in the world to solve each individual customer's problem. "To know me is to love me." Regardless of what obstacles you confront you will drive on to achieve the objective. The easiest thing to do is to justify failure. Don't make excuses in your mind which will make it impossible to correct your own personal weak areas (i.e., the people in my area are different, gas shortage, market conditions, weather, advertising, production problems and so on and so forth). Take aggressive action to solve your own problems. Problems which you are now experiencing, at one time or another, have been experienced by everyone. The strong will recognize their problems and correct them. The weak will cry, complain, make excuses and die. If you have a problem that is frustrating you, ask for help!!!

SERVICE TRACK (30)

_____, this is _____ at Cottman. Do you have a few minutes? We've just completed checking your transmission, and I'd like to go over it with you. OK?

Fine. We did locate the problem areas and it appears we can solve your problem in 1 of 2 ways. We feel the best solution is the Cottman Remanufactured Transmission with Torque Converter and the Lifetime Guarantee. This means that the transmission and the Torque Converter are completely guaranteed for as long as you own your car. The latest improvements and updated modifications are included in the Lifetime Guarantee. This is just a matter of $_____ or $_____ a month, and means that you will never have a transmission repair bill for as long as you own your car. This is really your best investment . . . (Pause). On the other hand, we can also suggest the Cottman Overhaul, which is an overhaul of your transmission. This is a matter of $_____ or $_____ a month, and carries a 90 Day or 4,000 mile guarantee on all parts and workmanship. As you can see, Mr. _____ for just an additional $_____, or a difference of only $_____ a month, you can have the Lifetime Guarantee. Which do you prefer, Mr. _____?

It is a lot of money, Mr. _____. However, when you consider that this Cottman Remanufactured Transmission includes the finest workmanship, the best parts, the latest updated modifications and is guaranteed for as long as you own your car, you can see, that in the long run, the Lifetime Guarantee is the least expensive thing to do. We can have that ready at _____, or would you need it sooner than that?

5. No, that's all we can do and give you the 90 Day or Lifetime Guarantee. Remember that the Lifetime Guarantee means that you will never have to worry about another transmission repair bill for as long as you own your car. (Yes Sequence) Which service do you prefer, Mr. _____?

6. I can certainly appreciate how you feel, Mr. _____. But in the long run, you will know what you did was the right thing. We will go ahead with the Cottman Remanufactured Transmission and Torque Converter with the Lifetime Guarantee. That's just a matter of $_____ or $_____ a month, and remember, the entire unit is completely guaranteed for as long as you own your car. We'll have it ready for you at _____. Fair enough?

7. You've made the right decision, Mr. _____. We'll go ahead with the Cottman Remanufactured Transmission and Torque Converter. This is just a matter of $_____, and remember, the entire unit is completely guaranteed for as long as you own your car. We'll have it ready at _____. Do you want to take care of this by cash or certified check?

Fine. We will call you when it's finished.

YES SEQUENCE! (20)

The "Yes Sequence" is a powerful selling device. It is to be used *only* when it will be most effective.

The *"Yes Sequence"* comprises a series of questions to

which the customer should reply with a *Yes* response. As the *"Yes Sequence"* is developing, the customer finds himself in agreement with everything we are saying. It then follows logically, that when we ask him to cooperate with whatever we are suggesting, he will also reply with a *YES* response.

It is most important that the *"Yes Sequence"* be developed upon information the customer has already mentioned to us. We must, as often as possible, develop the feeling that we are dealing only with this customer—we are dealing with him as an individual, working out his particular and unique problems.

After all, it is in the customer's best interest that he do business with us. Therefore, we will do what is right for him.

The following is an example of a typical *"Yes Sequence"*:

1. Well, _____, we have a problem with the transmission. Right?
2. You've been worrying about this for _____ now. Correct?
3. You thought it was going to let you stranded on the highway yesterday. Right?
4. You definitely need the problem corrected. Isn't that true?
5. Even your wife was upset driving the car the other day. Right?
6. For whatever you pay, you want to make sure you get a fair deal. Isn't that right?
7. You want to get the best job for the least amount of money. Isn't that true?
8. You want to be able to make the decision on how much you spend to repair it. Right?
9. When the job is completed, you want to be able to rely on the guarantee and the people that did the work. Right?
10. _____, you've come to the right place. Just OK the Repair Order and we can get started on it. Now, here's what will happen. I will call you at approximately _____.

7. *Yes Sequence*—The *Yes Sequence* comprises a series of statements or questions to which the customer must reply "yes". As the *Yes Sequence* develops, the *customer finds* himself in total *agreement* to *everything* you *are saying*. It follows logically that when we direct *him to comply* with our *recommendation,* he will reply *Yes*. This

is a powerful selling device and is to be used only when it is needed (As per class discussions).

8. *Based upon the information we have . . . (Yes Sequence) . . . we do know exactly what problem areas to check.* We are the experts. We do know exactly what to do . . . based upon the information given to us. Based upon the data given to us over the telephone, we will know exactly what to check on the Free Roadtest. Based upon the data we collect and observe from the Free Roadtest, we will know exactly which problem areas to check after we remove the transmission. Then, based upon all the data, we will make the proper recommendations to the customer.

9. *We will check it out together*—We are honest, open, above board. When the customer comes in, if he wishes, we will let him observe and be part of every step in our procedure. This is a full disclosure relationship. There is security for the customer if we check things *together.* This is to be used only with these customers who need this added personal touch. Not to be used or even mentioned to everyone.

10. *We'll be able to work out something*—This is a *Key Transitory Statement* exemplifying the concept that regardless of the customer's problems—personal, financial, whatever—we have the sensitivity and flexibility to be able to work out some solution that is satisfactory to all parties involved. *We can work it out.*

11. *Sensitivity*—The ability to selectively retain, remember, and use *in the "Yes Sequence"* all of the positive indicators given to us by the customer; as well as, the ability to transmit or ignore any negative or derogatory indicators that would tend to pull us off track or lose sight of the objective. The corner stone of this concept is—"To Know Me Is To Love Me."

12. *That's a good question . . . (Yes Sequence)*—When we sense that a customer is pressing for assurance or protection to a degree above the normal, it is imperative that we recognize this behavior and counter it by enhancing his self-esteem and self-assurance. Recognition of his cautiousness or concern will assure him that we are sensitive to his anxiety.

13. *Creative Anxiety*—The emotional state associated with the insecurities of change or confrontation.

15. Is that the cheapest job you can do? This is the least

expensive thing we can do and give you the Lifetime Guarantee . . .***

16. Are they the only *choices I have?* 'Yes'. . .***

17. Put it back together! Well, that's not going to solve the problem. (Yes Sequence) . . .***

18. You had better put it together or I will go to the BBB. Do you understand? Well, that's not going to solve the problem. (Yes Sequence) . . .***

19. How come your prices are so high? It is a lot of money, _____; however, . . .***

20. I can get the same thing for $115! Why should I pay you $325? I can certainly appreciate how you feel on that point, _____; however, I'm sure that you can understand exactly what we have here . . .***

21. Are you crazy! I'd never pay that much to fix any transmission! It is a lot of money, _____; however, . . .***

22. I just don't have that much money. It is a lot of money . . . (Yes Sequence) We can set this up on our Monthly Budget Plan. This would be just a matter of $_____ (month). Where do you work, _____? . . . ***

23. I can't afford it and I can't get credit! It is a lot of money, _____; however, you say you can't get credit. I'd like to suggest, let us give it a try. That way, it would be just a matter of $_____ (month). Fair enough? Where do you work, _____? . . .***

24. Where do you expect me to get that much money!? It is a lot of money, _____ . . . (Yes Sequence) . . . We can set this up on our Monthly Budget Plan. This would be just a matter of $_____ (Month). Where do you work, _____? . . .***

25. There must be something else you can do! There is nothing else we can do and give you the Lifetime Guarantee . . .***

26. For *Christ's sake, are you deaf?* I won't spend that much! It is a lot of money, _____; however, . . .***

27. My husband said if it's over $75.00, forget it! I see. Where can we reach your husband? (Call and make presentation to the husband). If you can not contact the husband now, wait and try to work out something.

28. I'll get another car before I pay that much. It is a lot of money, _____; however . . .***

29. I'm not going to keep the car. Just fix it as cheap as

you can. It is a lot of money, _____. What we want
to do now, is work out the least expensive solution
to your problem. Right, _____? . . .***
30. You had better do something else or the D.A. and I
will come down there (Yes Sequence). What we want
to do now, is work out the least expensive solution
to your problem. Right, _____? . . .***

The sales tactics practiced by Cottman's franchisers
are not unique. Many professional repair salesmen use
similar tactics with slight variations. Use Cottman's sales
literature as a guide to what not to do when shopping for
automobile repairs.

Repair Rackets: Self-Defense

The automotive-repair industry is basically fraudulent.
By using exorbitant flat-rate charges and replacing parts
that only need minor repairs, the average garage has a
license to steal. Few consumers have the time and resources required to discover this sophisticated style of
thievery. Nevertheless, some of the following suggestions may help in keeping that theft small:

   1. Demand the old parts—This is strictly a bluff—
unless you are able to get the parts checked out by an
independent mechanic who does not mind calling another mechanic a thief. Still, by asking for the old parts,
the customer leads the mechanic to believe that the
honesty and quality of his work is going to be verified by
someone else. The mechanic does not know who may
eventually inspect the work, so chances are that a better
job will be done during the initial repairs, and it will not
be necessary to come back to repair the repairs. In some
areas of the country the Attorney General, consumer
agencies, auto clubs, and the police fraud-squad will cooperate in catching crooked car mechanics by inspecting
the replaced parts.
   2. Make repair order specific—Never sign a blank
repair order, or simply ask the mechanic to do "whatever
is necessary."
   3. Sign a cost estimate—Insist that estimated cost for
a specific repair be written in the repair order. Draw an
arrow from your signature to amount estimated. Allow

for a 10 percent difference in final cost. Make it understood that additional work or a higher cost will not be accepted unless your permission has been obtained before the work is started.

4. Watch work being done—If time permits, remain with the car while repairs are being carried out. Don't interfere with mechanic, but make your presence known. This will encourage mechanic to work efficiently and also help you learn to perform some of the simple, basic repairs yourself. It is not true that owners are prohibited from repair bays because of insurance regulations for garage owners. Although this may be true in some isolated cases, most garage owners simply use this as an excuse to keep owners from repair bays while work is being done on their cars.

5. Get a proper diagnosis—Since the mechanic's diagnosis of the trouble is the starting point for all subsequent repairs, it is essential that the diagnosis be correct the first time it is made. Therefore, check out all preliminary diagnoses with other garages for confirmation. If you wait until the repairs have been completed, it will be too late. Once again, auto club diagnostic clinics can be very helpful in checking out the validity of a garage diagnosis.

6. Isolate repair categories—If the transmission, brakes, and muffler need fixing and a general tune-up is also required, don't get all the repairs done at once at the same garage. Isolate the different repairs according to cost and need. For example, the transmission should be fixed first because it prevents the car from being used. A good transmission specialist should be used for this repair. Brakes, a safety item, should then be repaired by an independent garage. The muffler should then be repaired because of the possibility of dangerous fumes leaking into the passenger compartment and the possible violation of noise laws. Muffler specialists should be used because they offer generally lower costs and more extensive warranties on parts and labor than do independent garages and automobile dealerships. A tune-up can be postponed until more money is available. It can also be done quite easily and cheaply by an independent garage.

7. Check for secret warranty extensions—Car makers often secretly extend the warranty on some models as much as 5 years or 50,000 miles because certain mechanical components have been found to have a high premature failure rate.

Since few car owners are aware of these secret warranty extensions, many repairs that could be charged to the manufacturer are routinely billed to the customer. Car dealers do not always inform customers of the existence of these special warranties because the automobile manufacturers do not pay promptly, and when they do pay, it is not at the full retail rate.

Some warranty extensions can be quite extensive. General Motors, for example, has extended the warranty on automatic transmissions of the 250, 350, and 400 series designation on its 1973–1975 model cars. The warranty extension is expected to cover more than 2.2 million vehicles and be applicable for 5 years or 50,000 miles. Toyota has a similar warranty extension on its 1971 and 1972 Corolla models afflicted with premature motor wear.

Purchasers of used cars may also be protected by secret warranty extensions. The 1971 through 1974 Vega/Astre models have such a warranty for second owners to cover premature motor wear for as long as 5 years or 50,000 miles.

8. Rust repairs are bad investments—Make minimal rust repairs on vehicles more than 5 years old. The cost of more extensive and expensive repairs is generally not worth the depreciated value of the car. Rust will usually reappear within a year, and no body repair shop will guarantee rust repairs for more than one year.

9. Refuse worthless warranties—The auto repair industry's average warranty covers parts and labor for 100 percent of the cost for a period of 90 days. Don't settle for anything less. Repair warranties of 50/50 are easily used to boost the bill to more than double the regular retail rate so the customer covered by such a warranty actually pays the full price for repairing faulty repair jobs. Remember, in most jurisdictions, the law states that anyone selling a defective product or service must rectify the fault or reimburse the amount paid. Under this rule of product liability, a mechanic's liability may go beyond the minimum expressed warranty if proof shows negligence is involved. Getting proof, though, may be difficult.

10. Request reconditioned or used parts—Cars older than two years do not need new parts, despite the claims of car manufacturers that new parts are more reliable.

The difference in cost between used parts and new ones is about 50 percent. Some scrapyards sell guaranteed used parts for about one-third the price of a new part.

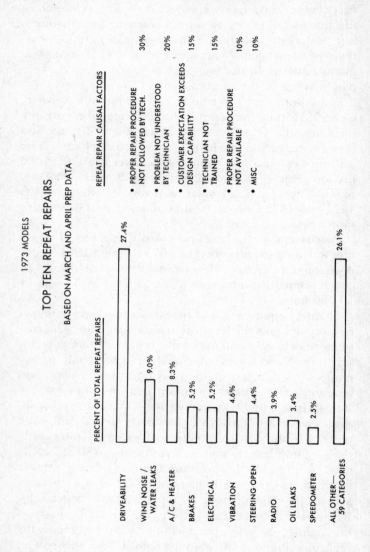

1973 MODELS

TOP TEN REPEAT REPAIRS

BASED ON MARCH AND APRIL PREP DATA

PERCENT OF TOTAL REPEAT REPAIRS

- DRIVEABILITY — 27.4%
- WIND NOISE / WATER LEAKS — 9.0%
- A/C & HEATER — 8.3%
- BRAKES — 5.2%
- ELECTRICAL — 5.2%
- VIBRATION — 4.6%
- STEERING OPEN — 4.4%
- RADIO — 3.9%
- OIL LEAKS — 3.4%
- SPEEDOMETER — 2.5%
- ALL OTHER— 59 CATEGORIES — 26.1%

REPEAT REPAIR CAUSAL FACTORS

- PROPER REPAIR PROCEDURE NOT FOLLOWED BY TECH. — 30%
- PROBLEM NOT UNDERSTOOD BY TECHNICIAN — 20%
- CUSTOMER EXPECTATION EXCEEDS DESIGN CAPABILITY — 15%
- TECHNICIAN NOT TRAINED — 15%
- PROPER REPAIR PROCEDURE NOT AVAILABLE — 10%
- MISC — 10%

Reconditioned parts may cost a bit more than used parts, but they are still less expensive than new ones.

Car manufacturers like to point out that one of the main reasons cars break down is because the public does not maintain its cars as it should. The industry even supports a Car Care Council to put out free-time spot commercials telling motorists to change their tires, spark plugs, air filter, etc., etc.

However, it does not seem to be true that poor owner maintenance is the chief reason for car breakdowns. In fact, the following confidential document sent by one Ford "whistle-blower," shows that the Ford Motor Company knows that 75 percent of the breakdowns are the company's fault:

If, as Ford seems to point out, the major cause of repeat repairs or breakdowns is the automobile dealer's servicing incompetence, then why should we take our cars back for even more servicing?

Hertz Boycotts Dealer Repairs

Everyone knows that the Hertz Corporation is the North American leader in the rent-a-car field; but Hertz also has more than 37,000 cars leased to individuals and fleets. For some time now, Hertz has sent its customers' cars to service stations for repairs rather than to new-car dealerships. The reason is price.

Hertz' vice-president and general manager, Jose Menendez, says, "Our experience has been that the independent gas station tends to be more price-responsive. Therefore, we encourage our customers to go to them . . . We do what we're supposed to do, which is to get things at the lowest possible price. If a new-car dealer will supply that, we will go along with that, of course, and if an independent station will supply that we'll go along . . ."

Could it be that Hertz knows something about dealership car repairs that the public doesn't?

CHAPTER IV

Legal Rights and Wrongs

•

During the past year, the courts have rendered a number of landmark decisions in favor of motorists seeking damages from automobile manufacturers, car dealers, and rustproofing firms.

The following court judgments may prove helpful in obtaining financial compensation if your case is similar to one listed here:

Misrepresentation

Model year deception

Throughout North America, many imported car firms, mobile and motor home manufacturers, snowmobile and motorcycle dealers, and truck distributors have sold their leftover last year's models as current models. However, since 1966, these manufacturers have been required by the United States government to affix a date-of-manufacture plate on the driver's door pillar, thereby curtailing substantially this "redating" deception.

In the United States Honda was forced to make an out-of-court class action settlement in *Henly* v *Honda,* (72 CIV, 4127, New York) because of allegations the company sold CB 350 and CB 750 models for the wrong model year.

A large number of car dealers and manufacturers have been successfully sued before the small claims courts for selling "updated" new and used cars. Most plaintiffs were awarded $400, the maximum amount permitted in Canada.

Quebec Cases

Lepage v *La Canardiere Datsun*, Quebec City, No. 73-1823

Manseau v *Colette*, 1955, C.S.

Bellerose v *Bouvier*, 1955, B.R. p.175

Legault v *Legare Auto*, 1924 Revue Légale n.s. p. 155, 1968, Revue Légale.

Pagnuelo v *Choquette*, Vol 34, C.R. p. 102

Twentieth Century Fox v *Roxy*, 1960 B.R. p. 547

Issenman & Al v *Wescrest*, 1961 C.S. p. 655

Feffergrad v *Weiner*, 1962 R.S. p. 513

Pinkus Construction v *MC Robert*, 1968 B.R. p. 520

Bellemare v *Dionne*, 1961 B.R. p. 524

Brodeur v *Garage Touchette*, 1960 C.S. p. 421

Lortie Ltd v *Jacques*, 35 B.R. p. 571

Morel v *Rousseau*, 54 B.R. p. 582

Lachance v *Ducharme*, 48 B.R. p. 213

Tye v *Fairman*, 1885 M.L.R. IQB, p. 504

Baily v *Reinhardt*, 20 C.S. p. 225

Breslow v *Carleton*, 1962, B.R., p. 267

Ferro Metal v *St-Germain*, 1956 B.R. p. 402

Boutin v *Pare*, 1959 B.R. p. 459

La Ferme Remi v *Joly*, 1972 C.S. p. 482

Potvin v *Gagnon*, 1966 B.R. p. 527

Poulin v *Thetford Toyota*, 73-0521, Mégantic Livre VIII C.P.

Fortin v *Thetford Toyota*, 73-0466, Mégantic Livre VIII C.P.

Pelletier v *Elegant Motors & Al*, 73-1581, Montréal, Livre VIII C.P.

Lalonde Automobile Ltée v *Ford Motor Co. & AL*, Montréal C.S. No. 05-015994-73

Normand v *Godbout*, Ste-Foy, 73-0875, Livre VIII C.P.

Boudrias v *Delisle Auto*, Montréal, C.P. No. 32-006807-73

In another important decision, Quebec's Superior Court, relying upon expert testimony by the Automobile Protection Association (APA), awarded $10,000 to the purchaser of a 1972 BMW that was fraudulently sold as a 1973 model. This case, *Ginn* v *Canbec Auto*, (No. 500-

05-014597-74-4, Montreal), dramatically affirmed that the European auto industry would not hesitate to defraud consumers in order to sell its vehicles.

Ontario and Newfoundland Cases

In Ontario, two separate lawsuits claiming that the Ford Motor Company systematically cheated Canadian consumers by selling 1970 model Cortinas as new 1971 models, were successful and each purchaser received $400 compensation from the small claims court.

In both these judgments (*Brosseau* v *Lewis Motors,* Ottawa-Carleton and *King* v *Paddy Shannahan Ford,* Toronto) the court agreed that Ford used deceptive and fraudulent sales tactics to cheat the public. The best summary of Ford's fraudulent behavior is provided by Justice George Davies in *King* v *Paddy Shannahan:*

> THE COURT: The plaintiff claims damages in the sum of $400.00 in respect to the purchase by her from the defendant of a Cortina motor vehicle manufactured by Ford Motor Company of either Britain or England.
>
> The plaintiff and her husband attended at the business premises of the defendant company and met one Goldberg, a salesman for the defendant. The plaintiff expressed a desire to purchase a 1971 Cortina. Goldberg offered a 1970 Cortina which the defendant had in stock with immediate delivery. The plaintiff declined the offer, insisting she did not want a 1970 Cortina but only a 1971 model. Goldberg agreed to deliver one in approximately two weeks. The buyer's order and the agreement appears in this action as Exhibit 1.
>
> Sometime after the delivery of this vehicle on January 15, 1971 according to Exhibit 2, the plaintiff and her husband became suspicious and finally, at a time which is not certain, enlisted the aid of a Mr. Edmonston of a Montreal based organization called "The Automobile Protection Association". Edmonston testified on behalf of the plaintiff and produced certain documentary evidence, notably a metal plate, which he took from the vehicle indicating the vehicle number, which appears as Exhibit 3.
>
> He also produced a Cortina Shop Manual, Ex-

hibit 4, which discloses the serial number to indicate that the vehicle was manufactured in July, 1970.

The plaintiff also called an employee of the Ford Motor Company of Canada who produced a letter dated October 7, 1970 which said letter inter alia authorized the dealers to reclassify or redesignate all new and unlisted 1970 Cortinas in stock effective October 15, 1970, to be 1971 models. That attached page of the said letter also identified the plaintiff vehicle and it was established through this witness that said car was manufactured in July, 1970 as a 1970 model.

If there was any doubt of the method of proof in respect to the plaintiff's assertion that this was a 1970 motor, that doubt was certainly removed by the evidence of the defense.

Goldberg testified that he knew that the 1970 models were being reclassified as 1971 models effective January 1, 1971. The purchase took place January 9th according to Exhibit 1. In addition to Goldberg's evidence, one Cummings, the sales manager of the defendant company was also called, and when shown Exhibit 7, he stated that all salesmen had been aware of the contents of that letter shortly after receipt by the company, either by memorandum or by information given at a sales meeting. In the Court's respectful opinion, the defendant through Goldberg was guilty of representation inducing the plaintiff to enter into a contract at the time when such representation was false. The Court therefore, finds that this was a fraudulent misrepresentation. In order to succeed in fraud or deceit, however, it must be specifically pleaded. In the absence of such pleading, the Court can afford no relief for fraud or deceit. The plaintiff's claim was hand drawn, and, if the plaintiff had not been represented by counsel who had been called to the Bar, perhaps in the exercise of equity and good conscience, the Court could perhaps have *exproprio motu* granted such an amendment. However, in view of the fact that the plaintiff at trial was represented by a member of the Bar, the Court did not feel it could on its own initiative, grant such an amendment and certainly none was asked for by counsel for the plaintiff.

In *Derry* v *Peek* 14 APP. Ca. 337, Lord Herschell included in his speech the following: "First, in order to sustain an action of deceit there must be proof of fraud, and nothing short of that will suffice. Secondly, fraud is proved when it is shown that a false representation has been made (1) knowingly, or (2) without belief in its truth, or (3) recklessly, careless whether it be true or false. Although, I have treated the second and third as distinct cases, I think the third is but an instance of the second, for one who makes a statement under such circumstances can have no real belief in the truth of what he states."

The doubt only of awarding exemplary or punitive damages for breach of contract appears to be by authority of *Addis* v *Gramophone Co. Ltd* (1909) A.C. 488 where Lord Atkinson stated at 496: "In many other cases of breach of contract there may be circumstances of malice, fraud, defamation or violence, which would sustain an action of tort as an alternative remedy to an action for breach of contract. If one should select the former mode of redress, he may, no doubt, recover exemplary damages of what is sometimes styled vindictive damages; but if he should choose to seek redress in the form of an action for breach of contract, he lets in all the consequences of that form of action."

In *Denison* v *Fawcett*, Schroeder, J.A. at 319, says: "Exemplary or aggravated damages are not, broadly speaking, awarded in actions for breach of contract, since damages for breach of contract are in the nature of compensation, and the motives and conduct of the defendant are not considered relevant to the assignment of damages. The action for breach of promise of marriage and an action upon a contract against a banker for wrongfully refusing to pay his customers' cheques constitute exceptions to this rule. Generally, however, such damages may be awarded in actions of tort such as assault, trespass, negligence, nuisance, libel, slander, seduction, malicious prosecution and false imprisonment. If, in addition to committing the wrongful act, the defendant's conduct is 'high-handed, malicious conduct showing a contempt of the plaintiff's rights, or disregarding every principle which actuates the conduct of a gentleman,' (to quote a few examples taken from the authorities) his conduct is an element to be considered as a circumstance of aggravation which may, depending upon its extent or degree, justify an award to the injured plaintiff in addition to the actual pecuniary loss which he has sustained. I do not think that it can be stated with any precision what may be classed as aggravating circumstances but malice, wantonness, insult and persistent repitition have always been regarded as elements which might be taken into account."

While the plaintiff's claim is capable of being framed in breach of contract, in my respectful opinion, it is equally capable of being framed in tort. While the representations of Goldberg cannot grant relief on the grounds of fraudulent misrepresentation, fraud not having been pleaded, therefore, one relies upon the second or third classification of a false representation as stated by Lord Herschell in *Dery* v *Peek suppra.*

It is clear law that the plaintiff would be entitled to recission of the contract pursuant to *Derry* v. *Peek* or restification according to later authorities. Rescission is out of the question in the instant case due to the delay. Restification is not available either for the uncontradicted evidence of the expert witnesses called for the defence were conclusive in that the vehicle in question upon a trade-in or resale would be treated as a 1971 model due to the registration that disclosed that fact, further, according to Exhibit 7 the price of the alleged 1971 models was not increased over the 1970 model.

There would appear to be one further problem the plaintiff must overcome and that is punitive damages were not claimed.

In two cases in the Ontario Court of Appeal, the Court unanimously held that punitive damages need not be claimed specifically. They are *Glenn* v *Brampton Poultry Co.* 18 D.L.R. (2d) 9; and *Starkman* v *Delhi Court Ltd,* 1961 28 D.L.R. (2d) 269.

The facts in this case are identical to an unreported decision of His Honour Judge Wilmot, former Chief Judge of the County Court, unreported in 1961, therefore, if I had any hesitation in respect to the propriety of awarding punitive damages, I am bound by his decision.

In the words of Mr. Justice Schroeder, paraphrased: "In the Court's respectful opinion, the conduct of the defendant's servant in the case at Bar was high-handed, conduct showing a contempt of the plaintiff's rights, and disregarding every principle which actuates the conduct of a gentleman."

I am therefore strongly of the opinion that this conduct merits censure by the Court, and the award of punitive damages in the sum of $400,000, costs and a counsel fee of $40.00.

In Newfoundland, *O.F. Lakerty* v *McKinley,* (D.L.R. (1953)514) and *McKinley* v *Cobb* (M.P.R. Vol. 51, 198) established that British Leyland had been redating its vehicles since 1951. Both lawsuits were successful.

Misleading Advertising As To Car Quality

In Toronto, General Motors was fined $20,000 for misleading newspaper ads showing its Firenza models traveling from Halifax to Vancouver without difficulty. During the trial, *R.* v *General Motors,* it was confirmed that the three vehicles had so many breakdowns that they barely lasted the entire trip. GM was found to have falsified these data and criminal charges for misleading advertising were successfully pleaded by the federal Department of Consumer and Corporate Affairs.

Misleading Advertising As To Gas Mileage (Dealer)

In *R.* v *Delisle Datsun,* a Montreal Datsun dealer was fined $500 after the federal Department of Consumer and Corporate Affairs laid criminal charges after he misleadingly advertised that a Datsun B210 could get thirty miles to a gallon of gas.

Misleading Advertising As To "Suggested Retail Price"

In *R.* v *Lanthier and Lalonde,* a Montreal Ford dealer was fined $300 for placing ads showing tremendous reductions on new cars sold at prices below the manufacturer's "suggested retail price." After criminal charges were laid, it was shown that the advertised savings were lies.

Misleading Advertising As To Gas Mileage (Dealer and Manufacturer)

The owner of a new 1978 Pinto/Bobcat sued both his dealer and Ford before the Thetford Mines small claims courts for financial compensation because his vehicle got only eleven miles to a gallon of gas despite promises by the dealer and publicity by Ford that he would get twenty-three miles to a gallon. Judge Bastien agreed that both Ford and the dealer intentionally cheated the plaintiff and awarded him $300 to cover the gas mileage difference (*Marchand* v *Grondin Ford,* No. 235-32-000387-758 Megantic).

Since most mileage claims are untrue, it appears that the small claims courts are the best recourse available to obtain compensation for this dishonest advertising gimmick.

Defective Used-Car Lemons

If every consumer had each car verified by an independent mechanic before purchasing it, most used-car lemons could be avoided. Unfortunately, few consumers take this simple precaution.

Once a lemon is bought, however, all is not lost. If you have proof the car was misrepresented to you verbally by the dealer, or misleadingly advertised in the newspaper, the dealer can be sued.

It is also against the law for car dealers to sell vehicles that contain "hidden defects." Therefore, if an independent garage is prepared to state that a used car is unsafe, or has so many defects it is worthless, chances are the contract can be canceled under the "hidden defects" sections of the law. A lawyer must always be consulted for cases of this type.

Odometer Tampering

It is against the law to turn back a car's odometer. Any dealer turning back the odometer is liable to prosecution.

Sold "As Is"

No dealer is permitted to sell an unsafe car to the public. Even if the car is sold "as is," the dealer has the obligation to recondition the vehicle to the extent where it is safe enough to be driven. "As is" provisions in contracts do not absolve the dealership of responsibility for the condition of each used car he sells.

Worthless Guarantee

Sometimes a used-car dealer will delay repairing a used car until after his guarantee runs out. To avoid this racket, send a registered letter to the dealer listing the defect needing repair. If the repairs are not done before the guarantee expires, take a copy of your letter to the small-claims court and claim the estimated amount the repair would cost elsewhere.

Oil companies sometimes give used-car guarantees through different used-car dealers. The dealer is required to guarantee his cars the first month, though. If the dealer does not guarantee the car or use a prescribed oil additive, he has broken his agreement with the oil company and the guarantee becomes worthless. If this happens, you may cancel your purchase because the dealer has failed to honor his guarantee.

Faulty Manufacture

Often a new or used car may contain performance-related and safety-related defects caused by the manufacturer. Usually, these cars are recalled by the manufacturer and corrected at no charge. Some used cars, though, may have been defective and never repaired. To check if your car has been recalled write to the Director, NHTSA, Department of Transportation, Washington, D.C.

Performance-related defects are not subject to recalls, because safety is not affected. However, consumers have canceled many contracts before the courts by listing such diverse defects as water leaks, transmission troubles, motor problems, etc.

Manufacturer's Responsibility for Used Cars

Just because a used car has been bought from a private seller and no longer falls within the limits of the normal new-car warranty expressed by the manufacturer, it does not necessarily mean that the manufacturer cannot be held liable for damages caused by the vehicle's defective design.

As mentioned before, the manufacturer is always liable for the replacement or repair of defective parts if independent testimony can show that the part was incorrectly manufactured or designed. Usually, the existence of a "secret" warranty extension will help prove the part had a high failure rate. In addition to replacing or repairing the part that failed, the automaker can also be held responsible for any consequential damages arising from the part's failure. In the past, this has meant that loss of wages, supplementary transportation costs, and damages for personal inconvenience could be awarded by the courts to owners of used cars.

Personal Injury Liability

Automobile dealers and manufacturers have been held responsible for injuries caused by used cars that had mechanical defects that *provoked* or *caused* an accident. In North America courts have upheld this principle of strict product liability on the part of the manufacturer or distributor of a product or service.

Recent court decisions from some of the higher courts have held automobile manufacturers responsible for the *design* of their vehicles. In essence, the courts have decided that a manufacturer of a new or used motor vehicle is responsible for the injuries arising from the accident, *aggravated* or *maximized* by faulty design. For example, even if an accident is *caused* by driver error and has nothing at all to do with a defective mechanical component, the manufacturer is responsible if injuries are caused by jagged protrusions in the passenger compartment, if fuel tanks exploded upon impact, or if any one of a thousand design features increased the severity of an injury in an automobile accident.

Probably the most recent court decision outlining this principle comes from the Supreme Court of Florida in *Ford Motor Company* v *Mary Jo Evancho,* NO: 45,844, District Court of Appeal NO: 73-764, Decision rendered February 11, 1976, Justices Adkins, England, Lee and Overton concur, with Justice Drew dissenting, with opinion.

Justice Overton gave the following reasons for dismissing the Ford Motor Company's pleas:

> This is a petition for writ of certiorari to review a decision of the Third District Court of Appeal reported as *Evancho v. Thiel,* 297 So. 2d 40 (Fla. App. 3d 1974), and its certification to us of a question of great public interest. We have jurisdiction.*
>
> The certified question concerns the liability of an automobile manufacturer for a defective design which enhances or causes injury but is not the cause of the accident. The certified question is as follows:
>
>> Whether a manufacturer of automobiles may be liable to a user of the automobile for a defect in manufacture which causes injury to the user when the injury occurs as the result of a collision and the defect did not cause the collision?
>
>> We hold that a manufacturer of automobiles may be liable under certain conditions for a design or manufacturing defect which causes injury but is not the cause of the primary collision.

In the above case the appellee, Mary Jo Evancho, brought an action for damages resulting from the death of her husband from injuries sustained as a passenger in an automobile collision. The decedent husband was ri-

*Art, V, § 3(b), Fla. Const.

ding in the rear seat of a 1970 Mercury Montego automobile when it collided with a parked automobile. It was alleged that as a result of the collision the decedent was thrown forward where he struck the back of the front seat of the automobile in which he was a passenger. The mechanism designed to lock the front seat to its carrier rail allegedly failed and caused the right side of the front seat to be thrown forward, exposing sharp and pointed edges of the rail upon which the decedent fell, striking his head and sustaining injuries from which he died.

The appellee brought her action for damages against the driver of the parked vehicle, the driver-owner of the automobile in which the decedent was a passenger, and its manufacturer, the appellant, Ford Motor Company. She contended the appellant negligently designed and manufactured the track-and-rail mechanism in such a manner that it could not withstand the impact of a person being thrown forward from the back seat in the course of a collision. Ford Motor Company moved to dismiss the complaint on the grounds that the alleged defect did not proximately cause the injuries and death, it appearing that the vehicle was operated in a manner beyond its intended use, and therefore no legal duty existed between Ford Motor Company and the plaintiff. The trial judge granted the motion, dismissing the complaint as to Ford Motor Company. The Third District, in a thorough opinion by Judge Pearson, reversed the trial court and certified the above question to us as an issue of great public interest.

Authority is divided whether automobile manufacturers can be held liable for defects in their cars which, although playing no part in causation of the primary automobile collision, nevertheless increase or bring about injury to occupants through secondary impacts. Two widely cited cases illustrating the opposing viewpoints on this issue are *Evans* v *General Motors Corporation,* 359 F. 2d 822 (7th Cir. 1966), and *Larsen* v *General Motors Corporation,* 391 F. 2d 495 (8th Cir. 1968).

In *Evans,* the plaintiff alleged that if the frame of his car had been designed differently, he would have sustained lesser injuries following a broadside collision. The majority opinion held that "A manufacturer is not under a duty to make his automobile accident-proof or fool-proof," and that the manufacturer has no duty to make the automobile "crashworthy." The controlling issue in this case was the breadth of the term "intended use." The majority held:

> The intended purpose of an automobile does not include its participation in collisions with other objects, despite the manufacturer's ability to foresee the possibility that such collisions may occur. As defendant argues, the defendant also knows that its automobiles may be driven into bodies of water, but it is not suggested that defendant has a duty to equip them with pontoons.
>
> *359 F. 2d at 825*

The *Evans* viewpoint has been followed by courts of several jurisdictions.

Schmel v. General Motors, 384 F. 2d 802 (7th Cir. 1967) (applying Ind. law)

McClung v. Ford Motor Co., 472 F. 2d 240 (4th Cir. 1973) (applying W. Va. law)

Walton v. Chrysler Motor Corp., 229 So. 2d 568 (Miss. 1969)

Alexander v. Seaboard Air Line Railroad Co., 346 F. Supp. 320 (W.D.N.C. 1971)

Shumard v. General Motors Corp., 270 F. Supp. 311 (S.D. Ohio 1967) (decided prior to *Larsen, supra*)

Burkhard v. Short, 28 Ohio App. 2d 141, 275 N.E. 2d 632 (Ct. App. Ohio 1971)

(The majority of jurisdictions appear, however, to follow *Larsen v. General Motors Corporation, supra.*)

Arbet v. Gussarson, 66 Wis. 2d 551, 225 N.W. 2d 431 (Wis. 1971)

Johnson v. American Motors Corp., 225 N.W. 2d 57 (N.D. 1974)

Mickle v. Blackman, 166 S.E. 2d 173 (S.C. 1969)

Grandmanis v. British Motor Corp., 308 F. Supp. 303 (E.D. Wis. 1970)

Engberg v. Ford Motor Co., 205 N.W. 2d 104 (S.D. 1973)

Brandenburger v. Toyota Motor Sales, U.S.A., Inc., 162 Mont. 506, 513 P. 2d 268 (1973)

Bolm v. Triumph Corp., 41 A.D. 2d 54, 341 N.Y.S. 2d 846 (App. Div. 1973), aff'd 33 N.Y. 2d 151, 350 N.Y.S. 2d 644 (1973)

Turner v. General Motors Corp., 514 S.W. 2d 497 (Tex. Ct. App. 1974) (application for writ of error refused by S. Ct., there being no reversible error)

Volkswagen of America, Inc. v. Young, 272 Md. 201, 321 A. 2d 737 (Md. 1974)

Badorek v. General Motors Corp., 11 Cal. App. 3d 902, 90 Cal. Rptr. 305 (Ct. App. 1970)

Perez v. Ford Motor Co., 497 F. 2d 82 (5th Cir. 1974) (applying La. law)

Turcòtte v. Ford Motor Co., 494 F. 2d 173 (1st Cir. 1974) (applying R.I. law)

Green v. Volkswagen of America, Inc., 485 F. 2d 430 (6th Cir. 1973) (applying Mich. law)

Passwaters v. General Motors Corp., 454 F. 2d 1270 (8th Cir. 1972) (applying Iowa law)

Dyson v. General Motors Corp., 298 F. Supp. 1064 (E.D. Pa 1969) (applying Pa. law)

Friend v. General Motors Corp., 118 Ga. App. 763, 165 S.E. 2d 734 (1968)

Baumgardner v. American Motors Corp., 83 Wash. 2d 751, 522 P. 2d 829 (1974)

Mieher v. Brown, 54 Ill. 2d 539, 301 N.E. 2d 307 (1973)

In *Larsen,* a head-on collision impacting on the left front corner of plaintiff's vehicle drove the steering shaft rearward into the plaintiff's head, causing his death. The court rejected the assertion by the automobile manufacturer that accidents are not readily foreseeable, and held that a manufacturer could not close his eyes to such eventualities. The *Larsen* court reasoned that the "intended use" of an automobile was "not just to provide a means of transportation" but held that the intended use of an automobile "is to provide a means of safe transportation." In doing so, it recognized the frequency with which automobiles are involved in collisions, and held that the probability must be taken into account by designers and manufacturers. It established liability on the automobile manufacturer for injuries sustained in secondary collisions between occupants and components of the vehicle in which they were riding when the injury was caused or enhanced by some such design or manufacturing defect and was reasonably foreseeable and reasonably could have been avoided. This theory does not impose liability on a basis of warranty or strict tort liability; rather, it recognizes a duty of reasonable care on automobile manufacturers based on common law negligence. The *Larsen* court, in establishing this doctrine, said:

> Accepting, therefore, the principle that a manufacturer's duty of design and construction extends to producing a product that is reasonably fit for its intended use and free of hidden defects that could render it unsafe for such use, the issue narrows on the proper interpretation of "intended use." Automobiles are made for use on the roads and highways in transporting persons and cargo to and from various points. This intended use cannot be carried out without encountering in varying degrees the statistically proved hazard of injury-producing impacts of various types. The manufacturer should not be heard to say that it does not intend its product to be involved in any accident when it can easily foresee and when it knows that the probability over the life of its product is high, that it will be involved in some type of injury-producing accident . . .
>
> . . . Where the manufacturer's negligence in design causes an unreasonable risk to be imposed upon the user of its products, the manufacturer should be liable for the injury caused by its failure to exercise reasonable care in the design. These injuries are readily foreseeable as an incident to the normal and expected use of an automobile. While automobiles are not made for the purpose of colliding with each other, a frequent and inevitable contingency of normal automobile use will result in collisions and injury-producing impacts. No rational basis exists for limiting recovery to situations where the defect in design or manufacture was the causative factor, as the accident and the resulting injury, usually caused by the so-called "second collision" of the passenger with the interior part of the automobile, all are foreseeable. Where the injuries or enhanced injuries are due to the manufacturer's failure to use reasonable care to avoid subjecting the user of its products to an unreasonable risk of injury, general negligence principles should be applicable. The sole function of an automobile is not just to provide a means of transportation, it is to provide a means of safe transportation or as safe as

is reasonably possible under the present state of the art.

This duty of reasonable care in design rests on common law negligence that a manufacturer of an article should use reasonable care in the design and manufacture of his product to eliminate any unreasonable risk of foreseeable injury. The duty of reasonable care in design should be viewed in light of the risk. While all risks cannot be eliminated nor can a crash-proof vehicle be designed under the present state of the art, there are many common-sense factors in design, which are or should be well known to the manufacturer, that will minimize or lessen the injurious effects of a collision. The standard of reasonable care is applied in many other negligence situations and should be applied here.

The option of the Third District Court is approved, and the certified question is answered affirmatively in accordance with our collective views. The petition for certiorari is discharged.

It is so ordered . . .

In so holding, however, the *Larsen* court recognized that manufacturers are not insurers and are under no duty to design a crash-worthy, accident-proof, or fool-proof vehicle.

We adopt the *Larsen* view, holding that the manufacturer must use reasonable care in design and manufacture of its product to eliminate unreasonable risk of foreseeable injury.

Unsafe New Cars

Since 1966 more than 70 million new cars that explode, careen out of control, lose wheels etc. . . . have been recalled by auto makers because of pressure from the federal government. Department of Transport figures show that only about two-thirds of those cars eligible for free recall repairs actually get repaired. That leaves on the road millions of lethal vehicles that can kill or maim innocent drivers, passengers, and pedestrians.

The following court decisions may be helpful if you wish to file suit for damages against an automobile manufacturer that has used an unsafe engineering design that increased the severity of accident injuries, or used defective components in the vehicle's assembly:

1. Rust causing chassis failure (Ford)—In *R.* v *Ford Motor Company of Canada,* the federal Ministry of Transport successfully pleaded that rusting of the undercarriage of Ford's 1965–1974 mid-sized models could cause the idler arms to become inoperative and lead to a complete loss of steering. Ford was fined $10,000. The company appealed the verdict and still informs its customers that there is no problem.

Under Canadian federal legislation *(Canadian Motor Vehicle Safety Act [1971]),* car companies do not have to recall their cars, or fix them free of charge, within a certain period of time. The law stipulates that the car companies only have to *notify* owners that their cars can kill them. American legislation requires notification and free correction.

This Ford safety hazard is of particular interest to owners of Datsun B210 and 240Z models, as well as 1971 and 1974 Fiat models, where chassis failure caused by rusting has been reported.

2. Gas Tank Fires—Once again, Ford has been on the receiving end of dozens of lawsuits claiming that its vehicles are unsafe. One case, *Buehler* v *Goodman,* (Illinois Supreme Court, Nos. 48949, 48956, December 12, 1977) is particularly striking in the way it shows how Ford deliberately misled the court about the dangers associated with flange-mounted gas tanks used by Ford since 1960.

In this fire injury lawsuit, Judge Dooley condemned Ford for "giving false answers to interrogatives under oath," and "secreting evidence damaging to its case." *Atkins* v *American Motors,* Alabama Supreme Court, No. S.C. 1488, May 21, 1976. 1970 Gremlin, fire fatality.

3. Accelerator—Woman sustained serious injuries when the accelerator return spring came loose and made car crash into a wall. Judgment in plaintiff's favor. (*Williams* v *Stewart Motor Company,* CA-DC, 1974), (*Heap* v *General Motors,* California Appeal Court, Second District, Division Three, No. 48043, December 29, 1976).

4. Rear Axle—Accident caused by rear axle failure judged to be responsibility of manufacturer (*Kuhbacker* v *Ford,* Wyoming Superior Court, 1974, *Townsend* v *Cleve Hugh Chevrolet–Buick,* Louisiana Appeal Court 1975, *Hatcher* v *American Motors Coporation,* Mississippi Supreme Court).

5. Brakes—School bus brake failure killed two children. Manufacturer held responsible (*Spurlin* v *General Motors*, CA-5 Ala, 1976).

Defective brake fluid caused brake failure. Manufacturer held responsible (*Begley* v *Ford*, CA-2 NY, 1973).

Brake failure, manufacturer and seller held responsible (*Baker* v *Ford*, Missouri Supreme Court, 1973).

Driver struck from rear by vehicle with defective brakes awarded damages from manufacturer of other car (*Ford* v *Zipper*, Kentucky Appeal Court, 1973).

Brakes of used car failed. Plaintiff awarded $40,000 for injuries. (*Tweedy* v *Ford*, Illinois Supreme Court, No. 47943, October 1, 1976.).

6. Cooling System—Ford Econoline cooling system hose ruptured due to defective design. Manufacturer held liable for injuries (*Ford* v *Russell and Smith Ford Company*, Texas Civil Court of Appeal, 1972).

7. Fan Blade—Breakage of fan blade rendered manufacturer responsible for injuries sustained (*Pouncey* v *Ford*, CA-5 Alabama, 1972). Since this judgment, the Ford Motor Company has recalled a number of its vehicles for the correction of defective fan blades. Unfortunately, one mechanic has already been killed, Henry Ford II called the recall delay "a regrettable error."

8. Gear Shift Components (Ford)—Driver awarded damages when vehicle suddenly jumped into gear while being started (*Ford* v *Lee*, Georgia Appeal Court, 1976).

A number of motorist injuries have been reported due to Ford's C-6 and FMX automatic transmissions jumping from "park" into "reverse" while the motor was running.

9. Head Restraints—Because a head restraint was defective, manufacturer as well as driver of other vehicle was held responsible for accident injuries (*Huddell* v *Levin*, DC NJ, 1975).

Absence of head restraints in 1973 Chevrolet LUV truck contributed to extent of injury. (*Buccery* v *General Motors*, California Court of Appeal, Second District, Division Three, Civ. No. 48051, July 27, 1976.).

10. Seatbelt—Defective seatbelt strap broke rendering manufacturer responsible for accident injuries (*Engberg* v *Ford*, South Dakota Supreme Court, 1973).

11. Hood Failure—Accident caused hood to enter passenger compartment and injure driver. Manufacturer held responsible (*Fink* v *Chrysler*, Illinois Appeal Court, 1974)

12. Shock Absorbers—Shock absorber failure ruled

cause of accident injuries. Manufacturer held responsible due to a defective left-front shock tower (*Ford* v *Bland,* Texas Civil Court of Appeal, 1974).

13. Steering Failure—Steering shaft separation caused accident injuries. Manufacturer held responsible (*Williams* v *General Motors,* Texas Civil Court of Appeal, 1973). (Also see *Coding* v *Paglia,* NY Appeal Court, 1973), (*Kohler* v *Ford,* Nebraska, Supreme Court, 1971).

(*Walczak* v *General Motors,* Illinois Appeal Court, 1976), (*Jastremsik* v *General Motors,* New Jersey Supreme Court, 1970), (*Stewart* v *Budget Rent-a-Car,* Hawaii Supreme Court, 1970), (*Culpepper* v *Volkswagen,* California Appeal Court, 1973), (*American Motors* v *Mosier,* CA-5 Texas, 1969), (*Cohen* v *Ford,* DC, NY, 1963), and (*Iadiccio* v *General Motors,* New York Supreme Court, Appelate Division No. 2460E., January 30, 1978), (*Jackson* v *General Motors,* New York Supreme Court, Appelate Division, Second Department, No. 1655E/76, March 7, 1977).

Although no defect evidence presented, damages awarded for accident injuries because car had a history of steering malfunction. (See *Stewart* v *Ford,* United States Court of Appeals, District of Columbia Circuit No. 75-1676, February 9, 1977). (*General Motors* v *Dillon,* Delaware Supreme Court, No. 102, November 3, 1976).

1968 Pontiac Firebird steering column collapsed. Driver awarded $65,000.

14. Transmission—Defective transmission that slipped from "park" into a forward gear caused serious injury. Rental company held responsible (*Bossons* v *Hertz,* Minnesota Supreme Court, 1970).

15. Wheel Failure—Rear wheel came off, manufacturer responsible for injuries (*Dumas* v *Chevrolet,* Louisiana DC, 1975).

Collapse of A-frame supporting front wheel of Mustang Mach I. (*Browder* v *Pettigrew Motor Company,* Tennessee Supreme Court, August 30, 1976).

16. Carburetor Defect—1970 Chevrolet pick-up equipped with defective quadrajet carburetor caused serious accident injuries. Driver recovered damages despite having tampered with carburetor (*Hopkins* v *General Motors,* Texas Supreme Court no. B-5986, February 23, 1977).

17. Seat Failure—(*Howell* v *General Motors,* New York Supreme Court, Appelate Division, Second Department, No. 1286, March 26, 1976).

1971 Fiats—seat failure from rear impacts. (*Smith* v *Fiat Roosevelt Motors*, N.S. District Court, Orlando Division, No. 73-228-ORL-C1V-R, October 20, 1975). (*Fredericks* v *General Motors*, Maryland Court of Appeals, No. 169, September 17, 1976.)

Damages awarded for unsafe seat-locking mechanism and poor roof design aggravating accident of secondary impact (See *Cronin* v *J.B.E. Olson Corp*, 104 Cal. Rptr. 433, 501 P 2d 1153).

18. Window Shattering—Blindness caused by window shattering on 1962 Chevrolet Impala during accident. Awarded $500,000. (*Simmons* v *General Motors*, Texas Court of Civil Appeals, No. 16,705, November 24, 1976).

19. Horn Cap Hazard— $45,000 awarded for facial injuries aggravated by striking horn cap in 1965 Chevrolet. Nonuse of seatbelt not pertinent. (*Horn* v *General Motors*, California Supreme Court, No. 30235, June 30, 1976).

20. Fire of Unknown Origin—1968 Truck caught fire while idle. (*Cornell Corporation* v *Ford*, Pennsylvania Superior Court, Pittsburg District, No. 508, June 28, 1976).

21. Motor Mounts—1969 Chevrolet Nova motor mount failure causing accident injuries (See *Murphy* v *General Motors*, New York Supreme Court Appellate Division, Third Judicial Department, No. 29510, January 27, 1977).

(*Barry-Manglass* v *General Motors*, New York Supreme Court, Appellate Division, Second Department, December 6, 1976).

22. Ignition Lock System—Seatbelt nonuse not pertinent. (*Fields* v *Volkswagen*, Oklahoma Supreme Courts, No. 46,805, July 27, 1976). $150,000 awarded for injuries caused by defective ignition lock affecting steering of 1971 VW. Driver drunk and speeding.

23. Tires—Goodyear "Super High-Miler" truck tire blow-out after only 9,000 miles, causing accident. (*Hughes Supply Inc.*, v *Goodyear*, Florida District Court of Appeal, Fourth District, No. 75-336, August 27, 1976).

24. Snowmobile—$100,000 awarded for injuries caused by Olympic 399 Ski-Doo with defective main-leaf springs. (*Sandowski* v *Bombardier*, U.S. Court of Appeals, Seventh Circuit, No. 75-1980, July 22, 1976).

25. Door Latch Failure—(*Melia* v *Ford*, Nova Scotia Court of Appeals, Eighth Circuit, No. 75-1316).

26. Warranty Compensation—(*Jagodnik* v *Renault*,

Florida District Court of Appeal, First District, No. Y-497, March 16, 1976).

27. "Lemon" Trailer Home—Couple awarded $8,750 damages for defective trailer home on theory of an implied warranty of reasonable fitness. (*Nobility Homes of Texas* v *Shivers,* Texas Court of Civil Appeals, Ninth Supreme Judicial District, No. 7808, July 15, 1976).

28. "Lemon" Motor Home—Defective Condor Motor Home purchase price of $16,867.92 refunded for breach of warranty. (*Christopher* v *Ford,* Utah Supreme Court, No. 14063, November 29, 1976).

Expert Witnesses

As a result of the thousands of product liability actions brought each year by American and Canadian motorists, the courts have used an increasing number of independent expert witnesses to counter industry testimony relating to the relative safety of their vehicles.

These independent experts are essential to winning a lawsuit. Their fees may be high, but there is really no alternative. Remember, in any product liability or negligence lawsuit, the car manufacturer will throw everything into the case. So, be well prepared.

The following people are recommended as expert witnesses in product liability lawsuits involving their own specialty. If the persons listed cannot take your case, see if they can supply your lawyer with the names of other competent expert witnesses capable of handling the intricacies of your case.

1. General Experts

ALLEN, J. Merril
Indiana University
(Optometry)

ANDERSON' P.E. John W.
Engineering Consultant
P.O. Box 8329
Portland, Oregon 97207
(503) 292-5547

AUGSPURGER, Quent
Consulting Mechanical Engr.

2311 E. Colter
Phoenix, Arizona 85016
(602) 956-9536

BACKLUND, H. Brandon
Backlund Engineering Co.
8610 Cass St.
Omaha, Nebraska 68114
(402) 393-8250

BETTINGER, Joseph L.
Bettinger Engineers

1289 Monroe Ave
Rochester, N.Y. 14620
(716) 442-1000

BODNER, Seymour S.
Consulting Engineer
27 Shadowlawn Drive
Livingston, N.J. 07039
(201) 994-3472

CAMPBELL, B.J. Dr.
Highway Safety
Research Center
North Carolina University
Chapel Hill, North Carolina

CHAPANIS, Alfonso
Human Factors Expert
Johns Hopkins University
Baltimore, Md.

CHRONIC, Bill M.
Chronic & Associates
707 N. 27th
Boise, Idaho 83702
(208) 345-0780

CLAFFEY, Paul J.
Civil Engineer
26 Grant St.
Potsdam, N.Y. 13676
(315) 265-3850
planning, research, traffic

DAMON, Henry E.
Associated Consultants, Inc
Box 5654
Meridian, Miss. 39301
(601) 693-6156

DUNLAP, Duane
Highway Safety Research Institute
University of Michigan
Ann Arbor, Michigan 48105
(313) 764-2168
quardrail design, placement & impact, accident reconstruction, site analysis, tire traction & road surfaces

EMERI, Richard I.
5800 A Boelter Hall
UCLA
L.A., Cal. 90024
(Auto Collision Mechanics & Reconstructions/Accidents)

FAILURE ANALYSIS ASSOCIATES
Engineering and Metallurgical Consultants
Dr. A. S. Tetelman (Professor of Materials Science)
University of California, Los Angeles
(213) 825-5664

FITZGERALD, John E.
Consulting Engineer
399 Beacon Hill Drive
Cheshire, Conn. 06410
(203) 272-6185

FLANAKIN, H.A. Mike
Civil Engineer
8702 Milford Ave
Silver Spring, Md. 20910
(301) 587-8243
city planning, research, traffic
engineering administration

FONDA, Albert
545 Hughes Rd
King of Prussia, Pa.
(215) 687-3311

FREEMAN, Ronald A.
Staunton & Freeman
101 Park Avenue
New York, N.Y. 10017
(212) 683-8865

HAISTEN, John L.
Applied Engineering
Laboratories, Inc,
Metallurgical & Consulting
Engineers
4925 First Avenue, South
Birmingham, AL 35212

595-1144
(Component failures: metal integrity)

HANAGUD, Satnya
Aeronautics Department
Georgia Tech
Atlanta, Georgia
(404) 894-3040 (3002)

HUMPHREYS, P.E.
Associate Professor
Dept. of Civil Engineering
112 Perkins Hall
University of Tennessee
Knoxville, Tenn. 37916
(615) 974-3188 office
(615) 593-4781
accident reconst., hwy safety,
traffic engr'g.

HUTCHISON, John, Dr.
Prof. of Traffic Engr's
Dept of Civil Engr'g
Univ. of Kentucky
Lexington, Ky. 40506

HYMAN, Harris
Engineer & Surveyor
Box 708
Middlebury, Vt. 05703
(802) 388-2174

JOHNSON, Howard R.
3204 Dexter Road
Ann Arbor, Michigan
(313) 769-2668
(Former Senior
Research Scientist for
Kelsey- Hayes;
willing to testify
as a brake lining expert)

KLEIN, Stanley J.
1694 Highland Avenue
Rochester, New York 14018

LEGGETT, James L.,
G. Reynolds Watkins
Consulting Engineers
3399 Tates Creek Rd

Lexington, Ky. 40502
(606) 269-4311

MANNING, Charles, Dr.,
North Carolina State University
Raleigh, North Carolina
(919) 737-2377

MANOS, Thomas, Dr.,
University of Detroit
4001 W. McNichols Rd
Detroit, Michigan
(313) 342-1000

MARTINEZ, John L.
12 Fontainebleau Drive
New Orleans, La. 70125
(Biomechanics-Whiplash
Phenomenon)

MASTERS, Frank M. Jr.,
Consulting Engineer
R.D. no. 4
Box 848,
Harrisburg, Pa. 17112
(717) 599-5123

MEISTER, Charles, P.E.
Meister & Associates
6200 B W. Fairfield Dr
Pensacola, Fla. 32506
(904) 455-2234

MORRIS, Alan D.
Morris and Ward
P.O. Box 5937
Washington, D.C. 20014
(301) 320-4900

MCCARTHY, S.M.
Tampa Bay Engineering Co.
Mechanical engineer
liability consulting dept.
1355 Shell Isle Blvd
(P.O. Box 7236)
St. Petersburg, Fla. 33734
(813) 896-1171
(retained as consultants in
law suit involving accident
of Dodge van-brakes).

NADY, Robert M.
Nady Engineering Service
1207 H Avenue
Nevada, Iowa 50201
(515) 382-4330

NUCCITELLI, Saul A.
Consulting Engineers & Architects
Suite 306 McDaniel Bldg.
Springfield, Mo. 65806
(417) 865-6247

OLSON, Nels R., M.D.
St. Joseph's Mercy Hospital
Ann Arbor, Mich. 48104
(313) 665-5330
(Expert in injuries of ear, nose, throat)

PETERS, George A.
15442 Ventura Blvd
Sherman Oaks, California 91403

POE, Lewis H. II
Consulting Engineer
815 Rio Vista St.
Santa Fe, New Mexico 87501
(505) 982-8926

PORTER Raughley L.
Kennedey-Bode Engineering
2319 Maryland Ave
Baltimore, Md. 21218
(301) 467-1645

PRESNELL ASSOCIATES
INC
100 E. Liberty St
Louisville, Ky. 40202
(502) 587-9611

PRITZKER, Paul E.
George L. Slack Co.
680 Hancock St.
Quincy, Mass. 02170
(617) 471-8282

RYAN, James J.
52 N. Mississippi River Blvd
St. Paul, Minn. 55104

(Impact crash worthiness, Occupant Restraint)

SAIBEL, Edward A., Dr.,
(vehicle skidding; vehicle steering)
Information: Roland King
Department of Public Relations,
Carnegie Mellon University,
Pittsburgh, Pa. 15213
(412) 621-2600 x318

SESSLER, John G.
121 Jean Ave
Syracuse, N.Y.
(315) 476-8190

SIMMONS/FLETCHER/
MURPHY & ASSOCIATES,
Inc
Investigative-Consultants
P.O. Box 2096
Monterey, California 93940
James L. Fletcher (408) 373-7733

SINGER, Robert H.
Testing Engineers, Inc
300 Montgomery St.
San Francisco, Calif. 94104
(415) 956-1400

SLEIGHT, Dr
Human Factors Expert
Century Research Corporation
Arlington, Va.
(703) JA 7-5373

STAHL, Robert E.
631 Overbrook Rd
Baltimore, Md. 21212
(301) 377-9624

STUBBLEFIELD, Bert
Buonaccorsi & Assoc.
215 Market St.
San Francisco, Calif. 94105
(415) 982-4370

SZOSTAK, Henry T.
Dept of Ind. Engr.

Berkeley, Calif. 94720
(Auto. Chassis, steering dynamics
namics
Direc/Engr. Program in
human facters)

TALBOTT, John A.
Talbott, Wong & Assoc.
2014 N.E. Sandy Blvd
Portland, Oregon 97232
(503) 233-6587

2. Flammability/Fuel System

ARNDT, Fred
S. Harry Robertson
Department of Engineering
Arizona State University
Tempe, Arizona
(602) 965-7749

BEDFORD, D. Ernie
10 W. Huron
Pontiac, Michigan 48058
(313) 338-6464

BELLES, Donald W.
116 Cloverdale Court
Hendersonville, Tenn. 37075
(615) 824-5974

BYRUS, Robert C.
11131 Emack Road
Beltsville, Maryland 20705
(301) 937-7068

CHRISTIAN, William J., Dr.,
Underwriters Laboratory
333 Pfingsten Road
Northbrook, Illinois 60062
(312) 272-8800

EINHORN, Irving, Dr.,
University of Utah
Salt Lake City, Utah 84112
(801) 581-8431

MANNING, Charles, Dr.,
North Carolina State University
sity
Raleigh, North Carolina
(919) 737-2377

PRUSSING, George F.
2911 Q. Street, N.W.
Washington, D.C. 20007
(202) 333-3660

STIEGLITZ, William I.
9 Howard Drive
Huntington, New York 11743
(516) 261-5360

STAM, Paul
P.O. Box 104 B
Greensboro, North Carolina
(919) 275-6333

WELKER, J. Reed, Dr.,
Flame Dynamics Laboratory
University of Oklahoma Research Institute
search Institute
1215 Westheimer Drive
Norman, Oklahoma 73069
(405) 325-7263

YUILL, Calvin H.
Southwest Research Institute
8500 Culebra Road
San Antonio, Texas 78284
(512) 684-5111

3. Handling/Stability

FONDA, Albert G.
545 Hughes Road
King of Prussia, Pa. 19406
(215) 687-3311

HEITZMAN, Edward
6 Moores Mill
Pennington, New Jersey 08534
(609) 466-2071

MANOS, Thomas, Prof.,
Dept. of Mechanical Engineering
University of Detroit
4001 McNichols Road, West
Detroit, Michigan 48221
(313) 342-1000

MILLIKEN, William R.,
Calspan Corp.
4455 Genesee Street
Buffalo, New York 14221
(716) 632-7500

McKIBBEN, Jon
250 North Nash Street
El Segundo, Calif. 90245
(213) 640-0576

O'SHEA, Paul
516 East 31st Street
Newport Beach, Calif. 92660
(714) 832-4877

SEGEL, Leonard
Highway Safety Research Institute
Huron Parkway & Baxter
Road
Ann Arbor, Michigan 48105
(313) 764-2168

SERGAY, Dimitry B.
427 Dorothy Drive
King of Prussia, Pa. 19406
(215) 265-4452

SMITH, Ralph H.
105 Mine Street
Flemington, New Jersey
08822
(201) 782-1630

WILDER, Stephen F.
249 West 18th Street
New York, New York 10011
(212) 989-7727

4. Motormount Experts

BURNSTINE, Murry, Dr.,
Hycor, Inc
1 Gill St.
N. Woburn, Mass. 01801

FLANNEGAN, James
211 Park Dale Plaza
Corpus Christi,
Texas 78411
(512) 853-5561

5. VW Specialists

BARZELAY, Martin
205 Janet Dr.
Syracuse, New York 13224,
(315) 446-1204, 476-5541

2172 Dupont Dr.
Irvine, Calif. 92664
(714) 752-7860
(also: Small cars, vans)

MCKIBBEN, Jon
McKibben Engineering Co.
Suite 18

STIEGLITZ, William
9 Howard Dr.
Huntington, N.Y. 11743
(516) 261-5360

6. Tire Experts

ARUTUNOFF, Anatoly
8117 E. 46th Street
Tulsa, Oklahoma 74145
(918) 622-5304

FONDA, Albert G.
545 Hughes Road
King of Prussia, Pa. 19406
(215) 687-3311

FORNEY, Loren J.
6819 Elm Street
McLean, Virginia 22101
(703) 356-2102, (703) 938-1882

FRAM, Adolph
347 Cayuga Street
Pittsburgh, Pa. 15224
(412) 681-8470 or (412) 681-3131

HEITZMAN, Ed
Forrestal Campus
Princeton University
Princeton, New Jersey 08540
(609) 452-5157 or (609) 466-2071

JORDAN, William
Tire Safety Registry
2011 I Street, N.W.
Washington, D.C. 20006
(202) 466-8693

KAMM, Erman
Stevens Institute
Hobokan, New Jersey 07030
(201) 792-2700

MEYER, Wolfgang
Pennsylvania State University
State College, Pa. 16802
(814) 237-7127

MILNER, Alan, Dr.,
1910 East Eight St.
Tucson, Arizona
(602) 623-5538

STIEHLER, Robert
3234 Quesada Road, N.W.
Washington, D.C. 20015
(202) 537-1859

WEIR, Kay
3863 Prospect
Culver City, Calif. 90030
(213) 836-6250 or 823-6618

7. Door Latch Design/Construction

ADAMS, Thomas
28334 Ridgebrook Road
Farmington, Michigan 48024
(313) 476-2084

GREEN, Elliott A.
156 Ardmore Road
Kensington, Calif. 94707
(415) 524-6841

HABBERSTAD, John L.
N. 7915 Excell Drive
Spokane, Washington 99208
(509) 328-9507

STIEGLITZ, William I.
9 Howard Drive
Huntington, New York 11743
(516) 261-5360

TEK, Mehmet Rasin, Dr.,
Prof. of Chemical and
Metallurgical Engineering
University of Michigan
Ann Arbor, Michigan 48104
(313) 764-3386

8. Canadian Experts

ARCON ENGINEERING
352 Consumers Rd
Willowdale, Ontario
(Electrical Components)

DELPLACE ASSOCIATES
LTD
4892 Victoria Avenue
Montreal. P. Que.
(Fires, mechanical)

GARAGE DUHAMEL
(J. Cantin)
0658 Joseph St.
Verdun, Quebec
(514) 768-5582
(Mechanical)

NATIONAL AUTO

ACCIDENT
615 Mount Pleasant
Toronto, Ontario
(Mechanical Failure)

MARC THERIAULT
6202 De Normandville
Montreal, Quebec
(Electrical components)

VINER, William C.
345 Victoria Ave
Westmount, Quebec
(514) 483-1242
(Fires, mechanical)

WILLIAMS, Prof.
McGill University
Montreal. Quebec
(Metal failure)

The Rustproofing Racket

Rusting is a serious affair, especially the premature rusting of a motor vehicle. Not only does it cause a vehicle to lose a great deal of its resale value, it also may create a serious safety hazard.

An effective rustproofing compound applied by competent experts could help reduce the severity of accidents caused by vehicles that are rust prone. Unfortunately, the industry is too busy selling franchises and offering phony guarantees to be concerned with offering North American motorists quality corrosion protection.

Ziebart USA, the godfather of the entire rustproofing industry, admits that it can no longer guarantee certain model cars, such as the Fiat and General Motors' Vega.

The Dura-Coat rustproofing company, based in Niagara Falls, has been chased out of Quebec, leaving numerous unpaid small-claims-court judgments, while at the same time having to defend itself against a fraud investigation initiated by Vermont's attorney general. No wonder rustproofing has a bad reputation.

The results of a recent survey indicate that a majority

of consumers feel they have been cheated by rust-proofing firms. These consumers complained of worthless guarantees, ineffective products, and misleading advertising.

Motorist Survey

The rustproofing questionnaires were answered by 308 motorists selected at random. Of this sample more than 60 percent of the motorists responding stated they were dissatisfied with the rustproofing product purchased.

Points of Dissatisfaction

The following consumer complaints are listed in order of their frequency.

1. Severe rusting despite rustproofing.
2. Unsatisfactory application of product.
3. Product sticky, stains clothing, slow drying, falls off.
4. Misleading advertising.
5. Warranty not respected.
6. Warranty conditions not explained.
7. Follow-up inspections not possible.
8. Variation of $80 for same rustproofing done elsewhere.

Rusting with Rustproofing

Rustproofing products appear to be completely ineffective on cars that have a tendency to rust due to design defects in construction and harsh climate. The following cars were found to be very rust prone:

Datsun 510 and 240Z
General Motors Vega and Astre
Renault 15
Peugeot
Volkswagen 411, 412, Beetle, and Super Beetle
Fiat 124, 128
Ford Maverick, Mustang, and Cougar
Toyota Corolla
Mercury Capri
Citroen

Jaguar XKE
Mercedes
Porsche 911

Rustproofing companies are aware of the ineffectiveness of their product on certain model cars, but often neglect to inform consumers. For example, Ziebart Rustproofing, one of the top rustproofing firms in North America, states, "Ziebart cannot guarantee the Astre, Fiat, or Vega due to a design defect in their construction."

Ziebart's director of marketing services did not state whether the average consumer is informed that his Vega, Astre, or Fiat cannot be guaranteed before purchasing Ziebart rustproofing, but a number of discontented Ziebart customers who took part in our survey complained that they were *not* told.

Unsatisfactory Application of Product

Consumers purchasing rustproofing may not only find that the product is ineffective; they may also find it has been improperly applied. Many consumers complained that the rustproofing compound was sprayed carelessly by incompetent technicians who even failed to clean the vehicle before beginning. Vital areas were not sprayed, leaving them vulnerable to rust. One dissatisfied customer wrote the following: "The quality of the work depends upon the quality of people. My car rusted because of incompetent, unconscientious employees."

Large companies also complained of the poor application of rustproofing products. One company spokesman states: "Of ten cars inspected among our group at the office, eight were incompletely coated."

In many cases consumers do not realize their car has been improperly rustproofed until the vehicle is inspected under warranty or following minor collision damage. One consumer received the following Ziebart inspection report: "We found that the rear quarter panels have not been sprayed, and doing a respray on the quarter panels would be thirty-three dollars."

Product Criticisms

A large number of consumers surveyed complained that the rustproofing compound caused noxious odors, was slow drying, stained clothing, peeled off, and stained their cars' finish. These problems continued for several months after application.

Misleading Advertising

Misleading advertising is a serious charge. In the rust-proofing survey, however, irate consumers repeatedly complained of being victimized by misleading statements from a variety of rustproofing firms.

One food-company president declared:

> We own a subsidiary company . . . and back in 1971 we had a couple of 1971 Ford Cars Ziebarted. One car was satisfactory, the other car cost us over three hundred dollars to repair rusted-out areas. The Ziebart dealer in Saint John refused to even refund our money, and it seems strange that they can continue to advertise giving the consumer the impression that their product is guaranteed for ten years, when in reality, all they are obligated to do is refund the money, and when they refuse to do this, we think it is time that an organization, like yours, brought the problems to the attention of the many unsuspecting consumers.

Another angry customer vented his dissatisfaction more directly:

> Outrageous, scandalous, manufacturer's rip-off —obviously a con game based on refusing my refund and waiting for the owner to scrap the car in disgust. I was a stupid ass who got taken for a ride in trying to protect his investment.

Warranty Not Respected

Although most companies advertise that they will refund your money if rusting occurs, many customers are denied refunds. One dissatisfied Vitalizing customer wrote: "The warranty is, of course, worthless." A frustrated Tuff-Coat customer wrote: "Tuff-Coat has ignored my correspondence into this matter, but the new-car dealer has corrected the matter himself."

Warranty Conditions Not Explained

From the survey responses, it appears that warranty conditions and limitations are not explained or, if explained, are stated in such vague terms that the consumer is never really sure what his warranty rights are. In one 12-page publicity pamphlet Ziebart does not mention the warranty once.

Tuff-Coat again comes in for some harsh criticism concerning its failure to fully outline its warranty limitations: "No one at Tuff-Coat mentioned the necessity of filling out the questionnaire to validate the guarantee."

Because a simple questionnaire was not filled out, this Tuff-Coat customer was refused his warranty coverage.

Follow-Up Inspections

A common requirement by most rustproofing firms surveyed stated that each rustproofed car must undergo a free follow-up inspection after two years, to insure that the rustproofing compound is effective and to respray those areas that may be especially vulnerable to rusting.

One of the major problems with mandatory follow-up inspections is that too often, consumers are apparently not told about them. Thus, the warranty becomes void. One consumer stated:

> He asked me whether I had proof of my two-year inspection, and when I stated I did not know about a two-year inspection being required . . . he informed me that Tuff-Coat would not pay for my repairs.
> Why require twenty-four-month inspection without any other warning? Agreed, I didn't maintain my part in having the auto inspected at twenty thousand miles, but did Ziebart attempt to contact me and have me bring it in?

A second problem with follow-up inspections occurs when the dealer goes out of business, or the customer moves away. Durable Coatings has a guarantee that states: "All claims of adjustments must be made by the dealer doing the original rustproofing job." This limitation of guarantee unfairly penalizes a consumer who rustproofs his car at a dealer that becomes bankrupt, or a consumer who has to move to a distant region. Both cases would invalidate the Dura-Coat guarantee.

Often consumers surveyed had to pay from $5 to $10 for their follow-up inspection, despite advertising saying the check-up was free.

Price Variations

Since rustproofing firms work on a franchised basis, it is not surprising to find price variations for the same product in a designated region. Nevertheless, it is hard to understand how prices can vary from $65 for the same application of Dura-Coat on a Volkswagen and to $120 on a Capri. Even Ziebart charged $120 to rustproof a 1973 Chevelle, while charging another owner $200 to rustproof his 1973 Volvo. Such price differences defy logic.

Rustproofing Profits

Rustproofing is profitable, though just how profitable is hard to tell. Nevertheless, the APA has found some sales literature, used to recruit undercoating dealers for Castrol Oils, that promises potential dealers an 80 percent profit on each sale! The Castrol company makes the following statements:

Simplicity

The undercoating of a vehicle is a simple operation which can be carried out in a relatively short time (less than one hour) and can very quickly be mastered by anyone in the service Department or P.D.I. Department.

Profitability

Despite its simplicity, undercoating remains a highly profitable venture and one which ought not to be neglected by the aggressive car dealer.

The figures which we show below are averages, but, nevertheless, serve to indicate the degree of profitability attributable to undercoating a vehicle with Castrol Surecoat.

Undercoating of Average-Sized Car

10 lbs. Castrol Surecoat at 29¢ per lb.	—$ 2.90
Labor—1 hour at $3 per hour	—$ 3.00
Allowance against overhead	—$11.00
Cost of job	—$ 6.90
Retail price of completed work	—$35.00
Profit	—$28.10
Profit as percentage of sales value	—80 percent

In spite of the high profitability of rustproofing, many rustproofing firms close up shop and either go into bankruptcy or simply disappear in the night. These firms vary from large, efficient, professional operations such as Eonizer and Ziebart to backyards and garages using part-time, inexperienced help. One consumer paid $112 for Ziebart rustproofing only to find:

> When I delivered the car I found the shop was not a shop at all but a garage in the backyard of a rundown house. The repairman was, to say the least, a "backyard mechanic." The car stands as a very poor example of Ziebart quality and workmanship.

In some areas, new-car dealers do their own rustproofing. We are skeptical of this practice, however, since a professional rustproofing application demands special tools, hoses, hydraulic lifts, and pumps. The investment in professional equipment and competent full-time rustproofing employees would be prohibitive for the average car dealer. This may be one reason why many car dealers applying their own "house" brand of rustproofing compounds reap large profits as well as large-scale consumer discontent.

In their haste to sell rustproofing franchises, many rustproofing firms apparently underestimate the time, money, and skill required. In one humorous recruiting ad placed in *Automotive News*, Quaker State made the following pitch:

> Drums of profit—if you'll just give 'em the air. No new car you sell is completely rustproofed. So

here's the Quaker State Rustproofing System with a money opportunity that's hard to overlook. And no investment to speak of, if you have a lift and an air compressor. Ask your distributor about Quaker Koat and Metal Gard—two quick, easy, inexpensive steps to higher gross on your new-car sales.

All of the rustproofing firms surveyed stress their warranties. However, upon close inspection, the warranties contained clauses that rendered them void if the product was not applied correctly, or repairs were not done by the selling agent, or mandatory inspection was missed, or rusting was exterior and not interior, or rusting was caused by stone chipping, or because of abusive use of vehicle, or extreme conditions, or damage by collision. With such a variety of excuses for voiding the warranty, the rustproofer has very little difficulty in picking and choosing arbitrarily those warranties he wishes to honor.

Breakdown of Informal Survey

Although it contains a small sampling, this survey does reflect the extent of consumer dissatisfaction.

	SATISFIED	DISSATISFIED	TOTAL
Ziebart	55	95	150

Not recommended. There were too many complaints of sloppy workmanship; 24,000 miles check-up voided guarantee if missed, ineffective against rust, sloppy public relations, warranty unsupported by performance.

Dura-Coat	4	26	30

Not recommended. Consumers complain of slow action on complaints, ineffective against rust, warranty invalid, product soft and sticky, wears off, stains.

Tuff-Coat	6	17	23

Not recommended. Consumers surveyed declared that the product was ineffective against rusting, customer complaints were ignored, product messy, careless application, warranty not honored.

Vital Rustproofing **(Vitalizing)**	6	9	15

Not recommended. Consumers noted product was ineffective against rust, improperly applied, peeling away, poor yearly inspections, cost irrelevant to task performed.

Miscellaneous 30 40 70

These companies had too small a sample of responses to evaluate. Companies involved are True-Guard, Superior, Rustop, Poly-Oleum, Quaker State and Goodyear.

Totals 101 187 288

Legal Recourse

If you cannot get satisfaction from the company that rustproofed your car, you may ask redress in the small-claims court.

Lawyers advise that if a dealer applied the rustproofing compound, send two registered letters to the dealer. The first letter should ask for reimbursement due to the ineffectiveness of the product, and the second letter should hold the dealer responsible for the rusting damages caused by the ineffective product. Remember, if you paid the dealer, he's responsible. Don't be afraid of the courts. Chances are excellent that the judge also has a rusty car.

Rust Hucksters In '79

Since the Canadian Automobile Protection Association blasted the rustproofing industry for ripping off the public a few years ago, three national dealer-affiliated rustproofers criticized in the APA study (Dura-Coat, Rustop, and Tru-guard) have gone out of business. Some of these companies have been operating in the United States, and Dura-coat in particular has been the object of a considerable number of complaints from Vermont motorists.

Many of the American dealer-affiliated franchised rustproofers are gearing up for the 1979 model year with a heavy advertising blitz aimed at American new-car purchasers.

Canadians are already protected by a 3-year federal voluntary rust code incorporated into all new car warranties. This federal warranty protection against premature rusting has taken away a considerable amount of the independent rustproofing market in Canada.

One innovative American rustproofing firm, the Daubert Chemical Company, is planning to push its ECP rustproofing compound with the aid of a cartoon-character rat the company calls its "corrodent." In a June 5, 1978 full-page ad in *Automotive News,* Daubert tells its car dealer readers ". . . We're on the Dealer's Side . . . We're stepping-up our media advertising with a newly developed character to help your customers remember 1-time "ECP": a dirty, rusty rat, aptly named a "Corrodent." He's a symbol for rust and corrosion no one will forget."

Perhaps Daubert's rusty rat will become unforgettable, but Daubert's ECP rustproofing compound and the hundreds of other rustproofing compounds sold through franchised car dealers do not deserve much attention.

Hundreds of motorists and car dealers alike have been cheated by rustproofing firms that sell their product through dealers, give unrealistic warranties, and then skip town after a few years, when rust claims start pouring into their offices. Often, the dealerships acting as agent for the rustproofer will be held responsible by the small claims courts either to reimburse the customer or to fix the rust damage. The rustproofer, however, is seldom caught.

Is Rustproofing Worthwhile?

There is very little independent data showing that rustproofing will actually prevent or retard rusting. In fact, some preliminary studies done in Canada by the Automobile Protection Association show that rust-prone cars that have been rustproofed will rust prematurely at the same rate as similar cars not rustproofed.

Nevertheless, rustproofing can be a good investment for reasons totally unrelated to its efficacy in preventing or retarding rust. For example, used cars are easier to sell and command higher prices if they were originally rustproofed. Cars that have been rustproofed also tend to ride more quietly. And, should the car rust prematurely, a small claims court judge may award damages against the auto maker, car dealer, and rustproofer, on the basis that the car owner did everything possible to prevent premature rusting. In this type of small claims litigation the rustproofer can be an excellent witness against the dealer and car manufacturer.

In conclusion, remember that rustproofing should only be purchased from an independent rustproofing firm that owns its own facilities. Stay away from car dealer operations. And, to prevent premature rusting despite rustproofing, keep your car in an unheated garage, don't frequent car washes that use recycled salt-contaminated water, and don't buy a new car with a history of being rust-prone.

FORD

Special Report—
Car Body Sheetmetal Corrosion
Naao Reliability—Quality Meeting*

Introduction

Recent reports from the Cleveland District, followed by a telephone survey of Ford Customer Service Division personnel in 20 districts located in Northern areas and along the Eastern and Gulf Coasts, plus results of customer direct-mail surveys indicate that **there is a serious vehicle rust problem on our 1969 through 1973 vehicles in a maximum corrosion environment.** Field surveys conducted in Cleveland and Detroit by representatives of the Automobile Assembly Division, Body Engineering Office, Ford Customer Service Division, and Product Development support this opinion. Further evidence of this problem is contained in the recently published annual "Paint and Corrosion Survey."

The General Product Acceptance Specification relating to rust and corrosion for highly visible panels allows no rust in one year and in two years only that rust that can be wiped off. Rust that can be wiped off in one year is permitted for other visible panels. **No metal perforation on exterior appearance panels if permissible for five years.**

The basic design and processing of corrosion protection has remained essentially unchanged in our cars for the past ten years with the exception of additional electrocoat facilities. **Why then has corrosion suddenly developed as a prominent product problem?** The answer at this time must be subjective but is judged to be a product of higher consumer expectation and competitive upgrading in corrosion protection, such as dip phosphate and primer, multiple coatings including alumi-

*Source: Ford quality control meeting, October 19, 1973.
(All boldface is the author's.)

num-filled wax and vinyl sealer, zinc chromate primer, and galvanized panels in tailgates. In a severe corrosion environment, our products do not satisfy the GPAS but seem competitive for the one- and two-year requirement. However, **perforation, which is the category of corrosion failure highest in customer concern, develops from one to two years earlier in our cars than in the competition's.**

The purpose of this Special Report is to specifically cover the major areas of corrosion now identified on Ford products in the postwarranty period and to discuss those corrective actions that are released or under investigation. Since the size of the problem relative to the total vehicle population has not been accurately established, additional investigations are discussed.

Description of Problem and Plan to Determine Scope

In severe corrosion environments in the U.S. and Canada, corrosion perforation of body sheet metal is occurring in the following areas prior to the five-year GPAS requirement.

Door inner and outer panel.
Quarter panel and wheelhouse.
Tailgate inner and outer panel.
Quarter and pillar to rocker panel joint.
Station wagon spare tire well and storage compartment.
Deck lid inner and outer panel.
Fender.

Four surveys have been conducted in the past month. These surveys were recognized to have statistical limitations due to sample size and method of sample selection. However, results of these surveys, when combined with previous survey data, Arizona Proving Ground corrosion test results, and Customer Service Division reports have provided a listing of individual body sheetmetal corrosion locations. Customer Service Division will complete an analysis of expenditures of extended policy funds by district, model year, car line, and major sheetmetal panel by November 30, 1973.

Statistically organized field surveys are planned in order to obtain a more accurate definition and scope of known problems, detect new problems, and provide a basis for field feedback and the effectiveness of corrective design and process changes. Survey participants will be included from all affected offices. Phase 1 completion is expected by December 15, 1973, with subsequent surveys to be regularly scheduled.

Correction Action to Date

Corrective action has eliminated four corrosion perforation problems identified in annual "Paint and Corrosion Survey."

- Quarter panel at fuel filler (Ford and Mercury—all models), effective January, 1973.
- Spare wheelwell (Ford, Mercury, Torino, and Montego—wagons), effective October, 1973.
- Quarter panel rear extension (Ford, Mercury, Torino, and Montego—wagons), effective October, 1973.
- Lower back panel (Mustang—all models), effective July 1, 1974. In addition the Excel Program was effective in all assembly plants July 1, 1973, to monitor body-sealing operations.

Unresolved Problems Pending Corrective Action

A joint effort involving Automotive Assembly Division, Body Engineering Office Ford Customer Service Division, Metal Stamping Division and Product Development is in progress to establish appropriate corrective action for the remaining presently identified corrosion problems.

- Quarter panel (all car lines—all models) perforations occur along the lower periphery—two to three years.
- Front and rear door inner and outer panel (all except electrocoat cars—all models) perforations occur along lower surfaces—two to three years.
- Tailgate inner and outer panel (Torino, Montego, Ford, Mercury—wagons) perforations occur along lower surfaces—two years.
- Tailgate window regulator mounting panel (Torino, Montego, Ford, Mercury—wagons) perforation causes detachment of lower end—two to three years.
- Rocker panel to quarter panel joints (all car lines—all

models) perforation is occurring at joints due to galvanic action caused by moisture entry through sealer cracks and skips—one year.

- Deck lid inner and outer panel (Ford, Mercury, Torino, and Montego—all models, less on wagons) perforations occur along the bottom edges—three years.
- Front fender (Pinto, Mustang, Maverick, Comet—all models) perforations occur along top surface and lower rear corner—two to three years.
- Quarter storage compartment (Ford and Mercury—wagons) perforations occur on lower surface—two to three years.
- Quarter wheelhouse (all car lines—all models) perforations occur at front and rear—two to three years.
- Perforations (Ford, Mercury, Torino, and Montego—wagons) occur at the rear outer corners—two years.
- Rear floor pan extension to quarter panel (Maverick, Comet—all models, and Ford, Mercury, Torino, Montego—wagons) perforations occur along the lower vertical surface—three years.
- Hood liner and outer panel (Pinto—all models) perforations occur along leading edge—three years.
- Pillar to rocker panel (all car lines—all models) perforations occur at joint—three years.

Future Model Programs

The design of corrosion protection on forward programs conceptually follows current programs, at times modified by field experience. Performance is evaluated after the fact on one- through five-year-old customer-owned vehicles by means of annual field surveys. Control of sheetmetal corrosion in future model programs requires a Design Verification Plan for measuring the effectiveness of corrosion protection prior to vehicle signoff.

The existing Arizona Proving Ground accelerated-corrosion test (P3-76) is used to gain information each year on new model prototype and early production vehicles. This test provides general information only because at present a correlation between the Arizona Proving Ground test and field service has not been established. The Body Engineering Office and Product Development are studying the test vs. field experience to determine proper correlation for subsequent GPAS utilization.

Other means of evaluating performance of corrosion protection at the prototype and early production stage are being considered; for example, laboratory salt spray testing of complete doors, tailgates, hoods, and deck lids.

Improvements in corrosion protection will be accomplished by reexamination of current practice in specifying barrier and sacrificial coatings, expanded use of spray-on vinyl sealers (ESB-M4G191) as a replacement for zinc-rich primer, plus improved water drainage in doors, quarters, tailgates, deep wells, etc., through sheet-metal design configuration and optimum drain-hole size, shape, and placement.

Consideration will be given to the use of special barrier protection for vehicles assembled in plants that normally supply customers in severe corrosion-producing areas.

Work Plan Summary

The following actions are scheduled for completion in the near future as indicated:

First Cleveland area survey	(A) 9-12-73
Second Cleveland area survey	(A) 9-19-20-73
Detroit area survey	(A) 9-22-73
Cleveland area Wixom car survey	(A) 10-15-17-73
Ford vs. competition corrosion protection study	11-15-73
Detroit area statistical survey	11-15-73
Interim action proposal	11-20-73
Customer Service Division extended policy analysis	11-30-73
Statistical field survey to determine problem frequency	12-15-73
Corrective action and cost-effectiveness	1-21-74

A follow-up meeting to review the results of the above actions will be scheduled the week of January 21, 1974.

Defect Investigation

Over 70 million cars have been recalled by their manufacturers for built-in defects, many of them deadly. Fires can break out. Engine mounts can break. Heaters can leak deadly carbon monoxide. Brakes can fail. Power steering can freeze.

Please check this list. If your vehicle is on it, you may be living dangerously. If you haven't had it repaired, get to your dealer—fast. In most cases he'll repair it for free. If he refuses, notify the government.

Those cases listed here are the subjects of current safety-related investigations now being conducted by the APA. When an investigation is begun, it should *not* be assumed that a defect exists, only that a safety-related problem has been reported with sufficient indication of its existence to justify investigation.

Manufacturer/ Make	Model	Year	Component	Possible Problems
Ford	F-250	1968–1969	16 × 5.5 Two Piece Wheel	Lock Ring Gutter Failure.
Ford	Ford Mercury	1965–1974	15 × 5-inch Single Piece Wheel	Alleged Wheel Rim Failure
General Motors	GMC ½-Ton Pickups	1960–1970	15 × 5.5-inch Single Piece Wheel	"
Ford	All	1967 and later	Dual Master Brake Cylinder	Failure of Cylinder Due to Corrosion
Volkswagen	All	Pre-1963	Heater	Engine Fumes
Ford	Ford Mercury	1969–1971	15 × 6.5 Single Piece Wheel	Disc Failure.
General Motors	Light Duty Trucks	1966–1971	Rear Axle Control Arm	Rear Axle Control Arm Failures.
International Harvester	Travelall 1110 4×4	1972–1973	Steering Arm Ball	Alleged Steering Instability.

Manufacturer/Make	Model	Year	Component	Possible Problems
General Motors	Cadillac Eldorado & Oldsmobile	1967–1973	Front Wheel Mounting Bolts	Failure of Front Wheel Mounting Bolts.
Ford	Ford, Mercury	1970–1971	Hood Latch	Failure of Latch.
Chrysler	Dodge Darts and Plymouth Valiants	1967–1972	Brake Proportioning Valve	Rear Wheel Lockup.
Winnebago	D24 Motorhome	1970–1971	Front End Suspension	Alleged Inadequate Front End Suspension.
Action Industries, Inc.	24 and 25-foot Motorhome	1971	Front End Suspension	"
Champion Home Builders	24-foot Motorhome	1971	Front End Suspension	"
Boise Cascade	Lifetime Premier 23-foot Motorhome	1969–1971	Front End Suspension	"
PRF Industries	Travco 220 Motorhome	1970	Front End Suspension	"

110

Manufacturer	Vehicle	Years	Component	Problem
General Motors	Chevrolet Series C, P, G-10 Trucks and GMC Series C, P, G-1500 Trucks	1971–1972	Steering Tie Rod	Separation of Ball From Socket
Ford	Fairlane and Ranchero Mercury Montego Ford Falcon Mercury Comet	1965–1969 1965–1969 1965–1970	Engine Mounts	Secondary Effects from Shearing of Engine Mounts.
General Motors	All Passenger Cars	1967–1973	Power Steering Gear	Alleged Power Steering Lockup and Self-Steering Problems.
Ford	All Pintos	1971–1972	Rack and Pinion Steering	Steering Difficulty
Ford	All With 4-Barrel Carburetors	1968–1974	Non-Metallic Fast Idle Cam	Breakage Causes Jamming of Throttle
Ford	School Bus B-700	1966–1974	Brake Drum	Front Brake Drum Failure.
Nissan	Datsun 510 Datsun 1200	1969–1971 1971	Filler Hose and Three-Way Connector	Leaks Could Result in Loss of Fuel and Fire.

Manufacturer / Make	Model	Year	Component	Possible Problems
Nissan	Datsun 510	1968–1971	Transverse Link	Alleged Transverse Link Failures.
General Motors	Rochester Carburetor Equipped	1965–1972	Carburetor Float	Carburetor Flooding Due to Float Saturation, Resulting in Fire.
Western Auto	Wizard A-5030	Various	Auto Jack Stand	Failure to Meet Load Rating.
International Harvester	Scout II Travelall and Pickup	1970–1973	Brake Lining	Alleged Erractic Service Brake Operation or Performance.
General Motors	Chevelle	1965–1969	Engine Mounts	Engine Mount Failure.

Volkswagen	VW Type 3 prior to August 1971; Porsche 914, 1.8, 1.7 and 2.0 Liter Engine; VW Type 4, 1.7 Liter Engine	1970–1972	Bosch Fuel Injector	Electronic Fuel Injector Leakage.
General Motors	Chevrolet Corvettes	1964–1974	Rear Wheel Bearing	Failure of Rear Wheel Bearings.
International Harvester	Travelalls and Pickups	1974	Battery Cable	Shorting of the Positive Battery Cable.
General Motors	Pontiac-all V8	1966–1972	Timing Gear and Chain	Failure of Timing Gear and Chain.
Toyota Motor Sales	Corolla and Carina Vehicle Equipped with 1600cc Engine	1971–1973	Throttle	Throttle Sticking.
Volvo	Volvo	1973	Front Bumper Bracket	Failure of Front Bumper Support Bracket.

Manufacturer/ Make	Model	Year	Component	Possible Problems
American Motors	Pacer	1975	Power Steering Gear	Leakage of Rack and Pinion Seal
Ford	F-250 and F-350 Series Trucks	1972–1974	Budd Duo-Rim & "C" Section Side Ring	Explosive Separation of "C" Section Side Ring From Budd Duo-Rim Wheels.
Ford	Mercury Capri	1971–1974 1976–1977	Front Stabilizer Bar	Front Stabilizer Bar Failures.
American Honda	750 & 1000cc Motorcycles	1975–1976	Disc Brakes	Poor Wet Braking Performance.
Volkswagen	Rabbit Scirocco Dasher Audi	1975–1976 1975–1976 1974–1975 1973–1975	Throttle Control System	Throttle Control System Malfunctions.

Manufacturer	Models	Years	System	Failure
General Motors	Chevrolet, Pontiac, Oldsmobile, Buick Cadillac, and GMC Trucks	1971–1977	Power Brake Booster	Power Brake Booster Failure.
Chrysler	All models	1971–1978	Carburetion and Emissions System	Vehicle Stalling.
Ford	Passenger Cars and Light Trucks	1970–1977	Flex-Fan (Engine Cooling Fan)	Flex-Fan Breakage
International Harvester	Heavy Trucks	1975–1977	Aluminum Hub Used on 10,800 and 12,000 Steering Axle.	Hub Cracks and Separates Between Bearings.
Fiat, Inc.	All	1970–1977	Undercarriage	Suspension and Undercarriage Failure Due to Corrosion.
British Leyland	Triumph Spitfire TR-7, MGB, MG Midget Jaguar XJ6, Jaguar XJ12	1975–1977 1971–1977	Ignition System	Stalling

Manufacturer/ Make	Model	Year	Component	Possible Problems
British Leyland	Triumph TR-7	1975–1977	Throttle Cable	Throttle Cable Failure Accelerator Sticks or Returns to Idle.
General Motors	Light Duty Trucks Chev., GMC C10, P10, K10, G20	1975–1977	Jack	Jacks May Fail.
British Leyland	Triumph—All	1969 thru 1976	Wiper Motor, Linkage Arm Blades and Switches	Failure of Wiper System
British Leyland	Triumph—All	1970 thru 1977	Headlamp Switches	Failure of Switch
General Motors	Vega, Subcompact	1970–1976	Gasoline Tank	Readily Damaged in Rear-end Collision.
Ford	Mercury Capri	1971–1972	Headlight Switch	Switch May Fall Apart.
British Leyland	Midget	1970–1974	Throttle Cable	Throttle May Break or Stick.

Manufacturer	Models	Year	System	Problem
General Motors		1975–1977	Electronic Fuel Injection System	Engine Compartment Fires.
Ford	All Models with V-8 Engines and C-6 or FMX Transmissions	1973–1978	Transmission Linkage	Assembly Grommets May Fail. Transmission May Jump From Park to Reverse.
Peugeot, Inc.	304 and 504	1972–1975	Seat Belt System	Retractor Fails to Operate Properly.
Ford	Ford, Mercury, Lincoln, Full-size and Intermediate	1968–1974	Idler Arm and Mounting Bracket	Bracket Pulls Out of Frame.
American Motors	Hornet Gremlin	1975 1976 1977	Power Steering Hose	Power Steering Hose Fails.
American Motors	All	1975, 1976	Ignition System	Stalling.
Firestone Tire & Rubber Co.	All Steel Belted Radial	Various	Tires	Tire Failure.

Manufacturer/ Make	Model	Year	Component	Possible Problems
Ford	Capri	1971–1978	Manual, Floor-Mounted Gear Shift Lever	Gear Shift Lever Breaks or Detaches From Transmission.
Ford	Granada Monarch	1975–1977	Power Steering Control Valve	Steering Instability.
General Motors	Olds Starfire V-6 Buick Skylark V-6 Chev Monza V-8	1975	Wheel Bearing	Wheel Can Separate From Vehicle.
Chrysler Corp.	Dodge Vans, Models B-300, MB-300, CB-400, MB-400	1973–1977	Front Disc Brakes	Loss of Front Brakes.
Ford	Heavy Trucks Models B,C,F,L,W, and DCL	1975–1978	Wiring Harness	Reduced Braking Capability.

General Motors	Cadillac	1959–1960	Steering Pitman Arm	Fatigue Failure
Ford	Mercury Capri	1971–1973	Windshield Wiper Arm Shaft and Motor	Arm Detaches From Drive Shift Motor;
GM/Ford	All Full-Sized	1975–1978	Catalytic converter	Exhaust overheating, fires.
Honda	Civic	1977	Steering	Steering could lock up.
Datsun	B210	1974–1978	Suspension	Undercarriage rusting
Datsun	240Z	1972–1973	Suspension	"

CHAPTER IV

The Art of Complaining

●

Complaining is a discouraging business. Tempers flare, harsh words are spoken, and both of the complaining parties usually take a solemn oath never to do business together again.

Not all complaints have to fall into the above category. Actually, there is an art to complaining that brings quick results and leaves tempers intact.

Most dealers hire a specialist to deal with customer complaints. This is the last person you should deal with. Customer-relations specialists are never in a policy-making position. They are required to apply warranty service within the strict confines of the manufacturer's or dealer's warranty. They know of 101 reasons to justify the cancellation of your guarantee. Since they hear complaints all day, only the most incredible, hard-luck, borderline cases get accepted under warranty.

The service manager is another individual not very helpful in settling warranty disputes. His job is to fix cars, not repair them gratuitously.

Whenever you are dissatisfied with a dealer's service, the best man to see is the owner of the dealership. This is the man everyone is afraid of. This is the man who likes to boast of his complaint-free servicing. This is also the man least likely to turn you away when you complain directly to him. The owner really does not want to hear customer complaints, but since very few complaints find their way to his office, he will probably attempt to settle those complaints that directly involve him.

When dealing with dealers, it is always a good idea to emphasize that the only reason you bought your car from this particular dealer was the good reputation he has in the community. Tell him how impressed you were with the competence and honesty of the garage—until you began having your present problems. Conclude by asking the dealer to personally verify your story before deciding to meet your demands. Before ending the conversation, repeat firmly and politely your demands.

If your problem has not been settled after a few days, send the dealer a registered letter, politely repeating your demands (see sample complaint letter). If after five days the dealer does not make a reasonable offer, send a final registered letter claiming the amount for corrective repairs if the car is only partially defective, or claim the entire purchase price, if the car is a real lemon. Make photocopies of this final letter and send copies to different government representatives on the local and federal level, consumer groups, and government consumer-protection agencies.

By now, no more than two weeks have passed since you first approached the dealer. You now are faced with three choices. One: You can admit that it was all a bluff and that you may as well keep your defective car. Two: You may get the car repaired elsewhere and sue the dealer in small-claims court for the cost of corrective repairs. Three: You may sue the dealer for your full purchase price plus expenses. This final alternative may not be desirable if court cases have more than a few months' waiting period.

SAMPLE COMPLAINT LETTER

Registered

Mr. Richard J. Jones
Honest Dick's Used Cars
El Centro, California

Dear Dick:
    I bought my _____ on _____. Since I purchased this car from you I have discovered the following defects:

1.
2.
3.

4.

5.

I have repeatedly asked that you fix these defects under warranty. This has not been done.

This car was purchased from your dealership with the understanding that it was a reliable means of transporation that would suit my needs.

I therefore request that you correct the defects mentioned above, failing which I shall correct the defects elsewhere and hold you responsible.

> Awaiting your earliest convenient reply, I remain,
> Sincerely yours,
> John Biggs

The following four general rules for an efficient and successful complaint strategy should be helpful in dealing with car dealers, or any other businessmen.

1. Write the Complaint

Telephone calls are forgotten as soon as the receiver is put down. Registered letters, though, intrude into the daily office routine, while telephone calls and personal visits can be later denied. A letter also helps you to formulate your complaint in clear, precise terms, for maximum impact. Try to keep your complaint within the confines of a two-page, double-spaced letter. Keep copies of all correspondence, since this will help you later if you go before the small-claims court.

2. Involve Others

Dishonest businessmen do not like publicity. Who knows, other unhappy customers may pick up the case. Write letters to your newspaper's "action-line," or directly to the editor. Some consumer complaints are so universal that many newspapers do feature stories on business abuses as a warning to their readers. The summer months are best for this approach.

Call "open-line" radio shows but be careful not to libel anybody. Call your priest and ask him to call the dealer for you. Call the police, fire department, and city health inspectors. If your dealer has a watchdog, call the dog catcher.

Sometimes it can be fun to form your own consumer-action group. Call a press conference and invite others with similar problems to write you (use a post office box, and give your home telephone number only to journalists). You will be surprised to see how quickly the dealer responds to your demands when you represent a dozen of his own discontented customers.

3. Use Humor

Although it may be difficult, try to interject a bit of humor into your negotiations. Businessmen often polarize their positions if the consumer comes on too strong.

4. Use the Courts

Consumers are more frequently using the small-claims court to settle disputes with merchants. In fact, some businessmen will settle out of court rather than risk the publicity of a court proceeding. In some jurisdictions, lawyers are not allowed to plead and the judge handles the case himself. Since cases brought before the small-claims court are quickly settled, and court costs are low, these courts are handling an increasing amount of consumer litigation.

The Art of Effective Complaining

1. **Write your complaint.** Letters intrude into the office routine, calls are forgotten, and meetings can be denied.

2. **Involve others.** Dishonest dealers dislike publicity and are afraid of anything that could turn into a group action.

3. **Act promptly.** Most complaints can be settled within two weeks. Take legal action if no settlement is made within one month of the initial complaint.

4. **See the top man.** If pollution flowed upstream, companies would cease polluting. Only the dealer can change policy and make compromises. The salesman sells; the service manager services; and the public relations department explains company policy.

5. **Be polite and firm.** Tell the dealer you chose his

place because he's the best dealer in town—but now you're having second thoughts.

6. **Use guerrilla warfare.** Send copies of your complaint to the APA, consumer affairs agency, newspaper "action-lines," radio "open-line" shows, the police, health department, fire department, and if the dealer has a roaming watchdog, call the dog catcher.

7. **Use the courts.** Small-claims courts are particularly lethal when used against unscrupulous dealers, so save all letters and documents.

8. **Form your own consumer group.** There is power in numbers, especially if many of the discontented consumers have been taken by the same dealer.

9. **Be persistent.** Complain to at least ten different agencies each day. Call the dealer daily. If the phone does not answer, send a night telegram.

10. **Keep your sense of humor.** If you are too serious or menacing, you may scare people away.

How to Start a Consumer Group

1. Rent a post office box.
2. Write a press release.
3. Call a press conference.
4. Invite consumer complaints, volunteers, and professional guidance.
5. Elect a board of directors.
6. Incorporate the association as nonprofit with low membership fees.
7. Start solving consumer complaints.
8. Call second press conference with details as to number and type of complaints received.
9. Establish contact with government and private agencies.
10. Contact industry and governmental "whistle-blowers."
11. Find an honest legal firm. (You may have several lawsuits by now.)
12. Keep the association small.
13. Call a monthly press conference exposing a documented abuse.

Consumer Pressure Tactics

The following consumer pressure tactics have been used successfully by individual motorists as well as by organized consumer groups throughout North America and Europe. Some of the more original tactics have been perfected by the late radical labor organizer Saul Alinsky, who spent his life organizing labor in America.

Parallel Auto Show

Whenever the local dealers present their annual auto exhibition, present a free parallel exhibition using public facilities. Exhibit cars that are prematurely rusted or that have other obvious defects. Demand that the media give equal time whenever the other auto exhibit is publicized. Choose ten worst cars and worst dealers, elect Miss Lemon, and even raffle off a scrapped car to some deserving dealer.

Malpractice Award

Give a malpractice award to that segment of the auto industry that distinguishes itself as most deserving.

Sample Press Release

Center for Auto Safety

800 National Press Building, Washington, D.C.

(202) 638-0420

For Immediate Release

CENTER FOR AUTO SAFETY GIVES AUTOMOTIVE
ENGINEERING MALPRACTICE AWARD TO GM'S COLE

The Center for Auto Safety today announced the selection of Edward N. Cole, President of General Motors Corporation, as the first recipient of the annual Automotive Engineering Malpractice Award.

The Ralph Nader-affiliated auto-safety group announced Cole's selection for the award at a press conference in Union Square (opposite the Hotel St. Francis) at 12:30 P.M. today. The annual award will be given by the Center for Auto Safety to the individual whose actions or inactions have had the most detrimental effect on auto safety. The press conference was preceded by a picket composed of local consumer groups, protesting Cole's presentation with an award of opposite intent—inside the hotel Cole was being given the National Motor Vehicle Safety Advisory Council's first annual award to an individual for contributions to auto safety.

The Washington-based Center said it would attempt to present Cole with a statue constructed of remnants of defective GM parts. The award consisted of a Pontiac "spinner" hubcap with protruding, unshielded, ornamental, knifelike blades; a piece of baling wire to signify GM's disregard for consumers in failing to replace defective engine mounts but rather installing wirelike restraint cables; a broken power brake vacuum check valve; a defective GM cruise control lever; a vial of carbon monoxide, symbolizing two large GM safety defect notification campaigns: the first for carbon monoxide leakage into the passenger compartment of 2½ million 1965 to 1969 Chevrolets, the second for the defective heaters on 600,000 Corvairs. The last item in the statue is a piece of gravel, representing an object that could cause steering lockup on any 1971 or 1972 full-sized GM car.

"This should serve as a fitting reminder to Mr. Cole of the large numbers of persons who are killed or injured each year by defective GM vehicles," commented a representative of the Center.

Midnight Telegrams

For dealers who refuse to answer their phone, or who otherwise fail to respond to consumer complaints, send a telegram. Send it "night-letter" rate (it's cheaper), and keep a copy.

Picketing

One of the most dangerous consumer tactics that can be employed, picketing should be used only as a last resort. It always presents the danger of mob rule, which can lead to criminal charges or a court injunction. Injunctions are counterproductive because they can create outrageous legal expenses that will quickly dry up a consumer group's finances. If picketing is used as a pressure tactic, be sure to get a permit, ask for police protection, call the media, use no more than ten picketers, and picket peacefully.

Misleading Advertising Complaints

An excellent pressure tactic to use in conjunction with other tactics. Don't expect to have the complaint taken seriously by an industry agency, though. The depositing of this type of complaint is useful in attracting media attention, getting additional consumer support, and tying up a company's lawyers and public relations people for weeks.

Press Conference

Write a press release (two pages, double-spaced, with telephone number) announcing a future press conference dealing with the formation of a consumer-protection group to combat the abuses you have personally experienced. Send out the release three days before holding the press conference. The day of the press conference, rent a meeting hall, dress conservatively, and meet the press around 2 P.M. so as to get on the six o'clock news. Be brief and precise. Present visual "treats" for the cameraman like signs, or a car painted like a lemon. If no one comes to the press conference, send out the text of your speech to all media people and list a post-office box where people may write.

"Lemon" Signs

As a last resort, put several lemon signs on your car and park it near the manufacturer or dealer. This tactic often gets quick results. Before getting out the paint and paper, though, check with the local university law society (free legal advice) whether such a sign could provoke an injunction or contravene a municipal bylaw. If trouble starts later, the law society may feel obliged to help out.

Classified Ads

Dealers and manufacturers use the classified ads to sell their cars. Any consumer placing satirical ads to criticize his own car is profaning sacred ground and attracts the attention of the car manufacturers, local dealers, and journalists looking for a human-interest story.

This consumer tactic was especially useful to one irate rusty-Ford owner who placed the following ad in one of the local newspapers:

RUSTED
1973 FORD CUSTOM

44,000 miles, requires about $2,200 worth of rust repairs and uses about 2 quarts of oil every 200 miles and gets about 8 miles per gallon. Does not at present pass safety inspection. Owner wants to get rid of. 865-7148.

As a result of this ad campaign, which cost approximately $13.50, Joe MacDonald, who placed the ad, received more than 200 telephone calls from other angry Ford owners and eventually found enough support to establish a Rusty Ford Owners Association, which is now pressing for a global settlement from Ford for all Ford owners victimized by Ford's rusting defect. The only negative result of MacDonald's ad was one telephone call from a local Ford salesman requesting that the ad be withdrawn because it was hurting his sales. The ad ran two days.

Complain to the Local Paper

Visit the news desk and try to interest a reporter in the story. Remember, chances are he has been cheated by garages and dealers fairly often himself.

"Action" Column

These consumer-help columns are of limited value. Most of them receive far too many requests for help to be really effective. Staffers may have become so jaded by hard-luck stories that motorists' complaints may have a very low priority. Another disadvantage with "action" columns is that the business community and journalists tend to disregard the impact the columns may have on the general public.

Creative Hysteria

As a last resort, it is often useful to appear completely irrational and dangerous to the dealer in private while maintaining a serene and peaceful comportment in public. This tactic is especially effective if you practice it by hanging around the showroom while the salesmen are showing new cars to customers.

While waiting for repairs that should be done under warranty, take a lunch along to the dealership and eat it inside one of the showroom cars (peanut butter and jelly sandwiches are the most cost-effective). Repairs will probably be completed in record time.

Write a Book About the Car

This will consolidate correspondence, alert the public and media, and possibly help pay for the legal expenses involved in a lawsuit. One consumer has written an automotive morality play in her book detailing the troubles she has experienced with her defect-prone, updated Toyota. Proceeds from the book have financed her lawsuit.

Burning the Car

Another last resort tactic that attracts the media and dramatizes the problem. A few years ago in California, Eddy Campos burned his new Lincoln Continental in front of Ford's regional headquarters. Public sympathy and media interest were so great that donations began pouring in from across North America. With these donations, Campos founded Motorists United, a nonprofit consumer-protection association for motorists. Be sure to check fire and pollution regulations before attempting a similar protest.

Government Hearings

Testify at government hearings investigating the automotive industry. This tactic will add pressure on the company as well as alert legislators to the problem.

Harass the Dealer's Bank

This is a last resort, quasi-legal tactic that is a group exercise. Find out which bank the dealer or garage uses and then send in a dozen individuals to open savings accounts with the minimum $5 deposit. Then have the same people go back and close their accounts. Keep opening and closing accounts until most of the bank's staff is tied up in the savings department alone, then ask for a heart-to-heart (pocketbook) talk with the bank manager.

Contact the Sales-Tax People

Businessmen do not like visits from the sales-tax investigator. The investigator probably has difficulties with his own dealer. Many dealers are confused over all the different sales-tax procedures, so the investigation by one agent will usually turn up something. Even if there is no violation of the law, the dealer will need a week to recover.

Contact the Internal Revenue Service

Calling in the Internal Revenue Service on a car dealer is like waving a cross in front of a vampire: the effect is immediate. Most businessmen are following tax plans established by their accountants without fully understanding what they mean. Therefore, visits by the IRS bring on a surge of pain because the dealer is poorly equipped to respond to precise inquiries as to his tax situation. The IRS agent may also be another aggrieved automobile owner.

Call the Health Department

Bathrooms are a good place to start. Even if there are no serious violations, the visit will have been unnerving enough.

Ask for Police Assistance

Usually the police have no powers to resolve civil disputes involving repair charges or the quality of used cars. In some areas, though, the police are well aware of the dishonest practices of certain car dealers or garages in their territory. Often the police will use their power of persuasion to convince the garage to release the car without being paid. Even if the police cannot do anything, their subsequent report can be used in court to show the dealer's attitude and to describe the events leading up to the lawsuit.

Stop the Check

If possible, give the dealer a check and stop the check later. Be sure to inform the dealer by registered mail that the reason the check was stopped was to liberate your car. Offer to renegotiate the bill at the dealer's earliest convenience.

Foreign Press Releases

Japanese and European auto makers are extremely sensitive to consumer criticism of their products directed against the parent company within their country of origin. By translating criticism into Japanese, German, French, Italian, or Swedish, and diffusing the material through that country's foreign correspondents, generally found at the National Press Building, Washington, D.C., effective consumer pressure is sustained.

Class Actions

Class-action lawsuits are initiated for a group of individuals seeking compensation from the same party for the same reasons. Although recent Supreme Court decisions have made class-action lawsuits more difficult to set up, they still remain an effective means whereby consumers can sue an automobile manufacturer together in one joint lawsuit and thereby minimize legal costs.

Just the simple act of filing a class-action lawsuit often pressures the automobile manufacturer to give compensation in an out-of-court settlement.

A good example of a manufacturer bowing to class-action pressure is the Ford Motor Company's recent decision to settle out of court a class-action lawsuit brought by 39 Michigan Ford owners claiming compensation for the premature rusting of their vehicles. Ford gave the plaintiffs $27,500 to drop the lawsuit. Another lawsuit for

$500 million is said to have been initiated against Ford in Illinois.

Class-action lawsuits require professional legal representation. Most lawyers, though, will take on a class-action prosecution on a contingency basis, in which they take no fees but share in the final award.

The best places to find other car owners with similar problems are newspaper "action" columns, the Washington-based Center for Auto Safety and Automobile Owners Action Council, and the Consumers Union.

Small-Claims Court

Businessmen dislike being sued before the small-claims courts. There are few delays, lawyers are not always present, and judges are experienced in hearing small claims. In some local court jurisdictions, the judge may have already heard similar cases against the same garage, car dealer, or automobile manufacturer, and even if you lose, the costs are minimal.

Because fraud is the foundation of the automobile industry in North America, consumers are victimized indiscriminately. Judges, too, are fair game, and frequently find themselves the target of incompetent mechanics or manufacturing defects. Usually, judges suffer this exploitation in silence, rather than create a disturbance. However, since these same judges preside over trials involving car dealers, they bring with them a keen sense of curiosity, cynicism, and prejudice based upon their own experiences. Therefore, as long as judges continue to get cheated by the automobile industry in their personal dealings, consumers will still find the courts understanding and equitable.

Of course, some judges may find their personal feelings against the automobile industry too overpowering and subsequently decide to excuse themselves from hearing the case. Recently, two small-claims court judges refused to preside over cases where consumers were asking $300 compensation each from Ford and Fiat because of damage due to premature rusting. Both judges had similar problems and publicly withdrew from the cases amid much courtroom laughter. In fact, the only persons not laughing in the courtroom were the representatives sent to testify on behalf of Ford and Fiat.

Many cases don't make it to trial, but are settled out of court as soon as the dealer gets a subpoena and thereby finds out his customer is serious in pursuing his claims. Records show that 33 percent of these cases are settled out of court.

Finally, small-claims courts are especially effective for consumer groups as a type of deferred class action. For example, Vega owners victimized by self-destructing motors and a biodegradable body have won hundreds of small-claims-court lawsuits against GM and its dealers throughout the United States, using GM "secret" warranty extensions on these items as the primary evidence for their claims. Initially, the judges were snowed under by GM's service representatives denying that such a warranty extension existed, and some consumers lost their cases. However, other, more alert judges found out the warranty extensions actually did exist and awarded compensation to the Vega owners bringing suit.

Each case that was won was then given extensive publicity in the media, due to the efforts of consumer groups in exploiting their victories. This publicity attracted other Vega owners to the courts to such an extent that now GM has found itself in the middle of a Vega-owner revolt. As a result of these small-claims-court victories, General Motors has decided to settle some of its Vega cases out of court rather than spend costly time before the courts.

This same tactic has been used successfully against Ford for premature rusting, General Motors for defective transmissions, and imported-car manufacturers for updating model years.

It is an effective tactic that radicalizes the judicial system and the general motoring public as well. And since many small-claims court judges also preside over courts of higher jurisdiction, a continuing series of small-claims court victories helps pave the way for consumers bringing similar cases before superior courts.

It should also be noted that small-claims courts allow consumers to subpoena important internal company documents that the manufacturer would prefer to keep secret. Many of the secret-warranty-extension documents found in this book were obtained by subpoena through the small-claims court.

United States Small-Claims Courts**

State	Claim Limit	Delay	Costs	Lawyers	Appeal/Rating*	
Arizona	$ 500	3 months	$ 5	optional	yes	C
Alabama	300	6 months	15	optional	yes	C
Alaska	1,000	2 weeks	15	optional	yes	B
Arkansas	500	1 month	3.50	optional	yes	C
California	750	2 weeks	3.50	excluded	yes	A
Colorado	500	3 weeks	7	optional	yes	B
Connecticut	750	1 month	8	optional	no	A
Delaware	1,500	3 weeks	10	optional	yes	B
District of Columbia	750	3 weeks	2.50	optional	yes	C
Florida	1,500	1 month	15	optional	yes	B
Georgia	200	2 months	6.50	optional	yes	C
Hawaii	300	3 weeks	8	optional	no	C
Idaho	200	1 month	7	excluded	yes	C
Illinois	1,000	6 weeks	11.50	optional	yes	B
Indiana	500	3 weeks	6	optional	yes	C
Iowa	300	2 months	5	optional	yes	C
Kansas	100	1 month	10	optional	yes	C
Kentucky	500	2 months	6.50	optional	yes	C
Louisiana	100	1 month	10	optional	yes	C
Maine	200	1 month	5	optional	yes	C
Maryland	1,000	1 month	10	optional	yes	B
Massachusetts	400	2 months	3	optional	no	C
Michigan	500	3 months	12	optional	yes	C
Minnesota	500	2 months	3	excluded	yes	B
Mississippi	200	2 months	6	optional	yes	C
Missouri	3,500	2 months	9	optional	yes	B
Montana	300	1 month	2.50	optional	yes	C
Nebraska	500	1 month	4	excluded	yes	B
Nevada	500	1 month	5	optional	yes	C
New Hampshire	300	1 month	3	optional	yes	C
New Jersey	200	1 month	10	optional	yes	C
New Mexico	2,000	3 months	8	optional	yes	B
New York	500	1 month	5	optional	yes	C
North Carolina	300	1 month	12	optional	yes	C
North Dakota	200	1 month	3	optional	yes	C
Ohio	150	1 month	3	optional	yes	C
Oklahoma	400	1 month	10	optional	yes	C
Oregon	500	1 month	6	optional	yes	C
Pennsylvania	500	3 months	6	optional	yes	C
Puerto Rico	2,500	1 month	5	optional	yes	B
Rhode Island	300	2 months	5	optional	yes	C
South Carolina	1,000	2 months	5	optional	yes	B
South Dakota	500	3 weeks	5	optional	yes	C
Tennessee	3,000	4 months	25	optional	yes	B
Texas	200	2 months	5	optional	yes	C
Utah	200	1 month	5	optional	yes	C
Virgin Islands	300	2 weeks	5	excluded	yes	B
Vermont	250	1 month	7	optional	no	C

State	Claim Limit	Delay	Costs	Lawyers	Appeal/Rating*	
Virginia	3,000	1 month	5	optional	yes	B
Washington	200	1 month	3	optional	yes	C
West Virginia	300	1 month	10	optional	yes	C
Wisconsin	500	2 months	7	optional	yes	C
Wyoming	100	1 month	3	optional	yes	C

*Many small-claims courts have been rated as substandard because of their low claims limits, acceptance of lawyers, and maintenance of appeal procedures. These factors increase the costs and bureaucracy of the simplest procedures thereby making it more difficult for consumers to have access to justice. Some of the courts listed may have recently undergone administrative changes, therefore, check with the courts to confirm essential information dealing with cost, delay, lawyers, claim limits, etc. A is highest rating, C the lowest.

**Verify data. Courts are constantly upgraded.

Lawsuit Materials

Sooner or later, you will file a lawsuit as the last resort to obtain compensation. Whether the action is initiated before the small-claims court or a higher judicial body, solid documentation is essential to winning the case. Usually, the dealer will be badly prepared and will not expect to see confidential internal company documents or industry research materials brought into the case.

The following documents have been used successfully by consumer groups before the courts. Remember that if some of these documents are unobtainable before the trial, they may still be subpoenaed through the manufacturer.

1. Extended Warranties, or Customer "Goodwill" Guidelines

These secret warranty extensions are admissions by the manufacturers of the existence of substandard mechanical components. Under a strict interpretation of product liability, the manufacturer cannot limit his liability to mileage, elapsed time, or number of prior owners. Be sure to subpoena the exact documents listed in this book.

2. The United States Motor Vehicle Safety Act, Department of Transportation, Washington, D.C.

This federal law states the government's powers and defines the responsibilities of auto manufacturers in correcting factory defects and complying with safety standards.

3. NHTSA Recall Register, Department of Transportation, Washington, D.C.

The Department of Transportation's National Highway Traffic Safety Administration publishes these quarterly guides that summarize *all* motor vehicle safety-related defects that have culminated in recall campaigns.

4. NHTSA Defect Investigations

Based upon consumer complaints, industry leaks, and independent investigation, the NHTSA publishes this monthly list of suspected defects so as to encourage motorist input into the inquiry. Note that an investigation is not an admission by the government or the automobile manufacturer that a defect actually exists.

5. NADA Guide to Used-Car Prices

This booklet is ideal for convincing judges that you overpaid the dealer or that the vehicle was sold for the wrong year. Insurance companies that offer unfair prices as compensation for vehicles "totaled" after major accidents should be confronted with this booklet in negotiating fairer compensation.

6. PDI Inspection Sheet

Every new car has to be carefully checked out by the dealer before delivery to the purchaser. This verification procedure is called the predelivery inspection and is paid for by the automobile manufacturer. The dealer is required to fill out a PDI sheet and keep it with the owner's file at the dealership. Many dealers do not carry out the PDI and pocket the profit instead. This practice may account for the poor condition of a new car throughout its first six months of use.

7. Dealer Franchise Agreement

Car dealers are *not* independent businessmen. In fact, the automobile manufacturers, through tough franchise agreements, keep a strict control over almost everything the dealer does. The dealer-franchise agreement will indicate whether the dealer follows company policy in his sales and services operations.

8. Warranty Claims Sheet

Each dealer has to claim his warranty costs from the manufacturer by submitting computer-coded warranty-claims sheets. These forms will show if the dealer was paid for warranty work that was not done, or if what was alleged to have been a "minor" engine adjustment was actually a complete motor overhaul.

9. Warranty Interpretation Manual

This dealer guide will show how dealers should process warranty claims. This guide is useful in showing if the dealer actually followed the correct procedures.

10. Dealer and Manufacturer Advertising

For both new- and used-car sales, checking the advertising is helpful in showing contradictions, exaggerations, misleading statements, or just plain lies. Very useful in cases where a new- or used-car sale is to be canceled. It also can be used to dispute claims for reliability, economy, or gas mileage. Recently, the Ford Motor Company was forced by a small-claims-court judge to reimburse the owner of a 1974 Bobcat $300 to cover the differences in gas mileage between what Ford advertised and what the driver actually got.

11. Dealer Invoice

This document shows how much the dealer paid for the vehicle and if there was a claim for transport damage. About one-third of all new cars are damaged in transport.

12. Prior Sales Contracts

These will verify for how much a used car was initially sold, when it was sold, the mileage, and what reconditioning was done to the vehicle. This information is essential in the cancellation of used-car sales. Try also to bring in the previous owner of the vehicle to testify about the poor condition of the car.

13. Service Work Orders

These are useful to find out what reconditioning was done to the vehicle, at which mileage, and at what cost to the dealer.

14. The Mitchell Manual, 4926 Savannah St., San Diego, Calif.

In disputes over car repairs, this guide shows parts cost and time allotted to perform repairs. This information can be devastating to garages that habitually "boost" repair bills or charge for fictitious "shop supplies."

15. Owner's Manual

This booklet is useful to show how carefully the car was maintained.

Where to Go for Help

1. Federal Government Agencies

National Highway Traffic Safety Administration, Department of Transportation, Washington, D.C.

These people will tell you all you ever wanted to know about your automobile, but were afraid to ask. Actually, the NHTSA is responsible for the recall of more than 60 million vehicles for safety-related defects. Staff engineers may be useful as expert witnesses in lawsuits alleging the presence of automotive defects.

This federal agency is interested in monitoring the advertising claims of companies and investigating their sales practices. Although the FTC does not have any real teeth and works chiefly through "cease and desist" orders, some auto makers prefer to change their advertising or warranty practices rather than get "gummed" by the FTC. Secret warranty extensions are now a hot issue with the FTC.

2. State Representatives

Each state representative tries to maintain close contact with the electors of his/her district, hoping to exploit popular causes that will facilitate reelection. Consumer complaints are often investigated, settled, or publicized by these politicians because they wish to show "the folks back home" that local issues are important.

State representatives can also be instrumental in establishing public hearings and drawing up legislation covering automobile-industry abuses.

One drawback in complaining to state representatives, though, is the possibility that the garage or dealer may be a financial contributor to the representative's election campaign. This problem can be overcome by using the media to publicize the cause so much that political action is rewarded by public support.

3. Private Consumer Agencies

Center for Auto Safety, 1223 Dupont Circle Building, Washington, D.C. 20036, (202) 659-1126

The Center for Auto Safety was founded in 1970 with a grant from Consumers Union. Its purpose is to probe the relationship between unsafe car design and highway deaths and injuries, to press for safer car design, and to monitor the effectiveness of government efforts to enact vehicle safety standards. Operating out of offices in Washington, D.C., the center keeps extensive files on consumer complaints about automobiles and is in continual contact with the auto industry and other private and federal sources.

In the course of its research, the Center for Auto Safety has acquired considerable expertise and a wide range of valuable information which is made available to subscribers through PLAR. The service offers technical reports and research studies, lists of attorneys handling similar cases, lists of potential expert witnesses, and complete records of federal recalls and defect investigations.

Specific Services

MOTOR VEHICLES

1. Names, addresses and telephone numbers of attorneys involved in related litigation.
2. List of engineers who have served as expert witnesses in litigation.
3. Review of recall campaigns for related defects.
4. Information on investigations of the subject model auto.
5. A compilation of the relevant Federal Motor Vehicle Safety Standards.
6. Any relevant petitions, docket submissions, tests, or compliance investigations from the Department of Transportation (DOT).
7. Highway safety literature related to the subject defect.
8. Information on any detailed investigations of accidents involving the subject vehicle.
9. Internal service bulletins that relate to the defect sent by the manufacturers to their dealers.
10. Copies of corroborative letters from the files at DOT and the Center for Auto Safety.
11. Names and addresses of persons who have complained of similar or related defects to the Center for Auto Safety, DOT, and Ralph Nader.

MOBILE HOMES

The Center recently published a book-length exposé of the mobile-home industry, including extensive documentation of severe fire and wind hazards. Copies of *Mobile Homes: The Low-Cost Housing Hoax* are available from the center for $10.95.

In the area of mobile-home fires, the center offers:

1. Information regarding specific mobile-home construction and safety standards existing at the time the unit was built.
2. Lists of attorneys who are handling or have handled similar lawsuits.
3. Detailed technical information regarding the flammability of mobile-home-interior finishes.
4. Detailed technical information regarding the aluminum-wiring fire hazard and name of potential expert witnesses on the subject.
5. Information about possible sources of ignition, including faulty wiring, gas explosions, and furnace and water heater malfunctions.
6. Information regarding escape and rescue provisions (e.g., egress windows) in mobile homes.

In addition, there is on file substantive technical information about mobile-home susceptibility to windstorm damage.

HIGHWAYS

The center monitors federal and state highway activities regarding the road design for safety. In December 1974, it published a 300-page report on highway safety: *The Failure of America's Roadside Safety Program;* available from the center for $12.50.

The center offers to attorneys handling highway-safety-design cases:

1. Specific information on roadside design.
2. Names of potential expert witnesses on proper roadside design.
3. Copies of design and construction standards relevant to a particular site.
4. Analysis of the respective federal and state roles in designing and constructing federal-aid roads.

BIMONTHLY NEWS BULLETIN

The Center's PLAR bimonthly news bulletin, *Impact,* keeps subscribers informed about current defects and recalls, federal regulatory actions, and the Center's monitoring activities.

Subscription Charges

The Product Liability Action Resource fees are designed to make the service self-sufficient. The subscription fee is $50 per year for an individual attorney and for firms with five or fewer lawyers. For firms with more than five lawyers, the charge is $250. In addition to this membership charge, subscribers are billed a modest hourly fee for initial research performed by the center on each request. Follow-up services will be supplied without additional charge, except when the center's technical staff generates substantial original analytical material. The subscription fee includes the charge for *Impact*. For safety-related defect probes, the center is the most dynamic group in the United States.

Automobile Owners Action Council, 1411 K Street NW Suite 800, Washington, D.C., 20005, (202) 638-5550

The Automobile Owners Action Council (AOAC) is a nonprofit membership organization, incorporated in the District of Columbia, for the purpose of assisting in the protection of the consumer interests of automobile owners. To this end, AOAC monitors and reviews the activities, policies, and practices of members of the automotive and other related industries for the purpose of identifying, isolating, and revealing to the public illegal, deceptive, unfair, usurious, or unconscionable acts and practices that are inimical to the interests of automobile consumers. AOAC is attempting to bring the concerted power and resources of honest, public-spirited attorneys, students, researchers, writers, and ordinary citizens to the aid of automobile owners in the United States.

Membership in AOAC is open to any person interested in the problems inherent in automobile ownership for an annual membership fee of $10. For their fee, members receive voting privileges (members elect the officers and directors of AOAC), a membership card, its newsletter (published quarterly), and individual assistance and support in settling claims and complaints against members of the automotive industry.

142

Rather ineffective in consumer advocacy for aggrieved car owners. Even its automobile ratings can be quite misleading as witnessed by its inaccurate ravings over the VW Rabbit and Fiat as recommended buys.

CU should concentrate less on product testing and establish more consumer-advocacy offices like its successful Washington operation. Consumer complaints are useful to CU in the planning of its editorial activities.

Automobile Protection Association, 292 St. Joseph Blvd. W.
Montreal, Quebec, (514) 273–1366.

The Automobile Protection Association is a non-profit, public-interest, consumer corporation founded 10 years ago to bring the powers of honest lawyers, mechanics, and journalists to the aid of motorists victimized by fraud or mechanic incompetency.

Corporate Ju-Jitsu to Make the Seller Beware. Every motorist's complaint goes through a committee of mechanics for verification, a publicity committee that exposes the dishonesty as a warning to the public, and a legal committee that uses ordinary laws in extraordinary ways to resolve the dispute.

If fraud or incompetency has been proven to exist, in a franchised gas station or within a well-known new car dealership, the APA takes the complaint through its three regular committees. If the garage or car dealer ignores the APA's demands for justice, a form of consumer corporate Ju-Jitsu is used by the Association. The APA may organize a boycott, press conference, picketing, or bring legal action all at once or spread the activities over several days.

APA Financing. The Automobile Protection Association is a non-profit, public-interest corporation financed in the following ways:

1. Selling of APA publications (*Justice for the Exploited Motorist,* and *Lemon-Aid*).
2. Lecture, radio and television appearances.
3. $10 membership fees.
4. Government research grants.

Because the APA is independently financed, it is also independently controlled. No donations are accepted from private interests such as oil, automobile manufacturers or automobile insurance companies.

APA Membership. Motorists may join the Automobile Protection Association for a yearly membership fee of $10.

For this membership fee, motorists receive the following services:

1. A list of recommended garages across Canada.
2. Membership card.
3. Window sticker showing APA membership.
4. Legal assistance from APA lawyers or before the small claims court.
5. Association support in settling claims.
6. Automobile repair inspections and price verification.
7. Counselling from honest mechanics.
8. New car purchase counselling on price, warranty and defects.
9. Used car purchase counselling on list prices and repair costs.
10. Insurance counselling on best and worst firms.
11. APA consumer bulletins.

APA Accomplishments. Over the past 10 years, the APA has been involved in numerous successful skirmishes with giant corporations and government bureaucrats.

1. Exposed Esso diagnostic clinics.
2. Investigated license bureau bribery and incompetence.
3. Picketed many auto dealers.
4. Probed worthless gasoline and oil additives.
5. Pushed for increased school bus safety.
6. Demanded the recall of millions of defective cars.
7. Exposed up-dating import car fraud (old cars sold as new).
8. Recovered millions of dollars for cheated consumers.
9. Prosecuted thousands of auto dealers.
10. Lobbied for stronger consumer protection laws.

In the past 10 years, the APA has grown to over 6,000 members. More than $7 million has been recovered in helping some 100,000 motorists.

Consumer Action,
26 Seventh Street
San Francisco, California,
(415) 626–2510

This California tax-exempt, nonprofit, community organization is one of the most effective grass-roots consumer advocacy groups in North America. Consumer Action, through its monthly *CA NEWS,* litigation, publicity compaigns, and mass demonstrations has successfully defended consumers' rights on a regional and national scale. Motorists have found CA particularly helpful in fighting auto-industry fraud and incompetenece.

CHAPTER V

"Secret"
Auto Warranty Extensions

●

Most consumers are aware of the 12,000-mile warranty applied to new cars. However, automobile manufacturers also have a system of secret warranty extensions for vehicles that have defective components. These warranty extensions often offer free parts and labor up to five years or 50,000 miles, regardless of the number of prior owners.

The following "secret" warranty extensions are presently in force. Nevertheless, most manufacturers will deny that extended warranties exist. If this happens, write The Federal Trade Commission, Washington, D.C. 20580, for copies of internal company documents sent to the government.

Also, if the extended warranty's arbitrarily established time limit has elapsed, consumers may still demand that the dealer or manufacturer pay part of the repairs. Usually a small-claims-court lawsuit will bring quick results if all else fails.

Defective GM Transmissions

General Motors, encountering some problems with leaking transmissions on its 1973, 1974, and some 1975 models, as a result of switching to a new type of transmission fluid, warrants cars with the problem for up to five years or 50,000 miles.

GM was forced to stop using whale oil in its automatic

transmission fluid because of a ban on the killing of sperm whales. Beginning in 1973, it adopted an alternate transmission oil.

Reports have come in from all GM divisions that the new fluid resulted in corrosion of a part of the automatic transmission oil cooler inside the radiator. This caused transmission fluid to leak into the cooling system, while antifreeze got into the transmission.

John C. Bates, GM service director, said the 400-series hydramatic transmission, used in about 2.1 million 1973 to 1974 standard models, resulted in about 5,000 leakages. On the company's 350-series automatic transmissions for its intermediates and compacts, about 500 failures have been reported.

According to *Automotive News,* the reports of failures have drifted downward since December 1975. Despite *Automotive News*'s optimistic prediction that General Motors would compensate motorists with defective automatic transmissions, consumer groups across the country have reported the contrary. In many cases, both GM's dealers and regional zone offices deny the *Automotive News* story and insist consumers pay from $300 to $600 for transmission repairs, even when the failures occur only a few thousand miles over the standard 12,000-mile-warranty period.

General Motors of Canada Limited
Oshawa, Ontario   L1G 1K7

April 18, 1975

TO ALL GENERAL MOTORS DEALERS

Attention: Service Manager

Dear Sirs:

SPECIAL   POLICY,   RE: COOLANT   LEAKS
CAUSED   BY   TRANS-
MISSION OIL COOLER
CORROSION

It has been determined that automatic transmission fluids used in certain 1973 and 1974 model GM vehicles may cause corrosion at the fittings of the tubular-type oil cooler, located in the radiator tank. Excessive corrosion can cause leaks which will allow transmission fluid to enter the cooling system and/ or coolant to enter the transmission. Therefore, a Special Policy has been established to avoid customer dissatisfaction in the event oil cooler fitting corrosion causes transmission or cooling system malfunction.

Special Policy

A dealer application for adjustment for parts and labour will be accepted by General Motors of Canada for cooling system and/or transmission failures, when caused by oil cooler corrosion, for 50,-000 miles. This policy applies to oil cooler related failure only.

All claims requesting reimbursement for transmission or cooling system repairs under this Policy must be supported by a no-charge invoice from an authorized radiator repair station, indicating replacement of an oil cooler assembly due to corrosion at the fitting.

Should a dealer sublet the oil cooler replacement to other than an authorized repair station, or make the replacement within the dealership, the defective cooler must be retained for inspection and scrapping by a factory representative, along with all other parts replaced under this Policy.

In the event an owner seeks a Policy adjustment for a previous failure of an automatic transmission or cooling system, which was caused by oil cooler fitting corrosion, the dealer should bring his case to the attention of his Zone District Service Manager and request a review.

A Dealer Technical Bulletin will be released shortly detailing model application, repair procedures and warranty data.

Yours truly,

M. J. Patrick,
General Service Manager.

JCT/am

When General Motors has been taken before the small-claims courts over this warranty "cover-up," more than 90 percent of the cases have been decided in favor of the plaintiff. So far, *Automotive News* has neglected to report GM's denial of its April and May 1975 articles, and the success of motorists using the transmission articles before the courts.

Ford Secret Warranty Extensions

1. Owners of 1977 Ford Granada/Monarch models can get free gas caps because they may leak if the car is hit from the rear. More than 322,000 '77 Granadas are involved. There is no mileage or ownership limitation.
  2. Ford's 1976–77 Granada/Monarch models are also eligible for the free replacement of the rear gas cap flap that often falls off due to a defective hinge. There is no mileage or ownership limitation.
  3. Ford has a "piston scuffing" defect in its 1974–1977 Pinto Bobcat, Comet Maverick, Granada/Monarch, and Mustang models. As a result, the company will make free repairs to cars affected by this motor defect. Ford has agreed to accept motor claims for vehicles that have as much as 36,000 miles, or 36 months of use. These is no ownership limitation.
  4. Defective motor components affect the following engines and models:

- 2.3-liter engines(1975–1976 Capri)
- 400-cubic-inch Windsor engines(1974–1977 cars and trucks)
- 351-cubic-inch Cleveland engines(1974–1977 cars and trucks)
- 360–390 FE truck engines(1974–1976 trucks and M450–500 motor homes)

Chrysler Paint Warranty Extended

The Chrysler company had quality-control problems with the paint used on its 1972 and 1973 models. Paint problems were especially severe on cars with the "Purple People Eater" paint style. Chrysler extended warranty through its Technical Bulletin.

Chrysler Vibrations

Chrysler has also extended its warranty coverage to correct suspension and tire defects that cause severe front-suspension vibrations on many of its 1975 and 1976 Cordoba and Charger models. Although Chrysler refers to the defect rather euphemistically as "Smooth Road Ride Complaints" the following internal Chrysler memo shows that both Goodyear and Chrysler may be responsible for the problem. Unfortunately for many owners, Chrysler has refused to correct the defect and has denied that the problem exists.

Chrysler Inter-Company Correspondence

To: All District Service Managers
Subject: Cordoba/Charger Smooth Road Ride Complaints

Goodyear and Chrysler Engineering are co-operating in an indepth investigation of the subject condition. It is to the advantage of all concerned to persevere for a short time when a field-service procedure will be made available.

Until the full procedure is released, most of the complaints can be resolved by what will be Step #1 of that procedure, namely the tire/wheel runout and balance correction procedure outlined in the attached Newsletter, No. 133.

These steps should be carefully followed by dealers that you select, where properly trained personnel and equipment are available.

After following this procedure, if tire(s) are isolated as a primary cause, the dealer should make contact with his tire manufacturer's store for additional assistance.

If after their assistance a problem still exists, your personnel should become involved.

KNG/bm   K. N. Gilboe
Attach.

What to Do?
Warranty Compensation Guidelines

Warranty extensions are made by manufacturers to compensate consumers for defective parts that either fail prematurely or never function properly from the start.

Lawyers advise consumers never to accept an automobile manufacturer's warranty limitation, whether it be for five years as with some Toyota and Vega-Astre warranty extensions, or the normal 12,000-mile/12-month warranty. The lawyers feel that since the warranty extensions are for repairs caused by defective parts, dealers and car manufacturers cannot arbitrarily limit the extent of their liability. The law holds manufacturers responsible for their negligence regardless of what a dealer or factory representative may say to the contrary. Therefore, be wary of "goodwill" settlements where the dealer or manufacturer agrees to assume only 50 percent of the bill, or agrees to pay only for parts but not for the labor to install the parts. This type of "goodwill" is hard to accept, since the labor would not be necessary if the part was not defective.

Consumers wishing to contest a repair bill that may be excessive or covered by a secret warranty extension should take the following steps:

1. Write a registered letter to dealer and car manufacturer asking that repairs be covered by the warranty or by an extended warranty.

2. If the request is refused, pay for repairs and then make a claim for reimbursement through the small-claims court.

3. Be sure to send a subpoena to the manufacturer ordering the deposit of all internal documents relating to the warranty extension for that model car. Refer to documents published in this book.

Consumer groups keep on file a list of small-claims court cases where consumers have forced manufacturers to extend their warranties for cars well after the normal warranty has expired. Some court judgments have extended the warranty far beyond the normal warranty period.

(taken from Original Confidential Documents)

Published by Ford of U.S.A. Ltd., General Motors of U.S.A. Ltd., Toyota U.S.A. Ltd.

General Motors Vega and Astre
1971 to 1974

GMC–328–3M 6–74–MBF

Vega–Astre "Special Policy"
Request for Reimbursement—
Special Engine Overheat Policy

This Special Policy applies to all 1971 through 1974 Vegas–Astres regardless of previous or present ownership and is retroactive for Overheat Services previously performed for which the owner may have been charged for all or parts of these services. Charges for parts and/or labor which may have been performed by a General Motors Dealer or an Independent Service Station prior to June 1, 1974, will be considered for adjustment.

Engine components eligible for Special Policy considerations include Head Gasket, Cylinder Head, Engine Block Replacement, Engine Block Reconditioning, Fitted Block Replacement, Partial Engine Assembly Replacement, necessary related gaskets, and labor allowances for installing the components.

The cost of parts and labor in connection with Maintenance Services normally considered owner responsibility as outlined in the applicable owner's Manual. General Motors New Vehicle Warranty is excluded from the provisions of this policy.

Purchasers must provide authentic documentation of repairs and proof of ownership of the vehicle in question.

Dealers are to assist owners in completing this application and insure all documentation required is attached.

Vega–Astre engine must have the coolant recovery system installed prior to submitting this application. Forward all applications to Zone Office for Zone Approval.

Toyota: Extended Policy 1
(1971 to 1972 Toyota Corollas with 2T–C Motors)

**Nature of repair applicable
for extended policy:**
   Head Crack

Applicable Vehicle Models:

Warranty coverage of 5 years/ 50,000 miles for Vehicles with Frame Numbers Prior to:	For Vehicles within Frame Number Range indicated below 36 months, 50,000 mile warranty is applicable
TE 21 059163	TE 21 059164 to 080836
TE 21 607044	TE 21 607045 to 631898
TE 27 049464	TE 27 049465 to 075030
TE 28 508364	TE 28 508365 to 530459
TA 12 062087	TA 12 062088 to 119325
	TA 12 700001 to 702941

**Policy period
and coverage:**
   Refer to the above Applicable Vehicle Models column.

Expiration date: June 30, 1975

OPERATION CODE F.R.H. DESCRIPTION OF REPAIR

**Operation Code
and flat rate hr.**
   Please refer to the Toyota Flat Rate Manual.

Failed Part No.

Authorization Number: HWG-3339

Toyota U.S.A.
Secret Motor Warranty

Remarks: This Bulletin replaces Extended Policy Bulletin

Feuille 153

**Nature of repair application
for extended policy:**
   Replace engine block in accordance with the
   Toyota Service Bulletin reference above.

**Applicable
Vehicle Models**

All vehicles 2T-C engines prior to engine
number 2T-0571850 or prior to frame
numbers indicated below:

TE 21 036625	TE 28 541264
TE 21 649076	TA 12 143028

Policy period and coverage: 100% parts and labor for 24 months or 24,000 miles.

Expiration date: June 30, 1975.

OPERATION CODE F.R.H. DESCRIPTION OF REPAIR
Operation Code and flat rate hr.
    Please refer to the Toyota Flat Rate Manual.

Failed Part No.

Authorization Number: EP 3-A

Remarks:
    This Bulletin replaces Extended Policy Bulletin.

Toyota Extended Policy

Subject:
    Differential Noise on Station Wagon Model

Nature of Repair Applicable for Extended Policy
    Repair due to excessive differential noise as indicated on the Toyota Service Bulletins referenced above.

Applicable Vehicle Models
    All vehicle models listed below:
    MX 28, MX 29
    RT 79, RT 89, RT 118
    TE 28.

Policy Period and Coverage
    100% parts and labor for 24 months or 24,000 miles.

Expiration date: June 30, 1975

OPERATION CODE F.R.H. DESCRIPTION OF REPAIR

Operation Code and Flat Rate Hour
    Refer to the Toyota Flat Rate Manual.

Failed Part No.

Authorization Number: EP-13

Remarks

Subject:
18R–C Carburetor Power Valve

Nature of Repair Applicable for Extended Policy
Correct rough engine idle and erratic hot engine stalling as indicated in the Toyota Service Bulletin.

Applicable Vehicle Models
All models with 18R–C engine within the frame number range indicated below:

All RT 63   All RT 85
All RT 73   All RT 95
All RT 79   All RT 89
RA 21 000001 to RA 21 121600
RN 22 000001 to RN 22 039855
RN 27 000001 to RN 27 006114.

For vehicles within the range indicated below, without EGR:
RT 104 000001 to RT 104 000815
RT 114 000001 to RT 114 006317
RT 118 000001 to RT 118 005094.

Policy Period and Coverage
100% parts and labor for 24 months or 24,000 miles.

Expiration date: June 30, 1975

OPERATION CODE F.R.H. DESCRIPTION OF REPAIR

Operation Code and Flat Rate Hour
Please refer to the Toyota Flat Rate Manual.

Failed Part No.

Authorization Number: HWG-3962

Remarks
This bulletin replaces extended policy Bulletin 6.

Subject:
Nippondenso Air Conditioner

Nature of Repair Applicable for Extended Policy
Repair of receiver dryer and related parts due to gas leakage from the receiver dryer. (Receiver dryer must be the original failed part number.)

Applicable Vehicle Models
All vehicles equipped with Nippondenso air conditioner.

Policy Period and Coverage
100% parts and labor for 24 months.

Expiration date: June 30, 1975

OPERATION CODE F.R.H. DESCRIPTION OF REPAIR

Operation Code and Flat Rate Hour
Please refer to the Toyota Flat Rate Manual.

Failed Part No.
Receiver dryer (88470-XXXXX) must be the original failed part number.

Authorization Number: EP-7A

Remarks
This bulletin replaces extended policy Bulletin 7.

Subject:
2M & 4M Carburetor Anti-Surge Correction

Nature of Repair Applicable for Extended Policy
Repair for carburetor surge as indicated in the Toyota Service Bulletin.

Applicable Vehicle Models
1972 Model (2M)
MX 12 000001 to 005191
MX 22 000001 to 003494
MX 28 000001 to 004655
1973 Model (4M)
MX 13 000001 to 009000
MX 23 000001 to 006000
MX 29 000001 to 009000
1974 Model (4M)
All models MX 13, MX 23, MX 29
Except California model

Policy Period and Coverage
100% parts and labor for 24 months or 24,000 miles.

Expiration date: June 30, 1975

OPERATION CODE F.R.H. DESCRIPTION OF REPAIR

Operation Code and Flat Rate Hour
360092   0.9 Hr.   Removal and Reinstallation of Power Piston.

Failed Part No.
21351-45010 (power piston)

Authorization Number: HSI-4035

Remarks
Please refer to the sample claim on reverse side for proper preparation procedure.
This Bulletin replaces extended policy Bulletin 8.

Subject:
F Engine Valve Failure

Nature of Repair Applicable for Extended Policy
Repair of burnt or sticking valve as indicated on the Toyota Service Bulletin.

Applicable Vehicle Models
All Vehicles with Frame Number prior to:
FJ40-160001
FJ55-037001

Policy Period and Coverage
100% parts and labor for the period of 24 months or 24,000 miles.

Expiration date: June 30, 1975

OPERATION CODE F.R.H. DESCRIPTION OF REPAIR

Operation Code and Flat Rate Hour
Please refer to the Toyota Flat Rate Manual.

Failed Part No.

Authorization Number: EP-12

Remarks

Toyota U.S.A.
Secret Motor Warranty

Remarks
This Bulletin replaces previous extended policy Bulletin.

Feuille 153

Nature of Repair Application for Extended Policy
Replace engine block in accordance with the Toyota Service Bulletin.

Applicable Vehicle Models
All vehicles 2T–C engines prior to engine number 2T–0571850 or prior to frame numbers indicated below:

TE 21 086625   TE 28 541264

```
TE 21 649076      TA 12 143028
TE 27 081612      TA 12 717221
TE 27 410638
```

Policy Period and Coverage
    100% parts and labor for 24 months or 24,000 miles.

Expiration date: June 30, 1975

OPERATION CODE F.R.H. DESCRIPTION OF REPAIR

Operation Code and Flat Rate Hour
    Please refer to the Toyota Flat Rate Manual.

Failed Part No.

Authorization Number: EP 3-A

Remarks
    This Bulletin replaces previous policy Bulletin.

Ford U.S.A.
Secret Rust Warranty, August 25, 1972

All Regional and District Managers, Ford Customer Service Division Limited Service Program J–67 for body rust on 1969 to 1972 model cars and light trucks—district information only.

Announcement of limited-service program covering body rust on 1969 to 1972 model cars and light trucks.

In our continuing efforts to assure customer satisfaction we are announcing a service program covering body rust on 1969 to 1972 model cars and light trucks.

This is a limited-service program **without dealership notification*** and should be administered on an individual-complaint basis. In effect, it enables you to handle body-rust complaints without utilizing your extended policy funds.

Under this program there will be 100% coverage of repair cost through the first 24 months and 75% from the 25th to the 36th month without regard to mileage. Approved claims should be noted J–67.

Your cooperation in administering this as a limited-service program will assure maximum benefits for all districts.

*Boldface is author's.

Defective Ford Components

(taken from Original Confidential Documents)
Published by Ford U.S.A. Ltd.

Besides maintaining a system of secret auto-warranty extensions, automobile manufacturers also compile confidential summaries of the major defective components used in each model year for each model car assembled.

The Ford Motor Company, for example, holds regular monthly meetings to discuss the reliability and quality of each car model as reflected by the number of warranty claims reported. The author has obtained copies of those reports submitted to the Ford North American Automotive Operations Quality Meeting held by Ford on October 19, 1973, November 16, 1973, and again on January 17, 1974. These highly confidential internal Ford documents show, for example, that Ford approved 33 "extended policy programs" between 1971 and 1973 that cost the company $22.4 million.

In addition to outlining the various "secret" warranty extensions paid for by Ford, the internal reports also give details on more than 2,000 separate defects affecting Ford models from 1969 to the 1974 model year. Ford owners who have paid for the repair of any defective mechanical components are urged to read the following selected documents carefully to determine if Ford has classified that component as defective. If so, a registered letter should be sent to the Ford Motor Company demanding a reimbursement for the repairs. If Ford refuses to give reimbursement, a small-claims-court lawsuit should be initiated using Ford's own confidential documents as proof.

Major Customer Product Problems*

Problem Area Current Model Problems	Car Lines	Description	Mo. of Review
Paint	All except Ford and Mercury	Mismatch and poor application	Nov.
Electrical Malfunctions	All except Mav., Comet and Pinto	Inoperative accessory and interior/exterior lights	Dec.

Major Customer Product Problems*

Problem Area Current Model Problems	Car Lines	Description	Mo. of Review
Air Conditioning	All	Windshield fogging, leaks, and compressor failures	Dec.
High Speed Vibration	T'Bird, Mark IV, Lincoln, Must. and Mercury	Improper tire balance	Dec.
Driveability	All with 2.3L, 2.8L and 250 CID	Dieseling, stalling, and rough idle	Nov.
Wind Noise and Water Leaks	Lincoln, T'Bird, Mark IV, Torino, Montego	Improper glass adjustment and poor sealing	–
Driveline Chunk	All	Noise on shift engagement	–
Front Suspension	All except Mav. Comet and Pinto	Noise and misalignment	–
Power Steering Gear	All w/XR-50 gear	Sticks and binds	Jan.
Locks, Handles, and Mechanism	Linc., Mustang, Comet, Torino, Montego and Cougar	Inoperative and improper adjustment	Jan.
Starter Interlock/ Seat Belts	All	No-start and twisted belts	Dec.
Sheet Metal	Ford, Mercury, Mark IV, Lincoln, Mustang, Comet and Montego	Poor fits, dents, dings, rough metal finish	Nov.
Radio	Mercury, T'Bird, Mark IV, Lincoln and Montego	Inoperative, static, poor reception	–
Shift Cable	Torino, Montego, T'Bird, Mark IV, Cougar	Cable freeze-up	–
Automatic Transmission	All	Erratic shifting	Dec.
Brakes	All	Master cylinder internal leakage	–
Solid State Ignition	All with 460, 400 CID engine	Module failure	Oct.
Past Model Problems			
Rust and Corrosion	All 1969–1973 car lines	Body rust and perforations	Oct.

Problem Area Current Model Problems	Car Lines	Description	Mo. of Review
Exhaust Manifold	1971–73 351W	Manifold cracking	Jan.
Valve Guides	1972–73 400 CID	Excessive guide wear	Jan.

*Source: Report of the Ford North American Automotive Operations Quality Meeting, January 17, 1974, p. 11a.

Ford 1974 Model Problem Description*

- **Driveability Complaints (All Car Lines)—** a detailed review and assessment of driveability complaints will be given following the major problem review.
- **Solid State Ignition System Failure (Thunderbird, Mark IV)—** this problem is identified by the customer as a "no start" condition or that the vehicle lacks top-speed performance. Replacement of the ignition system module is the most frequent dealer correction required.
- **Paint Discrepancies (Lincoln, Mark IV, Thunderbird, Mustang)—** the major problems are color mismatch, thin paint and dirt or foreign material in paint.
- **Sheetmetal Fits and Finish (Mustang, Lincoln, Mark IV, Thunderbird)—** this problem is identified as hood and deck lid misalignment and dents, dings and/or poor metal finish in sheet metal panels.
- **Electrical Malfunctions (Lincoln, Mark IV, Thunderbird, Mustang)—** the major complaints are inoperative electrical accessories or interior lights. Wiring quality and/or improper routing and connections are the most frequent causes.
- **High-Speed Vibration (Lincoln, Mark IV, Thunderbird, Mercury, Cougar, Mustang)—** customers report vehicle vibration at speeds above 45 mph. This problem is primarily caused by improper tire balance and is corrected by performing an on-car balance.**

A brief status report covering corrective actions

*Source: Report of the Ford North American Automotive Operations Quality Meeting, November 16, 1973, p. 9.
**Boldface is author's.

planned or underway in these areas will now be given by the affected activity.

U.S. Car and Truck
Extended Policy Payments by Major Area
(Total Through June 1973)

Model Year Cumulative Payments by Major Area	Car and Light Truck			Heavy Truck		
	1970	1971	1972	1970	1971	1972
Engine	26%	34%	28%	68%	47%	46%
Carb., Ign., Strg.	4	4	2	2	3	3
Transmission	9	18	20	5	8	6
Clutch	1	1	0	1	3	2
Chassis	19	21	32	18	30	34
Body	24	12	10	3	5	5
Electrical	17	10	8	3	4	4
Total	100%	100%	100%	100%	100%	100%
Memo: EP Programs As Percent of Total	3%	9%	31%	26%	10%	21%

Significant EP Programs*

Component	Maximum Coverage (Months/ Miles)	Vehicle Lines	Model Years	Estimated Program Costs (Mils.)
Valve Guide Wear	24/24	Cars and Light Trucks	1970–1972	$3.4
A/C Compressor	24/–	Torino and Montego	1972	3.2
330 HD FT Engine Bore Wear	–/50	Medium Trucks	1969–1973	2.9
361 & 391 FT Eng. Bore Wear and Oil Cons.	30/50	Med. and Heavy Trucks	1970–1973	2.1
C-4 A/T Band Slippage	24/40	Cars and Light Trucks	1971, 1972	1.8
Body Rust	36/–	Cars and Light Trucks	1969–1972	1.3
Bonded Ventless Window Glass	24/–	Cars Except Maverick	1969, 1970	1.2
A/C Evaporator Core	36/–	Ford and Mercury	1970–1972	1.1
Rear Axle "Chuckle"	24/24	Cars and Light Trucks	1972	1.1
Quarter Panel Rust Around Fuel Filter	24/–	Ford and Mercury	1969–1971	0.4
Power Window Motor and Drive Assy.	30/–	T'Bird and Mark III	1969, 1970	0.3
Subtotal				$18.8
All Other			1967–1974	3.6
Total				$22.4

*Source: Report of the Ford North American Operation Quality Meeting, October 19, 1973, p. 8a.

Volkswagen Warranty Extensions

Among all the domestic and import car manufacturers, Volkswagen is the least secretive about its warranty extensions. In fact, all of the following warranty extension bulletins were given to the author by Volkswagen officials:

VOLKSWAGEN ⬤ **Service Circular** April 21, 1977
PORSCHE ☐ *Circulaire du Service* No. 52
AUDI ☐ **Warranty/**Garantie

Subject: Crankcase Ventilation Modification
1975/76 Rabbit and Scirocco vehicles
— revised.
Supersedes No. 20, December 30, 1976

Evaluations indicate that only a small number of 1975/76 Rabbits and Sciroccos have been modified, as per our instructions given with Product Circular of February 9, 1976.

Icing in some carburetor tops caused performance problems during the previous winter season and, if this important modification has not been performed, the same could occur again.

We urge you to contact your customers to have subject modification done *now*.

In order to assist you and to give you a chance to encourage your customers to have this crankcase ventilation modification performed, *VWC will accept claims for vehicles out of warranty until further notice, regardless of time or mileage.*

Claims may be submitted as follows:

Labour operation: 1050 51A
Time allowance: 0030 T.U.

Parts

For 1975 models

| #ZVP 202 851 | Tubing and screw | 1 each |
| #055 103 493H | Hose | 1 |

For 1976 models

#ZVP 202 851	Tubing and screw	1 each
#211 129 101	PCV Valve	1
Local supplier	Hose clamps	2

Damage code: 1050 10 00
Warranty code: 2

H. Koch
Warranty Manager

VOLKSWAGEN ● **Service Circular** Sept. 14, 1977
PORSCHE ☐ *Circulaire du Service*   No. 82
AUDI ☐ **Warrranty/** *Garantie*

Subject: Volkswagen Metallic Paint—
          Adjustment Policy

We received reports that in certain geographic areas, or under unique atmospheric conditions, the clear coat may deteriorate on *Volkswagen vehicles through 1976 model year, painted with metallic.*

In order to assist customers who may experience this problem, we will accept claims for 100 per cent of refinishing costs up to 24 months from the date of delivery to the first retail customer, or first use.

After that, VWC will participate with 50 per cent of refinishing costs for vehicles in service up to 36 months.

Labour and material charges are to be based on the "Suggested Repair Times" manual for paint.

Naturally, deductions must be made for body panels which may have accident damage or are in any other way no longer in original factory condition. Indicate on the RFA repainting costs as applicable, minus deduction based on sheet metal damages.

Note: *If complete refinishing of a vehicle is necessary, and the customer requests the use of single coat acrylic ma-*

terial and procedures, you can perform the repair accordingly.

Please advise your personnel accordingly.

H. Koch
Warranty Manager.

HK:gd

VOLKSWAGEN	■	**Service Circular**	Feb. 3/77
PORSCHE	□	***Circulaire du Service***	No. 30
AUDI	■	**Warranty/*Garantie***	

Subject: Disc Brakes—Rabbit, Scirocco, Dasher and Audi Fox

In an effort to provide accurate quality control information, VWC will accept claims up to 24 months or 24,000 miles from date of original delivery or use, for the replacement of brake discs of Rabbit, Scirocco, Dasher and Audi Fox vehicles so equipped. However, discs damaged solely due to totally worn brake pads cannot be considered for reimbursement.

Claims must be completed as follows:

Labour Operation:	As applicable
Time Allowance:	As applicable
Parts:	As applicable
Damage Code:	4650 18 00
Warranty Code:	2

Please advise your personnel accordingly.

H. Koch
Warranty Manager
Directeur—garantie

HK/enb/mz

VOLKSWAGEN PORSCHE AUDI

☐ **Service Circular** Sept. 14, 1977
☐ *Circulaire du Service* No. 83
● **Warranty/** *Garantie*

Subject: Audi Metallic Paint—
Adjustment Policy

We received reports that in certain geographic areas, or under unique atmospheric conditions, the clear coat may deteriorate on *Audi vehicles through 1976 model year, painted with metallic.*

In order to assist customers who may experience this problem, we will accept claims for 100 per cent of refinishing costs up to 24 months from the date of delivery to the first retail customer, or first use.

After that, VWC will participate with 50 percent of refinishing costs for vehicles in service up to 36 months.

Labour and Material charges are to be based on the "Suggested Repair Times" manual for paint.

Naturally, deductions must be made for body panels which may have accident damage or are in any other way no longer in original factory condition. Indicate on the RFA repainting costs as applicable, minus deduction based on sheet metal damages.

Note: *If complete refinishing of a vehicle is necessary, and the customer requests the use of single coat acrylic material and procedures, you can perform the repair accordingly.*

Please advise your personnel accordingly.

H. Koch,
Warranty Manager.

HK:gd

Subject: Installation of Spur Belt Guide—
Types 17, 32, 53 and Audi Fox

Evaluations indicate that only a small number of the above vehicles have been modified as per our instructions given with Product Circular Group 15 of February 17, 1976.

In order to assist you, and to give you a chance to encourage your customers to have the spur belt guide installed, VWC will accept claims for vehicles as indicated below. This applies up to the following chassis numbers:

Rabbit	1763 316 023
Scirocco	5362 045 503
Dasher	3_62 175 953
Audi Fox	8_62 108 740
Audi Fox	
Station Wagon	3362 908 444

Claims may be submitted as follows:

Up to 24 months or 30 000 miles from date of delivery, —a regular Warranty claim.

Labour operation:	15 33 51A
Time allowance:	00.35 T.U.
Part number:	049 109 129 guide, Qty—1
Part number:	056 109 119A belt, Qty—1 (if nec.)
Damage code:	15 33 66 00 01
Account number:	2

For vehicles beyond 24 months or 30 000 miles—a goodwill claim using Account number #8

Please advise your personnel accordingly.

H. Koch
Warranty Manager

HK/enb

VOLKSWAGEN ☐ **Service Circular** Sept. 14, 1977
PORSCHE ● *Circulaire du Service* No. 81
AUDI ☐ **Warranty/***Garantie*

Subject: Metallic Paint—
Adjustment Policy

The Porsche factory changed the metallic paint material by adapting an acrylic clear coat beginning with the production of 1976 model 911 vehicles.

In order to satisfy owners of Porsche vehicles with metallic paint who experience deterioration of the clear coat, VWC will accept claims for 911 vehicles through 1975 model year and 914 vehicles through 1976 model year, as follows:

> A. 0–24 months 100% reimbursement
> B. 25–36 months 50% participation

Such reimbursement will be based on the labour and material allowances outlined in the "Suggested Repair Times" manual for paint or, in the event of sublet repairs, reasonable repainting charges. An RFA must be submitted to VWC, Toronto, before commencing repair.

Note: *If complete refinishing of a vehicle is necessary, and the customer requests the use of single coat acrylic material and procedures, you can perform the repair accordingly.*

Please advise your personnel accordingly.

H. Koch
Warranty Manager.

HK:gd

VOLKSWAGEN ☐ **Service Circular** Sept. 14, 1977
PORSCHE ● *Circulaire du Service* No. 84
AUDI ☐ **Warranty/***Garantie*

Subject: 1976/77 911 and 930 vehicles—
Adjustment Policy for Exhaust

Valve Guides for 24 month or 36,000 miles

Under severe operating conditions, some exhaust valve guides, installed into 911 and 930 vehicles within the chassis number ranges listed below, may wear prematurely.

The factory has made production changes of which you were advised with Product Circular 15 of July 6, 1977.

In an effort to satisfy those owners who experience such premature valve guide failure, VWC has implemented the following adjustment policy. Claims may be submitted up to 24 months or 36,000 miles, from date of delivery or first use, whichever comes first, as follows:

From 911 620 0010 to 911 620 2079
911 621 0010 to 911 621 2175
930 680 0010 to 930 680 0530

911 720 0010 to 911 720 1432
911 721 0010 to 911 721 1143

Labour Operation: as applicable

Time Allowance: as applicable

Parts: Exhaust valve guides #930 104 321 50 (Qty. as necessary)
Appropriate gasket set (Qty. 1)

Damage Code: 1576 18 00

Warranty Code: 2

Please advise your personnel accordingly.

H. Koch
Warranty Manager

HK/enb

Subject: Installation of Gasket kit on
1976/77 model 930 and 1977 model
911 Porsche vehicles equipped
with a Thermo Reactor

As part of our continuous efforts to improve our products for the benefit of our customers, we are introducing a special gasket kit to be utilized in the event of engine oil leaks, which may occur on some of the above listed model year vehicles, equipped with a thermo reactor.

With Product Circular Group 15 of September 20, 1977, you were given the necessary technical details, for which regular claims may be submitted until September 30, 1978, date of repair. It must be understood, however, that this special repair procedure will only be reimbursed once per vehicle.

The chassis number range for possibly affected vehicles is:

930 680 0010	930 680 0530
911 720 0010	911 720 3388
911 721 0010	911 721 2747
930 780 0010	930 780 0727

Please complete claims as follows:

Labour operation:	1531 12 A
Time allowance:	1050
Parts:	#930100909 00 kit (Qty. 1)
Damage code:	150150 00
Warranty code:	2

Note: Part numbers are listed for reference. Always verify with your Parts Department in case of changes.

Please advise your personnel accordingly.

H. Koch
Warranty Manager

HK/enb

VOLKSWAGEN ☐ **Service Circular** Nov. 24, 1977
PORSCHE ● *Circulaire du Service* No. 101
AUDI ☐ **Warranty/***Garantie*

Subject: Replacement of Chain Tensioners
on 1976/77 model 911 and 930
Porsche vehicles.

To accommodate customers who experience chain tensioner failure under certain operating conditions, we are
pleased to offer the following *Adjustment Policy.*

Up to 18 months or 24,000 miles, from date of first use
or retail delivery, the replacement of chain tensioners
can be claimed as follows:

Up to Chassis #911 720 1792
#911 721 1416
#930 780 0387

Labour operation: as applicable
Time Allowance: as applicable
Parts: chain tensioner—quantity
1 or 2 as required and, if
necessary, guide rail(s)
gaskets as applicable
Damage code: 1526 10 00
Warranty code: 2

Note: This adjustment policy does not apply if repairs
outlined with Warranty Circular No. 100 of November 24
—"Installation of Gasket Kit to prevent oil leaks," were
performed.

Please advise your personnel accordingly.

H. Koch
Warranty Manager

HK/enb

VOLKSWAGEN ☐ **Service Circular** Feb. 15, 1978
PORSCHE ● *Circulaire du Service* No. 15
AUDI ☐ **Warranty/***Garantie*

Subject: 1976/77 911 and 930 vehicles—
Adjustment Policy for Exhaust
Valve Guides for 24 months or
36,000 miles. Revised. Supersedes
S.C. 11 of February 9, 1978

Under severe operating conditions, some exhaust valve guides, installed into 911 and 930 vehicles within the chassis number ranges listed below, may wear prematurely.

The factory has made production changes of which you were advised with Product Circulars Group 15 of July 6, 1977, and Group 15 of January 9, 1978.

In an effort to satisfy those owners who experience such premature valve guide failure, VWC has implemented the following adjustment policy. Goodwill claims for the installation of new exhaust valve guides and exhaust valves may be submitted up to 24 months or 36,000 miles, from date of delivery or first use, whichever comes first, as follows:

From	911 620 0010	to	911 620 2079
	911 621 0010		911 621 2175
	930 680 0010		930 680 0530
	911 720 0010		911 720 1432
	911 721 0010		911 721 1143
	930 780 0010		930 780 0327

Labour Operation: as applicable
Time Allowance: as applicable

Parts:	Exhaust valve guides #930 104 321 50 (Qty. as necessary)
	Exhaust valve (Qty. as necessary)
	Appropriate gasket set (Qty. 1)
Damage Code:	1576 18 00 02
Warranty Code:	2

Please advise your personnel accordingly.

H. Koch
Warranty Manager

HK/enb

VOLKSWAGEN ☐ Service Circular April 6, 1978
PORSCHE ◉ *Circulaire du Service* No. 21
AUDI ☐ Warranty/*Garantie*

Subject: Porsche Turbo 930
Wastegate

Under certain driving and/or climatic conditions, it may become necessary to replace the wastegate. In the interest of good customer relations, VWC will accept claims for such replacement with a rebuilt wastegate on the following vehicles for a period of 24 months or 36,000 miles, whichever comes first, from the date the vehicle was first placed in service.

Porsche Turbo (930)—all 1976 and 1977 models up to chasis number 930 780 0561

Claims may be submitted as follows:

Labour Operation:	#2158 21 0
Time Allowance:	0110 T.U.
Parts:	930 123 060 07V, Wastegate, Qty. 1

Damage Code: 2158 66 000 2
Warranty Code: 2

> Note: Part numbers are listed for reference. Always verify with your Parts Department in case of changes.

H. Koch
Warranty Manager

HK/enb

CHAPTER VI

Used-Car Ratings

•

The following used-car ratings are based upon consumer complaints, garage interviews, and reports from seventeen different European and American testing agencies. Although some used cars are harshly criticized, this criticism does not mean that every single car in that model category will have the same defect. Even though a certain model may be listed as "not recommended" it may still be a good buy if an independent mechanic approves the vehicle before it is sold. Some cars may not be listed due to a lack of reliable information concerning that particular model.

Used-Car Price

This price is the actual retail selling price these cars command. Remember that a car dealer will always sell these cars for the amount listed. However, no car dealer will buy these cars for their full retail prices. To determine the wholesale price (dealer to dealer), subtract 30 percent from the retail figure. A $2,000 used car will be sold between dealers for $1,400 for a gross profit of $600. A smart shopper could cut the retail price down to $1,700 and still give the dealer a comfortable $300 profit.

The National Automobile Dealers Association "black book" and "red book" used-car listings have not been consulted because of their close affinity to the automobile industry and the contradictions found in their prices.

Also, many listed car prices appear to be grossly inflated.

For this book, prices have been determined by consumer interviews, newspaper advertising, automobile-auction reports, and negotiating for consumers.

Frequency of Repairs

The modern automobile has more than 15,000 separate moving parts. Some parts are weaker than others. Whenever consumers complain that one particular part constantly breaks down, that component is listed as having a higher-than-average frequency-of-repair rate.

Certain components, such as disc brakes, have a higher-than-average breakdown rate primarily because of the salt and extreme climate found in Canada and the Northern United States.

Body

Often a vehicle may be in perfect mechanical shape, but the body will be rusted out, will leak water, or will rattle. Rustproofing cars with these defects is just a waste of money.

Safety Defects

Over 70 million vehicles have been recalled for safety-related defects. It has been estimated that 30 percent of the recalled cars are never brought into the dealer for correction. If your car has been recalled for safety defects, the automobile manufacturer must correct those defects regardless of your car's mileage or number of different owners.

Check your used car for defects. Better that it be the manufacturer who pays for corrective repairs, rather than taking the money from your pocket.

Recommendations

Certain used cars have so many things going against them that they are risky buys for consumers wanting the most quality for the least amount of money.

Before deciding on a used car, check out its mechanical condition with a competent independent mechanic. **Do**

not depend upon this book's recommendation alone.
Some good cars may not be listed, since these car ratings
cannot cover every car manufactured. For additional information on any car not listed, please call the Center for
Auto Safety, Washington, D.C., (202) 659-1126.

Body Rusting

Many used cars may appear to be excellent buys, but
after a few weeks of ownership huge rust perforations
may appear through the new paint job applied by the
used-car dealer.

Since most cars have specific areas where premature
rusting is known to occur most frequently, we have decided to include diagrams of these areas so they can be
verified before the purchase of a used car.

Undoubtedly, automobile manufacturers will scoff at
the rust diagrams and try to attack their validity. Nevertheless, these diagrams were drawn in collaboration with
hundreds of body-shop interviews and in consultation
with thousands of angry motorists stuck with rusted-out
cars.

The following domestic-car-rusting diagrams have
been compiled from consumer complaints across North
America. Foreign-car-rusting diagrams will appear in the
foreign-car section. All diagrams are stylized and may not
correspond exactly to the true configuration of the
model indicated.

Gas Mileage

Gas mileage rates are only an indication of what a particular model may do under optimum conditions. Mileage
ratings are expressed in gallons.

Technical Data

The technical data may not be precise for every variation
of a particular model. Thus, the data are to be used only
as an approximation of available options.

GENERAL MOTORS
AREAS OF PREMATURE RUSTING

Monte Carlo (1974 to 1976)

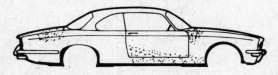

Cadillac (1970 to 1972)

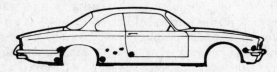

Cadillac (1973 to 1975)

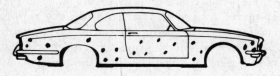

Buick Century (1973 to 1974)

Oldsmobile Cutlass (1970 to 1974)

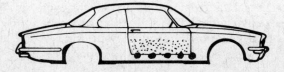

Firebird/Camaro (1971 to 1974)

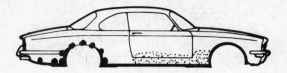

Toronado (1971 to 1973)

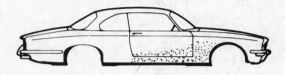

Chevelle (1970 to 1974)

Parisienne (1970 to 1974)

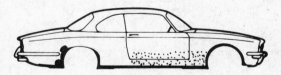

Ventura (1972 to 1975)

Buick Le Sabre (1972 to 1975)

Nova (1970 to 1974)

Grand Prix (1971 to 1974)

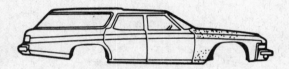

Vega/Astre (1971 to 1974)

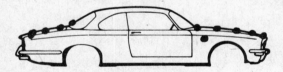

FORD
AREAS OF PREMATURE RUSTING
All Models (1969 to 1976)

Station Wagon or 4-Door

2-Door

Front   *Rear*

AMERICAN MOTORS
AREAS OF PREMATURE RUSTING

Javelin (1971 to 1973)

Matador (1971 to 1973)

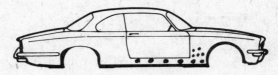

Pacer (1975)

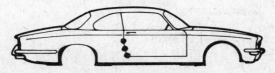

Gremlin (1971 to 1974)

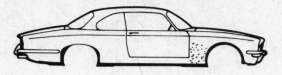

Hornet (1970 to 1974)

Ambassador (1970 to 1973)

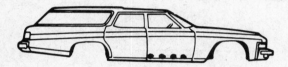

CHRYSLER
AREAS OF PREMATURE RUSTING

Plymouth Fury (1970 to 1974)

Satellite (1971 to 1973)

Polara, Monaco (1970 to 1974)

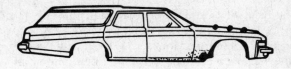

Challenger (1971 to 1973)

Newport (1971 to 1973)

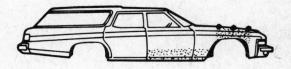

Colt/Cricket (1972 to 1975)

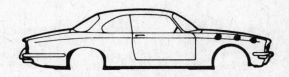

Dart/Scamp (1970 to 1974)

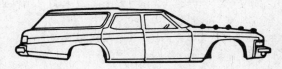

Rust diagrams for 1976—1977 models have not been provided as there has not been enough of a time lapse to determine exactly where rusting of these later-model cars might occur.

Mileage/Price Table

The price of a used car can vary considerably depending upon its mileage. So as to take the mystery out of mileage/price computations, the following mileage/price table has been calculated already. Remember, an average car does about 12,000 to 15,000 miles a year. Be suspicious of any used cars showing less than the normal amount of mileage.

Mileage Deduction Table

Mileage	1970	1971	1972	1973	1974	1975	1976
0 to 15,000	+$200	+$150	+$100	+$ 50	+$ 25	—	—
15,001 to 20,000	+$175	+$125	+$ 75	+$ 25	—	—	−$ 50
20,001 to 25,000	+$150	+$100	+$ 50	—	—	−$ 50	−$100
25,001 to 30,000	+$125	+$ 75	+ $25	—	—	−$100	−$150
30,001 to 35,000	+$100	+$ 50	—	—	−$ 50	−$150	−$200
35,001 to 40,000	+$ 75	+$ 25	—	—	−$100	−$200	−$250
40,001 to 45,000	+$ 50	—	—	−$ 50	−$150	−$250	−$300
45,001 to 50,000	+$ 25	—	—	−$100	−$200	−$300	−$350
50,001 to 55,000	—	—	−$ 50	−$150	−$250	−$350	−$400
55,001 to 60,000	—	—	−$100	−$200	−$300	−$400	−$450
60,001 to 65,000	—	−$ 50	−$150	−$250	−$350	−$450	−$500
65,001 to 70,000	—	−$100	−$200	−$300	−$400	−$500	−$550
70,001 to 75,000	−$ 50	−$150	−$250	−$350	−$450	−$550	−$600

Mileage Deduction Table

Mileage	1970	1971	1972	1973	1974	1975	1976
75,001 to 80,000	−$100	−$200	−$300	−$400	−$500	−$600	−$650
80,001 to 85,000	−$150	−$250	−$350	−$450	−$550	−$650	−$700
85,001 to 90,000	−$200	−$300	−$400	−$500	−$600	−$700	−$750
90,001 to 95,000	−$250	−$350	−$450	−$550	−$650	−$750	−$800
95,001 to 100,000	−$300	−$400	−$500	−$600	−$700	−$800	−$850

Model Year

The Gas Mileage Fairytale

Everybody wants to save money by cutting down on gas consumption. Congress has passed regulations forcing car manufacturers to make smaller and more fuel-efficient cars and the oil companies are helping us (?) by making gasoline more expensive.

Naturally, car manufacturers are using the gas-mileage estimates for different models as selling tools in their advertising. The only problem, though, is that few motorists will actually get the same fantastic number of miles per gallon of gas as promoted in the new car ads. The manufacturers explain this anomaly by usually putting small asterisks on all gas mileage printed ads saying that individual gas mileage may vary widely depending upon such variables as driving habits, atmospheric conditions, passenger weight, and even, perhaps, one's Zodiac sign.

Nevertheless, a good general rule for computing the estimated gas mileage of an advertised new car is to take the Environmental Protection Agency's listed mileage and subtract about 20 percent from that figure. This should be the gas mileage that one can realistically expect to have. The EPA's gas-mileage figures are not intentionally inflated through some government-industry conspiracy. Actually, the answer is much simpler. When the EPA does its gas mileage testing on new cars, the automobile manufacturers supply the agency with the best tuned and maintained cars money can buy. Of course, these are not the same cars that the average citizen can expect to purchase. But, the EPA does its testing, anyway, and publishes the test results each year. Sometimes the auto makers are not satisfied with just a normally inflated gas mileage rating of about 20 percent. Occasionally, they will tamper with the cars' engines illegally, hoping to slip by the EPA inspectors. Ford, Chrysler, and American Motors have all got caught by the EPA trying similar schemes.

So, don't place too much faith in gas-mileage claims. Remember, if the gas mileage is way off sue the auto maker in small-claims court for the difference. Some motorists have won!

Factors Influencing Gasoline Consumption

Vehicle weight and engine size are the most important items affecting overall fuel consumption. Generally speaking, in city driving, a 5,000 pound car will require twice as much gasoline to run as a 2,500 pound car. Optional equipment not only adds weight to the car but also requires power from the engine and thus requires fuel to operate. For example, using an air conditioner can reduce gas mileage by more than 10 percent in city driving.

Saving Gas Saves Money

· An automatic transmission usually reduces gas mileage as compared with a manual transmission.
· Rapid acceleration can reduce fuel economy by 15 percent over moderate acceleration.
· The best fuel economy occurs at speeds between 30 and 40 mph with no stops and no rapid speed changes.
· Using radial tires, instead of conventional or bias-ply tires, can result in a 3 percent improvement in gas mileage. Improper front-end alignment and tires inflated below the recommended pressure will reduce gas mileage.
· An idling engine burns about a half-pint of gas every six minutes, so don't idle your engine needlessly.
· A tuned car will average 6 percent better mileage than

an untuned one. And a properly maintained car also helps reduce air pollution.

· Unnecessary braking, excessive driving in low gears, dragging brakes and short trips all reduce fuel economy.

· Stay away from gas-saving gadgets. Not only may you waste money, but the engine can be damaged and the manufacturer's warranty can be revoked.

"Lemon" Used-Car Profiles

Consumer Groups Blast Vega

More than a half dozen North American consumer groups have joined forces to protest against General Motor's Vega and Astre models.

Both GM models were severely criticized for poor quality mechanical components leading to frequent breakdowns and a "biodegradable body" vulnerable to severe premature corrosion damage.

The groups feel that consumers throughout North America had been victimized by the Vega's "cruelly deceptive" advertising that touted the car as a reliable, economical, and highly durable subcompact vehicle.

Now, that Vega and Astre models have been dropped by General Motors, owners may find their cars impossible to sell and replacement parts inexistent.

"Biodegradable Body"

When the Vega was first launched in 1971, North American motorists were promised a "totally new, **unique** subcompact car." Yes, the Vega and Astre models are unique. Ziebart, for example, refuses to guarantee either model against premature rusting due to what the rustproofers call a "defective design."

Used car dealers often refuse to accept Vega/Astre models because of the possibility of hidden structural damage caused by premature rusting.

Even General Motors dealers have been reluctant to sell the car because of widespread consumer discontent caused by the rustprone chassis of the Vega and Astre.

Secret Warranty (Rust)

In response to the widespread consumer anger over the rust problem, General Motors initiated a secret warranty program to compensate Vega/Astre owners for premature rusting. This program called "goodwill adjustments" was supposed to compensate 1971–1974 Vega/Astre owners for rust repairs up to 5 years by supplying the body parts for free and charging only for labor.

Consumers attempting to take advantage of this compensation formula have reported that dealers often deny the program exists or overcharge so much on labor that the total repair cost is prohibitive. In some cases, owners have reported that the rust repairs only lasted one year and new repairs are now necessary.

It is interesting to note that General Motors has obviously been aware of the Vega/Astre's premature rusting problems since 1972. Yet, the company has refused to accept full responsibility for this defect, preferring to blame the problem upon snow, road salt, pollution, stone chips, etc. GM has seemingly ignored the complaints of hundreds of Florida Vega/Astre owners who have complained of premature corrosion damage occurring within only a few years of ownership.

The early rust-out of Vega and Astre models hits particularly the low-income consumer who cannot afford to replace the vehicle and yet cannot drive the vehicle to work unless it passes provincial or state safety inspection requirements.

Motor Madness

The Vega/Astre four-cylinder motor has been a disaster. It seems that each motor has a sophisticated timing mechanism that makes sure the engine does not self-destruct before the warranty period ends. When the motor begins taking a quart of oil every few hundred miles, dealers have said (if the vehicle is still under warranty) that such a high oil consumption is "normal" for that model car. However, when the warranty expires, these same dealers discover all of a sudden that a complete engine overhaul is needed.

Defective engines on the Vega and Astre are most frequent with the 1971–1974 models. Catastrophic failures are reported to occur between 13,000–50,000 miles. Repair cost averages to $600, but can go to a high of $1,200.

Secret Warranty (Motor)

Vega/Astre owners have become so incensed over GM's failure to build their cars with quality engine components, that General Motors has had to put into effect a secret warranty extension to compensate victims of the Vega/Astre motor madness.

This warranty extension is reproduced in its entirety on page 152. Note that the motor warranty extension is retroactive, applies to used Vega/Astres, and can be applied to work carried out by non-dealer repair agencies. Also, there is no limit to the number of free motor replacements.

Once again, this secret warranty extension is seldom applied except to the most persevering, and even obnoxious consumer complainers. In most cases, dealers simply deny that such a warranty extension exists.

Some consumers have reported that even when such engine repairs are performed under the warranty extension, dealers often fix charges in an arbitrary manner, or only make repairs that are temporary at best.

Conclusion

Vega advertisements lay claims that cannot be substantiated, while Vega owners are put through the "Vega run-around." General Motors has a responsibility to be responsive to its customers who have made General Motors Corporation the profitable business it is. One wonders whether GM realizes the obligation it owes to these customers. There is just so much that can be passed off as "improper usage," a "unique exception" and "poor upkeep" before Canadian consumers demand satisfaction. General Motors must assume a more realistic responsibility for its products.

Vega/Astre Consumer Protest Groups

Center for Auto Safety (Ralph Nader)
Washington, D.C. TEL: (1-202-659-1126)

Consumer Advocate Office,
Miami, Fla. TEL: (1-305-579-4206)

Consumer Education and Protection Association
Philadelphia, Pa. TEL: (1-215-424-1441)

Seattle Consumer Action Network
Washington. TEL: (1-206-324-1196)

Car Owners Action Council
Washington, D.C. TEL: (1-202-638-5550)

San Francisco Consumer Action Committee
San Francisco. Calif. TEL: (1-206-324-1196)

Volvo: A Monumental Deception

For the past several years, the Automobile Protection Association has received a steady stream of complaints from Volvo owners in the United States and Canada. The following letter is typical of the experiences other Volvo owners have reported to the Association:

"Last year on the 6th of May 1975, I purchased a Volvo Model 164-E at Héroux Automobile in Montréal. My reason for purchasing this particular model was the fact that it had been built in Sweden and I, naively enough, believed that this should be enough warranty of quality to make it an outstanding car. I was right in my conclusions but for the wrong reasons in as far as standard mechanical expenses and extra curricular expenses have to date amounted to $688.00 which divided by 22,000 miles, averages .03 cents per mile for maintenance. This figure is completely outrageous when compared to a 25-year use of American cars which did not cost me more than half a cent per mile over the years. I thought it might be enlightening to you to note the items that went wrong, some of which were under warranty, but largely were not.

Item 1: The right rear door inside had to be repainted within two months, improperly done at the factory.

Item 2: An external antenna had to be installed, the one in the windshield did not operate.

Item 3: The tank gauge was faulty and had to be replaced.

Item 4: Two window moldings had to be replaced completely.

Item 5: Two shock absorbers also had to be replaced.

Item 6: The front hood does not open because the release cable freezes or breaks inside.

Item 7: The radio went dead after a few months of use and had to be replaced. Even now, at times, it gently but firmly shuts off. However, this is compensated by the fact that the windshield wipers refuse to stop working.

Item 8: In the midst of winter on the highway, the battery completely discharged although the indicator did not show a malfunction at any time.

Item 9: In winter too, the trunk lid cylinder falls off. This may be a safety device on your part, but is a nuisance to the consumer.

Item 10: Ignition has always been difficult irrespective of service and consumption of 19 miles per gallon is way below what a six-cylinder engine should be able to perform at.

Item 11: The front wheel alignment, after 16,000 miles, went off so badly that within two weeks, two new front tires had to be purchased, something I usually only have to do when mileage reaches 40,000 miles.

Item 12: Recently the brakes went completely out of proper function and upon inspection I was told that the brake drums would have to be remachined at the same time being informed by your dealer that apparently I drove with my foot on the brakes. This is a technical insult which, having driven cars all of my life, and never having to have brake linings replaced, I find difficult to accept.

To summarize this whole matter, I must express my admiration for the Public Relations effort your Corporation puts out in promoting your product and I am convinced that if the product quality equalled this particular level, you would have an excellent car. The above facts prove it to be way below par.

P.S. This car is due to go in for its 22,000 miles

check and I tremble to think what the charge will be."

    cc: Department of Consumer Affairs—Ottawa
    Automobile Protection Association—Montréal
    Consumers' Union—U.S.A.

Documented complaints from other disenchanted and irate Volvo owners confirm that the expectations created by Volvo's clever advertising campaigns have not been fulfilled by either the car or the available dealer service. In fact, it appears to be obvious that Volvo has serious problems with persistent mechanical defects throughout the 1970–1976 model years and dealers that fail to adequately diagnose and repair these defects.

Defect-Prone

Angry Volvo owners report frequent mechanical defects affect all major components of their cars. Subsequent repairs at their dealers are said to be costly, inadequate, and often only temporary. For example, one dissatisfied Volvo owner had the following "adventure" after discovering his car's defects:

"Am reporting to your head Office. It is impossible to get any satisfaction from your local Representive about the above mentioned car.

Had the car only two months when the starter went out of order and, had to have that fixed. Shortly after that the transmission failed. Was presented with both bills, have never been paid for this and the car was under the Guarantee.

Five weeks ago, I was driving along Hauteurs Blvd. St. Hippolyte when the motor exploded and all the parts were dropped to the road. This was quite a shock and only, because I am a very calm person and a good Driver I advoided—what would have been a disasterous accident. The Gentleman driving behind me was very grateful for my quick thinking. He would be a good witness for same.

I am in business and I need the car to get here and there. Last week—Was told that they had sent to Volvo. Guy Martin's Garage, 437 Kennedy Bldv. St. Jerome Que. Parts to replace the ones exploded from the motor and that it would cost $400.00 to place same in motor. Why did they do that? why not send the whole motor? It would have been cheaper and faster. As this was no fault of mine I thought you would recall the car as I now know I had the bad luck of picking a LEMON. This does not reflect on the Volvo. It was my hard luck not to have bought a perfect one. In view of all the trouble I have had, could you get me a car to use until you have repaired mine? I really cannot add to the fast mounting Taxi Fares.

Was also told that the wrong tires were on the car when I bought same and they are not what is on the Volvo when a new car is bought."

Although, not all Volvos have the same number of defects and the severity of each defect may differ, owners writing to the APA invariably list some of the following defects as the most troublesome:

Defective Parts

1. Fuel injection system
2. Gas tank assembly and filler
3. Transmission breakdown
4. Premature rusting
5. Paint peeling
6. Muffler and exhaust system
7. Brakes
8. Shock absorbers
9. Heater fan motor
10. Heater control
11. Heater thermostat
12. Air conditioner
13. Motor
14. Camshaft
15. Spark plugs
16. Transmission clutch
17. Starter
18. Leaky trunk
19. Leaky windshield
20. Rapid tire wear
21. Windows
22. Windshield wipers and washers
23. Radio
24. Locks

25. Oil warning light
26. Fuel pump
27. Fuel filter
28. Battery
29. Seats
30. Regulator
31. Alternator
32. Carburetor
33. Gas gauge
34. Clutch
35. Fan clutch
36. Fuses
37. Wheel bearings
38. Handbrake
39. Turn indicators
40. Clock

In addition to the already mentioned defective parts, Volvo owners also complain about their cars having bizarre and abnormal performance characteristics that are unacceptable. Although quite a few of the problems associated with Volvo performance can be explained as being due to mechanical defects and inadequate corrective repairs by dealers, some of the frequently reported problems are most probably caused by dealers not adequately inspecting their cars before delivery. Nevertheless, regardless of the cause, Volvo owners report that their cars behave so erratically that they appear to be "possessed."

Performance Problems

1. Difficult starting
2. Excessive oil burning
3. Excessive gas consumption
4. Electrical system failures
5. Lack of power
6. High maintenance costs
7. Motor overheating
8. Oil leaks
9. Poor suspension
10. Unreliable
11. Poor quality control
12. Poor ignition
13. Engine knocking

14. Frequent breakdowns
15. Unreliable steering

It is interesting to note that one common complaint voiced by many Volvo owners concerned starting the car. This problem is further aggravated by the number of people who have trouble with **hot** weather starts. It is obvious that Volvo recognizes this problem since many owners can now purchase a "Hot Start Kit" to rectify these problems. It has not been confirmed whether Volvo has developed a "Cold Start Kit" yet, but one would certainly hope so.

Obviously, it is patently absurd for Volvo to have manufactured a starting system inappropriate for the climate of the country to which it is being exported in large numbers. Few owners appear to be aware of the starting kits existence. It is evident that Volvo has an obligation to inform its customers of the kits availability, and that it offer to install the kit, without charge, to owners who request it.

Gas and oil mileage is also the subject of frequent complaints by Volvo owners. The number of persons reporting low gas mileage, fuel leakage, and seemingly chronic oil burning appears to be at odds with Volvo's claim of gas mileage economy. In some cases, this problem may be directly attributable to air conditioning units, which can cut gas mileage significantly. Nevertheless, this certainly does not apply in all cases, and Volvo's customer relations personnel should no longer disclaim responsibility by claiming that excessive oil and gas consumption is "normal." The answer must lie in Volvo's engineering, and a review of recent improvements in such areas as exhaust system design and electronic fuel injection would seem mandatory if Volvo really wishes to avoid a reputation for shoddy workmanship.

The list of other complaints and defects is lengthy. Such poorly engineered components as exhaust systems and mufflers that corrode easily, air conditioning units which leak and reduce engine performance, leaking fuel injectors, and poorly designed heater assemblies are all recurring themes in APA addressed letters and phone transcripts. These tales of woe are all the more troublesome in light of Volvo's advertising campaign which promises economy, and trouble-free driving. One can only wish that Volvo's engineers were as competent as its ad men.

The purpose in analyzing the APA's complaints concerning Volvo is threefold. It seems that owners' complaints may not be getting to the right people at Volvo. From reading the complaint letters, one gains the impression that Volvo's customer relations efforts are Neanderthal at best. Is it really necessary for customers to sue Volvo, as three consumers already have done, in order to get treated decently? Is it appropriate for Volvo of Canada to threaten to sue the CBC program "Marketplace" in response to unfavorable criticism? Or, does it really help Volvo's image to sue a dissatisfied customer who tells his tale of mechanical frustration on television? This knee-jerk reaction to constructive criticism must be checked.

The second purpose of this report is to document the need for steps to be taken to review and analyze current Volvo quality control standards. Programs must be initiated to insure that this spate of unconscionable mechanical breakdowns ceases immediately. Surely an automobile manufacturer which has attained Volvo's level of technological competence should be able to easily identify, correct, and in the future, avoid problems which are annoying at best and lethal at worst. Obviously, the degree of defects that may be hazardous must take priority. Some of those defects reported by owners are:

Potentially Hazardous Defects

1. Gas tank leaks from flange of the drainage plug
2. Gas tank leaks from crack in the neck of the feed-in tube
3. Gas tank leaks from crack in crease
4. Windshield washers and wipers failing
5. Inadequate defrosting
6. Faulty steering
7. Inadequate locks
8. Exhaust system causing trunk and passenger floor to overheat
9. Steering wheel separation
10. Water leaking into side marker lights
11. Turn signal failures
12. Exhaust fumes in passenger compartment
13. Gasoline smell in passenger compartment

14. Windshield falling out
15. Emergency brake failure
16. Sudden steering loss
17. Imploded gas tank
18. Seatbelt warning light failure
19. Driver seat failure
20. Exhaust rubbing against car chassis
21. Concealed transport damage
22. Poor illumination of instrument panel
23. Wheel rims overheating
24. Exploding heater
25. Sticking gas pedal

Despite the fact that Volvo claims its cars are the safest vehicles they can make, a perusal of some owner complaints does not seem to support the claim that Volvo cars are completely safe.

Warranty Extensions

On April 30, 1976, Volvo Canada Ltd, extended their warranty on the Fuel Injection System Components, Heater Motor, and Viscous Fan Clutch for a period of 3 years or 36,000 miles from the original date the vehicle was placed in service. This special service adjustment program covers both parts and labour. Although Volvo says it informed owners of the warranty extension, it appears that not all owners are aware of the free repairs.

Volvo Safety Hazard

On July 8, 1976 Volvo Canada Limited sent a recall alert letter to the owners of its 1975 and 1976—240, 164, and 260 model cars. In the recall letter, Volvo fails to convey the notion that these vehicles may contain a highly dangerous safety defect. In fact, Volvo appears to skirt around the issue by using the following phrases:

"Volvo has determined, that a defect may exist in some of its 1975 and 1976—240, 164 and 260 model cars. Our records indicate that your vehicle is among those which could be affected.

The defect concerns the sealing of the fuel filler pipe which could allow fuel vapors or fumes to escape into the trunk area or passenger compartment.

Aside from the obvious odor, prolonged exposure while driving or riding could prove uncomfortable, however the flow-through ventilation system as well as keeping a window partially open can greatly reduce this condition . . .

. . . We regret any inconvenience caused by this campaign and thank you for cooperating in having this important correction to your car carried out".

Until Volvo improves its product quality control, complaint handling procedures, and style of recall notification, the APA cannot recommend its cars.

Finally, the analysis of consumer complaints directed against Volvo has shown that the expectations created by Volvo's national advertising campaign are monumentally misleading and deceptive when viewed against the often unpleasant realities of Volvo ownership. Specific contradictions include cost of ownership, reliability, and durability. Volvo should immediately take steps to insure that its advertising conform to this reality reported by far too many owners to ignore. Actually, Volvo should just concentrate more on improving its product than on maintaining its slipping image.

Service Complaints

1. Costly non-maintenance service
2. Incompetent repairs (would you believe a pair of pliers left in transmission?)
3. Lack of parts
4. Inadequate pre-delivery inspection
5. Refusal of warranty claim
6. Slow repairs
7. No courtesy car available
8. Rude personnel
9. Unauthorized repairs
10. Repairs not needed
11. Promises not kept
12. Incorrect owner registration card
13. No response to complaints
14. Bankrupt dealer
15. Poor diagnostic procedures

VOLVO
Volvo Canada Ltd.
Head Office, Toronto, Ontario

April 30, 1976.

Dear Volvo Owner:

The purpose of this letter is to advise owners of Volvo cars from 1974 models and up that Volvo Canada Ltd. has instituted a special Service Adjustment Program covering the following items.

> Fuel Injection System Components
> Heater Motor
> Viscous Fan Clutch

The adjustment period, which covers both parts and labour, is for a period of 3 years or 36,000 miles from the original date the vehicle was placed in service.

Beyond the revised limits of 3 years or 36,000 miles, repair to these items will be considered as normal maintenance and will be the responsibility of the owner.

The special Service Adjustment Program is to ensure that owners of Volvo cars from 1974 models and up will be covered for the costs of repairs to the specified items for the adjustment period should the need arise. This service advisory however, does not indicate that special inspection or replacement of these items is required.

All Volvo Canada Ltd. dealers have been notified of this program and any requests for service under the terms of this program should be made directly through your Authorized Volvo dealer.

We trust you will find this information helpful.

> Yours sincerely,
>
> VOLVO CANADA LTD.,
>
>
>
> M. Oosterhoff,
> Technical Service Manager.

MO/ws

Postal Address   *Telephone*   *Telex*
175 GORDON BAKER ROAD,   (416) 493-3700   06-966-535
WILLOWDALE, ONTARIO,
M2H 2N7

British Leyland

In March 1977, Thomas K. Wilka, a staff attorney with the Washington-based Center for Auto Safety discovered that British Leyland vehicles contained serious safety-related defects involving a large number of its models.

Wilka sent the following letter to BLM, where he referred to BCM confidential documents to support his demand for an independent inquiry and recall:

> . . . The need to examine safety defects in vehicles on a relative basis as opposed to an absolute number basis was recently pointed out by the United States Court of Appeals for the District of Columbia in **United States v. General Motors,** 518 F. 2d 420 (1975). There the Court stated in reference to whether a given number of vehicles failures represented an "unreasonable risk" of accident and injury: We use the term "significant" to indicate that there must be a minimum number of failures. The question whether a "significant" number of failures have taken place must be answered in terms of the facts and circumstances of each particular case. Relevant considerations include the failure rate of the component in question, failure rates of comparable components, and the importance of the component to the safe operation of the vehicle. **The number of failures need not be and normally will not be a substantial percentage of the total number of components produced.** (Emphasis added).

As the insider report concentrates on British Leyland Motors (BLM), the Center has researched its files and those of the NHTSA for consumer complaints on the specific BLM safety defects and hazards identified by the insider report. In the process, the Center has identified additional defects not specifically referenced in the report. The number of safety defects and hazards discerned total an incredible twenty-seven.

The inescapable conclusion of the Center's investigation is that British Leyland Motors, in addition to its callous disregard of owner complaints and warranty claims, has consistently exported to the U.S. passenger vehicles which present an ". . . unreasonable risk of accidents occurring as a result of the design, construction or performance." 15 U.S.C. no 1391. Consequently, the Center requests NHTSA to commence, pursuant to 15 U.S.C. no 1412, a comprehensive investigation of the following twenty-seven defects in the four makes of BLM cars regularly imported into this country.

The number of BLM cars imported into the United States each year may appear small when compared with the number domestically, but the potential for death and injuries caused by these cars is considerable. Likewise, the number of citizen complaint letters catalogued in the NHTSA computer system along with those at the Center (a total of 427) is deceptively very small compared to the total number of complaints on file but it is large when compared with the actual number of BLM vehicles imported. The Center requests this comprehensive defect investigation, cognizant that certain BLM models are currently subject to mandatory recall. It is the Center's position that many of the most dangerous defects have not been identified and acted upon by ODI.

Jaguar

The multitude of vehicle problems prevalent in British Leyland's most expensive make, the elite Jaguar, were so serious that BLM was compelled to make an internal investigation. The results of this, included as the major part of the insider report (see Attachments B-C), demonstrate the dangers presented by this make. Furthermore, BLM's corporate inability to deal with the problems is illustrated throughout the report, as noted in the following discussion of the MG. The two lists of "top ten" Jaguar U.S.A. warranty complaints included in the insider report, categorized by occurrence and cost, describe at least nine defects which in involve unreasonable risk of accident, injury and death in 1975 and 1976 Jaguars.

1. Defective Fuel Tank Change-over Switch The risk of stalling on moving traffic, exacerbated by the possibility that the stall may occur during adverse weather or on poorly constructed roadways, is presented by four specific Jaguar defects. Of the 7,000 to 8,000 Jaguars imported in 1975, 12% were reported to contain defective fuel tank change-over switches which regulates the Jaguar's dual gas tank system. This may be the problem described as a non-functioning right-gas tank by the owner of a 1975 XJ-12 in letter 033696.

2. Ignition Amplifier and Stalling A defective ignition amplifier also causes stalling in the 1975 Jaguar. The same problem apparently exists in earlier models; the NHTSA has received complaints from owners of 12 cylinder Jaguars manufactured in 1971 (015184), 1972 (044151), 1973 (02126) and 1974 (033083, 033729, 039838). The source of the problem may be a heat-induced malfunction of the ignition ampli-California, in letter 033083: "This amplifier is of the transistor type which seems to break down rapidly when exposed to wear. This car . . . ran well until the temperature outside reached 85–90 degrees—then the spark amplifier would no longer function correctly. I live in Fresno, California where Summer temperatures remain between 90–110 degrees for approximately four to five months . . . Last Summer three amplifiers were replaced by Arnold Wiebe within a four-month period. . . . Twice on the way . . . the car died—each time it being necessary to coast off the Highway and wait fifteen minutes to let the car cool down."

3. Defective Fuel Pumps, 1974–75 Jaguars An additional threat to stalling in traffic is posed by the fuel pump in 1975 Jaguars equipped with six cylindre engines. In the first third of 1976 alone, BLM received 703 complaints of such failures. A possible illustration of this is provided by letter H00124, describing a 1975 XJ-6L which stalls at 50 MPH. Another instance is described by Mr. Littrell, **supra,**

the owner of a 1974 Jaguar V-12E, who cited a faulty fuel pump which caused the car to stall in traffic, in one instance nearly causing a serious accident: "When reaching Arnold Wiebe's the Service Department Manager stated that the fuel filter was plugged, but upon his examination it was a faulty fuel pump causing the car to die. THIS SAME SYMPTOM OCCURRED EACH TIME THE SPARK AMPLIFIER WENT OUT.

I was passing a truck on a steep incline using second gear and there was on-coming traffic approaching. When my car reached 4,000 R.P.M. it **instantly died.** Fortunately, a JAGUAR does have good brakes and I managed—just barely—to slide in behind the truck. However, the engine could not be restarted at that time, even with the car in gear and moving forward. The situation was further complicated by the six cars in the rear waiting their turns to pass the truck. Again, fortunately, there was a turnout and my car had just enough speed to coast to the turnout. I decided that I should return home with the car for I felt that it was hazardous to drive. On my way home the car would run for about ten minutes and die." (Emphasis in original).

Another near accident has been reported by a 1974 V-12 owner who also noted that the fuel pump breakdown occurred almost simultaneously with failure of the ignition amplifier (039838). The relationship of these reports to the insider report points the need for a priority investigation into the fuel pumps in 1974–76 Jaguars. The similarity of these hazards to the defect necessitating recall 76-0007 must be investigated. That recall, involving 911 1976 Jaguar XJ-6 two and four door sedans with malfunctioning fuel pump nonreturn valves, may need expansion to include 1975 and 1974 models equipped with twelve and six cylinder engines.

4. EGR Pipe-Induced Engine Failure Another possible design defect is the cause of the fourth source of engine failure in Jaguars. This problem and the ensuing corporate response is best summarized by BLM itself: "It must be strongly recommended that there should be direct feed-back to the responsible Engineers/Managers at the plant. It is all very well having central Problem Control coordination, but if this policy fails then so does the chance of speedy problems rectification. A classic example of poor communication is the 6 cylinder EGR pipe C 43668, which can cause engine failure if the core plug falls out (a design fault). This problem was reported in September, 1975 and example sent to BLI Service. Several letters and further evidence obtained, the BL Problem Coordinator, decided that the problem would not be raised with Jaguar Engineering. I brought the problem up again on this trip and within hours the Power Unit Draftsman responsible had three different samples made up and a new drawing prepared for release.

The fact that there are no specific complaints alleging EGR core pipe falling out so as to cause engine failures is not surprising since all consumers know is that the engine failed."

5. Power Steering Failure British Leyland inability or refusal to deal with serious safety-related defects is further illustrated by the portion of the insider report entitled "4 month period January-April '76, Top Ten Jaguar USA Warranty. By Cost." Number one on the list is the power steering unit which loses fluid. According to the insider report, at least one serious accident was apparently caused by this defect.

The company presently has a lawsuit going on in New York where an owner ended up to be a vegetable. Her attorney claimed the power steering lost its fluid.

We have to of course, realize that a Jaguar could not be steered without the power steering, taking into consideration that it is not the same type of power steering as the domestic cars are equipped with.

BLM's response to this problem was to forward to dealers a supply of replacement parts which lasted only until July 1975. The company's voluntary failure to remedy by recalling being apparent, NHTSA's duty requires a mandatory recall to combat the severe safety hazard posed by a loss of steering. The need for this action for 1975 Jaguars is established by the internal BLM memoranda alone. NHTSA should also investigate the existence of the same defect in earlier models as is suggested by letters complaining of similar problems in a 1971 Jaguar (009357), a 1972 XJ-6 Sedan "power steering fluid reservoir . . . empty", 1973 V-12 Roadster (24 and 045654) and XJ-12 (032126), and a 1974 XJ-6 (033259). Since the BLM internal investigation was primarily a warranty analysis, it does not disclose the earlier model year problems as such earlier models were beyond the warranty cutoff point.

6. 1975 Jaguar Disc Brake Defects Another defect in 1975 Jaguars which requires NHTSA attention involves disc brakes, number five on Jaguar's top ten warranty cost list. Rather than take steps to correct the faulty Jaguar disc brakes, BLM satisfied itself with the internal admonishment, "Dealer/ Customer education required on basic brake bedding in policy." NHTSA must reject such an action as unsatisfactory and compel disclosure of the result of the engineering investigation by BLM to determine the scope of any accident potential posed by this brake defect.

7. Remote Control Door Linkage Failure With Door Lockup The large failure rate of the Jaguar remote control linkage and the concomitant safety hazard of a stuck door are aptly summarized by the insider report as follows:

(W)e are looking at 1098 failures of approximately 15% (of Jaguars sold in the U.S. in 1975). With this door linkage failure, in the case of an accident, the occupants cannot get out of the automobile, which is certainly a safety horror and hazard.

Given the high failure rate and the sharpened increased likelihood of injury in the event of an accident, a recall is mandated.

8. 1975 Windshield Wiper Failure The insider report also reveals the high frequency with which 1975 Jaguar windscreen washer motors fail: 862 failures in Jaguars (11%) and an astounding 5,329 failures in all BLM models were reported in the first four months of 1976. This presents an obvious visual hazard to all occupants of those vehicles, as well as pedestrians and other vehicle operators obscured from the view of the BLM driver. Windshield wipers with such failures obviously do not meet the performance requirements of Federal Motor Vehicle Safety Standard (FMVSS) 104.

NHTSA consumer letter 032126 from an XJ-12 owner exemplifies this defect in reporting four wiper motors failures.

9. Dash Electrical Harness Failure Both the insider report and consumer complaints indicate frequent failures and problems with the Jaguar dash harness. BLM received 929 dash harness failures reports in the January-April, 1976 period. A clear example of this is presented by letter 033696 from the owner of a 1975 XJ-12, who experienced failures of all indicator dials. The Center has received complaints describing dash harness failures from owners of pre-1975 models, indicating the failures documented by Jaguar itself for 1975 models existed previously. Owners of two 1973 Jaguar XJ-6's and a 1973 XJ-12 complainted of failures of all panel lights (045622046245, and 032136, respectively). Horn failures were the nineth most common warranty complaint reported to BLM in the January-April, 1976 period documented by the insider report with 482 reported failures. A variety of electrical problems were reported by the owners of a 1971 Jaguar V-12 (enclosed 23a, alternator, regulator, odometer and radio failures) and the 1974 XJ-6 (attached 20a and 033259, both citing "entire electrical system") and 1974 V-12 (039838). At the very minimum the NHTSA must determine whether these electrical failures result from a design common to the several Jaguar makes and models, e.g. improperly-placed fuse box as described below with respect to the MG, or design or performance problems in components manufactured by a single supplier, in this case Lucas Electric. (It should be noted here that the 1975 Triumph TR-7 exhibits a similar propensity for short-circuited panel lights and gauges; see letters H00749 and H00570, the latter additionally describing an incredible BLM failure to even install the windshield washer at all, once again in violation of FMVSS 104).

MG

10. MGB Engine Surge A defect exhibiting potential for serious accidents exists in the 1975 and 1976 MGB, of which approximately 20,000 were marketed in the U.S. in 1975 alone. According to the insider report, this model has a serious surge when driving which is particularly dangerous when passing and otherwise accelerating. This defect endangers not only the occupants of the vehicle, but pedestrians and other motorists as well. Thus, the potential for death and serious injury far outstrips that indicated by the number of cars involved.

The basic problems contributing to the MGB surge were identified and summarized by BLM employees in April, 1976:

"After extensive testing, it was established that three basic problems existed, all of which contribute directly to the surge.

1. Vacuum advance is required in top gear.
2. A new carburetor needle is required which will have a slightly richer configuration between 30 mph and 60 mph.
3. The carburetor air intake has to be relocated to a low pressure area due to an inbalance occuring (sic) with the existing set up."

Basically, the same problem exists on both 1975 and 1976 vehicles, and essentially the same approach will be required in order to overcome the surge.

The recommended steps were, for the most part, ignored by the BLM hierarchy. Their insensitivity to human losses and disregard for federal safety and emissions requirements is amply illustrated by a BLM internal memorandum dated May 10, 1976. "1. Although we would like to incorporate a new carburetor needle which has a slightly richer configuration between 30 mph and 60 mph, it has been decided to forego this in order to eliminate the necessary EPA clearance.

2. By relocating the anti-run-on valve drain tube from its current position to a new position just forward of the right hand radiator mounting basket, it is no longer necessary to modify the carburetor air intake inasmuch as it has been determined that it balance the pressure within the float chamber with that which exists at the carburetor air intake, in effect achieves the same things."

The insider report in the Center's possession concludes with this memo: ". . . shows clearly that the importer has taken no action since late 1974 when the 1975 MGB was marketed in the USA."

If such flagrant and intentional disregard of the law is to be discouraged, NHTSA must bring to bear upon BLM the full sanctions provided by law. BLM's failure to report this defect places it in violation of 15 U.S.C. 1397 (a) (4) and is therefore subject to the maximum civil penalty ($800,000) for this related series of violations. In addition the repair undertaken by BLM is a change of the emission control system which should require Environmental Protection Agency (EPA) approval. Failure to obtain such approval subjects BLM to an additional fine of $10,000 per vehicle under 205 of the Clean Air Act.

11. MG Midget Overheating and Stalling The 1975 MG Midget also presents an unreasonable risk of death and injury, specifically, stalling in traffic as a result of overheating. The insider report succinctly summarized the problem and the inadequacy of the BLM response:

"This model has a serious design fault in the cooling system with the result of severe overheating. The company came out with a corrective kit which is not successful. An exceedingly high amount of engines are imported as replacement for these engines which burned. A great amount of automobiles were repurchased by the dealers and the automobile manufacturer paid the losses to the dealers; these cars were again retailed as used cars.

The MG Midget is also so faulty that the manufacturer should have recalled them. Total 1975 sales volume made it possible for this importer to get away without any government pressure."

The Center urges NHTSA to commence a mandatory recall campaign of the 1975 MG Midget. Ten thousand automobiles are not insignificant; eight of the eleven most recent BLM recall campaigns involve fewer vehicles. Also, investigate whether this design defect exists in earlier models of the MG Midget. NHTSA's files include complaint letters 023164 and 019400 from owners of the 1971 MG who have experienced similar overheating and stalling problems! Letter 019400 includes an account of a near accident when the car stalled in the middle of an expressway.

12. MG Steering An examination of the consumer complaint letters received by the Center and NHTSA indicates that the various MG models contain additional defects of sufficient accident potential to justify an immediate NHTSA investigation with emphasis on certain components employed across BLM model lines and for several model years. Steering vibrations in the MGB present an obvious danger of loss of control, as well as accompanying increased deterioration of other components. Two owners of the 1971 MGB complained of this hazard in letters received by the Center, later given ODI numbers 017896 and 017917. Other steering complaints from 1971 MGB owners are numbered 027765, 016010, an 024195; whether this problem exists in MGB's made in other years, as indicated by letters 040986 (1972) and 006884 (1969) must be pursued. A complaint common to all of these letters is that continued realignments and tire replacements are of no avail.

A variety of steering problems experienced by Midget owners are serious enough to warrant NHTSA attention, especially to commonly-used components. Impeded steering columns were reported by 1971 Midget owners, described in letters 047722 (steering "froze up"), 028031 ("kidding") and 020082 (choke cable tangled with steering). Ernest R. Mijares of Huntington Beach, California, (017613) suggests a possible source of the steering problems in the 1970 Midget: "A fronted design which allows the steering line to 'fall off'—this occurred while driving when the three bolts on the right steering link bracket became unfastened. The left bracket faired a little better—its bolts were just loose. The net result of this situation was almost a complete loss of steering."

Steering hazards, in the 1973 Midget are also related in letters 041737 and 019624. The former describes a frightening situation in which the front wheels move sideways. Renee Scott of Placentia, California, (42a), provides a description of another spine-tingling episode resulting from an unidentified steering defect in a 1974 Midget:

"On Nov. 2, 1976, I was driving my '74 MG Midget down a bill on a clear, bright sunny day. The street was dry and visability perfect. All of a sudden I lost control of my car. I began to swerve from side to side or so I believed. I've never been in a car when a tire blow out, but that is what I thought had happened. Anyway, I'd lost control of the car, until it finally fish-tailed around and stopped; I was not speeding! Those cars behind we stopped and described to me what they saw and they all claimed I'd lost control for no apparent reason."

Similar hazards are described by 1976 Midget owners in letters 041737 and 019624.

13. MG Midget Sticking Accelerators Sticking accelerators have been reported in the 1973 Midget (041737), the 1971 Midget (038305, 047822, 017122, 04726, and 018221) and the 1970 Midget (017613, 017410). The hazard of this problem requires no elaboration. In fact, BLM recently recalled 9,299 1976 Midgets containing a defective throttle return spring, (the throttle butterflies will not close within the time specified by FMVSS 124) for a similar defect. Whether this or another serious defect exists in the earlier Midgets demands immediate, in-depth attention. The eight referenced consumer letters indicate a major problem exists.

14. MG Electrical Failures Problems with electrical components in BLM vehicles transcend all make and model distinctions. Electrical failures were cited as the cause of stalling in traffic and a near accident by the owner of a 1973 MGB, apparently from a faulty alternator (44). Other alternator complaints in NGTSA files are numbered 02974 (1970 MGB) and 017917 (1971 MGB). Margaret Lammond of Arlington, Virginia (017917) nearly had a serious vehicle accident caused by a defective alternator failure, Mrs. Lammond writes:

"Without warning, the car stopped in the middle of the highway. Fortunately for myself and rider, I was able to roll the car to the side of the road onto the shoulder. I just missed being hit from the rear by a large freight truck. A mile down the road and the car stopped in the middle once again—traffic screeching to a halt behind me."

Failures of panel lights, horn, fuel gauge, and

windshield wipers and washer were reported in various combinations by owners of 1970, 1971 and 1973 Midgets (017410, 019400, and 041867, respectively) and in 1972, 1973 and 1975 MGB's (040986, enclosed 44, and 34511 and enclosed 30). Letter 034511 attributed the similar failure of wipers, turn signals, and rear brake lights to a poorly-located and improperly-sealed fuse box which result in corroded contrats.

Triumph

Only an in-depth investigation will reveal whether the 1975 and 1976 Triumphs pose greaer safety hazards than those encountered in the MG and Jaguar models, but the need for immediate action is clear. Strong measures are needed to protect the public and cannot be expected to be initiated by British Leyland, especially in light of the fact that the TR-7 "was produced in Britain for export only and the USA public was used as test pilots and guinea pigs at their expense and inconvenience."

15. 1975–76 Triumph Ignition Amplifier Failure According to the internal BLM memoranda in the Center's possession, the faulty ignition amplifier exists in 1975–76 Triumphs as well as Jaguars, presenting the same danger of stalling in moving traffic. Consumer complaints received by the Center show not only the existence of this defect but also the fact that equally defective parts are used as replacements. Enclosed are letters from three owners of 1975 TR-7's. Larry Bishins of Fort Lauderdale, Florida (55c) provides further support for the Center's conclusion that BLM has itself long recognized the extent of Triumph ignition amplifier failures: "(Alpine Motors, a franchised BLM dealer) also told me that they had 11 or 12 other failures in the amplifier in the transistorized ignition. I checked out this fact and found out there was a great many failures in amplifiers in the TR-7 distributors . . . The fact that upset me mostly was that there was a great deal of failures and British Leyland knew this was a dangerous problem."

16. Gas Pedal Cable Breakage A loss of power in moving traffic is also threatened by the frequent gas pedal cable breakage exhibited by the Triumph TR-7 sold in this country in the beginning of 1975. The broken cable will result in a loss of control over the acceleration of the vehicle. The insider report indicates the TR-7 "has the highest level of gas pedal cable breakings, again a serious safety hazard." This defect was reported to the Center (letter 65g) for two 1976 TR–7's.

17. Windshield Wiper Failures As is the case with Jaguar and MG models, a variety of electrical problems abound in BLM's Triumph line. Safety related failure of the windshield wipers has been reported in the 1976 TR-7 (letters 55a and 55f) and the 1975 TR-7 (55g). The insider report also indicated that the TR-7 had "serious electrical problems. Earlier failures are reported in letters 043655 (1972 TR-6), 045725 (1971 Spitfire) and 044285 (1969 TR-6).

18. Lucas Headlight Switch Failure Lucas headlight switches from a variety of Triumph models have demonstrated a high rate of failure while the vehicle is in operation. A single dealer, A.BB. Freeman of Mobile, Alabama, has forwarded 48 such defective switches to NHTSA; Mr. Freeman advised the Center that he had resorted to using American parts as replacement since British Leyland is still using the same defective Lucas part for replacement.

19. 1974 TR-6's With Sticking Accelerators Sticking accelerators also result in an obvious loss of control over vehicle acceleration, but with an even higher potential for injury than gas pedal breakage. Although NHTSA has only three complaints, on this defect (032480, 033086 and 039522), one (039522) indicated that the accelerator sticking nearly caused an accident while another (033086) indicated the dealer knew about the defect and that another dealer also had experienced the problem on 1974 TR-6's. For a defect with such high potential for accident and injury, the NHTSA must investigate quickly without waiting for defect and accident reports to pick up.

20. TR-7 Hood Support Weakness The insider report cites "hood supports bending" as another common 1975 TR-7 defect. Any bending will result in a decrease in the hood (roof) resistance to crushing during roll-over crash of the hard-top TR-7 and constitutes a probable violation of FMVSS 216. This type of defect often cannot be anticipated by reference to consumer complaints and, following a roll-over crash, is difficult to prove without detailed structural analysis of the vehicle, which is seldom carried out. The information provided by the insider report is therefore of great utility to NHTSA as a starting point for an investigation into this obviously hazardous defect.

21. Faulty Suspension Break at Welding This report also provides the basis for an initial conclusion that the voluntary BLM recall of 13,081 1976 TR-7's for defective welding of the lower suspension link attachment brackets to rearaxle casings should be mandatorily extended to earlier models. The insider report, referring to the 1975 model, states: "The early TR-7 had a suspension bracket which was not properly welded to the rear axle resulting in loss of control of the car. No proper recall was instituted." A recent complaint (55d) from Harry Waldman of Philadelphia, the owner of a 1975 TR-7, is noteworthy: "Additionally, the car literally feels like its falling apart. There is something inherently wrong with the entire suspension, brakes and steering, something that I think can eventually cause a serious accident." The seriousness of this defect demands immediate NHTSA attention directed toward 1975 TR-7's, as well as close monitoring of the voluntary recall of 1976 models undertaken by BLM.

22. Spitfire Engine Fires Engine fires have been reported in several Triumph models, including the 1971 Spitfire IV (61,018218), the 1973 Spitfire (58,045730) and the 1975 Spitfire (61a); these were apparently caused by fuel leaks in the engine. Recall 74-0111 encompasses 1969–1974 TR-5 models which present the possibility of fuel leakage from any of several sources. In light of serious threats of accidents posed by engine fires, even the limited number of reports cited above suggest the need to investigate extending this recall to the Spitfire models manufactured in 1969–1975.

23. Austin Marina Accelerator The Austin Marina, last imported to the United States in 1975, exhibits several of the same defects common to other British Leyland models discussed above. One particularly dangerous example, according to the insider report, "its poorly constructed gas pedal cable resulted in a safety hazard when the cable broke in the middle of traffic." Several complaints about this have been received by NHTSA from owners of the 1974 Marina with consequent near-accidents. (H00020, 034595, 034440 and 032704). Letter 032704 describes the cable breakage as a "shredding of the wire", the cable broke at 75 MPH and the owner went through two red lights before bringing the car to a halt. To fully investigate the extent of these failures—NHTSA should invoke its authority under 15 U.S.C. 1401 (c) to obtain access to BLM records of the number of accelerator cables sold by BLM, to be compared with the number of Austin Marinas sold in 1974 and 1975. This should reveal the actual frequency of replacement of this component.

24. Defective Marina Carburetor Stalling in traffic is caused in 1974 Marinas by a poorly constructed carburetor. Letters 034595, 050496 and 0055738 describe this as a pin falling out of the carburetor which causes the engine to lose power. This is apparently caused by a faulty set screw which, when it becomes loose, allows the fuel metering pin to drop into the fuel jet, preventing fuel flow.

25. Marina Front and Alignment and Vibrations According to the insider report, an astounding "80% of all (Marina) owners complain about a dangerous vibration between 55 and 65 miles per hour. This vibration usually showed up after plus/minus 4000 to 6000 miles, after the front tires became cupped, due to an extremely weak front end combination. Owners paid through the nose for wheel alignments, tires, etc." which proved ineffectual to correct the problem. The Center and NHTSA have received an incredible 20 consumer complaint letters which consistently describe the vibration as occurring at 50–60 MPH, with no improvement felt following repeated realignment and three replacements. Owners have frequently been told by dealers that the problem results from a design defect which could not be corrected.

26. Marina Electrical Failures Electrical problems in the Austin models appear to be as common as those in other BLM models discussed above. The Center and NHTSA have received complaints from the owners of 1975 Marinas (3a) and 1974 Marinas (1 and 050469) complaining of windshield wiper failure, and about non-functioning windshield washers in 1974 Marinas (032004, 056164 and 034440). Chronic fuse problems, with accompanying failures of the interior and panel lights and horn, have been reported by 1974 Marina owners in letters 034081, 034595, and 050469. An identical failure in the 1973 Marina is described in letters 04502.

27. 1974 Marina Fuel Leaks Gasoline leaks into the trunk are also common in the 1974 Marina. Consumer complaint letters describe the cause of the leak as a hose disconnected or cracked at the filler pipe. (See letters 051292, 034363, 032519, 032565 and 034616.) Letter 034616 attributes the cracking in the hose to the use of a non-neoprene material in the hose transferring the gasoline. Finally, fuel leaks into the 1974 Marina engine, probably from the charcoal cannister, are described in letters 032337 and 034802. The potential of vehicle fire from these defects requires speedy investigation and resolution by NHTSA.

As a result of Wilka's investigation, the United States National Highway Traffic Safety Administration has begun a formal inquiry into British Leyland's hazardous defects.

A Lemon Is Born

During the past three years, complaints from frustrated and disappointed Chrysler Volare/Aspen owners have increased in proportionally greater numbers than for other manufacturers. Alarmed by this large and ever-increasing volume of complaints, the APA initiated a study of the Chrysler problem. First, 850 complaints on 1976–78 Volare/Aspen from all parts of Canada were examined in detail. The complaints were examined and tabulated for the problems most commonly experienced with the year and model in which they were found, so that defect patterns might be determined.

The results of this investigation reflect disturbing safety and consumer problems as well as poor quality control at Chrysler Corporation.

Safety Hazards

Stalling

Carburetor problems, especially stalling, present a potentially dangerous defect. Stalling when leaving an intersection, rounding a turn, or during acceleration can easily cause serious accidents. Several Volare/Aspen owners write:

*

My letter is a complaint. I hope it doesn't spoil your day, in spite of the fact that your company's product —to wit, a '76 Volare—has spoiled my last 410 days, give or take a day or two, when it actually went.

I considered myself fortunate the day I bought my Volare from Kingsway Plymouth Chrysler. I had checked the *Consumer's Report*, phoned the Auto Club and test drove the Aspen, Rabbit, and Volare. How could I possibly go wrong? Read on . . .

First, it stalled. Back it went, but still it stalled. In the heat, in the cold, in the rain, in the clear light of day, in the deep dark of the parking lot, there I sat, waiting for the Auto Club. The reason? Well, I heard a few, among them carburetor icing. I was also told in February Chrysler was putting out a kit to eliminate this. But in July, finally, the service department cleaned the spark plugs and blessed the carburetor, and charged me $21.95 for it. (Incidentally, it still stalls.)

*

I realize that the carburetor has nothing to do with the electrical system, but I had another problem. Everytime I slowed down to turn into a new road, then started to go again, the car would stall. A dangerous situation if another vehicle was coming in the opposite direction. I have heard that your cars in the U.S. have been recalled for this problem and I think our cars should be also. A Canadian life should be equal to an American!

As frequent as are complaints of close accidents as a result of this stalling problem, there is every indication that many of these turn into actual accidents. The recent announcement of the National Highway Traffic Safety Administration that it has 118 consumer complaints on 1975–77 Dart, Valiant, Aspen and Volare models stalling indicates that the problem is widespread.

Not only do faulty carburetors cause safety problems but they also cause emission standards to be violated. California, which has a diligent assembly-line test program, required Chrysler to make three recalls for correction of faulty carburetors and chokes on 1975 models, while the U.S. Environmental Protection Agency has issued a recall order for 208,000 more 1975 models with 360- and 440-cubic-inch engines. The number of carburetor complaints that the APA has received on 1976–77 Chrysler Volare/Aspen models indicates that emission violations exist in these years also.

Brakes

Serious safety hazards are presented by the brakes on late model Chrysler vehicles. Many Chrysler Aspen/ Volare owners writing the APA complain of brake problems ranging from pulling and grabbing brakes to excessive brake wear and weak brakes. Some of the owners complain of total brake failure—an obvious safety hazard. The following letter is typical:

I bought a Dodge Aspen station wagon on June 17, 1976. On June 20, 1977, just three days after the expiration of the year's warranty, while travelling back to Toronto along Highway #11, I noticed an ominous sound coming from the rear end on apply-

217

ing the brakes. I took the car to the nearby "Ted's Esso" service station (759 Eastern Avenue, Toronto), where upon examination of the braking system, the mechanic advised me not to drive the car as he considered it unsafe, and there was a great possibility of the rear brakes coming apart and causing a nasty accident. The service station (Ted's) findings, which I have documented, state that the left rear drum is cracked along with surface cracks on the right rear drum. The mechanic recommends replacing both drums and linings.

Steering

Motorists depend on and need safe and reliable steering. The steering problems found in these complaints—pulling to one side, sudden swerving or other loss of control, uncontrolled vibration and shimmy frequently causing tire wear—are not only disconcerting while driving but potentially dangerous.

Total loss of steering, as some individuals reported, obviously can cause accidents:

. . . car driven to Stoney Creek where noise and steering misbehaviour so apparent as to alarm client as to safety of car; car returned for fifth time for re-examination and correction: client advised by Service Advisor that the trouble eminated from a loose steering box; next day car driven for period without trouble until 4:30 P.M. when the same symptoms of noise and steering misbehaviour returned;

The purpose of this letter is to draw the above difficulties to your attention and to point out that my client has expressed concern about the roadworthiness of this car. On three occasions my client has returned the automobile to you with the same complaint, namely that the steering was defective and a loud noise appeared to be connected with the steering problem.

My client honestly fears for his safety should these difficulties re-occur in the course of his travels. In the event that loss of control of this automobile occurs and no other reasonable explanation can be found, it is my client's intention to hold the

parties responsible for the defect liable for any
damages incurred.

Fires

Many Volare/Aspen owners reported near-accidents
caused by the sudden seizing of the differential, crankshaft, and transmission. In some cases, the seizure
caused fires:

July 22nd—My 1977 Volare is now 40 days old and
has a little over 2,200 km on it. My family and I are
on a trip to a town called Manitowadge. After approximately 83 miles of travel I hear a tremendous
rattle underneath, the car slows down and the
speed control is racing the engine. I naturally stop
the vehicle and find to my chagrin that the drive
shaft has fallen down, at the differential and is *RED*
from heat for the approximate length of 1½ inches.
To add danger and terror to the situation, the differential, which is located very near the gas tank,
has flames shooting out of it. It naturally took only
a few seconds to evacuate the car, with my two
terrified young children being dragged out.
I fought the fire until it was out. (It is interesting to
note that afterwards someone suggested I should
have let the fire just work on the gas tank!)

The catalytic converter was also said to be the cause of
a number of sudden "flash" fires:

On Labour Day weekend because of a second
failure of the regulator, my wife was left without
lights or wipers during a dark rainy day returning
from Montreal. She stopped in Val d'Or and had
the battery charged, a $7 service charge. About 15
miles from Rouyn the car's engine began to sputter
and the car filled with smoke. A $35 towing charge.
The fire inside the car was caused, the dealers opinion, by the catalytic converter, which was installed
too close to the floor of the car. The resultant fire
melted a seat belt, peeled the paint off the floor and
sent noxious fumes into the rear seat area where my
two small children were strapped in.
Your representative has been most reluctant to

concern himself with the matter, the matter of the safety of my family. The suggestion was that the fire was caused by a cigarette tossed back of the seat. This continual shifting of responsibility is what prompted this letter. Neither my wife nor I have ever smoked and I am sure my six year old daughter doesn't.

Although no fires caused by the gas tank have yet been reported, several Volare/Aspen owners reported that gas tank defects could easily provoke a fire:

*

2. Gas Tank

The sales literature as well as the owner's handbook states that the tank holds 15 imp. gallons. This statement is correct, but it does not state that one cannot get it in. Normal filling by a gas station attendant invariably causes large splurges coming out of the filling pipe when the tank is filled to from 9 to 12 gallons. To fill it beyond 12 gallons requires patience, a pump nozzle which will fill very slowly, preferably a tilted car and still considerable spilling. Not only is it inconvenient, it is annoying, dangerous, and polluting.

2.1 The spill leaves up to a cupful of raw gasoline on the ground *every time* the tank is filled.

2.2 The spill leaves a dirty mark on the side of the car.

2.3 The spill occasionally hits the person filling the tank.

2.4 A person with gasoline on his clothes is a danger inside the car: the fumes may cause drowsiness and it is a fire hazard if somebody smokes.

2.5 The gas gauge indicates full at 12 imp. gallons while the tank is only 80% full.

U.S. laws limit raw gas evaporation from an entire car to 8 cm^3 per day. At an average spill of ½ cup (118 cm^3) the total allotted evaporation quantity is consumed if the car is filled only once every 14 days.

I am just as much concerned about the environment as about my own car and my own safety. This is such a serious deficiency that fixing is very necessary and I do not consider an answer, that "nothing can be done about it" as satisfactory.

Performance Defects

Carburetor

One of the most frequently replaced and adjusted parts of the Volare/Aspen is the carburetor. Despite these adjustments, stalling and post-ignition "dieseling" are cited in a high proportion of the complaints which the Automobile Protection Association has received. In addition, faulty fuel pumps, fuel-line leakage and sticking chokes cause Volare/Aspen owners untold and undue expense, hazard, and annoyance.

Accurate timing of the Volare/Aspen is almost impossible to maintain.

Transmission

On most new cars, the transmission is one of the last things to break down. Volare/Aspens, however, fall prey to strange "thumping and shuddering," slipping gears, and sticky shifts, often during the first months of ownership.

Leaks

Volare/Aspen owners are also plagued with oil, transmission, and coolant leaks. One owner is convinced that her Volare drank more than anyone over the New Year's season (three quarts of oil and one quart of transmission fluid per day).

Poor Gas Mileage

Chief among the many advertised "features" of the Volare/Aspen which many disgruntled owners now view with more than a bit of cynicism is the claim of "economy of performance." Poor gas mileage, frequent repairs and exorbitant depreciation have left the owners who thought they were buying a low-cost car bitterly disillusioned and well-nigh broke.

Volare/Aspens seem to have a voracious thirst for gas. They get substantially poorer fuel economy than the industry norm. More disturbing than the number of complaints on poor fuel economy of Chrysler vehicles is how poor the fuel economy of these cars is. Where Chrysler owners compare the Environmental Protection Agency rated fuel economy to their fuel economy, the average difference is 6.6 miles per gallon (MPG) in the city and 7.4 MPG on the highway.

The Chrysler Volare/Aspen complaints on poor fuel economy indicate that the consumers relied on Chrysler advertisements of good fuel economy when they bought cars that they thought would be saving gasoline for them and their country. Chrysler Volare/Aspen owners are outraged to find their Chrysler, advertised as fuel-efficient, ends up using more gasoline.

"Things That Go 'Bump' In the Dark"

A drive in a Volare/Aspen can be a traumatic experience. Numerous owners report being haunted by rattles and squeaks, jerks and shudders, which even their mechanics can't identify. Many report picking up loose bolts which had fallen out of their new car. Little problems multiplied countless times cause endless headaches for Volare/Aspen owners. Some heaters won't work; others won't turn off. Volare/Aspens seem to be keeping the spark plug manufacturing industry in business. The vinyl and upholstery is constantly being repaired. Speedometer and gas gauges are notorious for being defective. Motor noise is constant. One lady described the sound of her motor in cold weather as being like a skeleton rattling on a tin roof.

Owners of chronic "Volare/Aspen failures" live in daily fear of what will happen next. As one owner remarked, it is hard to know in which areas to watch for problems; the only thing you can be reasonably sure of is that your Volare/Aspen will break down.

Body Defects

Highlighting the lack of quality control on Chrysler assembly lines are tales of cars that are one model one side and another on the other. One appalled owner wrote:

On March 12, 1976 I thought I had received what I had ordered, a 1976 Dodge Aspen Special Edition. I did not inspect the car prior to taking delivery of it since it was purchased from Latil Motors (in) Biloxi, Mississippi, for whom we have had the highest esteem in the past.

I received a Dodge Volare Aspen. One side of the car bears a Volare nameplate, the other, an Aspen. Half of the seat belts in the rear are blue, half are black.

Other owners write:

*

All malfunctions of this new car were listed in my previous letter of June 20th 1977, the last problem being the water-leakage entering both doors, which was finally but not completely fixed.

I have been told that there was something wrong with the drainage system, but now, this water-leakage is entering *the inside of the car* onto the floor after each rainfall or car-wash, and there is now water right on the carpet of the car. The last time, while entering the car and starting to drive, water started to spurt-out from the Air-Vents in large amounts, to a point where my shoes and feet got literally soaked!

*

Aside of the usual breaking-in difficulties, I find myself plagued with a problem that my dealer can do nothing about. It has to do with the design of the molding on top of the doors.

When it rains and the windows have to be kept slightly open for air circulation, the rain drips heavily inside the car, from under the top molding. The gutter design was changed to a simple molding for an aesthetic reason maybe, but surely not for a safety one. Not to get flooded inside, I have to keep the windows completely closed, which makes driving hazardous (inside condensation and heat).

*

Dirty Windshield & Lights: Water somehow enters around headlights and hood, P/U dirt along way to windshield via fender flanges and keeps the windshield and entire front end of the car constantly dirty. This has been more of an irritation during the summer and fall period and could become treacherous during the coming winter. (This is a continuing problem.)

I wish to apologize if the above listing makes for somewhat odious reading, yet you can well imagine how I feel after having spent close to $5000 dollars (cash) for this auto. All of the above problem areas have been looked into at one time or another by the dealers without appreciable results. This car has spent more time on the dealers premises than on the road. I suspect that it's fallen in love either with the service manager or perhaps one of the more stylish cordobas.

*

I am the owner of a 1977 Volare, six cylinder, which was purchased on December 30, 1976, at Cornwall Chrysler, Pitt Street Cornwall, Ontario.

I've been having troubles with this car since day-one. One of the smaller problems is that the mud or dirty water coming from the front wheels somehow end up on the headlights and bumper. On the passenger side, which is the worse, the water flies on the windshield.

Chrysler's Anticonsumer Attitude

A frequent and disturbing complaint centers on Chrysler repair work and dealer attitudes. Vehicles were taken to the dealers for repair work, and often the problems reappeared. Many individuals have repeatedly taken their cars back to have the stalling problem fixed to no avail. Typical is the car that had to be taken in for repair work sixteen times in eleven months. Many owners found that repairs were delayed because parts were unavailable from Chrysler. This was most often experienced for carburetor repair kits. Such situations produced inconvenience, and sometimes a loss of wages for these car owners.

Along the same line, Chrysler's loaner policy was found to be inconsistent and unhelpful for the owners. Customers were told they would receive a loaner, when, in fact, they did not. Owners without the use of their defective cars for up to weeks at a time would have to provide their own transportation, frequently missing or being late for work and jeopardizing their jobs and economic stability because of this evasive loaner policy.

In today's fast-paced world, people comment on how the quality they once knew and respected is gone. Chrysler products are examples of this lack of quality control, and they exhibit inferior engineering and workmanship. The Volare was touted as being the sexy new European, the Aspen as being the Clincher, and the Van as providing nonstop fun. These expectations have not been met, and the consumers pay the price financially and in terms of personal safety. Consumers are losing faith in the Chrysler product. Many people believed Chrysler should provide them with new cars due to the extreme unreliability of what they originally purchased. People who once believed in Chrysler's superior engineering now say, "This is the last time I am purchasing a Chrysler vehicle."

Concern for the safety of motorists requires Chrysler to remedy the hazardous brakes, carburetors, steering systems, and transmissions in 1976–77 Chrysler Volare/Aspens. Concern for the consumer's welfare and Chrysler's reputation in the market require Chrysler to improve the fuel economy, quality control, and ease of repair of its vehicles. To do otherwise would expose Chrysler to mandatory government remedies, including recalls, product-liability litigation, and consumer rejection of the company's new and used cars.

Potentially Hazardous Defects

1. Seatbelt failure
2. Power steering loss
3. Steering failure
4. Seized differential
5. Electrical fires
6. Catalytic convertor fires
7. Differential fires
8. Loose hood
9. Brake failure
10. Gas tank filler pipe failure
11. Catastrophic stalling
12. Biodegradable tires
13. Heating and defrosting failure
14. Door lock failure
15. Loose and defective seats
16. Loose windshield
17. Exterior mirror defective

Defective Parts

1. Differential
2. Transmission
3. Motor oil leaks
4. Motor failure
5. Carburetor
6. Hood misaligned
7. Trunk misaligned
8. Door failure
9. Crankshaft
10. Alternator
11. Dashboard
12. Loose windshield
13. Front seat
14. Chrome deterioration
15. Automatic choke
16. Windows
17. Doors
18. Starter
19. Radio
20. Brakes
21. Accelerator pump
22. Heater and defroster
23. Door panels

24. Carpeting
25. Radiator

Performance Problems

1. Chronic stalling
2. Noisy brakes
3. Poor paint application
4. Premature rusting
5. Motor noise and vibrations
6. Water leaks in trunk
7. Water leaks from windshield
8. Water leaks from door/window/roof
9. Constant alignment
10. Starting difficulties
11. Frequent tune-ups
12. Lack of power
13. Water in headlights and tailights
14. Excessive oil consumption
15. Excessive gas consumption
16. Rear-end noise
17. Transmission slips
18. Uneven braking
19. Motor overheating
20. Power steering difficulties

Warranty and Service Complaints

1. Warranty repairs refused
2. Inadequate predelivery inspection (P.D.I.)
3. Poor customer relations
4. Recalls improperly carried out
5. Long repair waits
6. Repairs poorly performed
7. Parts not available
8. Safety defects disregarded
9. Bankrupt dealers
10. Discourteous treatment by Chrysler or dealer

CHRYSLER
CANADA LTD.

April 20, 1978

APA MONTREAL,
292 St-Joseph Boul. O.,
C.P. 117, Station E,
Montreal, 151, Quebec.

Attention: Mr. L.P. Edmonston
President, APA

Dear Sir:

We have received your letter of April 1, 1978 referring to a list of Chrysler Canada Ltd. customers, from whom you have received inquiries about their Chrysler built vehicles.

Chrysler Canada Ltd. intends to deal directly with all of the customers shown on this list within the terms of the warranty applying to their particular vehicle.

A policy to reimburse owners who have previously paid for repairs to correct a stalling condition, has already been established by Chrysler.

It is our view that a meeting between Chrysler Canada Ltd. and the APA would not serve any useful purpose at this time, since it will be our continuing policy to deal directly with our customers through the dealer organization.

Thank you for your concern in this matter and the time you have taken to write.

Yours very truly,
CHRYSLER CANADA LTD.

K.N. Gilboe
General Service Manager

The Diesel Dilemma

As a result of recent gasoline shortages, European and North American motorists are turning to the diesel motor as an economical alternative to conventional, inefficient gasoline engines. In Europe, vehicles equipped with diesel motors have jumped from only 2 per cent in 1970, to a present high of 5 per cent. The European car makers have jumped on the diesel bandwagon too, and now offer 11 different motors manufactured by Mercedes-Benz, Peugeot, Opel, Citroen, Datsun, and Volkswagen. It is rumored that Ford of England, Alfa Romeo, and the Russian Volga models will soon be diesel powered.

American car manufacturers are also participating, although a bit timidly, in the diesel's success in North America. International Harvester has a diesel in its Scout and General Motors has put diesels in its 1979 Oldsmobile passenger vehicles and its 1979 Chevrolet models. In fact, if American emission control standards are made less severe towards the emission of nitrogen dioxide (NOX) some industry experts predict that diesel-powered vehicles will count for at least 15 per cent of the North American new car market within the next 10 years.

Diesel Advantages

Diesel means economy. It has the highest mechanical efficiency of any internal-combustion engine. This mechanical efficiency can increase gas mileage by as much as 25 per cent. Low maintenance costs are achieved primarily by the simplicity of the diesel motor's design. Diesels have no spark plugs, ignition points, carburetors, coils, or distributors, so tune-ups are no longer necessary. Durability is another factor that cannot be ignored. Diesel engines have the reputation for running trouble-free for more than 300,000 miles without any major engine overhauls. Volkswagen has even boasted that its new diesel Rabbit's engine has a service life "twice as long as that of the spark-ignition engine." One of the last major advantages one finds with the diesel motor is the low cost of diesel fuel. However, the difference in cost between gasoline and diesel fuel only becomes an important factor in high mileage operation.

Diesel Disadvantages

Diesel motors give poor acceleration, are noisy at low speeds, produce foul-smelling emissions, cost $200–1,000 more than conventional engines, are overweight, and have a history of being hard to start in cold weather. Its future in North America is also clouded by the proposed pollution restrictions that the United States may adopt for 1978. The Environmental Protection Agency wants to reduce the emission of nitrogen dioxide from 2.0 grams per vehicle mile to 0.4 gpm in 1978. This restriction will effectively spell the end to any diesel motors marketed after 1978 because they cannot produce fewer than 1.5 nitrogen dioxide gpm using present technology. So, if the pollution controls are further tightened, the 1979 model year could be the first and last year for diesel sales in North America.

Conclusions

With its present imperfections, the diesel-powered car is a recommended buy only to those motorists who plan to drive at least 15,000 miles a year, keep their vehicles at least 5 years, and who live close to gas stations and garages where diesel fuel is sold and where minor repairs can be carried out. If all these criteria are met then some of the following models may be considered:

1. Oldsmobile Delta 88 This radically new diesel-equipped car is full of potential since it is built and marketed by General Motors, thereby guaranteeing good parts availability, normal rates of depreciation, good service, and the attractive Oldsmobile styling. The 350 diesel motor gives 135 HP and provides a fuel economy of 20 mpg in the city and 29 mpg for highway driving. This is an incredible increase in fuel economy when compared to the performance of the Oldsmobile's V8 gasoline engine that gives only 16 mpg in the city and 22 mpg for highway driving.

2. Volkswagen Rabbit Diesel This new model from Volkswagen's 1977 model offerings has already been on the market for a year. Judging from the absence of owner complaints directed against the diesel model, it seems that Volkswagen may have improved the quality control that was such a problem with earlier 1975–1976 Rabbits.

If this quality control is maintained with the 1979 Rabbit diesel models, they will then represent a cheaper alternative to the Oldsmobile diesel. The diesel Rabbit should sell for about $6,400 and give a fuel economy of 35 to 40 mpg depending upon where it is driven.

3. Mercedes-Benz Diesel The only reason why the Mercedes-Benz diesel has placed third is due to its high retail price. Aside from its original purchase cost, the Mercedes diesel represents the most refined diesel motoring that money can buy. Depreciation is low, replacement parts are plentiful, maintenance costs are reasonable, and the reliability of the diesel engine is without question. The Mercedes 240/300D models have been so well refined for 1979 that much of the noise and odors have been eliminated and the acceleration time improved. In fact, these refinements put both Mercedes a notch ahead of the Peugeot 504D which is their closest competitor that costs about $4,000 less to own.

4. Peugeot 504D After the Oldsmobile and the Volkswagen Rabbit diesel, the Peugeot diesel is one of the least expensive European models available on the market for 1979. Selling for about $9,000, the Peugeot gives its owner almost as much as the Mercedes, except for the greater parts availability of Mercedes and also the more rapid depreciation of its models. Peugeot's service after sales has also left much to be desired due to its weak dealer network and high cost for replacement parts. Gas economy is not too spectacular with an estimated fuel economy of 21 to 23 mpg split between city and highway driving.

5. Diesel Scout Traveller International Harvester has never been considered much of a rival to the major automakers. Nevertheless, in addition to making its reputation with the manufacturing of quality farm machinery, the company has also launched its own version of a four-wheel drive diesel vehicle called the Scout. Costing close to $8,500, this model lacks the refinement and sophistication found with other comparatively priced diesels. It combines some of the worst features of diesel motors with the Scout's trucklike handling and styling. International Harvester's quality control deficiencies, poor parts supply, and weak dealership servicing provide additional reasons for passing up the purchase of a Scout in 1979.

The Van Invasion

If Willys and American Motors are the pioneers in four-wheel-drive popularity, then Volkswagen is the acknowledged creator and marketer **par excellent** of the van. From its humble beginnings as a utility and delivery vehicle, the van has now become an intrinsic part of North America's mobile, free-wheeling lifestyle.

The van has become a sex symbol. Fitted with the right optional equipment, vans can become "rolling bedrooms" that provide both privacy and mobility. Today, van versatility will complement almost any lifestyle from cruising along the mainstreets of town to commuting to and from work.

Most vans require some customizing, and this is where expenses are likely to pile up. Most vans are sold with standard equipment that provides just the bare essentials (what plumber or electrician wants a van with wall-to-wall carpeting, water bed, and mirror on the ceiling?) since the traditional customers for vans used them mostly as utility vehicles.

Like four-wheel-drive vehicles, vans also sell close to their book value whether bought new or used. Unlike passenger cars, the accessories purchased with vans actually increase the van's resale value and may make the vehicle easier to sell. Remember, though, factory-ordered options are expensive and often the unadorned van purchased from stock and customized slowly through independent parts supply houses with the advice and help of professional van customizers is a cheaper alternative.

Safety is another aspect of van ownership that cannot be ignored. Since some vans have a high center of gravity, their handling characteristics will be quite different than with passenger vehicles. This requires some practicing in mastering the driving techniques required to operate vans safely. Shoulder belts and seat belts are also required equipment due to the little space separating driver and passenger from front collisions.

Vans represent a much better investment than front-wheel-drive vehicles and offer as much quality control as most passenger cars. Their purchase, however, represents a change in driving techniques and a commitment to purchasing some optional equipment.

CHEVY VAN

All data based on standard model

Used vehicle Price. $4,000–5,200
Based on standard equipped vehicle. Price assumes excellent
condition. Reduce price after August

Statistical Comparison
Average gas mileage
Below average depreciation
Parts available and inexpensive

Technical Data

Wheelbase	125	Standard Engine. . .	V8 (350)
Length	201	Standard Brakes . . .	Disc-Drum
Weight	4,250	Gasoline Mileage . .	11 M.P.G.
Width	79.5	(with unleaded fuel)	

Frequency of Repairs:
Excellent motor transmission and brakes. Some carburetor
problems.

Body:
Solid construction. Generalized paint peeling.

Safety Defects:
Possibility carburetor may be defective.

Recommendation:
Excellent choice new or used.

VANDURA

All data based on standard model

Used vehicle Price. $4,800–5,900
Based on standard equipped vehicle. Price assumes excellent
condition. Reduce price after August

Statistical Comparison
Very Ion depreciation
Parts inexpensive and available
Poor gas mileage

Technical Data

Wheelbase	125	Standard Engine. . .	V8 (400)
Length	201	Standard Brakes . . .	Disc-Drum
Weight	4,260	Gasoline Mileage . .	10 M.P.G.
Width	79.1		

Frequency of Repairs:
Excellent transmission. Some problems with motor and carburetor.

Body:
Paint defects and body rattles.

Safety Defects:
Possibility brakes may be defective.

Recommendation:
Recommended, practically identical with the Chevy Van

Ford Motor Company   **1978–1979**
Ford Division
ECONOLINE

All data based on standard model

Used vehicle Price. $3,500–4,800
Based on standard equipped vehicle. Price assumes excellent condition. Reduce price after August

Statistical Comparison
Average depreciation
Parts inexpensive and available
Average gas mileage

Technical Data

Wheelbase	138	Standard Engine. . .	V8 (351)
Length	206.8	Standard Brakes . . .	Disc-Drum
Weight	4,800	Gasoline Mileage . .	12 M.P.G.
Width	79.8		

Frequency of Repairs:
Good transmission and brakes. Minor problems with motor, steering, suspension, and electrical system.

Body:
Some premature rusting and paint peeling.

Safety Defects:
Possibility steering may be defective.

Recommendation:
Recommended. Body improved. Ford's response to the Chevy Van

Chrysler Corporation   **1978–1979**
Dodge Division
TRADESMAN

All data based on standard model

Used vehicle Price. $3,700–5,000
Based on standard equipped vehicle. Price assumes excellent condition. Reduce price after August

Statistical Comparison
Average depreciation
Parts available at average cost
Good gas mileage

Technical Data

Wheelbase	109	Standard Engine. . .	V8 (318)
Length	176	Standard Brakes . . .	Disc-Drum
Weight	3,950	Gasoline Mileage . .	14 M.P.G.
Width	79.8		

Frequency of Repairs:
Good motor. Problems with brakes, suspension and transmission.

Body:
Poor body construction. Water leaks, paint defects, rattles, and some rusting.

Safety Defects:
Possibility brakes may be defective.

Recommendation:
Not recommended. Dealer servicing inadequate.

The Four-Wheel-Drive Revolution

No one ever expected that the light four-wheel-drive vehicles that were used so extensively in 1940 for the military and later used as utility vehicles for recreational and commercial purposes would be as popular as they are today.

These special-interest vehicles have been in such great demand that many of them defy the auto industry's standard new vehicle depreciation rate of 30 per cent the first year of use and another 20 per cent after the second year of ownership. In fact, after a few years of use, owners may find their vehicles have depreciated no more than a third of the original selling price.

Because an inflated price structure exists with these vehicles, new car shoppers will find that salesmen will invariably stick close to the inflated suggested retail price and thereby keep bargaining to a minimum. As used cars, the same situation exists. There is so much demand for good used four-wheel-drive vehicles that a "black market" pricing mentality pervades causing owners to demand top dollar for their used vehicle.

The popularity of these vehicles has not been all that sudden. Precipated by the American Motors Jeep, car buyers have turned toward the four-wheel-drive models in protest against Detroit's generally bland model offerings. It has just been during the past 10 years that Detroit stylists and engineers (almost always found in that order of importance) discovered how to successfully cash in on the fad by marketing their own separate model lines.

Unfortunately, the stylists won over the engineers. Detroit's idea of what makes a successful four-wheel-drive vehicle, and the public's demand for a reliable and durable vehicle that would be adequate for expressway driving as well as navigate easily over primitive terrain, have failed to get any concessions from the manufacturers.

So, what we have now is a plethora of front-wheel-drive vehicles all promising more than they actually deliver, selling at outrageously inflated prices, and lacking the same quality control as other vehicles. As a result, the four-wheel-drive fad will pass and prices will inevitably plunge to more realistic levels. Once again, it will be the consumer who comes out the loser.

Advantages of Ownership

1. Safer and easier handling in Winter and over rough terrain
2. Pleasure of driving a "special interest" vehicle
3. Possibility of large cargo space
4. Present value depreciates slowly

Disadvantages of Ownership

1. Inflated new and used model prices
2. High fuel consumption
3. High insurance costs
4. Parking difficulties
5. Expensive service and costly parts
6. More frequent periodic maintenance than other vehicles
7. Road handling is different, driver must adapt
8. Accessories expensive and often necessary
9. Safety roll bar should be installed

Ford Motor Company   1978–1979
Ford Division
BRONCO

All data based on standard model

Used vehicle Price. $5,000–7,000
Based on standard equipped vehicle. Price assumes excellent
condition. Reduce price after August

Statistical Comparison
Rapid rate of depreciation
Expensive and rare parts
Poor gas mileage

Technical Data

Wheelbase	92	Standard Engine. . .	V8 (351)
Length	161	Standard Brakes . . .	Disc-Drum
Weight	3,860	Gasoline Mileage . .	8 M.P.G.
Width	74	(With unleaded fuel)	

Frequency of Repairs:
Problems with motor, carburetor, brakes, suspension and
steering.

Body:
Poor construction. Problems with rusting, rattles, and water
leaks. Little interior room.

Safety Defects:
Possibility steering may be defective. Poor visibility. Seat latch
failure.

Recommendation:
Not recommended.

Chrysler Corporation   1978–1979
Dodge Division
RAMCHARGER

All data based on standard model

Used vehicle Price. $4,200–6,400
Based on standard equipped vehicle. Price assumes excellent
condition. Reduce price after August.

Statistical Comparison
Rapid depreciation
Parts available and costly
Poor gas mileage

Technical Data

Wheelbase	106	Standard Engine. . .	V8 (318)
Length	184.6	Standard Brakes . . .	Disc-Drum
Weight	5,020	Gasoline Mileage . .	9 M.P.G.
Width	79.5	(With unleaded fuel)	

Frequency of Repairs:
Excellent motor and transmission. Problems with brakes, transmission, carburetor, steering, and suspension.

Body:
Poor body construction. Severe water leaks, rusting, and paint defects.

Safety Defects:
Possibility brakes may be defective.

Recommendation:
Not recommended. A mediocre model plagued by poor service.

American Motors Company   **1978–1979**
Jeep Division

JEEP/CJ-7

All data based on standard model

Used vehicle Price. $4,500–5,700
Based on standard equipped vehicle. Price assumes excellent condition. Reduce price after August.

Statistical Comparison
Below average depreciation
Parts available at average cost
Gas mileage average

Technical Data

Wheelbase	93.5	Standard Engine. . .	V8 (304)
Length	155	Standard Brakes . . .	Drum
Weight	3,100	Gasoline Mileage . .	10 M.P.G.
Width	78	(With unleaded fuel)	

Frequency of Repairs:
Excellent motor and electrical system. Brakes, suspension, transmission, and carburetor failure-prone.

Body:
Water leaks, rattles, and premature rusting

Safety Defects:
Possibility gas tank may leak and steering may fail.

Recommendation:
Recommended. The best of a bad lot.

International Harvester   **1978–1979**

SCOUT

All data based on standard model

Used vehicle Price. $4,200–6,100
Based on standard equipped vehicle. Price assumes excellent condition. Reduce price after August.

Statistical Comparison
Above average depreciation
Parts rare and costly
Average gas mileage
Inadequate service

Technical Data

Wheelbase	100	Standard Engine. . .	4 cyl (196)
Length	166	Standard Brakes . . .	Disc-Drum
Weight	4,250	Gasoline Mileage . .	10 M.P.G.
Width	69	(With regular fuel)	

Frequency of Repairs:
A good motor, steering, suspension, and transmission. Problems with starter and electrical system.

Body:
Solid construction, little rusting. Interior finish sloppy.

Safety Defects:
Possibility carburetor may be defective.

Recommendation:
Not recommended. Service not guaranteed.

Toyota Company   **1978–1979**
LANDCRUISER

All data based on standard model

Used vehicle Price. $4,300–5,900
Based on standard equipped vehicle. Price assumes excellent condition. Reduce price after August.

Statistical Comparison
Depreciation average
Parts costly and rare
Good gas mileage

Technical Data

Wheelbase	90	Standard Engine. . .	6 cyl (264)
Length	152.4	Standard Brakes . . .	Disc-Drum
Weight	3,765	Gasoline Mileage . .	12 M.P.G.
Width	66.5	(With regular fuel)	

Frequency of Repairs:
Excellent carburetor and electrical system. Problems with brakes, motor, transmission, steering, and suspension.

Body:
Severe rusting around doors and fenders

Safety Defects:
Information not available.

Recommendation:
Not recommended. Vehicle too small and lacks adequate quality control. Check date of manufacture plate on driver door.

General Motors Corporation   **1978–1979**
Chevrolet Division
BLAZER/JIMMY

All data based on standard model.

Used vehicle Price. $5,300–7,000
Based on standard equipped vehicle. Price assumes excellent condition. Reduce price after August.

Statistical Comparison
Excessive rate of depreciation
Parts costly and rare
Poor gas mileage

Technical Data

Wheelbase	106.5	Standard Engine. . .	V8 (350)
Length	221	Standard Brakes . . .	Disc-Drum
Weight	5,500	Gasoline Mileage . .	8 M.P.G.
Width	94	(With unleaded fuel)	

Frequency of Repairs:
Improved motor and transmission. High speed vibrations excessive. Serious problems with brakes, suspension, steering, and carburetor.

Body:
Severe rusting around doors, fenders, and rear end. Paint peeling, body rattles, water leaking into interior.

Safety Defects:
Possibility roof may be defective. Tires may be defective.

Recommendation:
Not recommended. Overpriced and overweight. The ideal vehicle for a rich masochist.

1970 MODELS

CHEVY II NOVA

All data based on four-door sedan

Used Car Price* $400
Based on standard equipped car with automatic transmission
and radio.
Price assumes excellent condition.

*Subtract $10 for each month after August for current price.

Statistical Comparison:
Excellent gas economy.
Excellent parts availability.
Low depreciation.
Low parts cost.

Technical Data

Wheelbase . .	111 in.	Standard Engine	6 cyl.
Length	189.4 in.	Standard Brakes	Drum
Weight	3,200 lbs.	Gasoline Mileage.	24
Width	72.4 in.	(with regular fuel)	

Frequency of Repairs:
Good brakes, good electrical system, good suspension and au-
tomatic transmission.
Minor problems with carburetion and ignition system.

Body:
The Nova escapes the more common body defects and is actually very durable.

Safety Defects:
Possibility of defective Rochester carburetor and power brake
vacuum check valve.

Recommendation:
A recommended good buy. Watch for rusting in trunk.

CHEVROLET (Full-sized)
Biscayne, Bel Air, Impala, Caprice

All data based on four-door sedan

Used Car Price* $500
Based on standard equipped car with automatic transmission
and radio.
Price assumes excellent condition.

*Subtract $10 for each month after August for current price.

Statistical Comparison:
Excellent gas economy.
Very slow rate of depreciation.

Average parts cost.
Excellent parts availability.

Technical Data

Wheelbase . .	119 in.	Standard Engine . . .	6 cyl.
Length	216 in.	Standaard Brakes . . .	Disc-Drum
Weight	4,100 lbs.	Gasoline Mileage . . .	19
Width	79.8 in.	(with regular fuel)	

Frequency of Repairs:
Clutch problems, exhaust problems, good brakes.

Body:
Body exterior problems. Body assembly poor.

Safety Defects:
Possibility of carbon monoxide gas leakage into passenger compartment.
Possibility of defective power brake vacuum check valve, defective steering wheel, Rochester carburetor and engine mount restraint.

Recommendation:
Recommended if car is driven with windows open and rusting has been checked.

Chevrolet Division   **1970**
General Motors

CAMARO

All data based on two-door coupe

Used Car Price* $900
Based on standard equipped car with automatic transmission and radio.
Price assumes excellent condition.

*Subtract $10 for each month after August for current price.

Statistical Comparison:
Average gas economy.
Slow rate of depreciation.
Average parts cost.
Average parts availability.

Technical Data

Wheelbase . .	108 in.	Standard Engine . . .	6 cyl.
Length	186 in.	Standard Brakes . . .	Disc-Drum
Weight	3,200 lbs.	Gasoline Mileage . . .	22
Width	74 in.	(with regular fuel)	

Frequency of Repairs:
Good motor. Transmission and brake problems reported.

Body:
Good resistance to rust. Well constructed body.

Safety Defects:
Possibility of defective Rochester carburetor and power brake vacuum check valve.

Recommendation:
A good buy if previous owner is not a "hot-rodder."

Pontiac Division   **1970**
General Motors
PONTIAC TEMPEST
Le Mans

All data based on four-door sedan

Used Car Price* $500
Based on standard equipped car with automatic transmission and radio.
Price assumes excellent condition.

*Subtract $10 for each month after August for current price.

Statistical Comparison:
Average depreciation.
Average parts cost.
Good gas economy.
Good parts availability.

Technical Data

Wheelbase . .	116 in.	Standard Engine	6 cyl.
Length	206.5 in.	Standard Brakes	Drum
Weight	3,700 lbs.	Gasoline Mileage	19
Width	76.7 in.	(with regular fuel)	

Frequency of Repairs:
Good drive-train and motor. Serious problems with ignition system and manual transmission.

Body:
Better rust resistance and quality of assembly than other Pontiac models.

Safety Defects:
Possibility of defective Rochester carburetor and power brake vacuum check valve.

Recommendation:
Recommended after mechanic verification.

PONTIAC (Full-Sized)
Catalina, Executive, Bonneville,
Laurentian, and Parisienne

All data based on four-door sedan

Used Car Price* $700
Based on standard equipped car with automatic transmission
and radio.
Price assumes excellent condition.

*Subtract $10 for each month after August for current price.

Statistical Comparison:
Average depreciation.
Good gas economy.
Good parts availability.
Low parts cost.

Technical Data

Wheelbase . .	125 in.	Standard Engine . . .	V8
Length	217.9 in.	Standard Brakes . . .	Disc-Drum
Weight	4,300 lbs.	Gasoline Mileage . . .	17
Width	79.8 in.	(with regular fuel)	

Frequency of Repairs:
Good motor and electrical system. Serious problems with cooling system, manual transmission, and clutch.

Body:
Rust resistant. Has a tendency to rattle.

Safety Defects:
Possibility of defective Rochester carburetor and power brake
vacuum check valve.

Recommendation:
Recommended. Laurentian and Parisienne are best buys.

PONTIAC FIREBIRD

All data based on hardtop coupe.

Used Car Price* $900
Based on standard equipped car with automatic transmission,
and radio.
Price assumes excellent condition.

*Subtract $10 for each month after August for current price.

Statistical Comparison:
Low depreciation.
Average parts availability.

Above-average parts cost.
Average fuel economy.

Technical Data

Wheelbase . . 108.1 in.   Standard Engine . . . 6 cyl.
Length . . . . 191.1 in.   Standard Brakes . . . Disc-Drum
Weight . . . . 3,500 lbs. Gasoline Mileage . . . 21
Width . . . . . 73.9 in.   (with regular fuel)

Frequency of Repairs:
Excellent brakes and motor. Problem with electrical system, cooling system, and automatic transmission. Hidden windshield wipers may fail.

Body:
Rust prone and rattle prone.

Safety Defects:
Possibility of unsafe defective throttle level, Rochester carburetor, and power brake vacuum check valve.

Recommendation:
Not recommended. High depreciation. May have been abused by racing.

Pontiac Division   **1970**
General Motors
PONTIAC GRAND PRIX

All data based on four-door sedan

Used Car Price* $700
Based on standard equipped car with automatic transmission and radio.
Price assumes excellent condition.

*Subtract $10 for each month after August for current price.

Statistical Comparison:
Rapid depreciation.
Average parts cost.
Average gas economy.
Average parts availability.

Technical Data

Wheelbase . . 118 in.   Standard Engine . . . V8
Length . . . . 210.2 in.   Standard Brakes . . . Disc-Drum
Weight . . . . 4,100 lbs. Gasoline Mileage . . . 17
Width . . . . . 75.7 in.   (with regular fuel)

Frequency of Repairs:
Good electrical system. Serious motor problems. Disc brakes are excellent.

Body:
Rust prone and rattle prone.

Safety Defects:
Possibility of defective Rochester carburetor and power brake vacuum check valve.

Recommendation:
Not recommended. GM has better family cars available.

Buick Division   **1970**
General Motors
BUICK (Full-sized)
Le Sabre, Custom, Wildcat, Electra

All data based on four-door sedan

Used Car Price* $800
Based on standard equipped car with automatic transmission and radio.
Price assumes excellent condition.

*Subtract $10 for each month after August for current price.

Statistical Comparison:
Very low rate of depreciation.
Excellent parts availability.
Average parts cost.
Good gas economy.

Technical Data

Wheelbase . .	124 in.	Standard Engine . . .	V8
Length	220.2 in.	Standard Brakes . . .	Disc-Drum
Weight	4,300 lbs.	Gasoline Mileage . . .	17
Width	80 in.	(with regular fuel)	

Frequency of Repairs:
Excellent brakes, fuel, and ignition systems. Some minor problem with automatic transmission and motor cooling system.

Body:
Well constructed. Very little rusting.

Safety Defects:
Possibility of defective Rochester carburetor, and power brake vacuum check valve.

Recommendation:
A good buy with V8 offering best economy.

OLDSMOBILE (Full-sized)

All data based on four-door sedan

Used Car Price* $600
Based on standard equipped car with automatic transmission
and radio.
Price assumes excellent condition.

*Subtract $10 for each month after August for current price.

Statistical Comparison:
Excellent parts availability.
Average depreciation.
Low parts cost.
Excellent gas economy.

Technical Data

Wheelbase . .	124 in.	Standard Engine . . .	V8
Length	219.1 in.	Standard Brakes . . .	Disc-Drum
Weight	4,300 lbs.	Gasoline Mileage . . .	18
Width	79.9 in.	(with regular fuel)	

Frequency of Repairs:
Excellent brakes, motor, fuel, and electrical system. All other
mechanical components above average. Numerous complaints
received on manual transmission and clutch assembly.

Body:
Very rust resistant. Excellent exterior finish. Well assembled
chassis.

Safety Defects:
Possibility of defective Rochester carburetor and power brake
vacuum check valve.

Recommendation:
An excellent buy. Check manual transmission before purchase,
A top-of-the-line family car.

Ford Division   **1970**
Ford Motor Company

FORD MAVERICK

All data based on two-door sedan

Used Car Price* $400
Based on standard equipped car with automatic transmission
and radio.
Price assumes excellent condition.

*Subtract $10 for each month after August for current price.

Statistical Comparison:
Good gas economy.
Excellent parts availability.

Low parts cost.
Fast depreciation rate.

Technical Data

Wheelbase . .	103 in.	Standard Engine	6 cyl.
Length	179.4 in.	Standard Brakes	Drum
Weight	2,600 lbs.	Gasoline Mileage.	24
Width	70.6 in.	(with regular fuel)	

Frequency of Repairs:
Problems with both automatic and manual transmission. Frequent complaints of stalling. Brakes are reported to wear out prematurely. Good motor, electrical system.

Body:
Rusting on fenders and doors. Well assembled. Good quality control.

Safety Defects:
Possibility of defective Firestone tires, defective seat belts, unsafe rear gas tank assembly, 15-by-5.5-inch single-piece wheel, brake master cylinder, 15-by-6.5-inch single-piece wheel, 4 barrel carburetor, and power brake vacuum check valve.

Recommendation:
A good buy. Little exterior difference between model years. Check frame and suspension for rust damage.

Ford Division   **1970**
Ford Motor Company
FORD MUSTANG

All data based on two-door hardtop

Used Car Price* $600
Based on standard equipped car with automatic transmission and radio.
Price assumes excellent condition.

*Subtract $10 for each month after August for current price.

Statistical Comparison:
High rate of depreciation.
Average parts cost.
Average parts availability.
Average fuel economy.

Technical Data

Wheelbase . .	108 in.	Standard Engine	6 cyl.
Length	187.4 in.	Standard Brakes	Drum
Weight	3,100 lbs.	Gasoline Mileage.	20
Width	71.7 in.	(with regular fuel)	

Frequency of Repairs:
Good motor, exhaust, and suspension system. Problems reported with automatic transmission and electrical system.

Body:
Extremely rust prone, especially around doors, front fenders, and rear gas tank.

Safety Defects:
Possibility of defective seat belt assembly, 15-by-5.5-inch and 15-by-6.5-inch single-piece wheel, 4 barrel carburetor, brake master cylinder, and power brake vacuum check valve.

Recommendation:
Not recommended. An average car with serious rusting problems. High rate of depreciation.

Ford Division   **1970**
Ford Motor Company
FORD (Full-sized)
Custom, Galaxie, LTD

All data based on four-door sedan

Used Car Price* $700

Based on standard equipped car with automatic transmission and radio.
Price assumes excellent condition.

*Subtract $10 for each month after August for current price.

Statistical Comparison:
Average parts availability.
Low parts cost.
Excellent gas economy.
Low depreciation rate.

Technical Data

Wheelbase . .	121 in.	Standard Engine	6 cyl.
Length	213.9 in.	Standard Brakes	Drum
Weight	3,900 lbs.	Gasoline Mileage	14
Width	79.7 in.	(with regular fuel)	

Frequency of Repairs:
Minor electrical and starting problems. Excellent motor. Minor brake problems.

Body:
Average body exterior. Metal is highly rust prone especially around doors, front fenders, and behind front wheels. Poor paint.

Safety Defects:
Defective seat belts. Possibility of defective power brake vacuum check valve, front wheel spindle, 15-by-6.5-inch single-piece wheel, 4 barrel carburetor, master cylinder, and hood latch.

Recommendation:
A good buy. A reliable family car with few exterior model changes. Learn to accept the rust.

Ford Division   1970
Ford Motor Company
                    FORD FAIRLANE

All data based on four-door sedan

Used Car Price* $500
Based on standard equipped car with automatic transmission and radio.
Price assumes excellent condition.

*Subtract $10 for each month after August for current price.

Statistical Comparison:
Average gas mileage.
Average depreciation rate.
Average parts cost.
Average parts availability.

Technical Data

Wheelbase . .	117 in.	Standard Engine	8 cyl.
Length	206.2 in.	Standard Brakes	Drum
Weight	3,300 lbs.	Gasoline Mileage	19
Width	76.4 in.	(with regular fuel)	

Frequency of Repairs:
Brake, clutch, steering, suspension, and manual transmission problems. Motor and electrical system better than average.

Body:
Low rust resistance. Body exterior poor quality. Paint problems.

Safety Defects:
Possibility of defective seat belts, hood latch, 15-by-5.5-inch and 15-by-6.5-inch single-piece wheel, brake master cylinder, 4 barrel carburetor and power brake vacuum check valve.

Recommendation:
Not recommended. A poorly-engineered vehicle.

MERCURY COUGAR

All data based on two-door hardtop

Used Car Price* $500
Based on standard equipped car with automatic transmission
and radio.
Price assumes excellent condition.

*Subtract $10 for each month after August for current price.

Statistical Comparison:
High depreciation.
Average parts cost.
Average gas economy.
Average parts availability.

Technical Data

Wheelbase . .	111 in.	Standard Engine . . .	V8
Length	196.1 in.	Standard Brakes . . .	Disc-Drum
Weight	3,500 lbs.	Gasoline Mileage . . .	19
Width	74.1 in.	(with regular fuel)	

Frequency of Repairs:
Average motor, automatic transmission, and fuel system. Serious problems with clutch, electrical system, cooling system, and suspension.

Body:
Extremely serious problem with rusting along front fenders, doors, and rear quarter panels. Overall chassis quality poor.

Safety Defects:
Possibility of defective power brake vacuum check valve, 15-by-5.5-inch single-piece wheel, brake master cylinder and 15-by-6.6-inch single-piece wheel.

Recommendation:
Not recommended. This is one Cougar that bites the hand that feeds it.

PLYMOUTH VALIANT
Duster

All data based on four-door sedan

Used Car Price* $800
Based on standard equipped car with automatic transmission
and radio.
Price assumes excellent condition.

*Subtract $10 for each month after August for current price.

Statistical Comparison:
Excellent gas economy.
Excellent parts availability.
Low depreciation.
Low parts costs.

Technical Data

Wheelbase . .	108 in.	Standard Engine	6 cyl.
Length	188.4 in.	Standard Brakes	Drum
Weight	3,000 lbs.	Gasoline Mileage.	24
Width	71.1 in.	(with regular fuel)	

Frequency of Repairs:
Excellent motor, ignition system, fuel and exhaust system.
Minor problems reported with clutch of manual transmission.

Body:
Good rust resistance, chassis well assembled. Some fender rust-ing.

Safety Defects:
Possibility of defective power-brake vacuum check valve, brake proportioning valve, and exhaust manifold cracking.

Recommendation:
Excellent car buy for a small family. Valiant should be kept a minimum of 5 years.

Dodge Division   **1970**
Chrysler Corporation
DODGE DART

All data based on four-door sedan

Used Car Price* $800
Based on standard equipped car with automatic transmission, and radio.
Price assumes excellent condition.

*Subtract $10 for each month after August for current price.

Statistical Comparison:
Excellent gas economy.
Good parts availability.
Low parts cost.
Low depreciation rate.

Technical Data

Wheelbase . .	111 in.	Standard Engine	6 cyl.
Length	196.2 in.	Standard Brakes	Drum
Weight	3,100 lbs.	Gasoline Mileage.	24
Width	69.7 in.	(with regular fuel)	

Frequency of Repairs:
Weak clutch and exhaust system. Excellent motor, suspension, ignition system, and fuel system. Check the manual transmission carefully.

Body:
All body components are of an excellent quality. A solid car. Some fender rusting.

Safety Defects:
Possibility of defective power-brake vacuum check valve, brake proportioning valve, and exhaust manifold cracking.

Recommendation:
An excellent buy. Low depreciation.

Plymouth Division 1970
Chrysler Corporation
PLYMOUTH BELVEDERE
Satellite

All data based on four-door sedan

Used Car Price* $600
Based on standard equipped car with automatic transmission and radio.
Price assumes excellent condition.

*Subtract $10 for each month after August for current price.

Statistical Comparison:
Average gas economy.
Average depreciation.
Average parts cost.
Average parts availability.

Technical Data

Wheelbase . .	116 in.	Standard Engine	6 cyl.
Length	204 in.	Standard Brakes	Drum
Weight	3,300 lbs.	Gasoline Mileage.	21
Width	76.4 in.	(with regular fuel)	

Frequency of Repairs:
Above average motor. Serious problems with clutch, drivetrain, exhaust system, steering and transmission.

Body:
Serious body problem including leaking and rattling. Fender rusting.

Safety Defects:
Possibility of defective power brake vacuum check valve and cracking exhaust manifold on V6 motor.

Recommendation:
Not recommended. Buy a Dart or Duster instead.

Dodge Division   **1970**
Chrysler Corporation
DODGE (Full-sized)
Polara and Monaco

All data based on four-door sedan

Used Car Price* $500
Based on standard equipped car with automatic transmission
and radio.
Price assumes excellent condition.

*Subtract $10 for each month after August for current price.

Statistical Comparison:
Average gas economy.
Rapid depreciation rate.
Average parts availability.
Average parts cost.

Technical Data

Wheelbase . .	122 in.	Standard Engine . . .	6 cyl.
Length	219.9 in.	Standard Brakes . . .	Disc-Drum
Weight	4,100 lbs.	Gasoline Mileage . . .	18
Width	79.2 in.	(with regular fuel)	

Frequency of Repairs:
Serious defects with brakes, drive-line, motor, fuel system, and
suspension.

Body:
Exterior quality poor; poorly assembled. Rusting is minimal.

Safety Defects:
Possibility of defective power brake vacuum check valve and
exhaust manifold cracking.

Recommendation:
Not recommended. A problem prone car.

Chrysler Division   **1970**
Chrysler Corporation
CHRYSLER (Full-sized)
Newport and "300"

All data based on four-door sedan

Used Car Price* $500
Based on standard equipped car with automatic transmission
and radio.
Price assumes excellent condition.

*Subtract $25 for each month after August for current price.

Statistical Comparison:
Rapid depreciation rate.
Average gas economy.

Average parts cost.
Average parts availability.

Technical Data

Wheelbase . .	124 in.	Standard Engine	V8
Length	224.7 in.	Standard Brakes	Drum
Weight	4,400 lbs.	Gasoline Mileage	16
Width	79.1 in.	(with regular fuel)	

Frequency of Repairs:
Serious deficiencies reported with electrical, cooling, fuel, ignition, steering, and suspension systems. Frequent brake repairs.

Body:
High frequency of body defects, though fender rusting is minimal.

Safety Defects:
Possibility of defective bumper jack and power brake vacuum check valve.

Recommendation:
Not recommended.

American Motors   **1970**
AMC HORNET

All data based on four-door sedan

Used Car Price* $600
Based on standard equipped car with automatic transmission and radio.
Price assumes excellent condition.

*Subtract $10 for each month after August for current price.

Statistical Comparison:
Slow rate of depreciation.
Good parts availability.
Good gas economy.
Average parts cost.

Technical Data

Wheelbase . .	108 in.	Standard Engine	6 cyl.
Length	179.26 in.	Standard Brakes	Drum
Weight	3,200 lbs.	Gasoline Mileage	23
Width	71.08 in.	(with regular fuel)	

Frequency of Repairs:
Engine and cooling system are excellent.
Minor problems with brakes and exhaust system.

Body:
Average body construction, some rusting.

Safety Defects:
Possibility of unsafe seating assembly and defective power brake vacuum check value.

Recommendation:
Recommended, after mechanic inspection.

American Motors 1970
AMC GREMLIN

All data based on two-door sedan

Used Car Price* $400
Based on standard equipped car with automatic transmission
and radio.
Price assumes excellent condition.

*Subtract $10 for each month after August for current price.

Statistical Comparison:
Slow rate of depreciation.
Good parts availability.
Good gas economy.
Average parts cost.

Technical Data

Wheelbase . .	96 in.	Standard Engine	6 cyl.
Length	161.25 in.	Standard Brakes	Drum
Weight	2,700 lbs.	Gasoline Mileage.	26
Width	70.6 in.	(with regular fuel)	

Frequency of Repairs:
Good reliable engine. Problems with clutch and manual transmission. Brakes may pull unevenly.

Body:
Premature fender rusting. Frequent body repairs.

Safety Defects:
Possibility of unsafe front seating assembly and power brake
vacuum check valve.

Recommendation:
Not recommended, unless thoroughly checked by a mechanic.

American Motors 1970
AMBASSADOR

All data based on four-door sedan

Used Car Price* $500
Based on standard equipped car with automatic transmission
and radio.
Price assumes excellent condition.

*Subtract $10 for each month after August for current price.

Statistical Comparison:
Lower than average parts availability.
Higher than average parts cost.

Average depreciation.
Average fuel economy.

Technical Data

Wheelbase	122 in.	Standard Engine	V8
Length	208 in.	Standard Brakes	Drum
Weight	3,700 lbs.	Gasoline Mileage	18
Width	77.24 in.	(with regular fuel)	

Frequency of Repairs:
Very rapid rate of depreciation. Fair gas economy. Serious problems with fuel system and suspension. Some transmission problems also reported.

Body:
Body construction causes accelerated rusting.

Safety Defects:
Possibility of defective power brake vacuum check valve.

Recommendation:
Not recommended. Buy a Hornet instead.

1971 MODELS

CHEVELLE

All data based on four-door sedan

Used Car Price* $700
Based on standard equipped car with automatic transmission
and radio.
Price assumes excellent condition.

*Subtract $15 for each month after August for current price.

Statistical Comparison:
Below average depreciation.
Excellent parts availability.
Below average parts costs.
Excellent gas mileage.

Technical Data

Wheelbase . .	116 in.	Standard Engine . . .	6 cyl. (250)
Length	206.9 in.	Standard Brakes . . .	Drum
Weight	3,550 lbs.	Gasoline Mileage . . .	17.9
Width	76.1 in.	(with regular fuel)	

Frequency of Repairs:
Excellent transmission, motor, and brakes. Some minor problems with the suspension and carburetor. Electrical system and
pollution control device often need adjustment.

Body:
Solid body construction. Excellent paint quality. Some rusting
to be expected around rear trunk and inside door frames.

Safety Defects:
Throttle rod to throttle lever retaining clip on carburetor may
have been incorrectly installed.

Recommendation:
Recommended. One of the best intermediate-sized used cars
on the market.

VEGA

All data based on two-door coupe

Used Car Price* $400
Based on standard equipped car with automatic transmission
and radio.
Price assumes excellent condition.

*Subtract $10 for each month after August for current price.

Statistical Comparison:
Very rapid depreciation.
Expensive parts cost.

Parts often unavailable.
Below average fuel economy.

Technical Data

Wheelbase . .	97 in.	Standard Engine . . .	4 cyl.
Length	169.7 in.	Standard Brakes . . .	Disc-Drum
Weight	2,200 lbs.	Gasoline Mileage . . .	23
Width	65.4 in.	(with regular fuel)	

Frequency of Repairs:
Brake problems, motor overheating, excessive oil consumption, and transmission failure.

Body:
Excessive rusting appearing after only a few months use. Ziebart refuses to guarantee Vegas and Astres.

Safety Defects:
Possibility of defective throttle lever, wheels, steering, Rochester carburetor and power brake vacuum check valve.

Recommendation:
Not recommended. If the rust and sticking accelerator don't get you, the depreciation will. Make GM pay for motor and fender defects through small claims court.

Chevrolet Division   **1971**
General Motors

CHEVY II NOVA

All data based on four-door sedan

Used Car Price* $600
Based on standard equipped car with automatic transmission and radio.
Price assumes excellent condition.

*Subtract $15 for each month after August for current price.

Statistical Comparison:
Excellent parts availability.
Below average depreciation.
Average parts cost.
Excellent fuel economy.

Technical Data

Wheelbase . .	111 in.	Standard Engine	6 cyl.
Length	189.4 in.	Standard Brakes	Drum
Weight	3,200 lbs.	Gasoline Mileage	19
Width	72.4 in.	(with regular fuel)	

Frequency of Repairs:
Good motor, transmission, brakes, and suspension. Troubles reported with carburetor and ignition system.

Body:
Very solid construction. Very few complaints.

Safety Defects:
Possibility of defective throttle lever, wheels, steering, Rochester carburetor and power brake vacuum check valve.

Recommendation:
An ideal used car for a small family.

Chevrolet Division   **1971**
General Motors
CHEVROLET (Full-sized)
Biscayne/Bel Air/Impala/Caprice

Used Car Price* $700

Based on standard equipped car with automatic transmission and radio.
Price assumes excellent condition.

*Subtract $15 for each month after August for current price.

Statistical Comparison:
Excellent parts availability.
Below average depreciation.
Average parts cost.
Excellent fuel economy.

Technical Data

Wheelbase . .	121.5 in.	Standard Engine . . .	6 cyl.
Length	216.8 in.	Standard Brakes . . .	Disc-Drum
Weight	4,000 lbs.	Gasoline Mileage . . .	14
Width	79.5 in.	(with regular fuel)	

Frequency of Repairs:
Minor problems with carburetor and manual transmission. Excellent motor, automatic transmission, and brakes.

Body:
Rusting problems. Also frequent complaints of rattles.

Safety Defects:
Possibility of defective throttle lever, wheels, and steering. Check for defective engine mounts. Possibility of defective power brake vacuum check valve, Rochester carburetor, steering wheel and engine mount restraint.

Recommendedation:
An excellent, inexpensive family car.

PONTIAC VENTURA II

All data based on four-door sedan

Used Car Price* $600
Based on standard equipped car with automatic transmission
and radio.
Price assumes excellent condition.

*Subtract $15 for each month after August for current price.

Statistical Comparison:
Average depreciation.
Low parts cost.
Good parts availability.
Average fuel economy.

Technical Data

Wheelbase . .	111 in.	Standard Engine	6 cyl.
Length	194.5 in.	Standard Brakes	Drum
Weight	3,000 lbs.	Gasoline Mileage	17
Width	72.4 in.	(with regular fuel)	

Frequency of Repairs:
Some minor engine problems, but overall mechanical components are good.

Body:
Good construction, but some rust and water leakage.

Safety Defects:
Possibility of defective tires, steering, throttle lever, and
wheels. Also possibility of defective Rochester carburetor and
power brake vacuum check valve.

Recommendation:
Not recommended. Try the Nova instead.

PONTIAC LE MANS

All data based on four-door sedan

Used Car Price* $700
Based on standard equipped car with automatic transmission
and radio.
Price assumes excellent condition.

*Subtract $25 for each month after August for current price.

Statistical Comparison:
Average parts cost.
Average parts availability.
Below average fuel economy.
Rapid depreciation.

Technical Data

Wheelbase . .	116 in.	Standard Engine	6 cyl.
Length	206.8 in.	Standard Brakes	Drum
Weight	3,400 lbs.	Gasoline Mileage	14
Width	76.7 in.	(with regular fuel)	

Frequency of Repairs:
Some small problems with motor and transmission. Brakes, electrical system, and carburetor are excellent.

Body:
Some rusting around doors. A few rattles reported.

Safety Defects:
Possibility of defective tires, steering, throttle lever, and wheels. Also possibility of defective Rochester carburetor and power brake vacuum check valve.

Recommendation:
Recommended.

Pontiac Division　　　　　　　　　　　　　　　　　**1971**
General Motors

PONTIAC (Full-sized)
Catalina/Executive/Bonneville/
Laurentian/Parisienne

All data based on four-door sedan

Used Car Price* $900
Based on standard equipped car with automatic transmission and radio.
Price assumes excellent condition.

*Subtract $15 for each month after August for current price.

Statistical Comparison:
Average depreciation.
Low parts cost.
Good parts availability.
Average fuel economy.

Technical Data

Wheelbase . .	123.5 in.	Standard Engine . . .	V8
Length	220.2 in.	Standard Brakes . . .	Disc-Drum
Weight	4,200 lbs.	Gasoline Mileage . . .	10
Width	79.5 in.	(with regular fuel)	

Frequency of Repairs:
Suspension and carburetor problems.

Body:
Rusting and rattles.

Safety Defects:
Possibility of defective tires, steering, throttle lever, and wheels. Also possibility of defective Rochester carburetor and power brake vacuum check valve.

Recommendation:
Recommended. A good family car.

Buick Division 1971
General Motors
BUICK (Full-sized)
Le Sabre/Centurion/Electra

All data based on four-door sedan

Used Car Price* $900
Based on standard equipped car with automatic transmission
and radio.
Price assumes excellent condition.

*Subtract $15 for each month after August for current price.

Statistical Comparison:
Average fuel economy.
Excellent parts availability.
Low parts cost.
Average depreciation.

Technical Data
Wheelbase . .	124 in.	Standard Engine . . .	V8
Length	220.74 in.	Standard Brakes . . .	Disc-Drum
Weight	4,200 lbs.	Gasoline Mileage . . .	12
Width	79.72 in.	(with regular fuel)	

Frequency of Repairs:
Excellent mechanical components. Brakes, suspension, and
motor are very durable.

Body:
The only weak point. Premature rusting around doors. Rattles
are common.

Safety Defects:
Possibility of defective wheels and steering. Le Sabre model
may have defective headlamp switch. Also possibility of defective Rochester carburetor and power brake vacuum check valve.

Recommendation:
Recommended, but check the safety defects.

Oldsmobile Division 1971
General Motors
OLDSMOBILE (Full-sized)

All data based on four-door sedan

Used Car Price* $900
Based on standard equipped car with automatic transmission
and radio.
Price assumes excellent condition.

*Subtract $15 for each month after August for current price.

Statistical Comparison:
Average depreciation.
Good parts availability.
Average parts cost.
Good fuel economy.

Technical Data
Wheelbase . .	124 in.	Standard Engine . . .	V8
Length	220.2 in.	Standard Brakes . . .	Disc-Drum
Weight	4,200 lbs.	Gasoline Mileage . . .	12
Width	79.5 in.	(with regular fuel)	

Frequency of Repairs:
Excellent motor, transmission, and brakes. Minor problems with suspension.

Body:
Excellent body construction.

Safety Defects:
Possibility of defective wheels and steering. Also possibility of defective carburetor and power brake vacuum check valve.

Recommendation:
Recommended. A good buy as a family car.

Ford Division   **1971**
Ford Motor Company
FORD PINTO/BOBCAT

All data based on two-door sedan

Used Car Price* $500
Based on standard equipped car with automatic transmission and radio.
Price assumes excellent condition.

*Subtract $20 for each month after August for current price.

Statistical Comparison:
Rapid depreciation.
Average parts cost.
Average parts availability.
Average fuel economy.

Technical Data
Wheelbase . .	94 in.	Standard Engine	4 cyl.
Length	163 in.	Standard Brakes	Drum
Weight	2,100 lbs.	Gasoline Mileage	22
Width	69.4 in.	(with regular fuel)	

Frequency of Repairs:
Good brakes and electrical system. Problems with transmission, carburetor, and motor.

Body:
Need for frequent door adjustments. Body is rust-prone.

Safety Defects:
Possibility accelerator may stick, clutch cable may cause loss of oil and engine damage or car may burst into flames.

Recommendation:
Not recommended. Car will easily fall to pieces.

Ford Division 1971
Ford Motor Company
FORD MAVERICK

All data based on four-door sedan

Used Car Price* $800
Based on standard equipped car with automatic transmission and radio.
Price assumes excellent condition.

*Subtract $10 for each month after August for current price.

Statistical Comparison:
Low depreciation.
Inexpensive parts.
Average parts availability.
Good fuel economy.

Technical Data

Wheelbase	109.9 in.	Standard Engine	6 cyl.
Length	186.3 in.	Standard Brakes	Drum
Weight	2,700 lbs.	Gasoline Mileage	22
Width	70.6 in.	(with regular fuel)	

Frequency of Repairs:
Excellent motor and electrical system. Problems with brakes, carburetor, and automatic transmission.

Body:
Excessive rusting in front fenders around door, on hood, and in trunk.

Safety Defects:
Possibility of defective 15 × 5.5 and 15 × 6.5 single-piece wheel, brake master cylinder, 4 barrel carburetor, power brake vacuum check valve, and gas tank.

Recommendation:
Not recommended. A waste of money.

FORD MUSTANG

All data based on two-door hardtop

Used Car Price* $800
Based on standard equipped car with automatic transmission
and radio.
Price assumes excellent condition.

*Subtract $25 for each month after August for current price.

Statistical Comparison:
Rapid depreciation.
Average parts cost.
Average parts availability.
Terrible fuel economy.

Technical Data

Wheelbase . .	109 in.	Standard Engine	6 cyl.
Length	189.5 in.	Standard Brakes	Drum
Weight	3,200 lbs.	Gasoline Mileage	14
Width	74.1 in.	(with regular fuel)	

Frequency of Repairs:
Problems with suspension, transmission, and heating system.
Excellent motor and electrical system.

Body:
Excessive rusting. "J-67" warranty extension applies.

Safety Defects:
Possibility of steering defects, wheel defects, and defective master cylinder and power brake vacuum check valve.

Recommendation:
Not recommended. Ford should not have changed the first
1965 Mustang.

FORD TORINO/MONTEGO

All data based on four-door sedan

Used Car Price* $800
Based on standard equipped car with automatic transmission
and radio.
Price assumes excellent condition.

*Subtract $25 for each month after August for current price.

Statistical Comparison:
Very rapid depreciation.
Average parts cost.
Average parts availability.
Below average fuel economy.

Technical Data

Wheelbase . .	117 in.	Standard Engine	6 cyl.
Length . . .	206.2 in.	Standard Brakes	Drum
Weight	3,400 lbs.	Gasoline Mileage	15
Width	76.4 in.	(with regular fuel)	

Frequency of Repairs:
Problems with brakes, transmission, suspension, and steering.

Body:
Excessive rusting. Complaints of rattles and paint peeling.

Safety Defects:
Possibility of defective seat belts, hood latch, 15 × 5.5 single-piece wheel, brake master cylinder, 4 barrel carburetor, and power brake vacuum check valve.

Recommendation:
Not recommended. Corrosion problems too extensive.

Ford Division   **1971**
Ford Motor Company
FORD (Full-sized)
Custom/Galaxie/LTD

All data based on four-door sedan

Used Car Price* $900
Based on standard equipped car with automatic transmission and radio.
Price assumes excellent condition.

*Subtract $15 for each month after August for current price.

Statistical Comparison:
Rapid depreciation.
Low parts cost.
Excellent parts availability.
Good fuel economy.

Technical Data

Wheelbase . .	121 in.	Standard Engine	6 cyl.
Length	216.2 in.	Standard Brakes	Drum
Weight	4,100 lbs.	Gasoline Mileage	14
Width	79.3 in.	(with regular fuel)	

Frequency of Repairs:
Problems with idler arms. Some complaints concerning carburetor and suspension.

Body:
Excessive rusting in front fenders and around doors. Not one of Ford's better ideas. Also paint quality inferior to other models.

Safety Defects:
Possibility of defective seat belts, power brake vacuum check valve, 15 × 5.5 and 15 × 6.5 single-piece wheel, 4 barrel carburetor, master cylinder, and hood latch mechanism.

Recommendation:
Not recommended. An average car with serious rust problems. Warranty extension "J-67" applies.

Plymouth Division   **1971**
Chrysler Corporation
PLYMOUTH VALIANT
Duster/Scamp

All data based on four-door sedan

Used Car Price* $1,000
Based on standard equipped car with automatic transmission and radio.
Price assumes excellent condition.

*Subtract $10 for each month after August for current price.

Statistical Comparison:
Low depreciation.
Low parts cost.
Excellent parts availability.
Excellent fuel economy.

Technical Data

Wheelbase . .	108 in.	Standard Engine	6 cyl.
Length	188.4 in.	Standard Brakes	Drum
Weight	3,000 lbs.	Gasoline Mileage	19
Width	71.1 in.	(with regular fuel)	

Frequency of Repairs:
Excellent mechanical components. Some transmission, brake, and clutch problems.

Body:
Excellent body construction, except for front fender rusting.

Safety Defects:
Possibility of defective brake linings and front wheel bearings. Also possibility of defective exhaust manifold, power brake vacuum check valve, and brake proportioning valve.

Recommendation:
Recommended. One of the best cars made. Six cylinder motor is best.

DODGE DART
Demon/Swinger

All data based on four-door sedan

Used Car Price* $1,000
Based on standard equipped car with automatic transmission
and radio.
Price assumes excellent condition.

*Subtract $10 for each month after August for current price.

Statistical Comparison:
Low depreciation.
Below average parts cost.
Excellent parts availability.
Excellent fuel economy.

Technical Data
Wheelbase . .	111 in.	Standard Engine	6 cyl.
Length	196.2 in.	Standard Brakes	Drum
Weight	3,000 lbs.	Gasoline Mileage.	19
Width	69.7 in.	(with regular fuel)	

Frequency of Repairs:
Serious brake problems. Transmission and clutch complaints.
Excellent motor, carburetor, and electrical system.

Body:
Excellent body construction. Very rust-resistant, except for
front fender rust perforations.

Safety Defects:
Possibility of defective brake linings and defective front wheel
bearings. Also possible defective power brake vacuum check
valve, cracking exhaust manifold, and brake proportioning
valve.

Recommendation:
Recommended. One of the best cars on the market. Six cylinder
superior to eight.

PLYMOUTH SATELLITE
Belvedere/Sebring

All data based on four-door sedan

Used Car Price* $900
Based on standard equipped car with automatic transmission
and radio.
Price assumes excellent condition.

*Subtract $15 for each month after August for current price.

Statistical Comparison:
Average depreciation.
Average parts cost.
Average parts availability.
Below average fuel economy.

Technical Data

Wheelbase . .	117 in.	Standard Engine	6 cyl.
Length	204.6 in.	Standard Brakes	Drum
Weight	3,400 lbs.	Gasoline Mileage.	17
Width	78.6 in.	(with regular fuel)	

Frequency of Repairs:
Problems with brakes, suspension, and electrical system.

Body:
Excessive rusting. Also complaints of rattles.

Safety Defects:
Possibility of defective brakes, front seats, disc brakes, and power steering. Possibility of defective power brake vacuum check valve and exhaust manifold cracking.

Recommendation:
Not recommended. Dodge Dart a better buy.

Dodge Division   **1971**
Chrysler Corporation
DODGE (Full-sized)
Polara/Monaco/Brougham

All data based on four-door sedan

Used Car Price* $900
Based on standard equipped car with automatic transmission and radio.
Price assumes excellent condition.

*Subtract $25 for each month after August for current price.

Statistical Comparison:
Rapid depreciation.
Average parts availability and cost.
Below average fuel economy.

Technical Data

Wheelbase . .	122 in.	Standard Engine . . .	V8
Length	220.2 in.	Standard Brakes . . .	Disc-Drum
Weight	3,900 lbs.	Gasoline Mileage . . .	13
Width	79.2 in.	(with regular fuel)	

Frequency of Repairs:
Serious complaints concerning brakes. Also problems with suspension and transmission.

Body:
Very rust prone, but good paint quality. Front fenders rust prone.

Safety Defects:
Possibility of defective front brakes and windshield defroster. Also possibility of defective power brake vacuum check valve and exhaust manifold cracking (V6).

Recommendation:
Not recommended. Too big, too wasteful, and too fragile.

Plymouth Division   **1971**
Chrysler Corporation
PLYMOUTH FURY

All data based on four-door sedan

Used Car Price* $900
Based on standard equipped car with automatic transmission and radio.
Price assumes excellent condition.

*Subtract $15 for each month after August for current price.

Statistical Comparison:
Average depreciation.
Average parts cost.
Average parts availability.
Below average fuel economy.

Technical Data

Wheelbase . .	120 in.	Standard Engine	6 cyl.
Length	215.1 in.	Standard Brakes	Drum
Weight	3,900 lbs.	Gasoline Mileage	13
Width	79.6 in.	(with regular fuel)	

Frequency of Repairs:
Brake, suspension, and electrical system problems.

Body:
Rusting and paint peeling. Front fenders rust-prone.

Safety Defects:
Possibility of defective brakes, exhaust manifold, and power brake vacuum check valve.

Recommendation:
Not recommended. A lot of old police cars around.

American Motors   **1971**
AMC HORNET

All data based on four-door sedan

Used Car Price* $800
Based on standard equipped car with automatic transmission and radio.
Price assumes excellent condition.

*Subtract $15 for each month after August for current price.

Statistical Comparison:
Average depreciation.
Average parts availability.
Average parts cost.
Good fuel economy.

Technical Data
Wheelbase . .	108 in.	Standard Engine . . .	6 cyl.
Length	179.26 in.	Standard Brakes . . .	Disc-Drum
Weight	2,800 lbs.	Gasoline Mileage . . .	19
Width	70.58 in.	(with regular fuel)	

Frequency of Repairs:
Serious clutch and fuel system problems. Problems reported with both automatic and standard transmissions.

Body:
Frequent complaints concerning rattles, rusting, and exterior body construction.

Safety Defects:
Possibility of defective door locks and leaking gas tank. Also possible defective power brake vacuum check valve.

Recommendation:
Not recommended. Frequent mechanical failures.

American Motors   **1971**
AMC GREMLIN

All data based on two-door sedan

Used Car Price* $600
Based on standard equipped car with automatic transmission and radio.
Price assumes excellent condition.

*Subtract $15 for each month after August for current price.

Statistical Comparison:
Average depreciation.
Average parts availability.
Average parts cost.
Good fuel economy.

Technical Data
Wheelbase . .	96 in.	Standard Engine	6 cyl.
Length	161.25 in.	Standard Brakes	Drum
Weight	2,700 lbs.	Gasoline Mileage	22
Width	70.6 in.	(with regular fuel)	

Frequency of Repairs:
Same problems as 1970 model, with the manual transmission still causing problems.

Body:
As with Ambassador, this model has an improved construction.

Safety Defects:
Possibility of defective door locks and leaking gas tank. Also, possibility of defective power brake vacuum check valve.

Recommendation:
Recommended, but don't pay very much for it.

American Motors   **1971**
AMBASSADOR

All data based on four-door sedan

Used Car Price* $600
Based on standard equipped car with automatic transmission and radio.
Price assumes excellent condition.

*Subtract $20 for each month after August for current price.

Statistical Comparison:
Rapid depreciation.
Average parts availability.
Average parts cost.
Below average fuel economy.

Technical Data
Wheelbase . .	122 in.	Standard Engine	V8
Length	210.78 in.	Standard Brakes	Drum
Weight	3,400 lbs.	Gasoline Mileage.	14
Width	77.24 in.	(with regular fuel)	

Frequency of Repairs:
Improved fuel system and better assembled body. Suspension problems still prevalent. Some problems with brakes.

Body:
Much improved assembly. Little exterior rusting, though exhaust system vulnerable to rust.

Safety Defects:
Possibility of leaking gas tank, and a defective jack. Also possibility of defective power brake vacuum check valve.

Recommendation:
Not recommended. Dart or Valiant a better buy.

1972 MODELS

VEGA

All data based on two-door sedan

Used Car Price* $500
Based on standard equipped car with automatic transmission
and radio.
Price assumes excellent condition.

*Subtract $20 for each month after August for current price.

Statistical Comparison:
Very rapid depreciation.
Expensive parts cost.
Parts often unavailable.
Below average fuel economy.

Technical Data

Wheelbase . .	97 in.	Standard Engine . . .	4 cyl.
Length	169.7 in.	Standard Brakes . . .	Disc-Drum
Weight	2,200 lbs.	Gasoline Mileage . . .	21
Width	65.4 in.	(with regular fuel)	

Frequency of Repairs:
Brake problems, major motor problems, excessive oil consumption. Reports of transmission failures.

Body:
Body was made for sunshine, not snow. Very excessive rusting
all over vehicle. Ziebart refuse to guarantee Vega and Astre.

Safety Defects:
Possibility of defective muffler, throttle cable, and rear axle.
Also possibility of defective steering relay rod.

Recommendation:
Not recommended. GM should be ashamed of itself for making
this car. Many court claims won against GM for defective motor
and fenders for 1971–1974 models. Warranty extended.

Chevrolet Division   **1972**
General Motors

CHEVY II NOVA

All data based on four-door sedan

Used Car Price* $800
Based on standard equipped car with automatic transmission
and radio.
Price assumes excellent condition.

*Subtract $15 for each month after August for current price.

Statistical Comparison:
Excellent parts availability.
Below average depreciation.

Average parts cost.
Excellent fuel economy.

Technical Data

Wheelbase . .	111 in.	Standard Engine	6 cyl.
Length	189.4 in.	Standard Brakes	Drum
Weight	3,200 lbs.	Gasoline Mileage	18
Width	72.5 in.	(with regular fuel)	

Frequency of Repairs:
8 cylinder is the better model. 6 cylinder has brakes, motor, and carburetor problems.

Body:
Solid construction with little rusting.

Safety Defects:
Possibility of defective steering and engine mounts. May not have Federal Motor Vehicle Safety Act stickers. Also possibility of defective Rochester carburetor and engine mounts restraint.

Recommendation:
Not recommended. Too many mechanical problems.

Chevrolet Division   **1972**
General Motors
CHEVELLE

All data based on four-door sedan

Used Car Price* $1,000
Based on standard equipped car with automatic transmission and radio.
Price assumes excellent condition.

*Subtract $15 for each month after August for current price.

Statistical Comparison:
Low depreciation.
Average parts cost.
Average fuel economy.
Excellent parts availability.

Technical Data

Wheelbase . .	116 in.	Standard Engine . . .	6 cyl.
Length	201.5 in.	Standard Brakes . . .	Disc-Drum
Weight	3,300 lbs.	Gasoline Mileage . . .	12
Width	75.4 in.	(with regular fuel)	

Frequency of Repairs:
8 cylinder motor better than 6. Minor brake problems. Excellent mechanical components.

Body:
Excessive rusting all over vehicle.

Safety Defects:
Possibility of defective steering and engine mounts. Also possibility of defective Rochester carburetor and engine mounts restraint.

Recommendation:
Recommended. Not as good as full-sized Chevrolet. Watch out for premature rusting.

Chevrolet Division   **1972**
General Motors
CHEVROLET (Full-sized)
Biscayne/Bel Air/Impala

All data based on four-door sedan

Used Car Price* $1,000
Based on standard equipped car with automatic transmission and radio.
Price assumes excellent condition.

*Subtract $15 for each month after August for current price.

Statistical Comparison:
Excellent parts availability.
Low depreciation.
Average parts cost.
Average fuel economy.

Technical Data

Wheelbase . .	121.5 in.	Standard Engine . . .	6 cyl.
Length	219.9 in.	Standard Brakes . . .	Disc-Drum
Weight	4,000 lbs.	Gasoline Mileage . . .	11
Width	79.5 in.	(with regular fuel)	

Frequency of Repairs
Minor problems with transmission and brakes.

Body:
Some rusting around fenders. Solid body construction.

Safety Defects:
Possibility of defective steering and engine mounts. Also possibility of defective Rochester carburetor, and engine mounts restraint.

Recommendation:
Recommended. First verify engine mounts.

PONTIAC VENTURA II

All data based on four-door sedan

Used Car Price* $900
Based on standard equipped car with automatic transmission
and radio.
Price assumes excellent condition.

*Subtract $20 for each month after August for current price.

Statistical Comparison:
Average depreciation.
Low parts cost.
Good parts availability.
Below average fuel economy.

Technical Data

Wheelbase . .	111 in.	Standard Engine	6 cyl.
Length	194.5 in.	Standard Brakes	Drum
Weight	3,300 lbs.	Gasoline Mileage.	12
Width	72.4 in.	(with regular fuel)	

Frequency of Repairs:
Serious problems with motor, carburetor, and transmission.

Body:
Excessive rusting, rattles, and water leakage in rear trunk.

Safety Defects:
Possibility of electrical fire, defective steering, tire, engine
mounts, and non-compliance with Federal Motor Vehicle
Safety Act. Also possibility of defective Rochester carburetor.

Recommendation:
Not recommended. May present serious safety hazards.

PONTIAC LE MANS

All data based on four-door sedan

Used Car Price* $1,000
Based on standard equipped car with automatic transmission
and radio.
Price assumes excellent condition.

*Subtract $25 for each month after August for current price.

Statistical Comparison:
Average parts cost.
Average parts availability.
Rapid depreciation.
Below average fuel economy.

Technical Data

Wheelbase . .	116 in.	Standard Engine	6 cyl.
Length	207.2 in.	Standard Brakes	Drum
Weight	3,400 lbs.	Gasoline Mileage	12
Width	76.7 in.	(with regular fuel)	

Frequency of Repairs:
Much improved motor and transmission. Minor problems with carburetor and pollution control device.

Body:
Some rusting and paint peeling.

Safety Defects:
Possibility of defective steering and motor mounts. May also catch on fire. Rochester carburetor could be defective.

Recommendation:
Not recommended. Car may be hazardous to your health.

Pontiac Division   **1972**
General Motors

PONTIAC (Full-sized)
Catalina/Executive

All data based on four-door sedan

Used Car Price* $1,000
Based on standard equipped car with automatic transmission and radio.
Price assumes excellent condition.

*Subtract $20 for each month after August for current price.

Statistical Comparison:
Average depreciation.
Low parts cost.
Good parts availability.
Below average fuel economy.

Technical Data

Wheelbase . .	123.5 in.	Standard Engine . . .	V8
Length	220.2 in.	Standard Brakes . . .	Disc-Drum
Weight	4,300 lbs.	Gasoline Mileage . . .	9
Width	79.3 in.	(with regular fuel)	

Frequency of Repairs:
Excellent motor and carburetor. Minor problems with transmission.

Body:
Good body construction. Some rattles still present. Minor paint problems.

Safety Defects:
Possibility of defective Rochester carburetor.

Recommendation:
Recommended. A much improved vehicle.

Buick Division   **1972**
General Motors
BUICK (Full-sized)
Le Sabre/Centurion/Electra

All data based on four-door sedan hardtop

Used Car Price* $1,100
Based on standard equipped car with automatic transmission
and radio.
Price assumes excellent condition.

*Subtract $20 for each month after August for current price.

Statistical Comparison:
Excellent parts availability.
Average parts cost.
Average depreciation.
Below average fuel economy.

Technical Data

Wheelbase . .	124 in.	Standard Engine . . .	V8
Length	220.9 in.	Standard Brakes . . .	Disc-Drum
Weight	4,400 lbs.	Gasoline Mileage . . .	11
Width	79.7 in.	(with regular fuel)	

Frequency of Repairs:
All mechanical components of good quality. Some minor transmission problems.

Body:
Body construction improved greatly. Still some rusting around
doors.

Safety Defects:
Possibility of defective steering components and Rochester carburetor.

Recommendation:
Recommended. One of GM's best.

Oldsmobile Division   **1972**
General Motors
OLDSMOBILE DELTA 88

All data based on four-door sedan

Used Car Price* $1,100
Based on standard equipped car with automatic transmission
and radio.
Price assumes excellent condition.

*Subtract $20 for each month after August for current price.

Statistical Comparison:
Average depreciation.
Good parts availability.
Good parts cost.
Average fuel economy.

Technical Data

Wheelbase . .	124 in.	Standard Engine . . .	V8
Length	22.1 in.	Standard Brakes . . .	Disc-Drum
Weight	4,300 lbs.	Gasoline Mileage . . .	11
Width	79.5 in.	(with regular fuel)	

Frequency of Repairs:
Excellent motor, electrical system, and carburetor. Problems with transmission.

Body:
Solid construction. Some paint problems.

Safety Defects:
Possibility of defective steering components and Rochester carburetor.

Recommendation:
Recommended. Excellent transportation as a family car.

Ford Division   **1972**
Ford Motor Company
FORD PINTO/BOBCAT

All data based on two-door sedan

Used Car Price* $700
Based on standard equipped car with automatic transmission and radio.
Price assumes excellent condition.

*Subtract $25 for each month after August for current price.

Statistical Comparison:
Rapid depreciation.
Average parts cost.
Average parts availability.
Average fuel economy.

Technical Data

Wheelbase . .	94.2 in.	Standard Engine . . .	4 cyl.
Length	163 in.	Standard Brakes . . .	Disc-Drum
Weight	2,100 lbs.	Gasoline Mileage . . .	22
Width	69.4 in.	(with regular fuel)	

Frequency of Repairs:
Good suspension and brakes. Problems with motor and transmission.

Body:
Problems with rattles, leakage, and severe rusting around doors, fenders, and trunk.

Safety Defects:
Possibility of defective bolts, rear wheel well, and rack and pinion steering.

Recommendation:
Not recommended. Too small, too rusty, and too expensive. Gas tank a mobile molotov cocktail.

Ford Division   **1972**
Ford Motor Company

FORD MAVERICK

All data based on four-door sedan

Used Car Price* $900
Based on standard equipped car with automatic transmission and radio.
Price assumes excellent condition.

*Subtract $15 for each month after August for current price.

Statistical Comparison:
Rapid depreciation.
Low parts cost.
Good parts availability.
Good fuel economy.

Technical Data

Wheelbase . .	109.9 in.	Standard Engine	6 cyl.
Length	186.3 in.	Standard Brakes	Drum
Weight	2,700 lbs.	Gasoline Mileage	20
Width	70.6 in.	(with regular fuel)	

Frequency of Repairs:
Excellent motor and transmission. Problems with brakes and carburetor.

Body:
Excessive rusting in front fenders, around door, and in rear trunk.

Safety Defects:
Unsafe placement of rear gas tank according to U.S. Army Engineers, and also defective 4 barrel carburetor.

Recommendation:
Not recommended. Premature rusting too extensive.

FORD MUSTANG

All data based on two-door hardtop

Used Car Price* $1,100
Based on standard equipped car with automatic transmission
and radio.
Price assumes excellent condition.

*Subtract $25 for each month after August for current price.

Statistical Comparison:
Rapid depreciation.
Average parts cost.
Average parts availability.
Terrible fuel economy.

Technical Data

Wheelbase . .	109 in.	Standard Engine	6 cyl.
Length	189.5 in.	Standard Brakes	Drum
Weight	3,200 lbs.	Gasoline Mileage	11
Width	74.1 in.	(with regular fuel)	

Frequency of Repairs:
Problems with transmission and suspension. Excellent brakes
and electrical system. Motor may have valve guide defects.

Body:
Excessive rusting around doors, front fenders, and trunk.

Safety Defects:
Unsafe placement of rear gas tank, also possibility of defective
4 barrel carburetor.

Recommendation:
Not recommended. Ford "J-67" warranty extension applies.

FORD TORINO/MONTEGO

All data are based on four-door sedan hardtop

Used Car Price* $1,000
Based on standard equipped car with automatic transmission
and radio.
Price assumes excellent condition.

*Subtract $25 for each month after August for current price.

Statistical Comparison:
Very rapid depreciation.
Average parts cost.
Average parts availability.
Below average fuel economy.

Technical Data

Wheelbase . .	118 in.	Standard Engine	6 cyl.
Length	207.7 in.	Standard Brakes	Drum
Weight	3,700 lbs.	Gasoline Mileage.	12
Width	79.3 in.	(with regular fuel)	

Frequency of Repairs:
Problems with brakes, transmission, and suspension. Good electrical system and motor.

Body:
Excessive door and fender rusting. Complaints of rattles and paint peeling.

Safety Defects:
Possibility of defective rear axle, seat belts, and wheel bearings. Also possibility of defective 4 barrel carburetor and rear axle assembly.

Recommendation:
Not recommended. This model can be very expensive to repair rusting damage. Ford extended rust warranty ("J-67").

Ford Division   **1972**
Ford Motor Company
FORD (Full-sized)
Custom/Galaxie/LTD

All data based on four-door sedan

Used Car Price* $1,200
Based on standard equipped car with automatic transmission and radio.
Price assumes excellent condition.

*Subtract $20 for each month after August for current price.

Statistical Comparison:
Rapid depreciation.
Low parts cost.
Excellent parts availability.
Good fuel economy.

Technical Data

Wheelbase . .	121 in.	Standard Engine	6 cyl.
Length	218.4 in.	Standard Brakes	Drum
Weight	4,100 lbs.	Gasoline Mileage.	12
Width	79.2 in.	(with regular fuel)	

Frequency of Repairs:
Excellent brakes and electrical system. Problems with idler arms and carburetor. Motor has valve guide defects.

Body:
Numerous rusting and paint problems, especially along fenders, doors and rear trunk.

Safety Defects
Possibility of defective bumper jacks and 4 barrel carburetor.

Recommendation:
Not recommended. An average car with serious rust problems.
Ford "J-67" warranty extension applies.

Plymouth Division   **1972**
Chrysler Corporation
PLYMOUTH VALIANT
Duster/Scamp

All data based on four-door sedan

Used Car Price* $1,300
Based on standard equipped car with automatic transmission
and radio.
Price assumes excellent condition.

*Subtract $15 for each month after August for current
price.

Statistical Comparison:
Very low depreciation.
Low parts cost.
Excellent parts availability.
Excellent fuel economy.

Technical Data

Wheelbase . .	108 in.	Standard Engine	6 cyl.
Length	188.4 in.	Standard Brakes	Drum
Weight	2,900 lbs.	Gasoline Mileage	20
Width	71 in.	(with regular fuel)	

Frequency of Repairs:
Minor problems with brakes, transmission, and anti-pollution
device. Excellent mechanical components.

Body:
Excellent body construction. Rusting perforations of front
fenders.

Safety Defects:
Possibility of defective alternator and front seats. Also possibility of defective exhaust manifold and brake proportioning
valve.

Recommendation:
Recommended. An excellent new or used car buy. Six cylinder
engine is preferred. Verify fender rusting.

DODGE DART
Demon/Swinger

All data based on four-door sedan

Used Car Price* $1,300
Based on standard equipped car with automatic transmission
and radio.
Price assumes excellent condition.

*Subtract $15 for each month after August for current price.

Statistical Comparison:
Very low depreciation.
Below average parts cost.
Excellent parts availability.
Excellent fuel economy.

Technical Data

Wheelbase	111 in.	Standard Engine	6 cyl.
Length	196.2 in.	Standard Brakes	Drum
Weight	2,900 lbs.	Gasoline Mileage	20
Width	69.6 in.	(with regular fuel)	

Frequency of Repairs:
6 cylinder better than 8. All other mechanical components excellent except automatic transmission. Some problems with
brakes locking in emergency stops.

Body:
Excellent body construction. No rusting except for front fenders.

Safety Defects:
Possibility of defective alternator and front seats. Also possibility of defective exhaust manifold and brake proportioning
valve.

Recommendation:
Recommended. There is no better car available.

PLYMOUTH SATELLITE
Sebring

All data based on four-door sedan

Used Car Price* $1,100
Based on standard equipped car with automatic transmission
and radio.
Price assumes excellent condition.

*Subtract $25 for each month after August for current price.

Statistical Comparison:
Average depreciation.
Average parts cost.
Average parts availability.
Below average fuel economy.

Technical Data
Wheelbase . .	117 in.	Standard Engine	6 cyl.
Length	204.6 in.	Standard Brakes	Drum
Weight	3,400 lbs.	Gasoline Mileage	14
Width	78.6 in.	(with regular fuel)	

Frequency of Repairs:
Problems with suspension (loose), brakes, and cooling system.

Body:
Some minor rusting. Body construction not up to average, especially front fenders.

Safety Defects:
Possibility of defective speedometer, suspension, and power steering. Also possibility of defective six cylinder exhaust manifold.

Recommendation:
Not recommended. Dart or Fury a better buy.

Dodge Division   **1972**
Chrysler Corporation
DODGE (Full-sized)
Polaro/Monaco

All data based on four-door sedan

Used Car Price* $1,200
Based on standard equipped car with automatic transmission and radio.
Price assumes excellent condition.

*Subtract $25 for each month after August for current price.

Statistical Comparison:
Rapid depreciation.
Average parts availability and cost.
Below average fuel economy.

Technical Data
Wheelbase . .	122 in.	Standard Engine . . .	8 cyl.
Length	219.4 in.	Standard Brakes . . .	Disc-Drum
Weight	4,000 lbs.	Gasoline Mileage . . .	11
Width	79.6 in.	(with regular fuel)	

Frequency of Repairs:
A much improved car. Brakes are still a minor problem.

Body:
Still very rust-resistant. Complaints concerning exterior finish. Front fenders rust-prone.

Safety Defects:
Possibility of defective front suspension and power steering.

Recommendation:
Not recommended.

Plymouth Division   **1972**
Chrysler Corporation
PLYMOUTH FURY (Full-sized)

All data based on four-door sedan

Used Car Price* $1,100
Based on standard equipped car with automatic transmission
and radio.
Price assumes excellent condition.

*Subtract $20 for each month after August for current
price.

Statistical Comparison:
Below average depreciation.
Average parts cost.
Average parts availability.
Below average fuel economy.

Technical Data

Wheelbase . .	120 in.	Standard Engine	6 cyl.
Length	217.2 in.	Standard Brakes	Drum
Weight	4,000 lbs.	Gasoline Mileage	12
Width	79.9 in.	(with regular fuel)	

Frequency of Repairs:
A much improved car. but still problems with steering, brakes
and electrical system. Excellent motor and transmission. Some
high-speed vibration.

Body:
Some rusting, but body construction much improved. Front
fenders rustprone.

Safety Defects:
Possibility of defective bumper jack and six cylinder exhaust
manifold.

Recommendation:
Recommended. Make sure vehicle is not an ex-taxi or police
car.

AMC HORNET

All data based on four-door sedan

Used Car Price* $1,000
Based on standard equipped car with automatic transmission
and radio.
Price assumes excellent condition.

*Subtract $20 for each month after August for current price.

Statistical Comparison:
Below average depreciation.
Average parts cost.
Average parts availability.
Good fuel economy.

Technical Data
Wheelbase . .	108 in.	Standard Engine	6 cyl.
Length	179.3 in.	Standard Brakes	Drum
Weight	2,700 lbs.	Gasoline Mileage.	18
Width	70.6 in.	(with regular fuel)	

Frequency of Repairs:
Same problems as '71 model. Motor is excellent.

Body:
Improved construction, but still causes problems.

Safety Defects:
Possibility of defective disc brakes and brake pedals.

Recommendation:
Not recommended.

AMC GREMLIN

All data based on two-door sedan

Used Car Price* $800
Based on standard equipped car with automatic transmission
and radio.
Price assumes excellent condition.

*Subtract $20 for each month after August for current price.

Statistical Comparison:
Below average depreciation.
Average parts cost.
Average parts availability.
Good fuel economy.

Technical Data
Wheelbase . .	96 in.	Standard Engine	6 cyl.
Length	161.3 in.	Standard Brakes	Drum

Weight . . . . 2,600 lbs. Gasoline Mileage 21
Width . . . . . 70.6 in.   (with regular fuel)

Frequency of Repairs:
Problems with carburetion, brakes, and transmission. Good motor, electrical system and automatic transmission.

Body:
Solidly constructed, few rust problems.

Safety Defects:
Possibility of defective disc brakes, brake pedals, and lamp reflectors.

Recommendation:
Recommended. Much improved over '71 model.

American Motors   **1972**
AMBASSADOR

All data based on four-door sedan

Used Car Price* $900
Based on standard equipped car with automatic transmission and radio.
Price assumes excellent condition.

*Subtract $25 for each month after August for current price.

Statistical Comparison:
Rapid depreciation.
Average parts availability.
Average parts cost.
Average fuel economy.

Technical Data

Wheelbase . .	122 in.	Standard Engine	8 cyl.
Length	210.8 in.	Standard Brakes	Drum
Weight	2,780 lbs.	Gasoline Mileage	12
Width	77.2 in.	(with regular fuel)	

Frequency of Repairs:
Suspension problems still reported. Exhaust system problems. Transmission complaints. Brakes and motor are good.

Body:
Excellent body construction. Highly rust-resistant.

Safety Defects:
Insufficient data.

Recommendation:
Not recommended. Not a good year for American Motors.

1973 MODELS

VEGA/ASTRE

All data based on two-door coupe

Used Car Price* $800
Based on standard equipped car with automatic transmission
and radio.
Price assumes excellent condition.

*Subtract $25 for each month after August for current price.

Statistical Comparison:
Incredibly rapid depreciation.
Unreasonable parts cost.
Parts often unavailable.
Terrible fuel economy.

Technical Data

Wheelbase . .	97 in.	Standard Engine . . .	V4 (140)
Length	172.2 in.	Standard Brakes . . .	Disc-Drum
Weight	2,268 lbs.	Gasoline Mileage . . .	13
Width	65.4 in.	(with regular fuel)	

Frequency of Repairs:
Premature brake wear, high oil consumption, and frequent
motor overheating. GM made a secret warranty extension for
motor repairs.

Body:
Excessive rusting all over vehicle. Ziebart refuses to guarantee
Vegas and Astres. GM warranty extension provides for free
fender replacement.

Safety Defects:
Possibility of steering lock-up due to foreign objects and defective steering relay rod.

Recommendation:
Not recommended. A masochist's dream car. Many motor and
rust claims won in small claims court.

CHEVY II NOVA

All data based on four-door sedan

Used Car Price* $1,200
Based on standard equipped car with automatic transmission
and radio.
Price assumes excellent condition.

*Subtract $25 for each month after August for current price.

Statistical Comparison:
Average depreciation.

Excellent parts availability.
Low parts cost.
Good fuel economy.

Technical Data

Wheelbase . . 111 in.   Standard Engine . . . V6 (250)
Length . . . . 194.3 in.   Standard Brakes . . . Drum
Weight . . . . 3,169 lbs.   Gasoline Mileage . . . 17
Width . . . . . 72.4 in.   (with regular fuel)

Frequency of Repairs:
Excellent motor. Some carburetion problems. Brakes are average. A much improved car. Transmission is failure-prone, so GM extended warranty to 50,000 miles.

Body:
Some rusting problems, but otherwise well constructed. Paint peeling off. Warranty also extended to cover this defect.

Safety Defects:
Possibility of deteriorated motor mounts.

Recommendation:
Recommended. GM's answer to the Ford Maverick for inexpensive and dependable transportation. Claim in court for transmission or paint compensation.

Chevrolet Division   **1973**
General Motors
CHEVELLE
Deluxe/Malibu/El Camino/Laguna

All data based on four-door hardtop sedan

Used Car Price* $1,300
Based on standard equipped car with automatic transmission and radio.
Price assumes excellent condition.

*Subtract $25 for each month after August for current price.

Statistical Comparison:
Average depreciation.
Excellent parts availability.
Average parts cost.
Average fuel economy.

Technical Data

Wheelbase . . 116 in.   Standard Engine . . . V6 (250)
Length . . . . 206.9 in.   Standard Brakes . . . Disc-Drum
Weight . . . . 3,545 lbs.   Gasoline Mileage . . . 13
Width . . . . . 76.6 in.   (with regular fuel)

Frequency of Repairs:
Minor suspension transmission and steering problems. Excellent V6 motor and electrical system.

Body:
Good body construction. Premature rusting caused by poor paint quality.

Safety Defects:
Possibility of defective steering.

Recommendation:
Recommended. An excellent buy equal to the Buick. Remember paint and transmission defects covered by extended warranty.

Chevrolet Division   **1973**
General Motors
CHEVROLET (Full-sized)
Bel Air/Impala/Caprice

All data based on four-door sedan

Used Car Price* $1,300
Based on standard equipped car with automatic transmission and radio.
Price assumes excellent condition.

*Subtract $25 for each month after August for current price.

Statistical Comparison:
Average depreciation.
Excellent parts availability.
Average parts cost.
Average fuel economy.

Technical Data

Wheelbase	121.5 in.	Standard Engine . . .	V8 (350)
Length	221.9 in.	Standard Brakes . . .	Disc-Drum
Weight	4,284 lbs.	Gasoline Mileage . . .	11
Width	79.5 in.	(with regular fuel)	

Frequency of Repairs
Some steering, suspension, transmission, and pollution control problems. Excellent motor and electrical system.

Body:
Good construction. Some rusting problems due to bad paint.

Safety Defects:
Possibility of defective steering.

Recommendation:
Recommended. Almost as good as the Chevelle. Use courts for paint and transmission damages.

PONTIAC VENTURA II

All data based on four-door sedan

Used Car Price* $1,400
Based on standard equipped car with automatic transmission
and radio.
Price assumes excellent condition.

*Subtract $25 for each month after August for current price.

Statistical Comparison:
Average depreciation.
Low parts cost.
Good parts availability.
Below average fuel economy.

Technical Data

Wheelbase . .	111 in.	Standard Engine . . .	V6 (250)
Length	197.5 in.	Standard Brakes . . .	Drum
Weight	3,234 lbs.	Gasoline Mileage . . .	11
Width	72.4 in.	(with regular fuel)	

Frequency of Repairs:
Carburetor and motor problems. Premature transmission wear,
so warranty was secretly extended by GM.

Body:
Frequent problems with rusting and water leaks. Paint defects
are chronic, but warranty extended.

Safety Defects:
Rochester carburetor.

Recommendation:
Not recommended. GM has better cars for the same price.
Many successful court claims over paint and transmission.

PONTIAC (Full-sized)
Catalina/Bonneville/Grandville

All data based on four-door hardtop sedan

Used Car Price* $1,400
Based on standard equipped car with automatic transmission
and radio.
Price assumes excellent condition.

*Subtract $25 for each month after August for current price.

Statistical Comparison:
Below average depreciation.
Average parts cost.

Average parts availability.
Below average fuel economy.

Technical Data

Wheelbase . .	124 in.	Standard Engine . . .	V8 (350)
Length	224.8 in.	Standard Brakes . . .	Disc-Drum
Weight	4,505 lbs.	Gasoline Mileage . . .	9
Width	79.6 in.	(with regular fuel)	

Frequency of Repairs:
Excellent motor. Some carburetor, transmission, and pollution control problems.

Body:
Solid construction. Some rusting around doors and fenders. Paint defects.

Safety Defects:
Possibility of defective fuel line and rear window defroster.

Recommendation:
Not recommended. Not the car for a gasoline shortage. Use the courts for paint and transmission compensation under extended warranties.

Pontiac Division   **1973**
General Motors
LE MANS/TEMPEST

All data based on four-door sedan

Used Car Price* $1,300
Based on standard equipped car with automatic transmission and radio.
Price assumes excellent condition.

*Subtract $25 for each month after August for current price.

Statistical Comparison:
Good parts availability.
Below average depreciation.
Average parts costs.
Good gas mileage.

Technical Data

Wheelbase . .	116 in.	Standard Engine . . .	V8 (350)
Length	212.8 in.	Standard Brakes . . .	Drum
Weight	3,800	Gasoline Mileage . . .	16.1
Width	77.9 in.	(with regular fuel)	

Frequency of Repairs:
Good motor, suspension, brakes, and manual transmission. Problems reported with automatic transmission and carburetor.

Body:
Solid body construction. Paint peeling. Minor rusting.

Safety Defects:
Inner tie rod end assembly may fail, resulting in loss of steering control of right front wheel.

Recommendation:
Recommended. A reliable family car.

Buick Division   **1973**
General Motors
BUICK (Full-sized)
Le Sabre/Custom/Centurion

All data based on four-door sedan

Used Car Price* $1,400
Based on standard equipped car with automatic transmission and radio.
Price assumes excellent condition.

*Subtract $25 for each month after August for current price.

Statistical Comparison:
Low depreciation.
Excellent parts cost.
Excellent parts availability.
Average fuel economy.

Technical Data

Wheelbase . .	124 in.	Standard Engine . . .	V8 (350)
Length	224.2 in.	Standard Brakes . . .	Disc-Drum
Weight	4,899 lbs.	Gasoline Mileage . . .	9
Width	79.6 in.	(with regular fuel)	

Frequency of Repairs:
Excellent motor and electrical system. Some problems with brakes and transmission. Transmission warranty extended.

Body:
Solid construction. Excellent body durability. Some rusting due to serious paint defects. Paint warranty extended.

Safety Defects:
Possibility of defective brakes.

Recommendation:
Recommended. An excellent family-sized car. Verify motor mounts. Many paint and transmission claims won in small claims court.

OLDSMOBILE DELTA 88

All data based on four-door sedan

Used Car Price* $1,400
Based on standard equipped car with automatic transmission
and radio.
Price assumes excellent condition.

*Subtract $25 for each month after August for current price.

Statistical Comparison:
Low depreciation.
Average parts availability.
Average parts cost.
Below average fuel economy.

Technical Data

Wheelbase . .	124 in.	Standard Engine . . .	V8 (350)
Length	226.2 in.	Standard Brakes . . .	Disc-Drum
Weight	4,420 lbs.	Gasoline Mileage . . .	8
Width	79 in.	(with regular fuel)	

Frequency of Repairs:
Excellent mechanical components. Some problems with automatic transmission (warranty extended).

Body:
Excellent body construction, but rusting and paint wear around
doors. Warranty extended for these defects.

Safety Defects:
Insufficient data.

Recommendation:
Recommended. Don't forget to use small claims court for paint
or transmission defects.

FORD PINTO

All data based on two-door sedan

Used Car Price* $900
Based on standard equipped car with automatic transmission
and radio.
Price assumes excellent condition.

*Subtract $25 for each month after August for current price.

Statistical Comparison:
Rapid depreciation.
Average parts cost.
Average parts availability.
Below average fuel economy.

Technical Data

Wheelbase	94.2 in.	Standard Engine	V4 (98)
Length	164.1 in.	Standard Brakes	Disc-Drum
Weight	2,216 lbs.	Gasoline Mileage	14
Width	69.4 in.	(with regular fuel)	

Frequency of Repairs:
Good brakes and steering. Problems with suspension, motor, and transmission.

Body:
Poor body construction. Much rusting. Some paint problems. Ford extended warranty "J-67" applies.

Safety Defects:
Possibility of defective rack and pinion steering and rear wheel well.

Recommendation:
Not recommended. Not a "better idea" from Ford. Maverick or Comet is much better car buy. Pinto rusting is worse than other models. Use small claims court for rust and high fuel consumption damages. Beware of fire-prone gas tank.

Ford Division   **1973**
Ford Motor Company
FORD MAVERICK

All data based on four-door sedan

Used Car Price* $1,200
Based on standard equipped car with automatic transmission and radio.
Price assumes excellent condition.

*Subtract $25 for each month after August for current price.

Statistical Comparison:
Average depreciation.
Low parts cost.
Good parts availability.
Good fuel economy.

Technical Data

Wheelbase	103 in.	Standard Engine	V6 (200)
Length	183.3 in.	Standard Brakes	Drum
Weight	2,852 lbs.	Gasoline Mileage	17
Width	70.5 in.	(with regular fuel)	

Frequency of Repairs:
Motor and transmission are excellent. Some minor problems with brakes. Starting problems caused by gearshift lever, poor contact in ignition. Correct by raising lever in "Park" position.

Body:
Excessive rusting along wheel fender skirts and around doors.

Safety Defects:
Possibility of defective tires, brakes, carburetor, and 4 barrel carburetor.

Recommendation:
Not recommended. Mechanically sound, but rust problems too serious. Ask for warranty extension compensation.

Ford Division   **1973**
Ford Motor Company
FORD MUSTANG

All data based on two-door hardtop

Used Car Price* $1,300
Based on standard equipped car with automatic transmission and radio.
Price assumes excellent condition.

*Subtract $25 for each month after August for current price.

Statistical Comparison:
Rapid depreciation.
Average parts availability.
Average parts cost.
Below average fuel economy.

Technical Data

Wheelbase . .	109 in.	Standard Engine . . .	V6 (250)
Length	193.8 in.	Standard Brakes . . .	Disc-Drum
Weight	3,229 lbs.	Gasoline Mileage . . .	10
Width	74.1 in.	(with regular fuel)	

Frequency of Repairs:
Some carburetor and suspension problems. Average motor and electrical system.

Body:
Excessive rusting around front fender skirts and doors.

Safety Defects:

Possibility that 4 barrel carburetor may cause throttle to jam.

Recommendation:

Not recommended. This behemoth barely resembles first Mustang so popular in 1965.

Ford Division 1973
Ford Motor Company
FORD TORINO/MONTEGO

All data based on four-door hardtop sedan

Used Car Price* $1,200
Based on standard equipped car with automatic transmission
and radio.
Price assumes excellent condition.

*Subtract $25 for each month after August for current price.

Statistical Comparison:
Rapid depreciation.
Average parts cost.
Average parts availability.
Below average fuel economy.

Technical Data

Wheelbase . .	114 in.	Standard Engine . . .	V6 (250)
Length	208 in.	Standard Brakes . . .	Drum
Weight	3,838 lbs.	Gasoline Mileage . . .	9
Width	79.3 in.	(with regular fuel)	

Frequency of Repairs:
Transmission, carburetor, and brake problems. Good motor.

Body:
Rusting around doors and front fenders. Paint defects caused
by faulty design.

Safety Defects:
Possibility of defective power steering, carburetor, brakes, and
fuel lines.

Recommendation:
Not recommended. Rust, rust, and more rust. Ford's biodegradable car. Ask for secret warranty extension "J-67" compensation.

Ford Division 1973
Ford Motor Company
FORD (Full-sized)
Custom/Galaxie/LTD

All data based on four-door hardtop.

Used Car Price* $1,400
Based on standard equipped car with automatic transmission
and radio.
Price assumes excellent condition.

*Subtract $25 for each month after August for current price.

Statistical Comparison:
Rapid depreciation.
Average parts cost.

Excellent parts availability.
Average fuel economy.

Technical Data

Wheelbase . .	121 in.	Standard Engine . . .	V8 (351)
Length	219.5 in.	Standard Brakes . . .	Drum
Weight	4,292 lbs.	Gasoline Mileage . . .	10
Width	79.5 in.	(with regular fuel)	

Frequency of Repairs:
Problems with steering, carburetion, and brakes. Good motor
and transmission. May have premature valve guide wear. Ford
has secret warranty extension for this motor defect.

Body:
Serious rusting problems around doors, fenders, and along
wheel fender skirts.

Safety Defects:
Possibility of defective power steering, distributors, and brakes
on Meteor models. Defective 4 barrel carburetor may jam
throttle in open position.

Recommendation:
Not recommended. Still an average car with serious rust prob-
lems. Seek rusting compensation in small claims court under
Ford's "J-67" secret warranty extension.

Plymouth Division   1973
Chrysler Corporation
PLYMOUTH VALIANT
Scamp/Duster

All data based on four-door sedan

Used Car Price* $1,500
Based on standard equipped car with automatic transmission
and radio.
Price assumes excellent condition.

*Subtract $25 for each month after August for current price.

Statistical Comparison:
Very low depreciation.
Excellent parts availability.
Low parts cost.
Excellent fuel economy.

Technical Data

Wheelbase . .	108 in.	Standard Engine	6 cyl.
Length	195.8 in.	Standard Brakes	Drum
Weight	2,440 lbs.	Gasoline Mileage	21
Width	71 in.	(with regular fuel)	

Frequency of Repairs:
Excellent mechanical components. Minor problems with carburetor and brakes.

Body:
Solid construction. No rusting, except for rust-prone front fenders.

Safety Defects:
Possibility of defective transmission fluid, steering, and fuel leakage.

Recommendation:
Recommended. The six cylinder version is the best new or used car on the market. Many motorists have won compensation from small claims court for rusting damages.

Dodge Division   **1973**
Chrysler Corporation
DODGE DART
Swinger

All data based on four-door sedan

Used Car Price* $1,500
Based on standard equipped car with automatic transmission and radio.
Price assumes excellent condition.

*Subtract $25 for each month after August for current price.

Statistical Comparison:
Very low depreciation.
Average parts cost.
Excellent parts availability.
Average fuel economy.

Technical Data

Wheelbase . .	111 in.	Standard Engine	6 cyl.
Length	203.8 in.	Standard Brakes	Drum
Weight	2,985 lbs.	Gasoline Mileage	21
Width	69.6 in.	(with regular fuel)	

Frequency of Repairs:
Some carburetion and motor problems caused by pollution control device. Other mechanical components excellent, except for rear brake defects.

Body:
Excellent body construction, no rusting other than front fenders.

Safety Defects:
Possibility of defective transmission fluid and defective steering.

Recommendation:
Recommended. The best family car on the market. When front fenders rust demand compensation through small claims court.

Plymouth Division   **1973**
Chrysler Corporation
PLYMOUTH SATELLITE
Road Runner/Satellite Custom/
Satellite Sebring

All data based on four-door hardtop

Used Car Price* $1,300
Based on standard equipped car with automatic transmission
and radio.
Price assumes excellent condition.

*Subtract $25 for each month after August for current price.

Statistical Comparison:
Average depreciation.
Average parts cost.
Average parts availability.
Below average fuel economy.

Technical Data

Wheelbase . .	117 in.	Standard Engine . . .	V-6 (225)
Length	213.3 in.	Standard Brakes . . .	Disc-Drum
Weight	3,625 lbs.	Gasoline Mileage . . .	11
Width	78.6 in.	(with regular fuel)	

Frequency of Repairs:
Problems with brakes, steering, and electrical system.

Body:
Good body construction. Very little rusting, except for front
fenders.

Safety Defects:
Possibility of defective transmission fluid, defective starter, and
fuel leakage.

Recommendation:
Not recommended. Fury is better buy.

Dodge Division   **1973**
Chrysler Corporation
DODGE (Full-sized)
Polara/Monaco

All data based on four-door sedan

Used Car Price* $1,400
Based on standard equipped car with automatic transmission
and radio.
Price assumes excellent condition.

*Subtract $25 for each month after August for current price.

Statistical Comparison:
Rapid depreciation.
Average parts cost.

Average parts availability.
Below average fuel economy.

Technical Data

Wheelbase . .	122 in.	Standard Engine . . .	V8 (318)
Length	226.6 in.	Standard Brakes . . .	Disc-Drum
Weight	3,980 lbs.	Gasoline Mileage . . .	9
Width	79.6 in.	(with regular fuel)	

Frequency of Repairs:
Problems with brakes, motor, carburetor, and suspension.

Body:
Fair overall body construction, but front fenders are rust-prone by design. Many small claims courts judgments against dealers for $300–$400 as compensation for defect.

Safety Defects:
Possibility of defective carburetor or air conditioner.

Recommendation:
Not recommended. Fenders and mechanical problems are too frequent.

Plymouth Division   **1973**
Chrysler Corporation
PLYMOUTH FURY
I, II, III

All data based on four-door sedan

Used Car Price* $1,400
Based on standard equipped car with automatic transmission and radio.
Price assumes excellent condition.

*Subtract $25 for each month after August for current price.

Statistical Comparison:
Average depreciation.
Average parts cost.
Average parts availability.
Below average fuel economy.

Technical Data

Wheelbase . .	120 in.	Standard Engine . . .	V8 (318)
Length	223.4 in.	Standard Brakes . . .	Drum
Weight	3,980 lbs.	Gasoline Mileage . . .	9
Width	79.8 in.	(with regular fuel)	

Frequency of Repairs:
Problems with brakes, carburetor, and fuel leakage.

Body:
Good body construction. Isolated rusting of front fenders.

Safety Defects:
Possibility of defective carburetor and fuel leakage.

Recommendation:
Recommended. Watch out vehicle is not an ex-taxi or police car by checking for roof holes or dashboard radio mounting screw holes.

American Motors   **1973**
AMC HORNET

All data based on four-door sedan

Used Car Price* $1,300
Based on standard equipped car with automatic transmission and radio.
Price assumes excellent condition.

*Subtract $25 for each month after August for current price.

Statistical Comparison:
Below average depreciation.
Average parts cost.
Average parts availability.
Average fuel economy.

Technical Data

Wheelbase	108 in.	Standard Engine	V6 (232)
Length	184.9 in.	Standard Brakes	Drum
Weight	2,884 lbs.	Gasoline Mileage	17
Width	71 in.	(with regular fuel)	

Frequency of Repairs:
Problems with carburetion, brakes, and suspension. Motor and transmission are excellent.

Body:
Excellent body construction. Some rattles reported.

Safety Defects:
Possibility of defective brake master cylinder and brake pedal.

Recommendation:
Recommended. Station wagon is top choice. Order heavy duty battery for reported cold-weather starting difficulties.

American Motors   **1973**
AMC GREMLIN

All data based on two-door sedan

Used Car Price* $1,100
Based on standard equipped car with automatic transmission and radio.
Price assumes excellent condition.

*Subtract $25 for each month after August for current price.

Statistical Comparison:
Below average depreciation.
Average parts cost.
Average parts availability.
Good fuel economy.

Technical Data
Wheelbase . .	96 in.	Standard Engine . . .	V6 (232)
Length	165.45 in.	Standard Brakes . . .	Drum
Weight	2,702 lbs.	Gasoline Mileage . . .	19
Width	70.6 in.	(with regular fuel)	

Frequency of Repairs:
Excellent motor, transmission, and electrical system. Problems with brakes and suspension.

Body:
Excellent body construction. Some paint-peeling reported.

Safety Defects:
Possibility of defective brake master cylinder, brake pedal.

Recommendation:
Recommended. A good compact car with inadequate interior space for tall adults. Verify braking performance.

American Motors   **1973**
AMBASSADOR

All data based on four-door sedan

Used Car Price* $1,300
Based on standard equipped car with automatic transmission and radio.
Price assumes excellent condition.

*Subtract $25 for each month after August for current price.

Statistical Comparison:
Above average depreciation.
Average parts availability.
Average parts cost.
Average fuel economy.

Technical Data
Wheelbase . .	122 in.	Standard Engine . . .	V8 (304)
Length	212.86 in.	Standard Brakes . . .	Drum
Weight	3,814 lbs.	Gasoline Mileage . . .	10
Width	77.28 in.	(with regular fuel)	

Frequency of Repairs:
Excellent motor and transmission. Problems with suspension and brakes. Exhaust system improved.

Body:
Excellent body construction. Very little rusting.

Safety Defects:
Possibility of defective suspension and brake pedal.

Recommendation:
Recommended, but model discontinued. So plan on visiting scrap yards frequently for parts.

1974 MODELS

VEGA/ASTRE

All data based on two-door sedan

Used Car Price* $1,100
Based on standard equipped car with automatic transmission
and radio.
Price assumes excellent condition.

*Subtract $25 for each month after August for current price.

Statistical Comparison:
Excessive depreciation.
Average parts supply.
Expensive parts.
Poor gas mileage.

Technical Data

Wheelbase . .	97 in.	Standard Engine . . .	4 cyl. (140)
Length	172.2 in.	Standard Brakes . . .	Disc-Drum
Weight	2,300 lbs.	Gasoline Mileage . . .	17
Width	65 in.	(with regular fuel)	

Frequency of Repairs:
Motor still may self-destruct. Excessive oil burning. Warranty
extended to cover premature motor defects up to 50,000 miles.
Chronic automatic transmission and carburetor problems.
Transmission warranty has been extended to 5 years for trans-
mission defects.

Body:
Premature rusting of front fenders, doors, and windshield
mouldings reported. GM dealers will replace fenders without
charge.

Safety Defects:
Original equipment tires (Goodyear) may be defective.

Recommendation:
Not recommended. A bicycle is more reliable.

Chevrolet Division   **1974**
General Motors

NOVA/CHEVY II

All data based on four-door sedan

Used Car Price* $1,500
Based on standard equipped car with automatic transmission
and radio.
Price assumes excellent condition.

*Subtract $25 for each month after August for current price.

Statistical Comparison:
Below average depreciation.
Excellent parts availability.
Parts inexpensive.
Average gas mileage.

Technical Data

Wheelbase . .	111 in.	Standard Engine . . .	6 cyl. (250)
Length	194.3 in.	Standard Brakes . . .	Drum
Weight	3,200 lbs.	Gasoline Mileage . . .	16
Width	72.4 in.	(with regular fuel)	

Frequency of Repairs:
Automatic transmission may be defective due to incorrect transmission fluid. Excellent 6 cylinder motor. Minor carburetor problems.

Body:
Average body construction. Minor paint problems reported.

Safety Defects:
Rear axle could be unsafe.

Recommendation:
Recommended. One of the Nova's best years. Be wary of transmission.

Chevrolet Division   **1974**
General Motors

CHEVELLE

All data based on four-door sedan

Used Car Price* $1,600
Based on standard equipped car with automatic transmission and radio. Price assumes excellent condition.

*Subtract $25 for each month after August for current price.

Statistical Comparison:
Below average depreciation.
Excellent parts availability.
Inexpensive parts.
Average gas mileage.

Technical Data

Wheelbase . .	116 in.	Standard Engine . . .	6 cyl. (250)
Length	210 in.	Standard Brakes . . .	Disc-Drum
Weight	3,680 lbs.	Gasoline Mileage . . .	16
Width	76.6 in.	(with regular fuel)	

Frequency of Repairs:
Good motor, electrical system, brakes, and suspension. Automatic transmission (350, 400 series) may fail prematurely.

Body:
Premature paint peeling on hood, trunk, and doors. Minor rusting reported.

Safety Defects:
Seatbelt may fail. Hood may open suddenly while car is in motion, thus blocking driver's vision.

Recommendation:
Recommended. The last model year where quality and reliability were maximized.

Chevrolet Division   **1974**
General Motors
CHEVROLET (Full-sized)
Bel Air/Impala/Caprice

All data based on four-door sedan

Used Car Price* $1,600
Based on standard equipped car with automatic transmission and radio.
Price assumes excellent condition.

*Subtract $25 for each month after August for current price.

Statistical Comparison:
Below average depreciation.
Excellent parts availability.
Inexpensive parts.
Average gas mileage.

Technical Data

Wheelbase	121.5 in.	Standard Engine	V8 (350)
Length	222.6 in.	Standard Brakes	Disc-Drum
Weight	4,666 lbs.	Gasoline Mileage	15
Width	79.5 in.	(with regular fuel)	

Frequency of Repairs:
Excellent motor, electrical system, and brakes. Automatic transmission is failure prone (350, 400 series).

Body:
Body very rust resistant except for doors and rear panels. Paint may peel off prematurely.

Safety Defects:
Rear brake pipe could be defective. Seatbelt may fail to hold during emergency stops.

Recommendation:
Recommended. One of the best buys in its category.

VENTURA

All data based on four-door sedan

Used Car Price* $1,500
Based on standard equipped car with automatic transmission
and radio.
Price assumes excellent condition.

*Subtract $25 for each month after August for current price.

Statistical Comparison:
Rapid depreciation.
Average parts availability.
Average parts costs.
Average gas mileage.

Technical Data

Wheelbase . .	111 in.	Standard Engine . . .	6 cyl. (250)
Length	197.5 in.	Standard Brakes . . .	Drum
Weight	3,250 lbs.	Gasoline Mileage . . .	15
Width	72.4 in.	(with regular fuel)	

Frequency of Repairs:
Good suspension and brakes. Problems with automatic transmission, motor, and electrical system.

Body:
Paint peeling affecting doors, hood, trunk, and fenders. Minor
rusting.

Safety Defects:
Rear springs may be broken.

Recommendation:
Not recommended. An average car with serious quality control
problems. Competing GM models are better buys.

LE MANS/TEMPEST

All data based on four-door sedan

Used Car Price* $1,700
Based on standard equipped car with automatic transmission
and radio.
Price assumes excellent condition.

*Subtract $25 for each month after August for current price.

Statistical Comparison:
Below average depreciation.
Good parts availability.
Average parts costs.
Average gas mileage.

Technical Data

Wheelbase . .	116 in.	Standard Engine . . .	V8 (350)
Length	212.8 in.	Standard Brakes . . .	Drum
Weight	3,800 lbs.	Gasoline Mileage . . .	15
Width	77.9 in.	(with regular fuel)	

Frequency of Repairs:
Good brakes. Excellent motor. Carburetor improved. Problems reported with automatic transmission.

Body:
Paint problems more extensive. Little rusting. Excellent body construction.

Safety Defects:
Possibility seatbelt may fail during emergency stop.

Recommendation:
Recommended. Although quality has been diminished, car still a good buy.

Pontiac Division   **1974**
General Motors

PONTIAC (Full-sized)
Catalina/Bonneville

All data based on four-door sedan

Used Car Price* $1,800
Based on standard equipped car with automatic transmission and radio.
Price assumes excellent condition.

*Subtract $25 for each month after August for current price.

Statistical Comparison:
Average depreciation.
Average parts availability.
Average parts costs.
Below average gas mileage.

Technical Data

Wheelbase . .	124 in.	Standard Engine . . .	V8 (455)
Length	226 in.	Standard Brakes . . .	Disc-Drum
Weight	4,300 lbs.	Gasoline Mileage . . .	12
Width	79.6 in.	(with regular fuel)	

Frequency of Repairs:
Good suspension and brakes. Problems with automatic transmission.

Body:
Minor paint problems. Little rusting. Solid body construction.

Safety Defects:
Brakes may fail due to defective power booster housing. Possibility of defective upper control arm.

Recommendation:
Recommended. The absence of fuel economy is made up in reliable performance.

Buick Division   **1974**
General Motors
BUICK (Full-sized)
Le Sabre/Electra

All data based on four-door sedan

Used Car Price* $1,800
Based on standard equipped car with automatic transmission and radio.
Price assumes excellent condition.

*Subtract $25 for each month after August for current price.

Statistical Comparison:
Average depreciation.
Good parts availability.
Average parts costs.
Average gas mileage.

Technical Data

Wheelbase . .	124 in.	Standard Engine . . .	V8 (350)
Length	224.2 in.	Standard Brakes . . .	Disc-Drum
Weight	4,600 lbs.	Gasoline Mileage . . .	12
Width	79.6 in.	(with regular fuel)	

Frequency of Repairs:
Good suspension, brakes, and electrical system. Problems with motor, carburetor, and automatic transmission.

Body:
Unacceptable paint defects causing premature rusting over entire car. Body is otherwise solidly constructed.

Safety Defects:
Possibility of defective rear brake pipe.

Recommendation:
Not recommended. For an average car, it is too costly to own.

Oldsmobile Division   **1974**
General Motors
OLDSMOBILE (Full-sized)
Oldsmobile 88/98

All data based on four-door sedan

Used Car Price* $1,900
Based on standard equipped car with automatic transmission and radio.
Price assumes excellent condition.

*Subtract $25 for each month after August for current price.

Statistical Comparison:
Slow depreciation.
Excellent parts availability.
Low parts costs.
Average gas mileage for engine.

Technical Data

Wheelbase	124 in.	Standard Engine	V8 (455)
Length	227 in.	Standard Brakes	Disc-Drum
Weight	4,500 lbs.	Gasoline Mileage	11
Width	79.5 in.	(with regular fuel)	

Frequency of Repairs:
Good carburetor, brakes, and suspension. Electrical system, motor, and automatic transmission are failure prone.

Body:
Severe paint flaking over entire car. Some rusting around doors and fenders.

Safety Defects:
Brake vacuum power booster housing may be defective.

Recommendation
Recommended. An excellent car for high mileage driving once motor and transmission have been verified.

Ford Division   **1974**
Ford Motor Company
PINTO/BOBCAT

All data based on two-door sedan

Used Car Price* $1,000
Based on standard equipped car with automatic transmission and radio.
Price assumes excellent condition.

*Subtract $25 for each month after August for current price.

Statistical Comparison:
Rapid depreciation.
Good parts availability.
Average parts costs.
Very poor gas mileage.

Technical Data

Wheelbase	94 in.	Standard Engine	4 cyl. (140)
Length	164.5 in.	Standard Brakes	Disc-Drum
Weight	2,200 lbs.	Gasoline Mileage	13
Width	69.4 in.	(with regular fuel)	

Frequency of Repairs:
Motor, automatic transmission, and brakes are main problem areas. Suspension and electrical system are fair.

Body:
Premature rusting perforations and severe "tuck under" design contribute to make the body practically biodegradable. A rust trap!

Safety Defects:
Original equipment tires (Firestone radials) may be defective.

Recommendation:
Not recommended. A four-cylinder infernal combustion machine. Gas Tank Fire-Prone.

Ford Division   **1974**
Ford Motor Company
MAVERICK/COMET

All data based on two-door sedan

Used Car Price* $1,500
Based on standard equipped car with automatic transmission and radio.
Price assumes excellent condition.

*Subtract $25 for each month after August for current price.

Statistical Comparison:
Slow depreciation.
Good parts availability.
Average parts costs.
Good gas mileage.

Technical Data

Wheelbase . .	103 in.	Standard Engine . . .	6 cyl. (200)
Length	183 in.	Standard Brakes . . .	Drum
Weight	2,350 lbs.	Gasoline Mileage . . .	19
Width	70.5 in.	(with regular fuel)	

Frequency of Repairs:
Good transmission and electrical system. Problems with rear brakes, carburetor, and motor. Excessive high speed vibrations at 60 mph reported.

Body:
Premature rusting of doors, fenders, and wheel wells. Paint flaking reported.

Safety Defects:
The carburetor used on 302, 351, and 400 CID engines with automatic transmission may be defective and cause throttle to stick. Brake pedal could be defective.

Recommendation:
Not recommended. Corrosion problems too severe. Car is well-made mechanically.

Ford Division   **1974**
Ford Motor Company
MUSTANG II

All data based on two-door sedan

Used Car Price* $1,500
Based on standard equipped car with automatic transmission and radio.
Price assumes excellent condition.

*Subtract $25 for each month after August for current price.

Statistical Comparison:
Rapid depreciation.
Below average parts availability.
High parts costs.
Poor gas mileage.

Technical Data

Wheelbase . .	96.2 in.	Standard Engine . . .	4 cyl.
Length	175 in.	Standard Brakes . . .	Disc-Drum
Weight	2,700 lbs.	Gasoline Mileage . . .	16
Width	70.2 in.	(with regular fuel)	

Frequency of Repairs:
Good brakes. Problems with suspension, motor transmission, electrical system, and carburetor. Excessive vibrations at 20–40 miles per hour.

Body:
Premature paint wear and severe rusting around fenders and door bottoms.

Safety Defects:
Original equipment (Firestone) tires may be defective. Brake pedal failures possible.

Recommendation:
Not recommended. A good-looking problem-prone car.

TORINO/FAIRLANE/MONTEGO

All data based on four-door sedan

Used Car Price* $1,700
Based on standard equipped car with automatic transmission
and radio.
Price assumes excellent condition.

*Subtract $25 for each month after August for current price.

Statistical Comparison:
Rapid depreciation.
Good parts availability.
Average parts costs.
Average gas mileage.

Technical Data

Wheelbase	118 in.	Standard Engine . . .	V8 (351)
Length	217 in.	Standard Brakes . . .	Disc-Drum
Weight	3,800 lbs.	Gasoline Mileage . . .	13
Width	79.3 in.	(with regular fuel)	

Frequency of Repairs:
Good suspension and brakes. Problems with motor and carburetor. Transmission and electrical system defects reported.

Body:
Severe premature rusting around doors, fenders, and wheel
wells.

Safety Defects:
Possibility that automatic speed control could bind leading to
sustained acceleration. Firestone HR 78-15 tires may be defective.

Recommendation:
Not recommended. One of Ford's worst intermediates.

FORD (Full-sized)
LTD/Galaxie

All data based on four-door sedan

Used Car Price* $1,900
Based on standard equipped car with automatic transmission
and radio.
Price assumes excellent condition.

*Subtract $25 for each month after August for current price.

Average depreciation.
Excellent parts availability.
Average parts costs.
Poor gas mileage.

Technical Data

Wheelbase	121 in.	Standard Engine	V8 (351)
Length	219.5 in.	Standard Brakes	Disc-Drum
Weight	4,631 lbs.	Gasoline Mileage	10
Width	79.5 in.	(with regular fuel)	

Frequency of Repairs:
Good transmission and brakes. Some motor problems reported. Carburetor and electrical system problems also reported.

Body:
Premature rusting affecting primarily fenders, doors, and wheel wells.

Safety Defects:
Automatic speed control may malfunction.

Recommendation:
Recommended. Check for rusting perforations and frame damage.

Plymouth Division   **1974**
Chrysler Corporation

VALIANT

All data based on four-door sedan

Used Car Price* $1,700
Based on standard equipped car with automatic transmission and radio.
Price assumes excellent condition.

*Subtract $25 for each month after August for current price.

Statistical Comparison:
Slow depreciation.
Excellent parts availability.
Low parts costs.
Excellent gas mileage.

Technical Data

Wheelbase	108 in.	Standard Engine	6 cyl. (225)
Length	195 in.	Standard Brakes	Drum
Weight	3,000 lbs.	Gasoline Mileage	19
Width	71.1 in.	(with regular fuel)	

Frequency of Repairs:
Excellent motor and transmission. Problems with electrical system, carburetor, brakes and suspension.

Body:
Little rusting except for front fenders. Solid body construction except for reports of water leaks into passenger compartment.

Safety Defects:
Possibility of defective transmission lever. Wheel bearings may have been incorrectly greased.

Recommendation:
Recommended. The best compact car on the market. Better than the Volare or Aspen.

Dodge Division   **1974**
Chrysler Corporation
DART

All data based on four-door sedan

Used Car Price* $1,700
Based on standard equipped car with automatic transmission and radio.
Price assumes excellent condition.

*Subtract $25 for each month after August for current price.

Statistical Comparison:
Slow depreciation.
Below average parts costs.
Excellent parts availability.
Good fuel economy.

Technical Data

Wheelbase	111 in.	Standard Engine	6 cyl. (225)
Length	203.8 in.	Standard Brakes	Disc-drum
Weight	3,000 lbs.	Gasoline Mileage	17
Width	69.6 in.	(with unleaded fuel)	

Frequency of Repairs:
Excellent motor, transmission, and suspension. Problems reported with brakes, electrical system, and carburetor.

Body:
Front fenders very vulnerable to early rust perforations. Few water leaks and rattles. Solid body construction otherwise. No serious paint problems.

Safety Defects:
Lower control arm and lower ball joint may be defective. Heating-defrosting system may malfunction.

Recommendation:
Recommended. An excellent compact car that beats the competition by far.

Plymouth Division 1974
Chrysler Corporation
SATELLITE/BELVEDERE

All data based on four-door sedan

Used Car Price* $1,900
Based on standard equipped car with automatic transmission and radio.
Price assumes excellent condition.

*Subtract $25 for each month after August for current price.

Statistical Comparison:
Below average depreciation.
Average parts costs.
Good parts availability.
Average gas mileage.

Technical Data

Wheelbase . .	117 in.	Standard Engine . . .	6 cyl. (225)
Length	212.4 in.	Standard Brakes . . .	Disc-drum
Weight	3,700 lbs.	Gasoline Mileage . . .	14
Width	78.6 in.	(with regular fuel)	

Frequency of Repairs:
Good motor, transmission, and electrical system. Problems with brake lock-up, loose suspension, and carburetor fuel mixture causing stalling and difficult starting.

Body:
Solid body construction. Few rattles. Front fenders are extremely vulnerable to rusting perforations. Water leaks common.

Safety Defects:
Transmission lever may malfunction causing difficulty in changing gears or giving a false reading as to gear that is engaged.

Recommendation:
Recommended. This model is much improved when compared with the 1973 model.

POLARA/MONACO (Full-sized)

All data based on four-door sedan

Used Car Price* $1,700
Based on standard equipped car with automatic transmission
and radio.
Price assumes excellent condition.

*Subtract $25 for each month after August for current price.

Statistical Comparison:
Rapid depreciation.
High parts costs.
Below average parts availability.
Poor gas mileage.

Technical Data

Wheelbase	122 in.	Standard Engine	V8 (360)
Length	222.7 in.	Standard Brakes	Disc-drum
Weight	4,300 lbs.	Gasoline Mileage	9
Width	79.3 in.	(with regular fuel)	

Frequency of Repairs:
Good transmission. Problems with brakes, motor, suspension,
carburetor, and electrical system. Heating-defrosting and air
conditioning are also defect-prone.

Body:
Poor body construction, although chassis is reasonably resistant to corrosion except for front fenders. Body panels may be
misaligned causing poor fits and excessive interior noise. Water
leaks are common.

Safety Defects:
Lower control arm and lower ball joint may separate causing
loss of steering control.

Recommendation:
Not recommended. A classic example of how not to make a car.

FURY

All data based on four-door sedan

Used Car Price* $2,000
Based on standard equipped car with automatic transmission
and radio.
Price assumes excellent condition.

*Subtract $25 for each month after August for current price.

Statistical Comparison:
Below average depreciation.
Average parts costs.
Good parts availability.
Average gas mileage.

Technical Data

Wheelbase . .	122 in.	Standard Engine . . .	V8 (318)
Length	228.8 in.	Standard Brakes . . .	Disc-drum
Weight	4,460 lbs.	Gasoline Mileage . . .	12
Width	79.4 in.	(with regular fuel)	

Frequency of Repairs:
Good transmission, motor, and electrical system. Brakes are a major problem with premature wear, lock-up, and uneven pull reported. Carburetor and suspension are still likely to malfunction.

Body:
Good body construction. Front fenders vulnerable to early rust-out. Model has more rattles than previous model years.

Safety Defects:
Lower control arm and ball joint connection may be defective causing the separation of the lower control arm from the lower ball joint. Heating-defrosting system may also malfunction.

Recommendation:
Recommended. Not an extraordinary buy, but a reliable average-performing car.

American Motors   **1974**
AMC HORNET

All data based on four-door sedan

Used Car Price* $1,700
Based on standard equipped car with automatic transmission and radio.
Price assumes excellent condition.

*Subtract $25 for each month after August for current price.

Statistical Comparison:
Below average depreciation.
Inexpensive parts.
Excellent parts availability.
Average fuel economy.

Technical Data

Wheelbase . .	108 in.	Standard Engine . . .	6 cyl. (232)
Length	189.4 in.	Standard Brakes . . .	Drum
Weight	2,880 lbs.	Gasoline Mileage . . .	18
Width	71.1 in.	(with regular fuel)	

Frequency of Repairs:
Excellent motor and transmission. Problems reported with uneven brake pull and carburetor malfunctioning.

Body:
Excellent body construction, though some minor rattling reported. Good rust resistance.

Safety Defects:
Possibility that tire pressure labels may be in error.

Recommendation:
Recommended. A cheap car that is reliable and requires little periodic servicing.

American Motors   **1974**
AMC GREMLIN

All data based on two-door sedan

Used Car Price* $1,300
Based on standard equipped car with automatic transmission and radio.
Price assumes excellent condition.

*Subtract $25 for each month after August for current price.

Statistical Comparison:
Average depreciation.
Average parts costs.
Good parts availability.
Excellent gas mileage.

Technical Data

Wheelbase . .	96 in.	Standard Engine . . .	6 cyl. (232)
Length	165.5 in.	Standard Brakes . . .	Drum
Weight	2,800 lbs.	Gasoline Mileage . . .	20
Width	70.6 in.	(with regular fuel)	

Frequency of Repairs:
Good motor and transmission. Problems reported with carburetor (stalling, hard starting), brakes, and electrical system.

Body:
Good body construction. Little rusting. Interior space may be inadequate for tall drivers.

Safety Defects:
Possibility original equipment tires may be defective.

Recommendation:
Recommended. An excellent urban subcompact car.

AMBASSADOR

All data based on four-door sedan

Used Car Price* $1,500
Based on standard equipped car with automatic transmission
and radio.
Price assumes excellent condition.

*Subtract $25 for each month after August for current price.

Statistical Comparison:
Very rapid depreciation.
Average parts costs.
Below average parts availability.
Below average gas mileage.

Technical Data

Wheelbase . .	122 in.	Standard Engine . . .	V8 (304)
Length	219.4 in.	Standard Brakes . . .	Disc-drum
Weight	4,118 lbs.	Gasoline Mileage . . .	10
Width	77.2 in.	(with regular fuel)	

Frequency of Repairs:
Excellent transmission. Problems with electrical system,
brakes, suspension, and carburetor. Motor has an average frequency of repair rating.

Body:
Average body construction with little rusting but some rattles.
Few paint problems.

Safety Defects:
Wheels on cars equipped with heavy-duty fleet package may be
defective.

Recommendation:
Not recommended. A good car victimized by poor quality control. This is its last year of production.

1975 MODELS

VEGA/ASTRE

All data based on two-door sedan

Used Car Price* $1,300
Based on standard equipped car with automatic transmission
and radio.
Price assumes excellent condition.

*Subtract $25 for each month after August for current price.

Statistical Comparison:
Worse than average depreciation.
Average parts supply.
Expensive parts.
Below average gas mileage.

Technical Data

Wheelbase . .	97 in.	Standard Engine . . .	4 cyl. (140)
Length	175.4 in.	Standard Brakes . . .	Disc-drum
Weight	2,495 lbs.	Gasoline Mileage . . .	20
Width	65.4 in.	(with regular fuel)	

Frequency of Repairs:
Motor improved, but still gives trouble. Starting and stalling
problems reported. Automatic transmission (250 series) is defect-prone. Warranty extension for 50,000 miles provided by
GM.

Body:
Fender rusting less severe. Doors and windshield mouldings
still vulnerable.

Safety Defects:
Tires on Vega and Astre may be incorrectly labeled. Tire size
BR 78-13 is really BR 70-13.

Recommendation:
Not recommended. Although car has been improved, its performance still leaves much to be desired. One still gets the
impression it's a disposable vehicle.

NOVA

All data based on four-door sedan

Used Car Price* $1,900
Based on standard equipped car with automatic transmission
and radio.
Price assumes excellent condition.

*Subtract $25 for each month after August for current price.

Statistical Comparison:
Average depreciation.
Good parts availability.
Inexpensive parts.
Poor gas mileage.

Technical Data

Wheelbase . .	111 in.	Standard Engine . . .	6 cyl. (250)
Length	196.7 in.	Standard Brakes . . .	Disc-drum
Weight	3,416 lbs.	Gasoline Mileage . . .	15.8
Width	72.2 in.	(with unleaded fuel)	

Frequency of Repairs:
Automatic transmission defects covered by extended warranty.
Motor is noisy and often stalls. Unleaded gas may not make a
smoother running engine.

Body:
Severe paint flaking causing slight exterior rusting. Body construction is solid.

Safety Defects:
Right and left front suspension lower control arm may have
improperly welded bracket. Suspension may fail causing loss of
steering control. Front seat back may not lock adequately.

Recommendation:
Recommended. Prior models are better buys.

Chevrolet Division   **1975**
General Motors

CHEVELLE

All data based on four-door sedan

Used Car Price* $2,200
Based on standard equipped car with automatic transmission
and radio.
Price assumes excellent condition.

*Subtract $25 for each month after August for current price.

Statistical Comparison:
Average depreciation.
Average parts availability.
Above average parts costs.
Atrocious gas mileage.

Technical Data

Wheelbase . .	116 in.	Standard Engine . . .	6 cyl. (250)
Length	209.2 in.	Standard Brakes . . .	Disc-drum
Weight	3,949 lbs.	Gasoline Mileage . . .	10
Width	76.6 in.	(with unleaded fuel)	

Frequency of Repairs:
Good brakes and carburetor. Problems reported with malfunctioning motors, automatic transmission, and electrical system.

Body:
Severe paint peeling and corrosion damage.

Safety Defects:
Original equipment radial tires (Goodyear) may be defective. Rear axle may be defective.

Recommendation:
Recommended. A classic car that has been sabotaged by cost-cutting on body hardware.

Chevrolet Division   **1975**
General Motors
CHEVROLET (Full-sized)
Bel Air/Impala/Caprice

All data based on four-door sedan

Used Car Price* $2,000
Based on standard equipped car with automatic transmission and radio.
Price assumes excellent condition.

*Subtract $25 for each month after August for current price.

Statistical Comparison:
Average depreciation.
Average parts availability.
Parts costs above average.
Poor gas mileage.

Technical Data

Wheelbase	121.5 in.	Standard Engine	V8 (350)
Length	222.7 in.	Standard Brakes	Disc-drum
Weight	4,318 lbs.	Gasoline Mileage	13
Width	79.5 in.	(with unleaded fuel)	

Frequency of Repairs:
Problems with motor, automatic transmission and electrical system. Motor is noisy and frequently stalls.

Body:
Serious paint defects affecting entire car. Little rusting.

Safety Defects:
Defective rear axle may malfunction. Original equipment radial tires may fail because of tread separation.

Recommendation:
Recommended. Not because it's such a great car, but because the competition is so bad.

VENTURA

All data based on four-door sedan

Used Car Price* $1,800
Based on standard equipped car with automatic transmission
and radio.
Price assumes excellent condition.

*Subtract $25 for each month after August for current price.

Statistical Comparison:
Rapid depreciation.
Average parts availability.
Average parts costs.
Poor gas mileage.

Technical Data

Wheelbase . .	111.1 in.	Standard Engine . . .	6 cyl. (250)
Length	199.6 in.	Standard Brakes . . .	Disc-drum
Weight	3,445 lbs.	Gasoline Mileage . . .	14
Width	72.4 in.	(with unleaded fuel)	

Frequency of Repairs:
Automatic transmission, motor, and electrical system frequently malfunction. Carburetor and suspension are improved.

Body:
Severe paint flaking probably caused by improper metal preparation. Minor rusting. Reports of water leaks in trunk.

Safety Defects:
Lower control arms may be defective. Possibility of tire failure
with FR 74-14 radial tires. Accelerator cable may jam.

Recommendation:
Not recommended.

LE MANS/TEMPEST

All data based on four-door sedan

Used Car Price* $2,100
Based on standard equipped car with automatic transmission
and radio.
Price assumes excellent condition.

*Subtract $25 for each month after August for current price.

Statistical Comparison:
Average depreciation.
Average parts availability.

Average parts costs.
Below average gas mileage.

Technical Data

Wheelbase . .	116 in.	Standard Engine . . .	V8 (350)
Length	212 in.	Standard Brakes . . .	Disc-drum
Weight	3,845 lbs.	Gasoline Mileage . . .	13
Width	77.4 in.	(with unleaded fuel)	

Frequency of Repairs:
Good suspension and brakes. Problems with carburetor, motor, automatic transmission, and electrical system.

Body:
Severe peeling of paint affecting entire body. Minor rusting.

Safety Defects:
Rear axle may be defective. Catalytic converter may cause fires.

Recommendation:
Not recommended. Too many mechanical defects may appear. No longer a reliable model.

Pontiac Division   **1975**
General Motors
PONTIAC (Full-sized)
Catalina/Bonneville

All data based on four-door sedan

Used Car Price* $2,200
Based on standard equipped car with automatic transmission and radio.
Price assumes excellent condition.

*Subtract $25 for each month after August for current price.

Statistical Comparison:
Rapid depreciation.
Average parts availability.
High parts costs.
Poor gas mileage.

Technical Data

Wheelbase . .	123.4 in.	Standard Engine . . .	V8 (400)
Length	226 in.	Standard Brakes . . .	Disc-drum
Weight	4,643 lbs.	Gasoline Mileage . . .	10
Width	79.6 in.	(with unleaded fuel)	

Frequency of Repairs:
Good brakes and suspension. Problem with motor, automatic transmission, carburetor, and electrical system.

Body:
Severe paint peeling. Some rusting. Good body construction.

Safety Defects:
The left front turn signal and parking lamp assembly may not comply with the Federal Motor Vehicle Safety Standards. Rear axle may be defective.

Recommendation:
Not recommended. Cost of ownership is too great.

Buick Division   **1975**
General Motors
BUICK (Full-sized)
Le Sabre/Electra

All data based on four-door sedan

Used Car Price* $2,300
Based on standard equipped car with automatic transmission and radio.
Price assumes excellent condition.

*Subtract $25 for each month after August for current price.

Statistical Comparison:
Rapid depreciation.
Average parts availability.
High parts costs.
Poor gas mileage.

Technical Data

Wheelbase . .	124 in.	Standard Engine . . .	V8 (350)
Length	226.9 in.	Standard Brakes . . .	Disc-drum
Weight	4,512 lbs.	Gasoline Mileage . . .	10
Width	79.9 in.	(with unleaded fuel)	

Frequency of Repairs:
Problems with fuel pump, motor, automatic transmission, and carburetor. Brakes and suspension perform well.

Body:
Severe paint peeling. Paint problems and surface rusting more extensive on this model than all other GM cars.

Safety Defects:
Rear axle may be defective. Possibility of wheel failure.

Recommendation:
Not recommended. An Oldsmobile or Le Mans is a better buy.

OLDSMOBILE (Full-sized)
Oldsmobile 88/98

All data based on four-door sedan

Used Car Price* $2,300
Based on standard equipped car with automatic transmission
and radio.
Price assumes excellent condition.

*Subtract $25 for each month after August for current price.

Statistical Comparison:
Below average depreciation.
Excellent parts availability.
Low parts costs.
Below average gas mileage.

Technical Data

Wheelbase . .	124 in.	Standard Engine . . .	V8 (350)
Length	226.7 in.	Standard Brakes . . .	Disc-drum
Weight	4,481 lbs.	Gasoline Mileage . . .	11
Width	79.9 in.	(with unleaded fuel)	

Frequency of Repairs:
Good electrical system, brakes, carburetor, and suspension.
Problems with automatic transmission and malfunctioning
motor.

Body:
Paint peeling over entire body. Some rusting on doors and
fenders.

Safety Defects:
Radial tires used as original equipment (Goodyear) may be
defective. Rear axle may be defective. Catalytic convertor may
be a fire hazard. Automatic cruise control may malfunction.

Recommendation:
Recommended. Be sure to examine motor and transmission
before purchase.

Ford Division   **1975**
Ford Motor Company
PINTO/BOBCAT

All data based on two-door sedan

Used Car Price* $1,200
Based on standard equipped car with automatic transmission
and radio.
Price assumes excellent condition.

*Subtract $25 for each month after August for current price.

Statistical Comparison:
Rapid depreciation.
Good parts availability.
Average parts costs.
Poor gas mileage.

Technical Data

Wheelbase . .	94.5 in.	Standard Engine . . .	4 cyl. (140)
Length	169 in.	Standard Brakes . . .	Disc-drum
Weight	2,562 lbs.	Gasoline Mileage . . .	18
Width	69.4 in.	(with unleaded fuel)	

Frequency of Repairs:
Motor improved. Suspension and electrical system are good.
Problems with carburetor, brakes, and automatic transmission.

Safety Defects:
Brake pedal could be defective. Firestone radial tires installed
as original equipment may be defective.

Recommendation:
Not recommended. An expensive economy car that only a masochist could support. Gas tank fire-prone.

Ford Division   **1975**
Ford Motor Company
MAVERICK/COMET

All data based on two-door sedan

Used Car Price* $1,800
Based on standard equipped car with automatic transmission
and radio.
Price assumes excellent condition.

*Subtract $25 for each month after August for current price.

Statistical Comparison:
Slow depreciation.
Average parts availability.
Average parts costs.
Average gas mileage.

Technical Data

Wheelbase . .	103 in.	Standard Engine . . .	6 cyl. (200)
Length	187 in.	Standard Brakes . . .	Drum
Weight	2,980 lbs.	Gasoline Mileage . . .	16
Width	70.5 in.	(with unleaded fuel)	

Frequency of Repairs:
Excellent transmission. Good brakes. Problems with motor and
carburetor. Some vibration problems still reported.

Body:
Doors, fenders, and wheel wells may rust prematurely. Paint defects common.

Safety Defects:
Engine wiring harness may have been routed incorrectly. Brake pedal may malfunction. Original equipment Firestone radial tires could be defective.

Recommendation:
Recommended. Car should not be driven in high corrosion environment.

Ford Division   **1975**
Ford Motor Company
MUSTANG II

All data based on two-door sedan

Used Car Price* $1,700
Based on standard equipped car with automatic transmission and radio.
Price assumes excellent condition.

*Subtract $25 for each month after August for current price.

Statistical Comparison:
Above average depreciation.
Average parts availability.
High parts costs.
Poor gas mileage.

Technical Data

Wheelbase . .	96.2 in.	Standard Engine . . .	4 cyl. (140)
Length	175 in.	Standard Brakes . . .	Disc-drum
Weight	2,776 lbs.	Gasoline Mileage . . .	16
Width	70.2 in.	(with unleaded fuel)	

Frequency of Repairs:
Suspension improved. Good brakes. Problems with carburetor, motor, transmission, and electrical system.

Body:
Premature rust and paint defects on doors, wheel wells, and fenders.

Safety Defects:
Potentially hazardous brake pedal and Firestone radial tires.

Recommendation:
Not recommended. A sad postscript to the original Mustang reputation.

Ford Division 1975
Ford Motor Company
TORINO/FAIRLANE/MONTEGO

All data based on four-door sedan

Used Car Price* $1,900
Based on standard equipped car with automatic transmission
and radio.
Price assumes excellent condition.

*Subtract $25 for each month after August for current price.

Statistical Comparison:
Rapid depreciation.
Average parts availability.
High parts costs.
Poor gas mileage.

Technical Data

Wheelbase . .	118 in.	Standard Engine . . .	V8 (351)
Length	218.4 in.	Standard Brakes . . .	Disc-drum
Weight	4,220 lbs.	Gasoline Mileage . . .	10
Width	79.3 in.	(with unleaded fuel)	

Frequency of Repairs:
Good brakes. Chronic motor, transmission, and carburetor
problems. High speed vibrations reported. Hard starting and
frequent stalling also reported.

Body:
Paint defects, premature rusting, and poor body construction
continue to plague this model.

Safety Defects:
Defective carburetor may jam throttle open. Original equipment Firestone radial tires could be defective. Brake pedal
could malfunction.

Recommendation:
Not recommended. The Torino is still a turkey.

Ford Division 1975
Ford Motor Company
FORD (Full-sized)
LTD/Galaxie

All data based on four-door sedan

Used Car Price* $2,200
Based on standard equipped car with automatic transmission
and radio.
Price assumes excellent condition.

*Subtract $25 for each month after August for current price.

Statistical Comparison:
Above average depreciation.
Average parts availability.
High parts costs.
Poor gas mileage.

Technical Data

Wheelbase . .	121 in.	Standard Engine . . .	V8 (351)
Length	223.9 in.	Standard Brakes . . .	Disc-drum
Weight	4,451 lbs.	Gasoline Mileage . . .	8
Width	79.5 in.	(with unleaded fuel)	

Frequency of Repairs:
Good suspension and brakes. Serious problems with motor, transmission, carburetor, and electrical system.

Body:
Paint defects, premature rusting, and body rattles reported.

Safety Defects:
Possibility that brake pedal pivot bolt nut may work free, resulting in a loss of brake pedal movement. Original equipment Firestone radial tires may be defective.

Recommendation:
Not recommended. General Motors models offer more value.

Ford Division   **1975**
Ford Motor Company
GRANADA/MONARCH

All data based on four-door sedan

Used Car Price* $1,900
Based on standard equipped car with automatic transmission and radio.
Price assumes excellent condition.

*Subtract $25 for each month after August for current price.

Statistical Comparison:
Rapid depreciation.
Average parts availability.
Above average parts costs.
Poor gas mileage.

Technical Data

Wheelbase . .	109.9 in.	Standard Engine . . .	V8 (302)
Length	197.7 in.	Standard Brakes . . .	Disc-drum
Weight	3,470 lbs.	Gasoline Mileage . . .	11
Width	74 in.	(with unleaded fuel)	

Frequency of Repairs:
Good brakes. Problems with carburetor (stalling, hard start-ing), suspension (excessive front-end vibrations), motor (fre-quent tune-ups), and transmission.

Body:
Paint mis-match and peeling. Reports of premature rusting. Rear gas tank cover often falls off due to defective spring and latch assembly. (Warranty extended to fix this design defect.)

Safety Defects:
Heater-defroster system may malfunction due to faulty connec-tion with air conditioning unit. Original equipment Firestone tires may be defective and blow out prematurely.

Recommendation:
Not recommended. Ford should be ashamed in comparing this lemon to a Mercedes-Benz.

Plymouth Division   **1975**
Chrysler Corporation
VALIANT

All data based on four-door sedan

Used Car Price* $1,800
Based on standard equipped car with automatic transmission and radio.
Price assumes excellent condition.

*Subtract $25 for each month after August for current price.

Statistical Comparison:
Slow depreciation.
Good parts availability.
Average parts costs.
Good gas mileage.

Technical Data

Wheelbase . .	111 in.	Standard Engine . . .	6 cyl. (225)
Length	199 in.	Standard Brakes . . .	Drum
Weight	3,100 lbs.	Gasoline Mileage . . .	18
Width	71 in.	(with unleaded fuel)	

Frequency of Repairs:
Good motor, transmission, and electrical system. Problems with carburetor (stalling), brakes (premature wear and locking), and suspension (loose).

Body:
Excellent corrosion resistance except for front fenders. No paint problems. Some water leaks into passenger compartment reported.

Safety Defects:
Original equipment Goodyear radial tires may be defective. Floor covering may interfere with accelerator pedal.

Recommendation:
Recommended. Still the best compact car on the market, although quality control has slipped.

Dodge Division   1975
Chrysler Corporation
DART

All data based on four-door sedan

Used Car Price* $1,900
Based on standard equipped car with automatic transmission and radio.
Price assumes excellent condition.

*Subtract $25 for each month after August for current price.

Statistical Comparison:
Below average depreciation.
Excellent parts availability.
Average parts costs.
Good gas mileage.

Technical Data

Wheelbase . .	111 in.	Standard Engine . . .	6 cyl. (225)
Length	203.2 in.	Standard Brakes . . .	Disc-drum
Weight	3,125 lbs.	Gasoline Mileage . . .	18
Width	69.8 in.	(with unleaded fuel)	

Frequency of Repairs:
Excellent motor. Problems reported with automatic transmission, short-circuiting starting mechanism, carburetor malfunctioning, brakes, and excessive road vibrations possibly caused by tires or suspension.

Body:
Solid body construction. Water leaks reported around windshield. Front fenders less vulnerable to rust-out than prior models. No serious paint problems.

Safety Defects:
Carpet or rubber mat may interfere with action of accelerator pedal. Original equipment tires (Goodyear) may fail prematurely.

Recommendation:
Recommended. Despite the 1975's poor quality control, it still has few defects that cannot be easily repaired.

SATELLITE/FURY

All data based on four-door sedan

Used Car Price* $2,300
Based on standard equipped car with automatic transmission
and radio.
Price assumes excellent condition.

*Subtract $25 for each month after August for current price.

Statistical Comparison:
Below average depreciation.
Average parts costs.
Average parts availability.
Below average gas mileage.

Technical Data

Wheelbase . .	117.5 in.	Standard Engine . . .	V8 (318)
Length	217.9 in.	Standard Brakes . . .	Disc-drum
Weight	3,835 lbs.	Gasoline Mileage . . .	12
Width	77.7 in.	(with unleaded fuel)	

Frequency of Repairs:
Motor, suspension, and electrical system very reliable. Problems reported with carburetor, transmission, and brakes. Vibrations reported at speeds of 20–60 mph.

Body:
Excellent body construction. Fenders less vulnerable to rust
perforations. Paint mis-matching common.

Safety Defects:
Front suspension lower control arm strut may disengage. Original equipment jack may malfunction. Original equipment tires
(Goodyear) may have premature catastrophic tread separation
at high speeds.

Recommendation:
Not recommended. Only the police and taxi models are better
constructed.

Dodge Division   **1975**
Chrysler Corporation

CORDOBA/CHARGER

All data based on four-door sedan

Used Car Price* $2,500
Based on standard equipped car with automatic transmission
and radio.
Price assumes excellent condition.

*Subtract $25 for each month after August for current price.

Statistical Comparison:
Above average depreciation.
Average parts availability.
Above average parts costs.
Poor gas mileage.

Technical Data

Wheelbase . .	115 in.	Standard Engine . . .	V8 (360)
Length	215.3 in.	Standard Brakes . . .	Disc-drum
Weight	4,400 lbs.	Gasoline Mileage . . .	8
Width	76.3 in.	(with unleaded fuel)	

Frequency of Repairs:
Good electrical system. Serious problems with brakes, suspension, transmission, carburetor, and motor. Excessive vibrations at speeds of 20–60 mph reported.

Body:
Premature rusting, body rattles, and paint defects reported by Cordoba owners. Water leaks also a common complaint.

Safety Defects:
Original equipment (Goodyear) radial tires may not be round or may fail at high speeds.

Recommendation:
Not recommended. A very attractive luxury LEMON.

Dodge Division   **1975**
Chrysler Corporation
MONACO (Full-sized)

All data based on four-door sedan

Used Car Price* $2,100
Based on standard equipped car with automatic transmission and radio.
Price assumes excellent condition.

*Subtract $25 for each month after August for current price.

Statistical Comparison:
Rapid depreciation.
High parts costs.
Below average parts availability.
Poor gas mileage.

Technical Data

Wheelbase . .	121.5 in.	Standard Engine . . .	V8 (360)
Length	225.6 in.	Standard Brakes . . .	Disc-drum
Weight	4,420 lbs.	Gasoline Mileage . . .	9
Width	79.8 in.	(with unleaded fuel)	

Frequency of Repairs:
Good transmission. Problems with premature brake wear and lock-up. Carburetor defects may cause hard starting and frequent stalling. Problems still reported with motor and electrical system.

Body:
Body construction still poor. Paint mis-match and rattles common problems. Front fenders still rust-prone. Excessive interior noise and water leaks reported.

Safety Defects:
Possibility of defective front lower control arm strut. Original equipment jack may malfunction. Original equipment tires (Goodyear) may be defective.

Recommendation:
Not recommended. Owning this car is like paying alimony— outrageous expenses for little performance.

American Motors   1975
AMC HORNET

All data based on four-door sedan

Used Car Price* $1,900
Based on standard equipped car with automatic transmission and radio.
Price assumes excellent condition.

*Subtract $25 for each month after August for current price.

Statistical Comparison:
Below average depreciation.
Average parts costs.
Average parts availability.
Average gas mileage.

Technical Data

Wheelbase . .	108 in.	Standard Engine . . .	6 cyl. (232)
Length	189.4 in.	Standard Brakes . . .	Drum
Weight	2,966 lbs.	Gasoline Mileage . . .	17
Width	71.1 in.	(with regular fuel)	

Frequency of Repairs:
Excellent transmission. Problems with carburetor and motor. Some minor problems reported with brake efficiency and electrical system.

Body:
Solid body construction. Good rust resistance. Few rattles.

Safety Defects:
Original equipment tires (Goodyear, Firestone, or Uniroyal) may be defective.

Recommendation:
Recommended. An average car that has been abused by the cost cutters of Detroit.

American Motors   **1975**
AMC GREMLIN

All data based on two-door sedan

Used Car Price* $1,500
Based on standard equipped car with automatic transmission and radio.
Price assumes excellent condition.

*Subtract $25 for each month after August for current price.

Statistical Comparison:
Average depreciation.
Average parts costs.
Excellent parts availability.
Good gas mileage.

Technical Data

Wheelbase . .	96 in.	Standard Engine . . .	6 cyl. (232)
Length	170.3 in.	Standard Brakes . . .	Drum
Weight	2,767 lbs.	Gasoline Mileage . . .	20
Width	70.6 in.	(with regular fuel)	

Frequency of Repairs:
Good transmission. Problems with motor and brakes. Some difficulties have been reported with the electrical system. Minor carburetor malfunctioning.

Body:
Solid body construction. Little rusting or rattles. Limited interior space.

Safety Defects:
Original equipment tires may fail at high speeds.

Recommendation:
Recommended. Although 1975 model is not as good as prior models, it is better than its nearest competitors.

American Motors   **1975**
PACER

All data based on two-door sedan

Used Car Price* $1,800
Based on standard equipped car with automatic transmission and radio.
Price assumes excellent condition.

*Subtract $25 for each month after August for current price.

Statistical Comparison:
Average depreciation.
Average parts costs.
Below average parts availability.
Average gas mileage.

Technical Data

Wheelbase	100 in.	Standard Engine	6 cyl. (232)
Length	171.5 in.	Standard Brakes	Disc-drum
Weight	2,995 lbs.	Gasoline Mileage	17
Width	77 in.	(with regular fuel)	

Frequency of Repairs:
Excellent motor, transmission, and suspension. Problems with carburetor, brakes, and electrical system. Rear window defrosting may malfunction due to faulty hose connection.

Body:
Unusual body configuration may accelerate rusting. Water leaks reported. Interior and exterior trim may be defective. Rear trunk lock can be easily disconnected.

Safety Defects:
Fuel line retainer clip may have been improperly installed. Original equipment tires may be defective.

Recommendation:
Not recommended. This year's Pacer has too many quality control "bugs" that need correcting.

1976 MODELS

VEGA/ASTRE

Used Car Price* $1,600
Based on standard equipped car with automatic transmission
and radio.
Price assumes excellent condition.

*Subtract $50 for each month after August for current price.

Statistical Comparison:
Terrible depreciation.
Average parts supply.
Expensive parts.
Poor gas mileage.

Technical Data

Wheelbase . .	97 in.	Standard Engine . . .	4 cyl. (140)
Length	175.4 in.	Standard Brakes . . .	Disc-Drum
Weight	2,523 lbs.	Gasoline Mileage . . .	27
Width	644 in.	(with regular fuel)	

Frequency of Repairs:
Motor noisy. Disc brakes wear prematurely. Some crankshaft
problems reported.

Body:
Paint adhesion poor causing rust blisters.

Safety Defects
Original equipment radial tires may be defective.

Recommendation:
Avoid this car like the plague.

NOVA/CONCOURS

Used Car Price* $2,400
Based on standard equipped car with automatic transmission
and radio.
Price assumes excellent condition.

*Subtract $30 for each month after August for current price.

Statistical Comparison:
Slow depreciation.
Excellent parts supply.
Average parts cost.
Poor gas mileage.

Technical Data

Wheelbase . .	111 in.	Standard Engine . . .	6 cyl. (250)
Length	196.7 in.	Standard Brakes . . .	Disc-Drum

Weight . . . . 3,331 lbs. Gasoline Mileage . . . 21
Width . . . . . 72.2 in.   (with regular fuel)

Frequency of Repairs:
Carburetor, electrical system, and transmission defects.

Body:
Rust blisters caused by poor paint adhesion.

Safety Defects:
Catalytic converter may overheat. Headlamps and reflectors
may be defective.

Recommendation:
Buy a Chevrolet Impala or Caprice V8 instead.

Chevrolet Division   **1976**
General Motors
CHEVELLE

Used Car Price* $2,400
Based on standard equipped car with automatic transmission
and radio.
Price assumes excellent condition.
*Subtract $30 for each month after August for current price.

Statistical Comparison:
Slow depreciation.
Excellent parts supply.
Inexpensive parts.
Good gas mileage.

Technical Data
Wheelbase . . 112 in.   Standard Engine . . . 6 cyl. (250)
Length . . . . 205.7 in.   Standard Brakes . . . Disc-Drum
Weight . . . . 3,766 lbs. Gasoline Mileage . . . 20
Width . . . . . 76.9 in.   (with regular fuel)

Frequency of Repairs:
6 cylinder motor a bit sluggish. Motor noisy.

Body:
Premature paint peeling.

Safety Defects:
Catalytic converter may overheat. Radial tires could be defective.

Recommendation:
A good, average car with average safety defects.

CHEVROLET (Full-sized)
Impala/Caprice

Used Car Price* $2,100
Based on standard equipped car with automatic transmission
and radio.
Price assumes excellent condition.

*Subtract $30 for each month after August for current price.

Statistical Comparison:
Slow depreciation.
Excellent parts supply.
Inexpensive parts.
Fair gas economy.

Technical Data

Wheelbase . .	121.5 in.	Standard Engine . . .	V8 (350)
Length	222.7 in.	Standard Brakes . . .	Disc-Drum
Weight	4,361 lbs.	Gasoline Mileage . . .	15
Width	79.5 in.	(with regular fuel)	

Frequency of Repairs:
Minor motor problems and some crankshaft defects.

Body:
Paint peeling a serious problem.

Safety Defects:
Problems with the catalytic converter and some radial tires.

Recommendation:
An excellent large-size car.

VENTURA

Used Car Price* $2,000
Based on standard equipped car with automatic transmission
and radio.
Price assumes excellent condition.

*Subtract $30 for each month after August for current price.

Statistical Comparison:
Average depreciation.
Average parts supply.
Average parts cost.
Poor gas economy.

Technical Data

Wheelbase . .	111.1 in.	Standard Engine . . .	6 cyl. (250)
Length	199.6 in.	Standard Brakes . . .	Disc-Drum

Weight . . . . 3,381 lbs. Gasoline Mileage . . . 20
Width . . . . . 72.4 in.   (with regular fuel)

Frequency of Repairs:
Transmission and motor problems.

Body:
Considerable paint peeling and poor body assembly.

Safety Defects:
Possibility of defective radial tires and catalytic converter.

Recommendation:
Don't buy. Try a Nova instead.

Pontiac Division   **1976**
General Motors
LE MANS

Used Car Price* $2,300
Based on standard equipped car with automatic transmission
and radio.
Price assumes excellent condition.

*Subtract $30 for each month after August for current price.

Statistical Comparison:
Average depreciation.
Good parts supply.
Inexpensive parts.
Poor fuel economy.

Technical Data
Wheelbase . . 112 in.   Standard Engine . . . 6 cyl. (250)
Length . . . . 208 in.   Standard Brakes . . . Disc-Drum
Weight . . . . 3,767 lbs. Gasoline Mileage . . . 19
Width . . . . . 77.4 in.   (with regular fuel)

Frequency of Repairs:

Motor and suspension system problems reported.

Body:
Premature paint peeling a problem.

Safety Defects:
Catalytic converter may overheat and radial tire tread could
separate.

Recommendation:
Choose the Oldsmobile Cutlass or Monte Carlo instead.

Pontiac Division   **1976**
General Motors
PONTIAC (Full-sized)
Catalina/Bonneville

Used Car Price* $2,500
Based on standard equipped car with automatic transmission
and radio.
Price assumes excellent condition.

*Subtract $30 for each month after August for current price.

Statistical Comparison:
Average depreciation.
Excellent parts supply.
Inexpensive parts.
Poor fuel economy.

Technical Data

Wheelbase . .	123.4 in.	Standard Engine . . .	V8 (400)
Length	226 in.	Standard Brakes . . .	Disc-Drum
Weight	4,416 lbs.	Gasoline Mileage . . .	15
Width	79.6 in.	(with regular fuel)	

Frequency of Repairs:
Motor, transmission, and suspension problems.

Body:
Premature rusting caused by paint flaking.

Safety Defects:
Catalytic converter and radial tires.

Recommendation:
Not recommended. A real gas-eater.

Buick Division   **1976**
General Motors
BUICK (Full-sized)
Le Sabre

Used Car Price* $2,800
Based on standard equipped car with automatic transmission
and radio.
Price assumes excellent condition.

*Subtract $30 for each month after August for current price.

Statistical Comparison:
Average depreciation.
Excellent parts supply.
Average parts cost.
Average fuel economy.

Technical Data

Wheelbase . .	124 in.	Standard Engine . . .	8 cyl. (350)
Length	226.9 in.	Standard Brakes . . .	Disc-Drum
Weight	4,238 lbs.	Gasoline Mileage . . .	15
Width	79.9 in.	(with regular fuel)	

Frequency of Repairs:
Motor and pollution control system failure prone. Transmission problems reported.

Body:
Excessive paint peeling (Buick Century most vulnerable).

Safety Defects:
Radial tires and catalytic converter.

Recommendation:
A good purchase.

Oldsmobile Division   **1976**
General Motors
OLDSMOBILE (Full-sized)

Used Car Price* $2,700
Based on standard equipped car with automatic transmission and radio.
Price assumes excellent condition.

*Subtract $30 for each month after August for current price.

Statistical Comparison:
Slow depreciation.
Excellent parts supply.
Low parts cost.
Excellent fuel economy.

Technical Data

Wheelbase . .	124 in.	Standard Engine . . .	V8 (350)
Length	226.7 in.	Standard Brakes . . .	Disc-Drum
Weight	4,481 lbs.	Gasoline Mileage . . .	15
Width	79.9 in.	(with regular fuel)	

Frequency of Repairs:
Some starting problems. Good motor.

Body:
Vulnerable to premature rusting and paint peeling.

Safety Defects:
Radial tires may fail and catalytic converter may overheat.

Recommendation:
An average buy, but watch out for the rusting.

PINTO/BOBCAT

Used Car Price* $1,300
Based on standard equipped car with automatic transmission
and radio.
Price assumes excellent condition.

*Subtract $30 for each month after August for current price.

Statistical Comparison:
Rapid depreciation.
Average parts supply.
Expensive parts.
Poor fuel economy.

Technical Data

Wheelbase . .	94.5 in.	Standard Engine . . .	4 cyl. (140)
Length	169 in.	Standard Brakes . . .	Disc-Drum
Weight	2,562 lbs.	Gasoline Mileage . . .	26
Width	69.4 in.	(with regular fuel)	

Frequency of Repairs:
Carburetor, transmission, and suspension problems reported.

Body:
Some rusting along door bottom. Generally more rust resistant.

Safety Defects:
Possibility fuel tank may be hazardous.

Recommendation:
Stay away. This is Ford's answer to the GM Vega and Astre.
This car can become an instant Molotov cocktail at the slightest
rear-end collision.

MAVERICK/COMET

Used Car Price* $1,800
Based on standard equipped car with automatic transmission
and radio.
Price assumes excellent condition.

*Subtract $30 for each month after August for current price.

Statistical Comparison:
Slow depreciation.
Excellent parts supply.
Inexpensive parts cost.
Good fuel economy.

Technical Data

Wheelbase	103 in.	Standard Engine	6 cyl. (200)
Length	187 in.	Standard Brakes	Disc-Drum
Weight	2,980 lbs.	Gasoline Mileage	20
Width	70.5 in.	(with regular fuel)	

Frequency of Repairs:
Good motor and transmission. Rear suspension is weak. Carburetor and brake problems are reported.

Body:
Some rust problems around doors and wheel wells.

Safety Defects:
Gas tank and radial tires may be defective.

Recommendation:
An excellent compact car.

Ford Division   1976
Ford Motor Company
MUSTANG II

Used Car Price* $1,900
Based on standard equipped car with automatic transmission and radio.
Price assumes excellent condition.

*Subtract $30 for each month after August for current price.

Statistical Comparison:
Rapid depreciation.
Average parts supply.
High parts costs.
Fair fuel economy.

Technical Data

Wheelbase	96.2 in.	Standard Engine	4 cyl. (140)
Length	175 in.	Standard Brakes	Disc-Drum
Weight	2,735 lbs.	Gasoline Mileage	26
Width	70.2 in.	(with regular fuel)	

Frequency of Repairs:
Front suspension and carburetion problems.

Body:
Paint defects and rusting reported.

Safety Defects:
Fuel tank may be hazardous and radial tires may fail.

Recommendation:
Not a wise buy.

TORINO/MONTEGO

Used Car Price* $2,200
Based on standard equipped car with automatic transmission
and radio.
Price assumes excellent condition.

*Subtract $30 for each month after August for current price.

Statistical Comparison:
Rapid depreciation.
Average parts supply.
Average parts cost.
Poor fuel economy.

Technical Data

Wheelbase	118 in.	Standard Engine . . .	V8 (351)
Length	219 in.	Standard Brakes . . .	Disc-Drum
Weight	4,259 lbs.	Gasoline Mileage . . .	15
Width	78.6 in.	(with regular fuel)	

Frequency of Repairs:
Motor and suspension problems reported.

Body:
Some premature rusting reported.

Safety Defects:
Radial tires may fail.

Recommendation:
Not a wise buy.

GRANADA/MONARCH

Used Car Price* $2,100
Based on standard equipped car with automatic transmission
and radio.
Price assumes excellent condition.

*Subtract $30 for each month after August for current price.

Statistical Comparison:
Rapid depreciation.
Average parts supply.
Expensive parts cost.
Poor fuel economy.

Technical Data

Wheelbase	109.9 in.	Standard Engine . . .	V8 (302)
Length	197.7 in.	Standard Brakes . . .	Disc-Drum

Weight . . . . 3,500 lbs. Gasoline Mileage . . . 15
Width . . . . . 74 in.   (with unleaded fuel)

Frequency of Repairs:
Motor and carburetor problems reported.

Body:
Premature rusting reported.

Safety Defects:
Fuel tank may be hazardous. Front suspension and shoulder belts also might fail.

Recommendation:
This car has more style than quality.

Plymouth/Dodge Division   **1976**
Chrysler Corporation
VALIANT/DART

Used Car Price* $2,000
Based on standard equipped car with automatic transmission and radio.
Price assumes excellent condition.

*Subtract $30 for each month after August for current price.

Statistical Comparison:
Little depreciation.
Excellent parts supply.
Low parts cost.
Excellent fuel economy.

Technical Data
Wheelbase . . 108 in.   Standard Engine . . . 6 cyl. (225)
Length . . . . 200.9 in.   Standard Brakes . . . Disc-Drum
Weight . . . . 3,045 lbs. Gasoline Mileage . . . 21
Width . . . . . 71.7 in.   (with unleaded fuel)

Frequency of Repairs:
Suspension, stalling, vibrations, and brakes are most criticized.

Body:
Water leaks into car interior.

Safety Defects:
Radial tires could fail.

Recommendation:
Best compact car Chrysler makes. The last year for the Dart/Valiant nameplate is 1976. Both models renamed Aspen and Volare.

FURY

Used Car Price* $2,500
Based on standard equipped car with automatic transmission
and radio.
Price assumes excellent condition.

*Subtract $30 for each month after August for current price.

Statistical Comparison:
Average depreciation.
Average parts supply.
Average parts cost.
Excellent fuel economy.

Technical Data

Wheelbase	117.5 in.	Standard Engine . . .	V8 (318)
Length	218.4 in.	Standard Brakes . . .	Disc-Drum
Weight	4,025 lbs.	Gasoline Mileage . . .	21
Width	77.7 in.	(with unleaded fuel)	

Frequency of Repairs:
Vibrations, brake problems and transmission failures.

Body:
Severe leaking of water into interior.

Safety Defects:
Radial tires may be defective.

Recommendation:
A good average car.

CORDOBA/CHARGER

Used Car Price* $2,700
Based on standard equipped car with automatic transmission
and radio.
Price assumes excellent condition.

*Subtract $30 for each month after August for current price.

Statistical Comparison:
Rapid depreciation.
Poor parts supply.
High parts cost.
Poor fuel economy.

Wheelbase . .	115 in.	Standard Engine . . .	V8 (318)
Length	215.3 in.	Standard Brakes . . .	Disc-Drum
Weight	4,005 lbs.	Gasoline Mileage . . .	15
Width	77.1 in.	(with unleaded fuel)	

Frequency of Repairs:
Vibrations and brakes most common problem.

Body:
Frequent water leaks into interior.

Safety Defects:
Radial tires may fail.

Recommendation:
Not recommended. Needs more quality control by the factory.

Dodge Division   **1976**
Chrysler Corporation
MONACO (Full-sized)

Used Car Price* $2,500
Based on standard equipped car with automatic transmission
and radio.
Price assumes excellent condition.

*Subtract $30 for each month after August for current price.

Statistical Comparison:
Rapid depreciation.
Average parts supply.
Average parts cost.
Poor fuel economy.

Technical Data

Wheelbase . .	121.5 in.	Standard Engine . . .	V8 (318)
Length	225.7 in.	Standard Brakes . . .	Disc-Drum
Weight	4,250 lbs.	Gasoline Mileage . . .	15
Width	79.8 in.	(with unleaded fuel)	

Frequency of Repairs:
Motor stalling; brakes locking or premature wear reported.
Some reports of transmission failures.

Body:
Frequent water leaks into interior.

Safety Defects:
Radial tires could be defective.

Recommendation:
Not recommended.

AMC HORNET

Used Car Price* $2,100
Based on standard equipped car with automatic transmission
and radio.
Price assumes excellent condition.

*Subtract $30 for each month after August for current price.

Statistical Comparison:
Average depreciation.
Average parts supply.
Low parts cost.
Average fuel economy.

Technical Data

Wheelbase . .	108 in.	Standard Engine . . .	6 cyl. (232)
Length	186 in.	Standard Brakes . . .	Disc-Drum
Weight	2,905 lbs.	Gasoline Mileage . . .	19
Width	71 in.	(with regular fuel)	

Frequency of Repairs:
Motor and transmission problems.

Body:
Solid body construction, except for bumpers.

Safety Defects:
N/A

Recommendation:
Recommended. A reliable economy car.

AMC GREMLIN

Used Car Price* $1,800
Based on standard equipped car with automatic transmission
and radio.
Price assumes excellent condition.

*Subtract $30 for each month after August for current price.

Statistical Comparison:
Average depreciation.
Good parts supply.
Average parts cost.
Excellent fuel economy.

Technical Data

Wheelbase . .	96 in.	Standard Engine . . .	6 cyl. (232)
Length	169.4 in.	Standard Brakes . . .	Disc-Drum
Weight	2,761 lbs.	Gasoline Mileage . . .	21
Width	70.1 in.	(with regular fuel)	

Frequency of Repairs:
Brakes and steering problems reported.

Body:
Slight rusting on bumpers. Solid body construction.

Safety Defects:
N/A

Recommendation:
Recommended. An excellent subcompact urban car.

American Motors 1976
PACER

Used Car Price* $2,000
Based on standard equipped car with automatic transmission
and radio.
Price assumes excellent condition.

*Subtract $30 for each month after August for current price.

Statistical Comparison:
Rapid depreciation.
Average parts supply.
Expensive parts.
Average fuel economy.

Technical Data

Wheelbase . .	100 in.	Standard Engine . . .	6 cyl. (232)
Length	170 in.	Standard Brakes . . .	Disc-Drum
Weight	3,180 lbs.	Gasoline Mileage . . .	19
Width	77 in.	(with regular fuel)	

Frequency of Repairs:
Electrical and suspension problems.

Body:
Poor assembly of sheet metal. Door frames and bottoms highly
vulnerable to rusting.

Safety Defects:
N/A

Recommendation:
Not recommended. This is one original idea that has been
rejected by the public.

1977 MODELS

VEGA/ASTRE

Used Car Price* $1,800
Based on standard equipped car with automatic transmission
and radio.
Price assumes excellent condition

*Subtract $75 for each month after August for current price.

Statistical Comparison:
Wildly fluctuating depreciation.
Good parts supply.
Expensive parts.
Poor gas mileage.

Technical Data

Wheelbase . .	97 in.	Standard Engine . . .	4 cyl. (140)
Length	175.4 in.	Standard Brakes . . .	Disc-Drum
Weight	2,636 lbs.	Gasoline Mileage . . .	27
Width	65.4 in.	(with regular fuel)	

Frequency of Repairs:
Motor stalling, premature brake wear, and carburetor problems.

Body:
Poor paint adhesion still a problem.

Safety Defects:
Possibility of defective tires and electrical system.

Recommendation:
Don't be a sucker for this car. Even GM has dropped it from its
future models.

NOVA/CONCOURS

Used Car Price* $2,900
Based on standard equipped car with automatic transmission
and radio.
Price assumes excellent condition.

*Subtract $50 for each month after August for current price.

Statistical Comparison:
Slow depreciation.
Excellent parts supply.
Average parts cost.
Poor gas mileage.

Technical Data

Wheelbase . .	111 in.	Standard Engine . . .	6 cyl. (250)
Length	196.7 in.	Standard Brakes . . .	Disc-Drum
Weight	3,284 lbs.	Gasoline Mileage . . .	21
Width	65.4 in.	(with regular fuel)	

Frequency of Repairs:
Some minor motor and transmission defects.

Body:
Reports of mismatched and peeling paint.

Safety Defects:
Catalytic converter may overheat. Headlamps and reflectors may be defective. Power brake booster.

Recommendation:
A Chevy Impala or Caprice V8 still a better buy.

Chevrolet Division   **1977**
General Motors

CHEVELLE

Used Car Price* $2,600
Based on standard equipped car with automatic transmission and radio.
Price assumes excellent condition.

*Subtract $50 for each month after August for current price.

Statistical Comparison:
Slow depreciation.
Excellent parts supply.
Inexpensive parts supply.
Good gas economy.

Technical Data

Wheelbase . .	112 in.	Standard Engine . . .	6 cyl. (250)
Length	205.7 in.	Standard Brakes . . .	Disc-Drum
Weight	3,667 lbs.	Gasoline Mileage . . .	20
Width	76.9 in.	(with regular fuel)	

Frequency of Repairs:
Minor starting problems. Some motors maladjusted.

Body:
Paint peeling.

Safety Defects:
Catalytic converter may overheat. Radial tires may be defective. Power brake booster.

Recommendation:
Buy it. A good family-sized car.

CHEVROLET (Full-sized)
Impala/Caprice

Used Car Price* $2,300
Based on standard equipped car with automatic transmission
and radio.
Price assumes excellent condition.

*Subtract $50 for each month after August for current price.

Statistical Comparison:
Slow depreciation.
Excellent parts supply.
Inexpensive parts.
Fair gas economy.

Technical Data
Wheelbase . .	116 in.	Standard Engine . . .	V8 (350)
Length	212.1 in.	Standard Brakes . . .	Disc-Drum
Weight	3,771 lbs.	Gasoline Mileage . . .	15
Width	76 in.	(with unleaded fuel)	

Frequency of Repairs:
Carburetor and minor motor problems.

Body:
Paint peeling still a problem.

Safety Defects:
Radial tires and catalytic converter may be defective.

Recommendation:
The best of the large-size cars.

VENTURA

Used Car Price* $2,300
Based on standard equipped car with automatic transmission
and radio.
Price assumes excellent condition.

*Subtract $50 for each month after August for current price.

Statistical Comparison:
Average depreciation.
Good parts supply.
Inexpensive parts.
Poor gas economy.

Technical Data
Wheelbase . .	111.1 in.	Standard Engine . . .	6 cyl. (231)
Length	199.3 in.	Standard Brakes . . .	Disc-Drum

Weight . . . . 3,277 lbs. Gasoline Mileage . . . 22
Width . . . . . 72.4 in.   (with unleaded fuel)

Frequency of Repairs:
Motor stalling and some crankshaft problems.

Body:
Some paint defects.

Safety Defects:
Possibility of defective radial tires and catalytic converter.
Power brake booster.

Recommendation:
Not a good buy. Other GM models are better.

Pontiac Division   **1977**
General Motors
LE MANS

Used Car Price* $2,900
Based on standard equipped car with automatic transmission
and radio.
Price assumes excellent condition.

*Subtract $50 for each month after August for current price.

Statistical Comparison:
Average depreciation.
Good parts supply.
Inexpensive parts.
Poor fuel economy.

Technical Data
Wheelbase . . 112 in.   Standard Engine . . . 6 cyl. (231)
Length . . . . 208 in.   Standard Brakes . . . Disc-Drum
Weight . . . . 3,666 lbs. Gasoline Mileage . . . 20
Width . . . . . 77.4 in.   (with unleaded fuel)

Frequency of Repairs:
Motor noisy and sluggish. Some crankshaft problems.

Body:
Some paint flaking reported.

Safety Defects:
Catalytic converter and radial tires may be defective. Power
brake booster.

Recommendation:
Buy the Oldsmobile Cutlass instead for a better resell value.

PONTIAC (Full-sized)
Catalina/Bonneville

Used Car Price* $3,200
Based on standard equipped car with automatic transmission
and radio.
Price assumes excellent condition.

*Subtract $50 for each month after August for current price.

Statistical Comparison:
Average depreciation.
Average parts supply.
Average parts cost.
Average fuel economy.

Technical Data

Wheelbase . .	115.9 in.	Standard Engine . . .	V6 (231)
Length	214.3 in.	Standard Brakes . . .	Disc-Drum
Weight	3,583 lbs.	Gasoline Mileage . . .	19
Width	75.7 in.	(with unleaded fuel)	

Frequency of Repairs:
Motor noisy. Much improved mechanical components.

Body:
Some paint defects.

Safety Defects:
Catalytic converter and radial tires. Power brake booster.

Recommendation:
Recommended. Vast improvement over earlier V8 model.

BUICK (Full-sized)
Le Sabre

Used Car Price* $3,000
Based on standard equipped car with automatic transmission
and radio.
Price assumes excellent condition.

*Subtract $50 for each month after August for current price.

Statistical Comparison:
Slow depreciation.
Excellent parts supply.
Average parts cost.
Good fuel economy.

Technical Data

Wheelbase . .	115.9 in.	Standard Engine . . .	V8 (350)
Length	218.2 in.	Standard Brakes . . .	Disc-Drum
Weight	3,900 lbs.	Gasoline Mileage . . .	18
Width	77.2 in.	(with unleaded fuel)	

Frequency of Repairs:
Improved motor. Some suspension problems. Some transmission problems.

Body:
Paint peeling reported (worse on Buick Century).

Safety Defects:
Catalytic converter and radial tires. Power brake booster.

Recommendation:
A good choice. Car is much improved.

Oldsmobile Division   **1977**
General Motors
OLDSMOBILE (Full-sized)

Used Car Price* $3,100
Based on standard equipped car with automatic transmission and radio.
Price assumes excellent condition.

*Subtract $50 for each month after August for current price.

Statistical Comparison:
Slow depreciation.
Excellent parts supply.
Low parts cost.
Excellent fuel economy.

Technical Data

Wheelbase . .	119 in.	Standard Engine . . .	V8 (350)
Length	220.4 in.	Standard Brakes . . .	Disc-Drum
Weight	3,985 lbs.	Gasoline Mileage . . .	17
Width	76.8 in.	(with unleaded fuel)	

Frequency of Repairs:
Good motor. Some starting problems.

Body:
Paint peeling reported.

Safety Defects:
Catalytic converter may overheat and radial tires may fail. Power brake booster.

Recommendation:
An average good car. Make sure GM did not put a Chevrolet motor in your Oldsmobile. If so, GM will extend your motor warranty or exchange the car.

Ford Division 1977
Ford Motor Company
PINTO/BOBCAT

Used Car Price*. $1,600
Based on standard equipped car with automatic transmission and radio.
Price assumes excellent condition.

*Subtract $50 for each month after August for current price.

Statistical Comparison:
Rapid depreciation.
Average parts supply.
Expensive parts.
Poor fuel economy.

Technical Data

Wheelbase . .	94.5 in.	Standard Engine . . .	4 cyl. (140)
Length	169 in.	Standard Brakes . . .	Disc-Drum
Weight	2,428 lbs.	Gasoline Mileage . . .	26
Width	69.4 in.	(with unleaded fuel)	

Frequency of Repairs:
Motor is weak and sometimes hard to start. Steering and suspension problems reported.

Body:
Minor paint peeling.

Safety Defects:
Fuel tank may be hazardous.

Recommendation:
Don't buy. This car was never one of Ford's "Better Ideas."

Ford Division 1977
Ford Motor Company
MAVERICK/COMET

Used Car Price*. $2,000
Based on standard equipped car with automatic transmission and radio.
Price assumes excellent condition.

*Subtract $50 for each month after August for current price.

Statistical Comparison:
Slow depreciation.
Good parts supply.
Inexpensive parts cost.
Good fuel economy.

Technical Data

Wheelbase . .	103 in.	Standard Engine . . .	6 cyl. (200)
Length	187 in.	Standard Brakes . . .	Disc-Drum
Weight	2,986 lbs.	Gasoline Mileage . . .	20
Width	70.5 in.	(with unleaded fuel)	

Frequency of Repairs:
Some steering problems. Excellent motor and transmission.

Body:
A sound body, much improved from previous models.

Safety Defects:
Gas tank and radial tires may be defective.

Recommendation:
Still one of the best compact cars on the market.

Ford Division   **1977**
Ford Motor Company
MUSTANG II

Used Car Price* $2,400
Based on standard equipped car with automatic transmission
and radio.
Price assumes excellent condition.

*Subtract $50 for each month after August for current price.

Statistical Comparison:
Average depreciation.
Average parts supply.
Average parts cost.
Fair fuel economy.

Technical Data

Wheelbase . .	96.2 in.	Standard Engine . . .	4 cyl. (140)
Length	175 in.	Standard Brakes . . .	Disc-Drum
Weight	2,776 lbs.	Gasoline Mileage . . .	26
Width	70.2 in.	(with unleaded fuel)	

Frequency of Repairs:
Suspension vibrations and motor stalling reported.

Body:
Some reports of paint defects.

Safety Defects:
Fuel tank may be hazardous.

Recommendation:
Look at the Camaro instead.

Ford Division   1977
Ford Motor Company
TORINO/LTD II

Used Car Price* $2,900
Based on standard equipped car with automatic transmission
and radio.
Price assumes excellent condition.

*Subtract $50 for each month after August for current price.

Statistical Comparison:
Rapid depreciation.
Average parts supply.
Average parts cost.
Poor fuel economy.

Technical Data

Wheelbase . .	118 in.	Standard Engine . . .	V8 (351)
Length	219.5 in.	Standard Brakes . . .	Disc-Drum
Weight	4,220 lbs.	Gasoline Mileage . . .	13
Width	78 in.	(with unleaded fuel)	

Frequency of Repairs:
Motor, carburetor, and suspension problems.

Body:
Body well-assembled. Much more rust resistance.

Safety Defects:
Fuel tank could be hazardous.

Recommendation:
Not a good buy. The Torino is a turkey.

Ford Division   1977
Ford Motor Company
GRANADA/MONARCH

Used Car Price* $2,800
Based on standard equipped car with automatic transmission
and radio.
Price assumes excellent condition.

*Subtract $50 for each month after August for current price.

Statistical Comparison:
High depreciation.
Average parts supply.
Expensive parts cost.
Average fuel economy.

Technical Data

Wheelbase . .	109.9 in.	Standard Engine . . .	V8 (302)
Length	197.7 in.	Standard Brakes . . .	Disc-Drum
Weight	3,514 lbs.	Gasoline Mileage . . .	17
Width	74 in.	(with unleaded fuel)	

Frequency of Repairs:
Brakes, motor, steering, and carburetor problems reported.

Body:
Much improved resistance to premature rusting.

Safety Defects:
Fuel tank may be hazardous. Also front suspension and shoulder belts may fail.

Recommendation:
This car needs a lot of improvement.

Plymouth Division   **1977**
Chrysler Corporation

FURY

Used Car Price* $3,000
Based on standard equipped car with automatic transmission and radio.
Price assumes excellent condition.

*Subtract $50 for each month after August for current price.

Statistical Comparison:
Average depreciation.
Average parts supply.
Average parts cost.
Fair fuel economy.

Technical Data

Wheelbase . .	117.4 in.	Standard Engine . . .	V8 (318)
Length	218.4 in.	Standard Brakes . . .	Disc-Drum
Weight	4,025 in.	Gasoline Mileage . . .	18
Width	77.7 in.	(with unleaded fuel)	

Frequency of Repairs:
Motor stalling and brake problems. Some transmission failures.

Body:
Some water leaks into passenger compartment.

Safety Defects:
Radial tires could fail. Transmission defect due to catalytic converter.

Recommendation:
Recommended. Be sure to get an independent mechanic's appraisal before purchase.

VOLARE/ASPEN

Used Car Price* $2,400
Based on standard equipped car with automatic transmission
and radio.
Price assumes excellent condition.

*Subtract $30 for each month after August for current price.

Statistical Comparison:
Little depreciation.
Excellent parts supply.
Low parts cost.
Excellent fuel economy.

Technical Data

Wheelbase . .	108.7 in.	Standard Engine . . .	6 cyl. (225)
Length	197.5 in.	Standard Brakes . . .	Disc-Drum
Weight	3,275 lbs.	Gasoline Mileage . . .	21
Width	72.8 in.	(with regular fuel)	

Frequency of Repairs:
Minor motor problems and some serious transmission failures.

Body:
Water leaks have worsened.

Safety Defects:
Radial tires may have tread separation.

Recommendation:
A poor choice, because quality has gone down considerably.

CORDOBA/CHARGER

Used Car Price* $3,100
Based on standard equipped car with automatic transmission
and radio.
Price assumes excellent condition.

*Subtract $50 for each month after August for current price.

Statistical Comparison:
Rapid depreciation.
Fair parts supply.
Parts expensive.
Poor fuel economy.

Technical Data

Wheelbase	115 in.	Standard Engine	V8 (318)
Length	215.3 in.	Standard Brakes	Disc-Drum
Weight	4,030 lbs.	Gasoline Mileage	15
Width	77.1 in.	(with unleaded fuel)	

Frequency of Repairs:
Minor problems with motor and transmission.

Body:
Water leaks frequent complaint.

Safety Defects:
Radial tires may be defective.

Recommendation:
Don't buy. Look to a Fury or Monte Carlo instead.

Dodge Division   **1977**
Chrysler Corporation
MONACO (Full-sized)

Used Car Price* $2,900
Based on standard equipped car with automatic transmission and radio.
Price assumes excellent condition.

*Subtract $50 for each month after August for current price.

Statistical Comparison:
Rapid depreciation.
Average parts supply.
Average parts cost.
Poor fuel economy.

Technical Data

Wheelbase	117.4 in.	Standard Engine	V8 (318)
Length	218.4 in.	Standard Brakes	Disc-Drum
Weight	4,024 lbs.	Gasoline Mileage	15
Width	77.7 in.	(with unleaded fuel)	

Frequency of Repairs:
Brakes, suspension and carburetor remain problem areas.

Body:
Few water leaks.

Safety Defects:
Radial tires may be defective. Transmission defect due to catalytic converter

Recommendation:
Try a Fury or Monte Carlo instead.

AMC HORNET

Used Car Price* $2,500
Based on standard equipped car with automatic transmission
and radio.
Price assumes excellent condition.

*Subtract $30 for each month after August for current price.

Statistical Comparison:
Average depreciation.
Average parts supply.
Average parts cost.
Good gas economy.

Technical Data
Wheelbase . .	108 in.	Standard Engine . . .	6 cyl. (232)
Length	186.1 in.	Standard Brakes . . .	Disc-Drum
Weight	3,049 lbs.	Gasoline Mileage . . .	19
Width	71 in.	(with regular fuel)	

Frequency of Repairs:
Electrical system and brakes are problem-prone.

Body:
Solid body construction.

Safety Defects:
N/A

Recommendation:
A recommended compact car.

AMC GREMLIN

Used Car Price* $1,900
Based on standard equipped car with automatic transmission
and radio.
Price assumes excellent condition.

*Subtract $50 for each month after August for current price.

Statistical Comparison:
Average depreciation.
Average parts supply.
Average parts cost.
Good gas economy.

Technical Data
Wheelbase . .	96 in.	Standard Engine . . .	6 cyl. (232)
Length	166.8 in.	Standard Brakes . . .	Disc-Drum
Weight	2,806 lbs.	Gasoline Mileage . . .	21
Width	70.6 in.	(with unleaded fuel)	

Frequency of Repairs:
Brakes and motor problems.

Body:
Good solid construction.

Safety Defects:
N/A

Recommendation:
Both the 6 and 4 cylinder models are recommended.

American Motors   **1977**
PACER

Used Car Price* $2,300
Based on standard equipped car with automatic transmission
and radio.
Price assumes excellent condition.

*Subtract $50 for each month after August for current price.

Statistical Comparison:
Rapid depreciation.
Average parts supply.
Average parts cost.
Poor gas mileage.

Technical Data

Wheelbase . .	100 in.	Standard Engine . . .	6 cyl. (232)
Length	170.2 in.	Standard Brakes . . .	Disc-Drum
Weight	3,162 lbs.	Gasoline Mileage . . .	19
Width	77 in.	(with unleaded fuel)	

Frequency of Repairs:
Motor and carburetor problems.

Body:
Body construction and rusting may cause problems.

Safety Defects:
N/A

Recommendation:
Not recommended. Try a Nova

1978 MODELS

Chevrolet Division
General Motors Corporation
CHEVETTE/ACADIAN

All data based on two-door sedan

Used Car Price* $2,500–3,400
Based on standard equipped car with automatic transmission
and radio.
Price assumes excellent condition.

*Subtract $35 for each month after August for current price.

Statistical Comparison:
Average depreciation
Expensive parts
Inadequate, but improved, parts supply
Average gas mileage

Technical Data
Wheelbase . .	94.3 in.	Standard Engine	L4(98)
Length	159.7 in.	Standard Brakes	Disc
Weight	1,991 lbs	Gasoline Mileage	30
Width	61.8 in.	(with unleaded fuel)	

Frequency of Repairs:
Brakes, motor, and suspension problems.

Body:
Fair body construction, though some premature rusting and
paint peeling reported.

Safety Defects:
Possibility gas tank placement unsafe.

Recommendation:
Not recommended. Although a much better car than its defect-
ridden Vega/Astre cousins, this model still cannot compete
with the Honda, Arrow, or Rabbit subcompacts.

Chevrolet Division   **1978–1979**
General Motors Corporation
MONZA/SKYHAWK/STARFIRE/SUNBIRD

All data based on two-door sedan

Used Car Price* . . . . $2,900–$3,900
Based on standard equipped car with automatic transmission
and radio.
Price assumes excellent condition.

*Subtract $35 for each month after August for current price.

Statistical Comparison:
Rapid depreciation
Average parts availability
Average parts cost
Poor gas mileage

Technical Data

Wheelbase . .	97 in.	Standard Engine	L4
Length	179.3 in.	(Skyhawk), (V6-231)	
Weight	2,800 lbs	Standard Brakes	Disc
Width	65.4 in.	Gasoline Mileage	26
		(4 cyl.), 21 (6 cyl.)	
		(with unleaded fuel)	

Frequency of Repairs:
Noisy motor and crankshaft failures. Poor ventilation, suspension, and excessive motor (V6) vibrations. Brakes may wear out prematurely.

Body:
Poor body construction. Fair rust resistance, but some problems with paint chipping along sides.

Safety Defects:
Possibility suspension and tires could be defective. Chance of steering control loss.

Recommendation:
Not recommended. Ever since the ill-fated Corvair, General Motors' subcompact cars have been subcompact disasters. Just ask any Vega/Astre owner (one can always be found stranded along the side of the road with the car's hood up).

Chevrolet Division **1978–1979**
General Motors Corporation
NOVA/SKYLARK

All data based on two-door sedan

Used Car Price* $3,500–4,100
Based on standard equipped car with automatic transmission and radio.
Price assumes excellent condition.

*Subtract $35 for each month after August for current price.

Statistical Comparison:
Very low depreciation
Excellent parts availability
Low parts cost
Fair gas mileage

Technical Data

Wheelbase . .	111 in.	Standard Engine	L6(250),
Length	196.7 in.	Skylark V6(231)	
	220.2 in.	Standard Brakes	Disc
Weight	3,300 lbs	Gasoline Mileage	21
Width	72.2 in,	(with unleaded fuel)	
	72.7		

Frequency of Repairs:
Frequent 6 cylinder motor failures. Eight cylinder motor preferred. Inadequate suspension and interior ventilation.

Body:
Solid body construction. Few rattles. Some complaints on paint cracking, bubbling, and peeling. Some premature rusting also reported.

Safety Defects:
Wheels may fly off.

Recommendation:
Recommended. Although GM's quality control has declined, the Nova still is a good car buy.

Chevrolet Division   **1978–1979**
OMEGA/PHOENIX

All data based on two-door sedan

Used Car Price* $3,100–4,400
Based on standard equipped car with automatic transmission and radio.
Price assumes excellent condition.

*Subtract $40 for each month after August for current price.

Statistical Comparison:
Rapid depreciation
Average parts supply
Average parts cost
Poor gas mileage

Technical Data

Wheelbase	111 in.	Standard Engine	V6(231)
Length	199.6 in., 203.4 in.	Standard Brakes	Disc
		Gasoline Mileage	17
Weight	3,300 lbs	(with unleaded fuel)	
Width	72.9 in., 73.2 in.		

Frequency of Repairs:
Premature brake wear, poor steering, and suspension problems reported. Motor noisy and creates annoying excessive vibrations. Eight cylinder preferred.

Body:
Fair body construction. Some rattles. Numerous reports of premature rusting and paint defects.

Safety Defects:
Wheels may fly off.

Recommendation:
Not recommended. The Nova, Fairmont, or Skylark is a better buy.

Chevrolet Division   **1978–1979**
General Motors Corporation
               CAMARO/FIREBIRD

All data based on two-door sedan

Used Car Price* $4,800–5,400
Based on standard equipped car with automatic transmission and radio.
Price assumes excellent condition.

*Subtract $30 for each month after August for current price.

Statistical Comparison:
Little depreciation
Excellent parts supply
Low parts cost
Fair fuel economy

Technical Data

Wheelbase . .	108 in.,	Standard Engine	V8(305)
	108.2 in.	Standard Brakes	Disc.
Length	197.6 in.,	Gasoline Mileage	17
	196.8 in.	(with unleaded fuel)	
Weight	3,500 lbs		
Width'.	74.5 in.,		
	73.4 in.		

Frequency of Repairs:
Motor noisy and frequent V6 motor problems. Weak suspension. Good transmission and carburetor.

Body:
Poor body fitting. Paint application uneven.

Safety Defects:

Wheels may fly off.

Recommendation:
Recommended. Both cars are average vehicles, but their "sports car" image and reliability keep their resale value high. Excellent choice as a "sports car" for novice drivers who really don't know what a real sports car is.

OLDSMOBILE CUTLASS

All data based on four-door model

Used Car Price*. $4,800–5,800
Based on standard equipped car with automatic transmission
and radio.
Price assumes excellent condition.

*Subtract $40 for each month after August for current price.

Statistical Comparison:
Below average depreciation
Excellent parts availability
Average parts cost
Average gas mileage

Technical Data

Wheelbase . .	108.1 in.	Standard Engine	V8(260)
Length	197.7 in.	Standard Brakes	Disc
Weight	3,300 lbs	Gasoline Mileage	15
Width	71.9 in.	(with unleaded fuel)	

Frequency of Repairs:
Crankshaft problems with V8 motor and excessive vibrations
with the V6 motor. Early production diesel eight cylinder 350
motors are failure-prone.

Body:
Poor body construction apparently caused by downsizing the
Cutlass. Very poor paint adhesion along sides, wheel wells,
trunk, roof, and hood.

Safety Defects:
Wheels may fly off.

Recommendation:
Recommended with the reserve that motor and chassis get a
thorough going-over by an independent garage.

OLDSMOBILE 98

All data based on two-door sedan

Used Car Price*. $5,800–6,900
Based on standard equipped car with automatic transmission
and radio.
Price assumes excellent condition.

*Subtract $90 for each month after August for current price.

Statistical Comparison:
Average depreciation
Good parts supply

Average parts cost
Poor gas mileage

Technical Data

Wheelbase . .	119 in.	Standard Engine	V8(350)
Length	220.4 in.	Standard Brakes	Disc
Weight	4,124 lbs	Gasoline Mileage	10
Width	76.8 in.	(with unleaded fuel)	

Frequency of Repairs:
Diesel motor flaws. Crankshaft failures.

Body:
Uneven paint application. Poor paint adhesion. Premature rusting due to excessive paint peeling

Safety Defects:
Wheels may fly off.

Recommendation:
Not recommended, unless used as a business vehicle where gas expenses are tax deductible, high mileage service required, and car traded-in before it's too rusty.

Buick Division   **1978–1979**
General Motors Corporation
LE SABRE

All data based on four-door model

Used Car Price* $3,800–5,800
Based on standard equipped car with automatic transmission and radio.
Price assumes excellent condition.

*Subtract $60 for each month after August for current price.

Statistical Comparison:
Average depreciation
Good parts supply
Average parts cost
Average fuel economy

Technical Data

Wheelbase . .	115.9 in.	Standard Engine	V8(301)
Length	218.2 in.	Standard Brakes	Disc
Weight	3,600 lbs	Gasoline Mileage	17
Width	77.2 in.	(with unleaded fuel)	

Frequency of Repairs:
Noisy motor. Some crankshaft failures. Improved transmission

Body:
Paint peeling worse this year. Premature rusting all over the vehicle.

Safety Defects:
Wheels may fly off.

Recommendation:
Recommended, but quality has declined.

Buick Division   **1978–1979**
General Motors Corporation
MONTE CARLO/GRAND PRIX

All data based on four-door model

Used Car Price* $4,200–5,900
Based on standard equipped car with automatic transmission
and radio.
Price assumes excellent condition.

*Subtract $50 for each month after August for current price.

Statistical Comparison:
Below average depreciation
Good parts supply
Average parts cost
Average fuel economy

Technical Data

Wheelbase . .	108 in.,	Standard Engine	V6(231),
	108.1 in.		V8(301)
Length	200.4 in.,	Standard Brakes	Disc
	201.2 in.	Gasoline Mileage	21(V6),
Weight	3,400 lbs		17(V8)
Width	71.5 in.,	(with unleaded fuel)	
	72.8 in.		

Frequency of Repairs:
Crankshaft problems with eight cylinder. Excessive vibrations
caused by V6 motor. Eight cylinder (305) more reliable motor.
Good transmission

Body:
Very poor body construction. Poor fits, paint peeling and
premature rusting.

Safety Defects:
Possible rear brake failure. Wheels may fly off.

Recommendation:

Recommended with reserve that independent mechanic checks
out body and motor defects.

Buick Division
General Motors Corporation
CENTURY/REGAL/LE MANS

All data based on two-door sedan

Used Car Price* $4,200–5,500
Based on standard equipped car with automatic transmission
and radio.
Price assumes excellent condition.

*Subtract $60 for each month after August for current price.

Statistical Comparison:
Rapid depreciation
Average parts supply
Average parts cost
Poor fuel economy

Technical Data

Wheelbase . .	108.1 in.	Standard Engine	V8(305),
Length	196 in.,	Regal V6(196)	
199.3 in.		Standard Brakes	Disc
Weight	3,350 lbs	Gasoline Mileage	15(V8),
Width	70.1 in.,	19(V6)	
72.6 in.		(with unleaded fuel)	

Frequency of Repairs:
Motor, transmission, and carburation problems.

Body:
Body components fitted poorly. Poor paint adhesion to metal
causing excessive paint peeling and premature rusting on roof,
trunk lid, and hood.

Safety Defects:
Possible rear brake failure. Wheels may fly off. Tires may be
mis-labled.

Recommendation:
Not recommended. Although these cars are identical to other
GM models, they exhibit more chassis and mechanical defects
for some uncanny reason that only General Motors knows.

Chevrolet Division
General Motors Corporation
MALIBU

All data based on two-door sedan

Used Car Price* $3,700–5,400
Based on standard equipped car with automatic transmission
and radio.
Price assumes excellent condition.

*Subtract $40 for each month after August for current price.

Statistical Comparison:
Average depreciation
Average parts cost
Good parts supply
Fair fuel economy

Technical Data
Wheelbase . .	108.1 in.	Standard Engine	V6(200)
Length	192.7 in.	Standard Brakes	Disc
Weight	3,250 lbs	Gasoline Mileage	16
Width	71.5 in.	(with unleaded fuel)	

Frequency of Repairs:
Transmission, motor and brake problems reported. The V8(305) motor is more reliable.

Body:
Poor body construction. Water leaks in trunk. Paint peeling and rusting on hood, trunk, and roof.

Safety Defects:
Possible rear brake failure. Wheels may fly off.

Recommendation:
Recommended. Despite a decline in quality, possibly caused by downsizing, the Malibu is still not as bad as its competition.

Cadillac Division **1978–1979**
General Motors Corporation
CADILLAC SEVILLE

All data based on four-door model

Used Car Price* $9,000–11,000
Based on standard equipped car with automatic transmission and radio.
Price assumes excellent condition.

*Subtract $130 for each month after August for current price.

Statistical Comparison:
Rapid depreciation
Poor parts supply
Expensive parts
Terrible gas mileage

Technical Data
Wheelbase . .	114.3 in.	Standard Engine	V8(350)
Length	204 in.	Standard Brakes	Disc
Weight	4,289 lbs	Gasoline Mileage	10
Width	71.8 in.	(with unleaded fuel)	

Frequency of Repairs:
Noisy motor. Some crankshaft failures. Brake problems reported. Transmission improved.

Body:
Poor paint adhesion. Uneven paint application. Serious rust problems due to massive paint peeling along door bottoms, trunk, hood, and roof.

Safety Defects:
Electronic fuel injector may be fire-prone. Windshield washer may fail. Wheels may fly off.

Recommendation:
Not recommended. General Motors' luxury "lemon".

Chevrolet Division   1978–1979
General Motors Corporation
CORVETTE

All data based on two-door sedan

Used Car Price* $8,500–11,000
Based on standard equipped car with automatic transmission and radio.
Price assumes excellent condition.

*Subtract $40 for each month after August for current price.

Statistical Comparison:
Insignificant depreciation
Excellent parts supply
Expensive parts cost
Poor gas mileage

Technical Data

Wheelbase . .	98 in.	Standard Engine	V8(350)
Length	185.2 in.	Standard Brakes	Disc
Weight	3,572 lbs	Gasoline Mileage	9
Width	69 in.	(with unleaded fuel)	

Frequency of Repairs:
Minor carburation and motor problems. Good transmission. Suspension improved.

Body:
Fiber-glass well fitted. Excellent paint adhesion. Reports of metal roof rack carrier being in short supply.

Safety Defects:
Rear wheel mounting bolts may be defective.

Recommendation:
Excellent new or used car buy. Hard to lose money on a Corvette purchase due to its traditional high resale value.

FAIRMONT/ZEPHYR

All data based on two-door sedan

Used Car Price* $3,000–4,100
Based on standard equipped car with automatic transmission
and radio.
Price assumes excellent condition.

*Subtract $35 for each month after August for current price.

Statistical Comparison:
Below average depreciation
Average parts cost
Inadequate parts supply
Average fuel economy

Technical Data

Wheelbase . .	105.5 in.	Standard Engine	L6(200)
Length	193.8 in.	Standard Brakes	Disc
Weight	2,870 lbs	Gasoline Mileage	22
Width	71 in.	(with unleaded fuel)	

Frequency of Repairs:
Some motor failures reported. Good suspension, brakes, and
transmission.

Body:
Improved body construction. Poor paint adhesion along door
bottoms and wheel wells. Fair rust resistance.

Safety Defects:
Brake rotors could be cracked. May have excessive brake fade.
Transmission may fail in park. Air conditioner may be hazard-
ous.

Recommendation:
Recommended. Six cylinder preferred over eight. Station
wagon model is best body style.

PINTO/BOBCAT

All data based on two-door sedan

Used Car Price* $2,000–3,300
Based on standard equipped car with automatic transmission
and radio.
Price assumes excellent condition.

*Subtract $40 for each month after August for current price.

Statistical Comparison:
Rapid depreciation
Average parts supply

Average parts cost
Poor gas mileage

Technical Data

Wheelbase	94.5 in.	Standard Engine	L4(140)
Length	169.3 in.	Standard Brakes	Disc
Weight	2,425 lbs.	Gasoline Mileage	25
Width	69.4 in.	(with unleaded fuel)	

Frequency of Repairs:
Transmission and motor defects.

Body:
Improved rust resistance. Paint adhesion inadequate due to poor body design.

Safety Defects:
Tires may be defective. Seatbelt retractor may fail to lock.

Recommendation:
Stay away. This Ford subcompact is a turkey.

Ford Division   **1978–1979**
Ford Motor Company
MUSTANG II

All data based on two-door sedan

Used Car Price* $2,900–4,400
Based on standard equipped car with automatic transmission and radio.
Price assumes excellent condition.

*Subtract $30 for each month after August for current price.

Statistical Comparison:
Below average depreciation
Average parts supply
Average parts cost
Poor gas mileage

Technical Data

Wheelbase	96.2 in.	Standard Engine	L4(140)
Length	175 in.	Standard Brakes	Disc
Weight	2,700 lbs	Gasoline Mileage	20
Width	70.2 in.	(with unleaded fuel)	

Frequency of Repairs:
Minor motor and transmission defects. Improved interior and exterior finish.

Body:
Poor paint adhesion, but, improved rust resistance.

Safety Defects:
Automatic transmission may fail and jump from park to reverse.
Accelerator cable defective.

Recommendation:
Recommended. Make sure independent garage checks out motor and transmission.

Ford Division   **1978–1979**
Ford Motor Company
GRANADA/MONARCH

All data based on two-door sedan

Used Car Price* $3,700–4,700
Based on standard equipped car with automatic transmission and radio.
Price assumes excellent condition.

*Subtract $50 for each month after August for current price.

Statistical Comparison:
Rapid depreciation
Good parts supply
Average parts cost
Poor gas mileage

Technical Data

Wheelbase . .	109.9 in.	Standard Engine	V8(302)
Length	197.7 in.	Standard Brakes	Disc
Weight	3,350 lbs	Gasoline Mileage	13
Width	74 in.	(with unleaded fuel)	

Frequency of Repairs:
Motor, electrical and suspension problems. Good automatic transmission.

Body:
Poor paint adhesion along door bottom and lower fenders.

Safety Defects:
Automatic transmission may jump from park to reverse.

Recommendation:
An inferior "better idea" from Ford that should be rejected in favor of a Nova.

Ford Division   **1978–1979**
Ford Motor Company
LTD/THUNDERBIRD

All data based on two-door sedan

Used Car Price* $4,000–5,800
Based on standard equipped car with automatic transmission and radio.
Price assumes excellent condition.

*Subtract $40 for each month after August for current price.

Statistical Comparison:
Average depreciation
Poor parts supply
Expensive parts
Atrocious gas mileage

Technical Data

Wheelbase	114 in.	Standard Engine	V8(302)
Length	215.5 in.	Standard Brakes	Disc
Weight	4,050 lbs	Gasoline Mileage	12
Width	78.5 in.	(with unleaded fuel)	

Frequency of Repairs:
Crankshaft, valve and piston defects. Carburation and starting problems.

Body:
Poor paint adhesion. Good rust resistance

Safety Defects:
Automatic transmission, tires. Tilt-steering may fail. Cast aluminum wheels may be defective.

Recommendation:
Not recommended. Motor failures too common.

Lincoln Division   **1978–1979**
Ford Motor Company
VERSAILLES

All data based on two-door sedan

Used Car Price* $8,500–13,500
Based on standard equipped car with automatic transmission and radio.
Price assumes excellent condition.

*Subtract $125 for each month after August for current price.

Statistical Comparison:
Incredibly fast depreciation
Expensive parts
Poor parts supply
Terrible gas mileage

Technical Data

Wheelbase	109.9 in.	Standard Engine	V8(302)
Length	200.9 in.	Standard Brakes	Disc
Weight	3,913 lbs	Gasoline Mileage	13
Width	74.5 in.	(with unleaded fuel)	

Frequency of Repairs:
Rapid brake wear. Motor, carburetor and ignition problems reported. Fair transmission. Rear suspension inadequate.

Body:
Poor paint application and matching. Paint peeling reported. Average rust resistance.

Safety Defects:
Automatic transmission, tires, and tilt-steering may fail. Electronic engine control may be defective.

Recommendation:
Who needs it? This gas guzzler is a tasteless, over-priced imitation of the cheaper Granada/Monarch. Buyers of this mobile monstrosity can be found listening to Musak, caressing their pet rocks, and drinking Chivas Regal with Diet Tab as a mixer.

Lincoln Division   **1978–1979**
Ford Motor Company
CONTINENTAL

All data based on two-door sedan

Used Car Price* $7,100–11,300
Based on standard equipped car with automatic transmission and radio.
Price assumes excellent condition.

*Subtract $100 for each month after August for current price.

Statistical Comparison:
Very rapid depreciation
Expensive parts
Inadequate parts supply
Poor gas mileage

Technical Data

Wheelbase . .	127.2 in.	Standard Engine	V8(400)
Length	233 in.	Standard Brakes	Disc
Weight	4,830 lbs	Gasoline Mileage	11
Width	80 in.	(with unleaded fuel)	

Frequency of Repairs:
Motor and carburation problems. Good transmission. Poor suspension.

Body:
Uneven paint application. Average rust resistance.

Safety Defects:
Automatic transmission, and tilt-steering may fail. Electronic engine control may be defective.

Recommendation:
A luxury "lemon". Its cousin, the Mark V, is no better.

OMNI/HORIZON

All data based on two-door sedan

Used Car Price* $2,800–3,950
Based on standard equipped car with automatic transmission
and radio.
Price assumes excellent condition.

*Subtract $60 for each month after August for current price.

Statistical Comparison:
Rapid depreciation
Poor parts supply
Average parts cost
Average gas mileage
Poor warranty performance

Technical Data

Wheelbase . .	99.2 in.	Standard Engine	4 cyl.
Length	163.2 in.	Standard Brakes	Disc.
Weight	2,137 lbs	Gasoline Mileage	31
Width	66.2 in.	(with regular fuel)	

Frequency of Repairs:
Carburation, brake, and suspension problems. Frequent steering complaints. Good transmission.

Body:
Good rust resistance. Poor interior and exterior finish. Numerous rattles.

Safety Defects:
Defective lower control arms, fuel tank leaks, fuel line abrasions
and inferior emergency handling. Front wheel may fly off.

Recommendation:
Stay away. More of a "lost Horizon", than an economy car.

VOLARE/ASPEN

All data based on two-door sedan

Used Car Price* $2,800–4,200
Based on standard equipped car with automatic transmission
and radio.
Price assumes excellent condition.

*Subtract $50 for each month after August for current price.

Statistical Comparison:
Rapid depreciation
Average parts supply
Expensive parts

Unbelievably bad gas mileage
Anti-consumer warranty performance

Technical Data

Wheelbase . .	108.7 in.	Standard Engine	L6(225)
Length	197.2 in.	Standard Brakes	Disc
Weight	3,200 lbs	Gasoline Mileage	13
Width	73.3 in.	(with unleaded fuel)	

Frequency of Repairs:
Major motor, transmission, and differential defects. Chronic stalling and brake problems.

Body:
Premature rusting. Myriad water leaks. Rattles.

Safety Defects:
Hood latch, brakes, carburetor, and steering may fail. Defective fuel supply tube. Brake tubes may break. Tilt-steering may be defective.

Recommendation:
Not recommended. Both the Volare and Aspen models are more "Ass-pain," than economy car.

Plymouth Division   **1978**
Chrysler Corporation
FURY

All data based on two-door sedan

Used Car Price* $3,900
Based on standard equipped car with automatic transmission and radio.
Price assumes excellent condition.

*Subtract $40 for each month after August for current price.

Statistical Comparison:
Below average depreciation
Average parts cost
Inadequate parts supply
Average fuel economy
Poor warranty performance

Technical Data

Wheelbase . .	114.9 in.	Standard Engine	L6(225)
Length	213.2 in.	Standard Brakes	Disc
Weight	3,700 lbs	Gasoline Mileage	19
Width	77.7 in.	(with unleaded fuel)	

Frequency of Repairs:
Motor hesitation, poor carburation, and transmission/differential failures.

Body:
Poor body construction. Uneven paint application, premature rusting, and serious water leaks.

Safety Defects:
Tilt-steering may be defective.

Recommendation:
Not recommended. The '77 Fury is a much better buy.

Dodge Division   **1978–1979**
Chrysler Corporation
LE BARON/DIPLOMAT

All data based on two-door sedan

Used Car Price* $4,500–5,600
Based on standard equipped car with automatic transmission and radio.
Price assumes excellent condition.

*Subtract $40 for each month after August for current price.

Statistical Comparison:
Average depreciation
Poor parts supply
High parts cost
Poor gas mileage

Technical Data

Wheelbase	112.7 in.	Standard Engine	L6(225)
Length	204.1 in.	Standard Brakes	Disc
Weight	3,500 lbs	Gasoline Mileage	14
Width	73.5 in.	(with unleaded fuel)	

Frequency of Repairs:
Starting, stalling and suspension problems. Transmission/differential defects common.

Body:
Poorly fitted chassis components. Uneven and inadequate paint application. Water leaks are paramount.

Safety Defects:
Steel brake tubes may break. Tilt-steering may be defective. Hood latch may fail.

Recommendation:
Not recommended. There is nothing regal or "diplomatic" about this car's defects.

CORDOBA/CHARGER

All data based on two-door sedan

Used Car Price* $4,300–5,800
Based on standard equipped car with automatic transmission
and radio.
Price assumes excellent condition.

*Subtract $60 for each month after August for current price.

Statistical Comparison:
Rapid depreciation
Poor parts supply
High parts cost
Poor gas mileage
Poor warranty performance

Technical Data

Wheelbase . . 114.9 in.   Standard Engine . . . . V8(318)
Length . . . . 215.8 in.   Standard Brakes . . . . Disc
Weight . . . . 4,100 lbs   Gasoline Mileage 13
Width . . . . . 77.1 in.   (with unleaded fuel)

Frequency of Repairs:
Chronic electrical failures and stalling reported. Transmis-
sion/differential failure-prone.

Body:
Premature paint peeling and rusting. Water leaks everywhere.
Rattles.

Safety Defects:
Tilt-steering may fail.

Recommendation:
Not recommended. A high-priced, over-rated luxury lemon.

MONACO

All data based on two-door sedan

Used Car Price* $3,500
Based on standard equipped car with automatic transmission
and radio.
Price assumes excellent condition.

*Subtract $50 for each month after August for current price.

Statistical Comparison:
Rapid depreciation
Poor parts supply
High parts cost

Poor gas mileage
Poor warranty performance

Technical Data

Wheelbase	. . 114.9 in.	Standard Engine	L6(225)
Length	. . . . 213.2 in.	Standard Brakes	Disc.
Weight	. . . . 3,717 lbs	Gasoline Mileage	14
Width	. . . . . 77.7 in.	(with unleaded fuel)	

Frequency of Repairs:
Chronic stalling, suspension vibrations, inadequate brakes, and transmission/differential failures.

Body:
Poor body construction. Considerable number of water leaks into passenger compartment.

Safety Defects:
Tilt-steering may fail.

Recommendation:
Not recommended. Design defects coupled with Chrysler's poor warranty performance, make the Monaco a poor choice.

American Motors Division   **1978–1979**
GREMLIN/SPIRIT

All data based on two-door sedan

Used Car Price* $2,600–3,400
Based on standard equipped car with automatic transmission and radio.
Price assumes excellent condition.

*Subtract $30 for each month after August for current price.

Statistical Comparison:
Average depreciation
Poor parts supply
Average parts cost
Poor gas mileage

Technical Data

Wheelbase	. . 96 in.	Standard Engine	L6(232)
Length	. . . . 166.6 in.	Standard Brakes	Disc
Weight	. . . . 2,823 lbs	Gasoline Mileage	18
Width	. . . . . 71.1 in.	(with unleaded fuel)	

Frequency of Repairs:
Carburation and brake problems.

Body:
Poor body construction. Interior space limited and poor body finish.

Safety Defects:
Possibility of fire in instrument panel.

Recommendation:
Not recommended. The Gremlin/Spirit is one "spook" that has little going for it in '78.

American Motors Division　　　　　　**1978–1979**
CONCORD

All data based on two-door sedan

Used Car Price*. $2,900–4,100
Based on standard equipped car with automatic transmission and radio.
Price assumes excellent condition.

*Subtract $40 for each month after August for current price.

Statistical Comparison:
Below average depreciation
Poor parts supply
Average parts cost
Average gas mileage

Technical Data

Wheelbase . .	108 in.	Standard Engine	L6(232)
Length	183 in.	Standard Brakes	Disc
Weight	3,062 lbs	Gasoline Mileage	17
Width	71.1 in.	(with unleaded fuel)	

Frequency of Repairs:
Brakes and carburation problems. Electrical failures reported. Good transmission and suspension.

Body:
Good paint adhesion and rust resistance. Poorly fitted body parts.

Safety Defects:
Front brakes may be inadequate.

Recommendation:
Average used car buy. The Concord is a Hornet in disguise.

American Motors Division　　　　　　**1978–1979**
PACER

All data based on two-door sedan

Used Car Price*. $2,800–4,600
Based on standard equipped car with automatic transmission and radio.
Price assumes excellent condition.

*Subtract $50 for each month after August for current price.

Statistical Comparison:
Rapid depreciation
Poor parts supply
Average parts cost
Poor gas mileage

Technical Data

Wheelbase . .	100 in.	Standard Engine	L6(232)
Length	172 in.	Standard Brakes	Disc
Weight	3,207 lbs	Gasoline Mileage	15
Width	77 in.	(with unleaded fuel)	

Frequency of Repairs:
Numerous electrical, motor, and brake problems.

Body:
Poor body construction. Interior and exterior finish inadequate. Rattles, premature rusting and paint peeling common problems.

Safety Defects:
Steering may lock up.

Recommendation:
Not recommended. Apart from unique styling, the Pacer has little to offer.

American Motors Division   1978–1979
AMX

All data based on two-door sedan

Used Car Price* $3,400–5,200
Based on standard equipped car with automatic transmission and radio.
Price assumes excellent condition.

*Subtract $50 for each month after August for current price.

Statistical Comparison:
Average depreciation
Good parts supply
Average parts cost
Average gas mileage

Technical Data

Wheelbase . .	108 in.	Standard Engine	6
Length	183 in.	cylinder (258)	
Weight	N/A	Standard Brakes	Disc
Width	71 in.	Gasoline Mileage	16
		(with unleaded fuel)	

Frequency of Repairs:
Excellent motor and transmission. Reports of premature brake wear and uneven braking.

Body:
Excellent rust resistance. Poor interior finish.

Safety Defects:
Front brakes may be inadequate.

Recommendation:
Average used car buy. Good second choice to Camaro or Firebird.

FOREIGN USED CARS
1970 to 1978

Domestic vs. Import

There is still a lot of controversy surrounding the relative merits of foreign and domestic cars. Before deciding which car is best, it would be wise to forget all the popular mythology and try to get solid facts.

Almost without exception, foreign-car parts will be much more expensive than those for a domestic equivalent, despite the similar initial retail price. A good way to check these prices is to comparison shop prices on certain items one would expect to replace frequently. Exhaust systems, brake pads, tires, and electrical components are the best indicators. Time permitting, verify replacement costs for major items, such as the transmission and motor, as well.

Servicing also needs to be investigated since this has traditionally been the "bête noire" of the importer in North America. For example, a vehicle can have the best engineering features in the world, but if the servicing is lousy, that vehicle will quickly deteriorate and fall into a lemon category. Volkswagen, Fiat, and Volvo are well aware of this problem and are trying to improve servicing procedures at the dealership level. British Leyland, though, may be already too far gone for any help to be useful.

Verify how often the vehicle needs to be serviced, and whether there is a franchised dealer nearby who has mechanics that are both reliable and inexpensive. Of course, no dealer is going to admit that he has recurring problems on a particular model and thereby lose a potential sale. So check servicing costs with other car owners driving similar models and be on the lookout for cars showing the dealer's nameplate on the trunk. Ask owners to evaluate the quality of service found at their dealership. It also might be worthwhile to check with fleet owners about the servicing problems they are encountering with their foreign or domestic vehicles. Finally, question closely regional and national automobile consumer-protection groups as to which vehicles receive the most complaints and what mechanical components are the most failure-prone. Remember that most consumer groups need at least six months' worth of complaints in order to properly evaluate new cars.

BRITISH IMPORTED CARS

British Leyland

England's British Leyland auto manufacturer answers the important consumer question "Can an automobile manufacturer that consistently makes inferior vehicles, with a parts-replacement system that moves by stagecoach, and a dealer network that is practically nonexistent, survive and still be profitable?" with both a yes and a no.

BLM is in pitiful shape, as is most of the British automobile industry. British Leyland, however, has suffered a steeper decline in sales and reputation than most of its English compatriots, owing primarily to the misjudging of the American foreign-car market by its chief executive, Lord Stokes. Consequently, British Leyland is surviving, but just barely.

The Austin Marina is the English revenge against its former American colonies. It uses the same infernal combustion engine that generations of MG owners loved to hate. The Jaguar 6-cylinder is a waste of money, while the Jaguar V-12 is doubly wasteful.

The Triumph is British Leyland's answer to the Ford Edsel and the Vauxhall Viva. It is the ideal car to teach young sports-car enthusiasts the therapeutic value of walking. It's an all-around bad car that has all the problems endemic to British Leyland automotive decline.

The remaining BLM products are also not recommended, owing to the high cost of servicing and parts replacement. British Leyland's warranty performance is judged to be poor by many of its hapless customers who have complained to American, British, and Canadian consumer groups.

Best Models

MG 1972–1976
Mini 1971–1978

Worst Models

Jaguar 1972–1979
Marina 1973–1979
Triumph 1974–1978

BRITISH LEYLAND
AREAS OF PREMATURE RUSTING

Austin Marina (1973 to 1975)

MG (1970 to 1973)

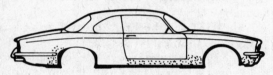

Jaguar (1971 to 1973)

Rover (1971 to 1973)

Triumph (1970 to 1973)

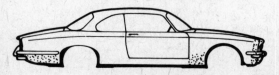

Make	Model	Model Year	Brief Description of Defect (Manufacturer's Corrective Action)	Number of Pages on File	Number of Vehicles Recalled
MG	MG— Midget MGB— Roadster MGB—GT	1970	Possibility that locking bolt of steering column lock may have been ineffectively secured in assembly. Under certain circumstances, this could engage lock causing immediate loss of directional control of vehicle.	6	6,000
Rover	3500S	1970	Possibility that hood safety and main latches were misaligned. If this condition exists, could cause hood assembly to lift while in motion.	5	1,292
Austin	American Model	1968 thru 1971	Possibility that inertia valve in rear brake system may not operate correctly. If this condition exists and front brake system fails, would cause rear brake system to be less efficient. (Correct by replacing valve where necessary.)	7	41,006
Jaguar	XJ6	1970	Possibility that hand brake cable may become displaced from intermediate lever, causing loss of handbrake operation.	4	920

Make	Model	Model Year	Brief Description of Defect (Manufacturer's Corrective Action)	Number of Pages on File	Number of Vehicles Recalled
Triumph	GT–6 and GT–6+	1968 1969 1970	Possibility that lap-type seatbelt instead of shoulder-type seatbelt was installed in vehicle. (Correct by replacing with proper belt.)	5	3,236
Austin MG	Healey/ Sprite Midget	1968 thru 1971	Possibility that if front brake system fails in dual-braking systems, rear brake system may not operate at full efficiency, thereby increasing vehicle-stopping distance and possibly affecting safety in handling vehicle.	5	32,386
Triumph	GT6MK III	1971 1972	Possibility that two rear brake hoses may contact rear wheel arch flanges when rear suspension is in full "bump" position. If condition exists, hoses could chafe through and result in decreased braking efficiency.	12	3,335
Austin	Marina	1974 and 1975	Possibility that outer rubber casing of front brake hose may be subject to cracking. Cracking is due to suspension/brake hose movement which is characteristic of this model when operated under arduous conditions.	3	14,000

Model & Body Type	Wholesale Price	Retail Price
1978		
MIDGET Roadster	$3800	$4500
MGB Roadster	4700	5700
1977		
MIDGET Convertible	2900	3400
MGB Convertible	3800	4200
1976		
MIDGET	1900	2400
MGB	2300	2800
1975		
MIDGET 4 Cyl. 80″ W.B.		
Convertible	1,800	2,200
MGB 4 Cyl. 91.13″ W.B.		
Convertible	2,000	2,300
1974		
MIDGET 4 Cyl. 80″ W.B.		
Convertible	1600	2000
MGB 4 Cyl. 91.1″ W.B.		
Convertible	2000	2400
Coupe GY	2300	2700
1973		
MIDGET 4 Cyl. 80″ W.B.		
Convertible	1200	1600
MGB 4 Cyl. 91″ W.B.		
Convertible	1700	2100
Hardtop	1800	2200
Coupe GT	2000	2400
1972		
MIDGET 4 Cyl. 80″ W.B.		
Convertible	900	1200
MGB 4 Cyl. 91″ W.B.		
Convertible	1400	1700
Hardtop	1500	1800
Coupe GT	1600	1900
1971		
MIDGET 4 Cyl. 80″ W.B.		
Convertible	800	1000

Model & Body Type	Wholesale Price	Retail Price
MGB 4 Cyl. 91" W.B.		
Roadster	1100	1400
Coupe GT	1300	1600
1970		
MIDGET 4 Cyl. 80" W.B.		
Convertible	500	800
MGB 4 Cyl. 91" W.B.		
Roadster	900	1200
Coupe GT	1000	1300

USED CAR PRICES (APPROXIMATE)

Rover

Model & Body Type	Wholesale Price	Retail Price
1974		
LAND ROVER 4 Cyl. 88" W.B.		
88 Hardtop Deluxe	$2100	$2400
1973		
LAND ROVER 4 Cyl. 88" W.B.		
88 Hardtop Deluxe	1800	2100
1972		
LAND ROVER 4 Cyl. 88" W.B.		
88 Hardtop	1400	1700
1971		
2000TC 4 Cyl. 103.4" W.B.		
4 Door Sedan	1100	1300
LAND ROVER 4 Cyl. 88" W.B.		
88 Hardtop	1000	1200
1970		
2000 4 Cyl. 103.4" W.B.		
4 Dr Sedan (Auto. Trans.)	900	1100

Model & Body Type	Wholesale Price	Retail Price
1975		
AUSTIN MARINA 4 Cyl. 96″ W.B.		
4 Door Sedan	$1200	$1400
2 Door GT Coupe	1200	1400
1974		
MARINA 4 Cyl. 96″ W.B.		
2 Door GT Coupe	1000	1100
4 Door Sedan	1000	1200
1973		
MARINA 4 Cyl. 96″ W.B.		
2 Door GT Coupe	900	1100
4 Door Sedan	800	1000
1972		
1971		
MARINA 4 Cyl. 96″ W.B.		
2 Door Coupe	700	900
4 Door Sedan	700	900
2 Door GT	800	1000
AUSTIN 4 Cyl. 93.5″ W.B.		
Coach	1100	1300
Coupe	1100	1300
AUSTIN AMERICA 4 Cyl. 93.5″ W.B.		
2 Door Sedan	200	500
2 Door Sedan (Auto. Trans.)	300	500
1970		
AUSTIN AMERICA 4 Cyl. 93.5″ W.B.		
2 Door Sedan	200	400
2 Door Sedan (Auto. Trans.)	200	400

Model & Body Type	Wholesale Price	Retail Price
1978		
XJ6 Sedan (LWB) (Auto & P.S.)	$14822	$17500
XJ·12LWB Sedan	16244	19200
XJS 2 Plus 2 Coupe	19213	22750
1977		
Coupe 2D (2+2)	10775	12125
Sedan 4D	10625	11950
Sedan 4D	NA	NA
Coupe (2+2) GT	NA	NA
1976		
AT/PS/AC		
2D Cpe. XJ6C	6000	7500
4D Sdn. XJ6L	6500	8000
2D Cpe. XJ12L	7000	8500
4D Sdn. XJ12L	7000	8500
1975		
XJ66 Cyl. 108.8″ W.B.		
(Cpe) 113″ W.B. (Sdn)	5700	6700
XJ6-6 L 4 Dr Sdn (Long W.B.)	5500	6500
XJ6-C 2 Dr Cpe (Short W.B.)	5800	6800
XJ12 12 Cyl. 108.8″ W.B.		
(Cpe) 113″ W.B. (Sdn)		
XJ12-L 4 Dr Sdn (Long W.B.)	6500	7600
XJ12-C 2 Dr Cpe (Short W.B.)	7000	8400
1974		
XKE 12 Cyl. 105″ W.B.		
Convertible	6000	7000
Convertible (Auto. Trans.)	6100	7100
XJ6 Cyl. 108.8″ W.B.		
Sedan (Auto. Trans.)	6500	7500
1973		
XKE 12 Cyl. 105″ W.B.		
Convertible	4100	4900
Coupe	4300	5100
XJ6 Cyl. 108.9″ W.B.		
Sedan (Automatic Trans.)	5300	5800
XJ 12 Cyl. 108.9″ W.B.		
Sedan (Automatic Trans.)	5700	6200

Model & Body Type	Wholesale Price	Retail Price
1972		
XKE 12 Cyl. 105″ W.B.		
Roadster	3500	4000
Coupe	3100	4200
XJ6 Cyl. 108.9″ W.B.		
Sedan	3900	4400
1971		
XKE 6 Cyl. 96″ W.B.		
Roadster	1900	2300
Coupe	2100	2500
XJ Sedan	3300	3700
1970		
XKE 6 Cyl. 96″ W.B.		
(Exc. 2 + 2) 105″ W.B.		
(2 + 2)		
Convertible Roadster	1500	1800
Coupe	1600	1900
Coupe 2 + 2	1800	2100
Coupe 2 + 2 (Auto. Trans.)	1900	2200
XJ6 Cyl. 108.9″ W.B.		
Sedan	2900	3400

USED CAR PRICES (APPROXIMATE)
Triumph

Model & Body Type	Wholesale Price	Retail Price
1978		
Spitfire 1500 Convertible	$4200	$4800
TR-7 Coupe	5400	6000
1977		
Coupe	3800	4300
Convertible Spitfire	3000	3500
1976		
TR6 Convertible	3000	3800
TR7 Coupe	2900	3700
1975		
SPITFIRE 4 Cyl. 83″ W.B.		
1500 Convertible	2000	2500

Model & Body Type	Wholesale Price	Retail Price
TR-7 4 Cyl. 85″ W.B.		
Hardtop	2500	3000
TR-6 6 Cyl. 88″ W.B.		
Convertible	2600	3100
1974		
SPITFIRE 4 Cyl. 83″ W.B.		
1500 Convertible	1600	2100
TR 6 6 Cyl. 88″ W.B.		
Convertible	2300	2800
1973		
SPITFIRE 4 Cyl. 83″ W.B.		
1500 Roadster	1300	1700
GT-6 6 Cyl. 83″ W.B.		
Mark III Fastback Coupe	2000	2400
TR 6 6 Cyl. 88″ W.B.		
Convertible	2200	2600
Hardtop	2300	2700
1972		
SPITFIRE 4 Cyl. 83″ W.B.		
Mark IV Roadster	1000	1300
GT-6 6 Cyl. 83″ W.B.		
Mark III Fastback Cpe	1400	1700
TR6 6 Cyl. 88″ W.B.		
Convertible	1500	1800
Hardtop	1700	2000
1971		
SPITFIRE 4 Cyl. 83″ W.B.		
Mark IV Softtop	500	900
Mark IV Hardtop	600	1000
TR-6 6 Cyl. 88″ W.B.		
Convertible	1200	1500
Hardtop	1200	1500
GT-6 6 Cyl. 88″ W.B.		
Mark III Fastback	900	1200
1970		
SPITFIRE 4 Cyl. 83″ W.B.		
Mark III Softtop	400	800
Mark III Hardtop	500	900
TR-6 6 Cyl. 88″ W.B.		
Convertible	1000	1300
Hardtop	1100	1400
GT-6 6 Cyl. 83″ W.B.		
Fastback	800	900

FRENCH IMPORTED CARS

Citroen

Citroen makes the most advanced car on the American market. Unfortunately, owing to Citroen's feuding with the National Highway Traffic Safety Administration over its headlight and bumper design, the last Citroen imported into the United States was the 1974 SM model. Therefore, the wise consumer will steer clear of any used Citroen purchases, since the reported parts shortage is bound to become a chronic problem.

Recall Campaigns

Model	Year	Defect	Number Recalled
DS–21 Sedans and Station Wagons	1971–1972	Hydraulic brake lines to front and rear brakes reversed, which could, under certain conditions, result in irregular braking.	496

CITROEN
AREAS OF PREMATURE RUSTING

All Models (1970 to 1973)

Model & Body Type	Wholesale Price	Retail Price
1974		
SM 6 Cyl. 116.2" W.B.		
2 Door Coupe	$4800	$5500
2 Door Coupe (Auto. Trans.)	5000	5700
1973		
SM 6 Cyl. 116.2" W.B.		
2 Door Coupe	4000	4500
2 Door Coupe (Auto. Trans.)	4500	5200
1972		
D Special 4 Cyl.		
4 Door Sedan	1000	1300
DS-21 4 Cyl.		
4 Door Sedan	1500	2000
4 Dr Pallas Sdn	1600	2100
D-21 4 Cyl.		
Station Wagon	1700	2000
Station Wagon (Auto. Trans.)	1800	2100
SM 6 Cyl.		
2 Door Coupe	3500	4000
2 Door Coupe (Auto. Trans.)	3800	4300
1971		
D-19 4 Cyl.		
Special Grand Route Sedan	700	1000
DS-21 4 Cyl.		
Aero Super Sedan	1000	1500
Pallas Grand Route Sedan	1200	1700
Pallas Aero (Auto. Trans.)	1200	1700
Station Wagons 4 Cyl.		
21 Grand Route	900	1300
21 Aero Super (Auto. Trans.)	1100	1500
Mehari 4 Cyl. 123" W.B.		
Jeep	700	1100
1970		
ID-19 4 Cyl. 123" W.B.		
Special Grand Route Sedan	400	600
DS-21 4 Cyl. 123" W.B.		
Aero Super Sedan	700	1000
Pallas Grand Route Sedan	800	1100

Model & Body Type	Wholesale Price	Retail Price
Pallas Aero Super (Auto. Trans.)	800	1100
Station Wagon 4 Cyl. 123″ W.B.		
21 Luxe	700	1000
21 Comfort	800	1100
21 Comfort (Auto. Trans.)	800	1100
Mehari 4 Cyl. 123″ W.B.		
Jeep	500	900

Peugeot

In France, Peugeot is considered the poor man's Citroen. Embodying sophisticated engineering, with economical performance, makes this the perfect car for . . . France! In North America, the dealer body is too weak and the parts supply too haphazard for the needs of most motorists. Parts prices as well as long waiting periods for repairs have also come in for strong owner criticism.

Of all the Peugeot offerings, owners report that the 304 model gave the best value for its price. Unfortunately, that model has been discontinued, so parts may be a real problem. The new Peugeot models with the diesel engine should be shunned in favor of a good secondhand Mercedes diesel, which sells for the same price.

Best Models

Peugeot 504 (gas) 1972–1973

Worst Models

Peugeot 504 (diesel) 1974–1978

Make	Model	Model Year	Brief Description of Defect (Manufacturer's Corrective Action)	Number of Pages on File	Number of Vehicles Recalled
Peugeot	504 Sedan	1970 thru 1973	Possibility that rubber windshield moldings have hardness level below design specifications.	5	13,255
Peugeot	404 504	1967 thru 1971	Possibility that seal on first piston of dual brake master cylinder may fail. If condition exists, will cause loss of rear brakes. Front braking system will be unaffected.	5	14,817
Peugeot	304, 404 & 504	Jan. 1968 thru Mar. 1974	Possibility that interior rear view mirror mounting stems may be defective. (Correct by inspecting and modifying mirror mounting stem.)	1	35,000

PEUGEOT
AREAS OF PREMATURE RUSTING

All Models (1971 to 1974)

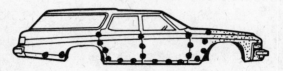

USED CAR PRICES (APPROXIMATE)
Peugeot

Model & Body Type	Wholesale Price	Retail Price
1978		
504SL (Gas)		
A91 Sedan	$6100	$7500
A93 Sedan (Auto)	6600	7900
504 (Gas)		
D91 Wagon	6600	8000
D93 Wagon (Auto)	7000	8400
504 (Diesel)		
AC0 Sedan	7300	8800
AC5 Sedan (Auto)	7600	9200
DC0 Wagon	7700	9300
DC5 Wagon (Auto)	8100	9700
604SL (Gas)		
AA1S Sedan	9000	11000
AA3S Sedan (Auto)	9500	11500
1977		
Sedan 4D	5800	6300
Station Wagon	6200	6600
Sdn. 4D (Diesel)	7000	7800
Station Wagon		
(Diesel)	7500	8300
1976		
GL504 4D Sdn.	3500	4000
SL504 4D Sdn.	3700	4200
504 St. Wgn.	3800	4300
504 4D Sdn.		
(Diesel)	4000	4500
504 St. Wgn.		
(Diesel)	5000	5500
1975		
504 4 Cyl. 108″ W.B. (Sdns)		
114″ W.B. (Wgns)		
4 Door Sedan	2500	3000
5 Door Station Wagon	1900	3400
4 Door Diesel Sedan	3200	3700
4 Door Diesel Station Wagon	3500	4000

Model & Body Type	Wholesale Price	Retail Price
1974		
504 4 Cyl. 108″ W.B. (Sdns)		
114.8″ W.B. (Wgns)		
4 Door Sedan	2000	2500
5 Door Wagon	2300	2800
4 Door Diesel Sedan	2400	2900
4 Door Diesel Wagon	2700	3200
1973		
504 4 Cyl. 108″ W.B.		
4 Door Sedan	1800	2200
5 Door Wagon	2000	2400
1972		
304 4 Cyl. 101.9″ W.B.		
4 Door Sedan	500	700
4 Door Wagon	700	900
504 4 Cyl. 109″ W.B.		
4 Door Sedan	1300	1500
4 Door Wagon	1500	1900
1971		
304 4 Cyl. 101.8″ W.B.		
4 Door Sedan	400	600
4 Door Wagon	600	800
504 4 Cyl. 108″ W.B.		
4 Door Sedan	900	1100
4 Door Sedan (Auto. Trans.)	1000	1200

Renault

Known as the General Motors of France, Renault makes the best-engineered low-priced, economical compact and subcompact vehicles in Europe. All of its vehicles maximize both comfort and driving performance while maintaining a solid reputation for fuel economy.

Renault's marketing experience in the United States and Canada has been marked by low sales and an inability to find a substantial number of quality dealers capable of servicing its products. As a result of these rather formidable obstacles, the French auto maker practically abandoned the American market in 1965 and concentrated upon its Canadian sales. In retrospect, it was a poor marketing decision prompted by the American motorist's spurning of the defect-prone Renault Dauphine. Renault had the right idea—but the wrong car. Nevertheless, in 1959, it sold 93,000 cars and became the leader in imported-car sales in the United States. This popularity was cut short, however, when other importers, such as Volkswagen, offered better-quality cars at lower prices. Competition got so bad that Renault's total sales in the United States for 1975 were only 7,287 vehicles.

Best Models

Renault 12 1971–1978
Renault 5 1978–1979

Worst Models

Renault 10 All Years
Renault 15 All Years
Renault 17 All Years

Because of a generally weak dealer network in the United States and Canada, parts replacement has always been inadequate and has contributed to the rapid depreciation in value of Renault models throughout North America. Servicing is another problem area, according to many Renault owners interviewed. Poor diagnostic procedures, mechanical defects that are repaired and then reappear, and difficulty in getting service from independent garages were the major complaints listed. This last problem is a common complaint with many European cars.

Owners report mechanical defects affecting primarily the motor (burning oil and seizing), suspension (front suspension may wear out prematurely from road-spray contaminants), and outer body shell, which is prone to early rusting. Many Renault owners also report they were sold the wrong model year by both new- and used-car dealers. Check the manufacturer's date-of-manufacture plate affixed to the door on the driver's side to determine the true model year.

Although Renault has some very serious problems in servicing its cars, no other auto maker, either European or American, offers such inexpensive, well-engineered vehicles to the North American buying public. However, because of the rapid depreciation and poor dealer servicing of new models, the only new Renault model that represents good value for the money spent is the Renault 5. This model competes favorably with the Chevrolet Chevette (an American car requiring European metric tools), Fiat 128, and the Volkswagen Rabbit, because of its low initial cost, simplified construction, and moderate depreciation.

Anyone looking for an excellent used-car buy should carefully consider the Renault 12. Although this model's best years were from 1970 through 1972, when pollution-control regulations were less stringent, subsequent model years remain good used-car buys because of their low retail prices caused by a devastatingly rapid depreciation rate. Plenty of spare parts are available, since the Renault 12 has had few basic design changes through the years.

The worst used Renault one can buy is the Renault 16 model, which has recently been discontinued. Parts are impossible to find, mechanical defects abound, and even Renault dealers have been known to refuse service on this vehicle. The Renault 16, and, also, to a lesser extent, the Renault 12, has a front-wheel-drive assembly that is failure prone, owing to its defective "cardan," or rubber protector. Since these failures, which are not safety-related, occur between 24,000 and 36,000 miles, Renault France has secretly extended warranty coverage on these parts and also applied the warranty extension to second owners.

Selected Recall Campaigns
Renault

Model	Year	Brief Description of Defect	Number Recalled
Renault 12 Sedans and station wagons	1971, 1972, 1973	Door latches may not meet strength requirements set by the Federal Motor Vehicle Safety Act.	12,726

RENAULT
AREAS OF PREMATURE RUSTING

Renault 12 (1970 to 1973)

Renault 12 (1974 to 1975)

USED CAR PRICES (APPROXIMATE)
Renault

Model & Body Type	Wholesale Price	Retail Price
1978		
EAST		
Renault 5 GTL "LeCar" (Base)	$3100	$3500
EAST		
Renault 5 TL "Le Car" (Deluxe)	3400	4000
EAST		
Renault 17 Gordini Convertible	6100	7400
1977		
Sedan 2D LeCar	2200	2700
Sedan 2D LeCar	2400	2900
Sedan 4D	2700	3300
Station Wagon	2900	3500
Cpe. Convertible	3600	4400
Cordini Cpe./Conv.	4200	4900
1976		
R5TL 2D Sedan	1800	2300
R5GTL 2D Sdn.	2000	2700
R12TL 4D Sdn.	2100	2800

Model & Body Type	Wholesale Price	Retail Price
R12GTL 4D Sdn.	2300	2900
R12 St. Wgn.	2500	3000
R15TL 2D Cpe.	3000	3500
R17TL Cpe./Conv.	3500	4100
R17 Gordini		
Cpe./Conv.	4000	4600
1975		
4 Cyl. 96″ W.B.	1500	1900
12 4 Door Sedan	1700	2100
12L 4 Door Sedan	1700	2100
12 TL 4 Door Sedan	1900	2300
12 4 Door Station Wagon	2100	2500
15TL 2 Door Coupe	2300	2700
17 Gordini 2 Door Coupe	2700	3200
17 Gordini Convertible	2900	3400
1974		
4 Cyl. 96″ W.B. (Exc. Gordini)		
95.5″ W.B.		
(Gordini)		
12 Sedan	1100	1500
12 L Sedan	1200	1600
12 TL Sedan	1300	1700
12 Station Wagon	1400	1800
15 Coupe	1500	1900
17 TL Coupe	1700	2100
17 TL Coupe/Convertible	1800	2200
17 Gordini Coupe	1900	2300
17 Gordini Coupe/Conv.	2100	2600
1973		
4 Cyl. 96″ W.B.		
12 Sedan	800	1200
12 Station Wagon	900	1300
15 Coupe	1000	1400
17 Sport Coupe	1500	2000
16 4 Door	700	900
1972		
4 Cyl. 96″ W.B. (Exc. 16's)		
106.6″ W.B. (16's)		
12 Sedan	400	700
12 Station Wagon	500	800
16 Sedan/Wagon	400	600

Model & Body Type	Wholesale Price	Retail Price
16 Sedan/Wagon (Auto. Trans.)	400	600
15 Coupe	800	1100
15 Coupe (Auto. Trans.)	900	1200
10 Sedan	600	700
1971		
4 Cyl. 89″ W.B. (10)		
105.8″ W.B. (16)		
10 Sedan	300	500
10 Sedan (Auto Trans.)	400	600
16 Sedan/Wagon	300	500
16 Sedan/Wagon (Auto. Trans.)	300	500
12 Sedan	600	800
12 Wagon	700	900
4 4 Door	300	500
4 Fourgonette	300	500
1970		
4 Cyl. 89″ W.B. (10)		
105.8″ W.B. (16)		
10 Sedan	200	300
10 Sedan (Auto. Trans.)	300	400
16 Sedan/Wagon	300	400
16 Sedan/Wagon (Auto. Trans.)	300	400
8 Gordini 4 Door	500	700
4 Wagon	400	500
4 Fourgon	300	400

GERMAN IMPORTED CARS

BMW (Bavarian Motor Works)

Good reliability, sophisticated engineering, and a slow rate of depreciation combine to make the BMW an expensive and popular dream machine. Owners have complained of inadequate dealer service facilities and many drivers have switched over to independent garages to avoid being stuck with high repair bills. Parts are so scarce and expensive that a black market in used parts presently exists among scrapyards along the northeast coast of the United States.

BMW used-car prices are inflated due to fluctuating European currency rates, the increased retail prices for new models and BMW's well-earned reputation for quality. The best used-car model is the 2002, manufactured before the 1973 emission-control regulations. The 530i 6-cylinder model is not recommended, because of early production problems with the fuel-injection system and the problems with finding replacement parts.

Best Models

BMW Bavaria 1972–1975
BMW 530i 1976–1977

Major Recall Campaigns
Bayerische Motoren Werke (BMW)

Make	Model	Model Year	Brief Description of Defect (Manufacturer's Corrective Action)	Number of Pages on File	Number of Vehicles Recalled
BMW	Six cylinder Model 2500 and 2600	Imp. since Jan. 1 1969	Possibility that headlights may not comply with Federal Safety Standard 108, because minimum height from ground level to center of head lights may need to be modified. (Correct by modifying head lights to meet Standard 108.)	3	1,306

Make	Model	Model Year	Brief Description of Defect (Manufacturer's Corrective Action)	Number of Pages on File	Number of Vehicles Recalled
BMW	6 cylinder 182 CID engines	1972	Possibility that carburetor malfunction may occur, which in certain cases could result in engine compartment fire.	3	4,000
BMW	R75/5 motorcycle	1973	Possibility that bolts used to retain flywheel may not have been properly torqued. If condition exists, bolts could break under stress causing loss of driving power through clutch to transmission and rear wheel.	4	1,136

USED CAR PRICES (APPROXIMATE)
BMW
(West Germany)

Model & Body Type	Wholesale Price	Retail Price
1978		
BMW 320i Sedan 2D	$7500	$8700
BMW 530i Sedan 4D	11500	13600
BMW 733i 4D	18100	21400
1977		
Sedan 2D	6900	7900
Sedan 4D	9000	10000
Coupe 2D	17500	19000
1976		
BMW PS/AC		
2002 2D Sdn.	5400	6400
2002A 2D Sdn.	5600	6500
5301 4D Sdn.	8200	9200

Model & Body Type	Wholesale Price	Retail Price
5301A 4D Sdn.	8400	9400
3.0Si 4D Sdn.	9800	11000
3.0SiA 4D Sdn.	10200	11400
1975		
2002 4 Cyl. 98.4″ W.B.		
2 Door Sedan	3900	4500
2 Door Sedan Automatic	4400	4900
530 i 6 Cyl. 103.8″ W.B.		
4 Door Sedan	6000	6500
5 Door Sedan Automatic	6200	6700
3.0 Si 6 Cyl. 106″ W.B.		
4 Door Sedan	9700	10300
4 Door Sedan Automatic	10000	10600
1974		
2002 4 Cyl. 98.5″ W.B.	3000	3500
2 Door Sedan	3000	3500
Tii 2 Door Sedan	3400	3900
3.0 6 Cyl. 106″ W.B. (Sdns)		
103.3″ W.B. (Cpes)		
Bavaria 4 Door Sedan	5600	6100
Bavaria 4 Dr Sdn. (Auto. Trans.)	5100	6000
S 4 Door Sedan	7500	8100
S 4 Door Sedan (Auto. Trans.)	7600	8200
CS 2 Door Coupe	7700	8300
CS 2 Door Coupe (Auto. Trans.)	8000	8500
1973		
2002 4 Cyl. 98.5″ W.B.		
2 Door Sedan	2400	2900
Tii 2 Door Sedan	2700	3200
3.0 6 Cyl. 106″ W.B. (Exc. CS)		
103.3″ W.B. (CS)		
Bavaria 4 Door Sedan	3500	4000
Bavaria 4 Dr Sdn. (Auto. Trans.)	3600	4100
CS 2 Door Coupe	5000	5500
CS 2 Door Coupe (Auto. Trans.)	5200	5800
1972		
2002 4 Cyl. 98.5″ W.B.		
2 Door Sedan	1700	2300
Tii 2 Door Sedan	2100	2600

Model & Body Type	Wholesale Price	Retail Price
Bavaria & 3.0 6 Cyl.		
106" W.B. (Bavs)		
103.1" W.B. (Cpes)		
Bavaria 4 Door Sedan	3000	3500
Bavaria 4 Dr Sdn (Auto. Trans.)	3100	3600
3.0 CS 2 Door Coupe	4200	4700
3.0 CSA 2 Door Coupe	4400	4900
1971		
1600 & 2002 4 Cyl. 98.5" W.B.		
1600 2 Door Sedan	1100	1500
2002 2 Door Sedan	1300	750
Bavaria & 2500 & 2800 6 Cyl.		
106" W.B. (Exc. Cpes)		
103.3" W.B. (Cpe)		
Bavaria 4 Door Sedan	1800	2300
2500 4 Door Sedan	2100	2600
2800 4 Door Sedan	2500	3000
2800 CS 2 Door Coupe	3500	4000
280 CSA 2 Dr Cpe (Auto. Trans.)	3700	4200
1970		
1600 & 2002 4 Cyl. 98.5" W.B.		
1600 2 Door Sedan	800	1200
2002 2 Door Sedan	1100	1500
2002 2 Dr Sdn (Auto. Trans.)	1200	1500
2500 & 2800 6 Cyl. 106" W.B.		
2500 4 Door Sedan	1700	2300
2800 4 Door Sedan	2300	2800
2800 CS 2 Door Sedan	3200	3700
2800 CA 2 Door Sedan	3500	4000

Capri

Ford's best European car. After all, with the Cortina disaster, Ford of Europe had to make some move to bolster its European import reputation in the United States. Unfortunately, the early 1971 and 1972 models had many quality-control defects affecting the front disc brakes, windshield wipers, heater, defroster, alternator, and regulator. These Capri models also had problems with an excessive shimmy in the front suspension, a high oil consumption, hood-cable breakage, and door adjustments. For many of the above-noted problems, Ford has made several special secret warranty extensions.

Anyone wishing to purchase a used Capri would be prudent to stick with the post-1973 models. In that category, the 1975 Capri 2 looks like the best used car buy, with the 1974 6-cylinder Capri placing second. In overall driving performance, Ford's European Capri makes the American Ford Mustang II look like it contracted hoof and mouth disease.

CAPRI
AREAS OF PREMATURE RUSTING

(1972 to 1974)

Best Models

   Capri 1974–1978

Worst Models

   Capri 1972–1973

Fiesta

Ford's Fiesta has the potential for becoming a North American automotive fiasco. Depreciation is high, parts are expensive and rare, and repairs must be done by mechanics specialized in working on European cars.

Ford is not expected to keep the Fiesta around much later than 1980. Should this be the case, parts will become even more rare and the car's resale value will plummet.

WORST MODELS

   Fiesta 1978

Make	Model	Model Year	Brief Description of Defect	Number of Pages on File	Number of Vehicles Recalled
Mercury	Capri	1973	Possibility of gasoline or gas fumes leakage.	N/A*	N/A
Mercury	Capri	1974 2.8 mtr	Possibility of defective brake lines or master cylinder	N/A	N/A
Mercury	Capri 1 Capri 2 Manufactured in Germany	1974 and 1976	Front brake system may be defective.	N/A	N/A

*N/A means not applicable.

USED CAR PRICES (APPROXIMATE)
Capri
(West Germany)

Model & Body Type	Wholesale Price	Retail Price
1978		
Capri II 3-door Sport Coupe	$3800	$4400
Capri II Ghia 3-door Sport Coupe	4000	4600
1977		
Coupe 3D Sport	2900	3500
Coupe 3D Sport Ghia	3100	3700
1976		
Coupe 3D Sport	2600	3200
Coupe 3D Ghia	2800	3400
1975		
Capri II 4 Cyl. 100.8" W.B.		
3 Door Sport Coupe	2400	2900
Ghia 3 Door Sport Coupe	2600	3200

Model & Body Type	Wholesale Price	Retail Price
1974		
2000 4 Cyl. 100.8″ W.B.		
2 Door Sport Coupe	1600	2100
2600 6 Cyl. 100.8″ W.B.		
2 Door Sport Coupe	1900	2400
1973		
2000 4 Cyl. 100.8″ W.B.		
2 Door Sport Coupe	1300	1800
2600 6 Cyl. 100.8″ W.B.		
2 Door Sport Coupe	1500	2000
1972		
1600 & 2000 4 Cyl. 100.8″ W.B.		
1600 2 Door Sport Coupe	900	1400
2000 2 Door Sport Coupe	1000	1500
2600 6 Cyl. 100.8″ W.B.		
2 Door Sport Coupe	1100	1600
1971		
4 Cyl. 100.8″ W.B.		
2 Door Sport Coupe	800	1000
1970		
4 Cyl. 100.8″ W.B.		
2 Door Sport Coupe	400	700

Mercedes-Benz

The married man's BMW. Actually, the Mercedes-Benz models are even more reliable than the BMW, with a slower rate of depreciation, too. Servicing and parts supply appear adequate, probably owing to the large numbers of models sold in North America and the demands made by some of the more affluent Mercedes owners.

The diesel models are the best buy, either new or used. Some owners have reported that the diesel fuel may jell at low temperatures, but Mercedes-Benz is working on an additive to correct the problem.

The only negative reports concerning Mercedes have been regarding the frequent replacement of the exhaust system in colder climates, and the charges for periodic maintenance work. Some customers have reported that

Mercedes will pay 50 percent of the bill for the replacement of the exhaust system within the first two years of ownership. This alleged warranty extension has not been confirmed, however.

Best Models

Mercedes Diesel 1972–1974
Mercedes Gasoline 1972–1973

MERCEDES-BENZ
AREAS OF PREMATURE RUSTING

All Models (1970 to 1974)

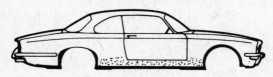

Major Recall Campaigns
Mercedes-Benz of North America, Incorporated

Make	Model	Model Year	Brief Description of Defect (Manufacturer's Corrective Action)	Number of Pages on File	Number of Vehicles Recalled
Mercedes-Benz	220/9 to 300SEL/8 6.3	Mfg from mid Mar. to Sept. 30, 1970	Possibility that check valve of vacuum line from brake booster to intake manifold might develop cracks, causing booster system assist reduction and resulting in possible reduced braking capacity. (Correct by replacing line and check valve.)	9	16,107

Make	Model	Model Year	Brief Description of Defect (Manufacturer's Corrective Action)	Number of Pages on File	Number of Vehicles Recalled
Mercedes-Benz	280SE Convert. 3.5 280SE Coupe 3.5 300SEL 3.5 Sedan	1971	Possibility that fuel supply connecting hoses and fuel injection nozzle hose may develop leaks at connecting point creating possibility of fuel escaping which could ignite causing fire damage.	10	2,281
Mercedes-Benz	280 & 280 Coupe	1973	Possibility that brake line from master cylinder to right front wheel may rub against automatic transmission filler pipe causing line to rupture and leak.	9	6,300
Mercedes-Benz	220D, 220 250, 250c, 280, 280c	1972 & 1973	Possibility that seat belts fail to meet requirements of Federal Motor Vehicle Safety Standard No. 208. Condition exists because length of belt, when front seat is in most forward position, prevents or impedes belt usage by certain individuals who might find seat belt uncomfortably tight.	15	29,228

USED CAR PRICES (APPROXIMATE)
Mercedes-Benz

Model & Body Type	Wholesale Price	Retail Price
1978		
230 Sedan (Auto)	$11500	$14400
240D Sedan (Diesel)	10500	13200
240D Sedan (Diesel-Auto)	11400	14300
280E Sedan (Auto)	15100	18900
280CE Coupe (Auto)	17000	21200
280SE Sedan (Auto)	17900	22300
300D Sedan (Diesel-Auto)	14700	18300
300CD Coupe (Diesel-Auto)	16500	20600
450SEL Sedan (Auto)	22400	28000
450SL Coupe/Roadster	20400	25500
450SLC Coupe	24900	31100
6.9 Sedan (Auto)	34200	42700
1977		
Sedan 4D	9500	10700
Sedan 4D	8500	9500
Sedan 4D	13000	14000
Sdn. 4D (280E)	14000	15000
Sedan (280SE)	17000	19000
Sedan 4D		
(450 SEL)	21000	23000
Cpe./Rdstr. 2D	17000	19000
Coupe 2JD	22000	24000
Sedan 4D (6.9)	31000	34000
1976		
AT/PS/AC		
Mercedes-Benz		
230 4D Sdn.	8200	9200
240D 4D Sdn.	8600	9700
300D 4D Sdn.	10100	11400
280 4D Sdn.	9700	11000
280C 2D Cpe.	10400	11700
280S 4D Sdn.	11200	12600
450SD 4D Sdn.	14600	15900
450SEL 4D Sdn.	15300	16600
450SL Cpe./		
Rdstr. 2D	15000	16400
450SLC 2D Cpe.	17500	19000

Model & Body Type	Wholesale Price	Retail Price
1975		
4 Cyl. 108.3" W.B.		
230 Sedan Automatic	8000	8600
240D Sedan	7500	8000
240D Sedan Automatic	8100	8700
5 Cyl. 108.3" W.B.		
300D Sedan Automatic	10300	11000
6 Cyl. 108.3" W.B. (Exc. S)		
112.8" W.B. (S)		
280 Sedan Automatic	10500	11300
280C Coupe Automatic	10900	12000
280S Sedan Automatic	12000	13600
8 Cyl. 112.6" W.B. (SE)		
116.5" W.B. (SEL)		
96.9" W.B. (SL)		
111" W.B. (SLC)		
450SL Coupe Roadster Auto.	13200	14800
450SE Sedan Automatic	14100	15900
450 SEL Sedan Automatic	15000	17400
450 SLC Coupe Automatic	17200	18200
1974		
4 Cyl. 108.3" W.B.		
230 4 Dr Sedan (Auto. Trans.)	5700	6300
240 D 4 Dr Sedan	5800	6400
240 D 4 Dr Sdn (Auto. Trans.)	6100	6900
6 Cyl. 108.3" W.B.		
280 4 Dr Sedan (Auto. Trans.)	6900	7700
280 C 2 Door Coupe (Auto. Trans.)	7300	8300
8 Cyl. 112" W.B. (SE)		
116" W.B. (SEL)		
96.6" W.B. (SL) 111" W.B. (SEL)		
450 SE 4 Door Sedan (Auto. Trans.)	11900	12900
450 SEL 4 Door Sedan (Auto. Trans.)	12800	14000
450 SL Coupe/Roadster (Auto. Trans.)	11300	12500
450 SLC Coupe (Auto. Trans.)	15200	17400

Model & Body Type	Wholesale Price	Retail Price
1973		
4 Cyl. 108.3″ W.B.		
220 4 Door Sedan (Auto. Trans.)	4200	5000
220 D 4 Door Sedan	4300	5100
220 D 4 Door Sedan		
(Auto. Trans.)	4400	5200
6 Cyl. 108.3″ W.B.		
280 4 Door Sedan		
(Auto. Trans.)	5400	6100
280 C 2 Door Coupe (Auto. Trans.)	5700	6400
8 Cyl. 108.3″ W.B. (SE)		
112.2″ W.B. (SEL)		
96.9″ W.B. (SL) 111″ W.B. (SLC)		
450 SE 4 Door Sedan		
(Auto. Trans.)	11000	12000
450 SEL 4 Door Sedan		
(Auto. Trans.)	11600	12600
450 SL Coupe/Roadster		
(Auto. Trans.)	10500	11500
450 SLC 2 Door Coupe		
(Auto. Trans.)	13100	14100
1972		
4 Cyl. 108.3″ W.B.		
220 4 Door Sedan		
(Auto. Trans.)	3300	3900
220 D 4 Door Sedan	3400	4000
220 D 4 Door Sedan		
(Auto. Trans.)	3500	4100
6 Cyl. 108.3″ W.B.		
250 4 Door Sedan		
(Auto. Trans.)	3800	4400
250 2 Door Sedan		
(Auto. Trans.)	4200	4800
280 SE 4 Door Sedan		
(Auto. Trans.)	5000	5600
8 Cyl. 108.3″ W.B. (SE)		
112.2″ W.B. (SEL)		
96.9″ W.B. (SL)		
280 SE 4.5 Sedan		
(Auto. Trans.)	5200	6000
280 SEL 4.5 Sedan		
(Auto. Trans.)	5400	6200

Model & Body Type	Wholesale Price	Retail Price
300 SEL 4.5 Sedan		
(Auto. Trans.)	6300	7400
350 SL 4.5 Coupe/Roadster		
(Auto. Trans.)	6300	7400
600 4 Door Sedan	8500	9900
1971		
4 Cyl. 108.3″ W.B.		
220 4 Door Sedan	2200	2500
220 D 4 Door Sedan	2300	2600
6 Cyl. 108.3″ W.B.		
(Exc SE & SL's)		
112.8″ W.B. (SEL)		
94.5″ W.B. (SL's)		
250 4 Door Sedan	2700	3200
250 2 Door Coupe	3100	3700
280 S 4 Door Sedan	3100	3700
280 SE 4 Door Sedan	3200	3900
280 SEL 4 Door Sedan	3600	4500
280 SL Roadster	4600	5300
280 SL 2 Door Coupe	4100	4900
280 SL Coupe/Roadster	4000	4800
1970		
4 Cyl. 108.3″ W.B.		
220 4 Door Sedan	1800	2300
220 D 4 Door Sedan	1900	2400
6 Cyl. 108.3″ W.B.		
(Exc. SEL's & SL's)		
112.8″ W.B. (SEL)		
95.4″ W.B. (SL)		
250 4 Door Sedan	2000	2500
250 2 Door Coupe	2400	2900
280 S 4 Door Sedan	2400	2900
280 SE 4 Door Sedan	2500	3000
280 SEL 4 Door Sedan	2700	3200
280 SL 2 Door Roadster	3300	4000
280 SL 2 Door Coupe	3400	4200
280 SL 2 Door Coupe/		
Roadster	3500	4300
280 SE 2 Door Coupe	4800	5800
280 SE Convertible	5500	6500
300 SEL 2.8 4 Door Sedan	4700	5700

Opel

A German import that has disappointed many North American motorists, with its reputation for mechanical failures and inadequate servicing. General Motors has never been very lucky with its European imports, ever since its Vauxhall fiasco (yes, Virginia, GM is *now* selling its Vauxhall Viva and Firenza in—South Africa).

Opel owners complain of an inadequate parts supply, rapid depreciation rate, and repeated malfunctioning of the electrical system.

Best Models

Opel 1974–1976

Worst Models

Opel 1972–1973

Major Recall Campaigns
General Motors Corporation-Buick Division-Opel

Make	Model	Model Year	Brief Description of Defect (Manufacturer's Corrective Action)	Number of Pages on File	Number of Vehicles Recalled
Opel	Kadetts Model 31, 31D, 36, 36D and 39-1900 Series	1970 1971 1972	Possibility that windshield may not have been mounted to conform with retention requirement of Federal Motor Vehicle Safety Standard No. 212. If condition exists and vehicle is involved in high impact frontal collision, windshield may come out. (Correct by inspecting and securing with improved adhesive where necessary.)	12	100,661

Model & Body Type	Wholesale Price	Retail Price
1978		
2-door Coupe (T77)	$3100	$3500
2-door Deluxe Coupe (Y77)	3300	3800
4-door Deluxe Sedan (Y69)	3400	3900
2-door Sport Coupe (W77)	3400	3900
1977		
Sedan 4D	2500	2900
Coupe 2D	2200	2600
Coupe 2D		
Deluxe	2500	2900
1976		
Opel Isuza		
2 Door Coupe	2200	2600
2D Cpe. Deluxe	2400	2800
1975		
1900 4 Cyl. 95.1″ W.B.		
2 Door Sedan	1800	2300
2 Door Station Wagon	2000	2500
MANTA 4 Cyl. 95.7″ W.B.		
2 Door Sport Coupe	1800	3300
1974		
MANTA 4 Cyl. 95.7″ W.B.		
2 Door Coupe	1400	1900
Luxus 2 Door Coupe	1600	2100
Rallye 2 Door Coupe	1500	2000
1900 4 Cyl. 95.7″ W.B.		
2 Door Wagon	1400	1900
1973		
1900 4 Cyl. 95.7″ W.B.		
2 Door Wagon	1000	1400
MANTA 4 Cyl. 95.7″ W.B.		
2 Door Sport Coupe	900	1300
Rallye 2 Door Sport Coupe	1000	1400
Luxus 2 Door Sport Coupe	1000	1400
GT 4 Cyl. 95.7″ W.B.		
Coupe	1500	2000
1972		
31 & 39 4 Cyl. 95.1″ W.B.		
31 2 Door Sedan	500	800
31 D 2 Door Deluxe Sedan	600	900

Model & Body Type	Wholesale Price	Retail Price
39 2 Door Deluxe Wagon	700	1000
1900 4 Cyl. 95.7″ W.B.		
2 Door Sedan	700	1000
4 Door Sedan	800	1100
2 Door Wagon	800	1100
2 Door Sport Coupe	700	1000
2 Door Rallye Coupe	800	1100
GT 4 Cyl. 95.7″ W.B.		
Coupe	1200	1600
1971		
4 Cyl. 95.1″ W.B.		
31 2 Door Sedan	300	500
31 D Deluxe Sedan	400	600
36 4 Door Sedan	400	600
36 D Deluxe Sedan	500	800
39 Deluxe Wagon	600	900
53 4 Door Sedan	600	900
1900 4 Cyl. 95.7″ W.B.		
Sedan	500	800
Station Wagon	700	1000
Sport Coupe	600	900
Rallye Coupe	700	1000
GT 4 Cyl. 95.7″ W.B.		
Coupe	900	1300
1970		
4 Cyl. 95.1″ W.B.		
2 Door Standard Sedan	200	400
Deluxe Sport Sedan	300	500
Deluxe Wagon	400	600
Super Deluxe Sport Coupe	400	600
Rallye Kadett Coupe	500	700
GT Coupe	700	1100

Volkswagen

The Beetle has always been Volkswagen's ideal city car, with a solid reputation for economy, reliability, and defective heaters that almost never worked in the winter.

Unfortunately, VW's love affair with North American motorists has come to a sad and untimely end. Japanese and other European models are now taking an increasingly larger share of the imported-car market.

Since Volkswagen abandoned the Beetle, it has repeatedly struck out with its subsequent models. The Audi, Dasher, VW 411 and 412 have all been losers, and Volkswagen appears to be intent on continuing that tradition with its new Rabbit and Scirocco.

Rabbit owners complain of chronic starting problems, inoperative door locks, defective interior trim and finish, body rattles, transmission clunks, and exhaust-system thumps. Rubber dampers used to protect the exhaust system from striking the chassis also have a high failure rate. In addition to serious mechanical defects, Rabbit and Scirocco owners also report that dealer service is expensive and spare parts are scarce. Fires have been reported in Volkswagens in California and Canada, owing to a defective catalytic-converter system in California, and a defective rubber damper used on the non-catalytic-converter-equipped model in Canada. Both models have been recalled.

Because of Volkswagen's serious shortcomings with its Rabbit/Scirocco models, the company has extended the warranty on its 1975 models to "upgrade the 1975s to the level of the 1976s," according to Josef L. Metz, vice president in charge of corporate service, Volkswagen of America. Rabbit/Scirocco owners will receive free repairs for problems in the following areas: brakes, poor driveability, carburetor malfunctioning, exhaust system rattles, cold-starting difficulties, and plastic door trim defects. This major warranty extension program is expected to cost VW more than $5 million and could possibly affect more than 100,000 vehicles.

VW 411 and 412

Even Volkswagen dealers admit that these models were commercial duds, owing to the countless number of mechanical defects and poor dealer servicing. Both models have now been discontinued, so they are definitely not recommended as used-car choices.

Best Models

VW Beetle 1971–1975
VW Rabbit 1977–1979

Worst Models

VW 411 and 412 1972–1974
VW Dasher 1974–1975
VW Rabbit 1975
Audi 1972–1976

Major Recall Campaigns
Volkswagen of America, Incorporated

Make	Model	Model Year	Brief Description of Defect (Manufacturer's Corrective Action)	Number of Pages on File	Number of Vehicles Recalled
VW	Type 1, 3, 4 and Super Beetle	1971	Possibility that guide pin in steering column lock may have been damaged in assembly. Also, ignition switch may have manufacturing defect. These conditions could result in difficulty in unlocking steering and starting engine. (Correct by replacing locks and switches where necessary.)	21	78,100
			Possibility that left front hood hinge may rub against wiring harness causing damage to wiring.		

Make	Model	Model Year	Brief Description of Defect (Manufacturer's Corrective Action)	Number of Pages on File	Number of Vehicles Recalled
VW	Type 1	1975	Possibility that rear axle shaft could break in vicinity of spline/thread junction due to improper heat treatment.	6	1,760
VW	Model 14 Karmann Ghia	1968 1969 1970 1971 1972	Possibility that fuel vapors or small amounts of liquid fuel may enter passenger compartment through small opening in wall which separates the car's interior from luggage compartment.	5	112,000

USED CAR PRICES (APPROXIMATE)
Volkswagen

Model & Body Type	Wholesale Price	Retail Price
1978		
STANDARD		
1511 Convertible	$4700	$5500
1701 Rabbit 2D Hatchback Standard	3700	4000
1721 Rabbit 2D Hatchback Custom	3900	4500
1723 Rabbit 2D Hatchback Custom (Auto.)	4100	4800
1725 Rabbit 2D Hatchback (Custom Diesel)	4000	4700
1741 Rabbit 4D Sedan Custom	4000	4700
1743 Rabbit 4D Sed. Custom (Auto.)	4200	4900
1745 Rabbit 4D		

Model & Body Type	Wholesale Price	Retail Price
Hatchback (Custom Diesel)	4100	4900
1761 Rabbit 2D Hatchback Deluxe	4300	5100
1763 Rabbit 2D Hatchback Deluxe (Auto.)	4300	5000
1765 Rabbit 2D Hatchback (Deluxe Diesel)	4300	5000
1781 Rabbit 4D Sedan Deluxe	4400	5100
1783 Rabbit 4D Sedan Deluxe (Auto.)	4400	5200
1785 Rabbit 4D Sedan (Deluxe Diesel)	4700	5500
DASHER		
3241/81 Dasher 2D Hatchback	4900	5800
3243/83 Dasher 2D Hatchback (Auto.)	5200	6000
3441/81 Dasher 4D Sedan	5000	5900
3443/83 Dasher 4D Sedan (Auto.)	5300	6100
3641/81 Dasher 4D Wagon	5300	6100
3643/83 Dasher 4D Wagon (Auto.)	5500	6400
WAGONS		
2211 Station Wagon, 7-S	5500	6400
2213 Station Wagon 7-S (Auto.)	5700	6600
2231 Station Wagon, 9-S	5500	6400
2361 Kombi w/3-Pass Rear Bench Seat	5200	6000
2391 Campmobile Basic	5200	6000
2393 Campmobile Basic (Auto.)	5500	6300
SCIROCCO		
5311 Scirocco 2D Sedan	5000	5900
5313 Scirocco 2D Sedan (Auto.)	5200	6100
1977		
Sedan 2D	2900	3700
Convertible	3600	4400

Model & Body Type	Wholesale Price	Retail Price
Sedan 4D Dasher	3700	4500
Sedan 2D Dasher		
(Hatchback)	3800	4600
Sta. Wgn. Dasher	4200	5000
Coupe 2D Scirocco	3900	4700
Hatchback 2D Rabbit	2900	3700
H'bk 2D Rabbit Custom	3100	3900
H'bk 4D Rabbit Custom	3200	4000
H'bk 2D Rabbit Delux	3300	4100
H'bk 4D Rabbit Delux	4300	5200
Kombi	4500	5300
Station Wagon	4500	5300
Station Wagon 9P	5000	5900
Campmobile	5000	5400
1976		
Volkswagen		
2 Door Sedan	2400	3100
Convertible	3000	3800
4D Dasher Sdn.	3000	3800
2D Dasher Sdn.		
(Hatchback)	3100	3900
St. Wgn. Dasher	3400	4200
2D Cpe. Scirocco	3100	3900
2D Rabbit	2400	3100
2D Rabbit Cust.	2500	3300
4D Rabbit Cust.	2600	3300
2D Rabbit Dlx.	2700	3400
4D Rabbit Dlx.	2700	3500
Volkswagen Transporte		
Kombi	3700	4500
St. Wgn. 7P	3800	4700
St. Wgn. 9P	3900	4700
Campmobile	4400	5300
1975		
BEETLE 4 Cyl. 94.5" W.B.		
2 Door Sedan	1700	2200
2 Door Super Beetle	1900	2400
2 Door Sedan Le Grande	2200	2700
Convertible	2600	3200
RABBIT 4 Cyl. 94.5" W.B.		
2 Door Hatchback Sedan	1900	2400

Model & Body Type	Wholesale Price	Retail Price
4 Door Hatchback Sedan w/Perf. Pkg.	2400	2900
DASHER 4 Cyl. 97.2″ W.B.		
2 Door Sedan	2400	2900
4 Door Sedan	2500	3000
4 Door Station Wagon	2600	3100
SCIROCCO 4 Cyl. 94.5″ W.B.		
2 Door Sedan	2600	3100
TRANSPORTERS 4 Cyl. 94.5″ W.B.		
Campmobile Basic	2900	3400
Kombi	2900	3400
7 Seat Station Wagon	3000	3500
9 Seat Station Wagon	3000	3500
Panel Delivery	3000	3500
1974		
VOLKSWAGEN 4 Cyl. 94.5″ W.B. (Exc. Super) 95.3″ W.B. (Super)		
2 Door Beetle Sedan	1400	1700
2 Door Super Beetle Sedan	1500	1600
Super Beetle Convertible	1900	2400
Karmann Ghia Coupe	1900	2400
Karmann Ghia Convertible	2000	2500
DASHER 4 Cyl. 97.2″ W.B.		
2 Door Sedan	2000	2500
4 Door Sedan	2100	2600
4 Door Wagon	2200	2700
412 4 Cyl. 98.4″ W.B.		
2 Door Sedan	2000	2500
4 Door Sedan (Auto. Trans.)	2200	2700
Station Wagon (Auto. Trans.)	2300	2800
STATION WAGONS 4 Cyl. 94.5″ W.B.		
Panel Delivery	2200	2700
7 Passenger Wagon	2200	2700
9 Passenger Wagon	2200	2700
Kombi Wagon	2000	2500
Campmobile w/Equipment	2900	3400

Model & Body Type	Wholesale Price	Retail Price
1973		
VOLKSWAGEN 4 Cyl.		
94.5" W.B. (Exc. Super)		
95.3" W.B. (Super)		
2 Door Beetle Sedan	1000	1500
2 Door Super Beetle Sedan	1100	1600
Super Beetle Convertible	1300	1800
Karmann Ghia Coupe	1300	1800
Karmann Ghia Convertible	1400	1900
2 Door Squareback Sedan	1400	1900
Type 3 Fastback Sedan	1300	1800
'The Thing'	1300	1800
412 4 Cyl. 98.4" W.B.		
2 Door Sedan	1000	1200
4 Door Sedan (Auto. Trans.)	1100	1300
Station Wagon (Auto. Trans.)	1200	1400
STATION WAGONS 4 Cyl.		
94.5" W.B.		
Panel Delivery	2000	2500
7 Passenger Wagon	1900	2400
9 Passenger Wagon	2000	2500
Kombi Wagon	1700	2200
Campmobile	1700	2200
1972		
VOLKSWAGEN 4 Cyl.		
94.5" W.B. (Exc. Super)		
95.3" W.B. (Super)		
2 Door Beetle Sedan	800	1100
2 Door Super Beetle Sedan	1000	1200
Super Beetle Convertible	1200	1400
Karmann Ghia Coupe	1000	1300
Karmann Ghia Convertible	1100	1400
2 Door Fastback Sedan	900	1200
2 Door Squareback Sedan	1000	1300
Type 3 2 Door Sedan	1000	1300
411 4 Cyl. 98.4" W.B.		
4 Door Sedan	900	1100
3 Door Sedan	900	1100
STATION WAGONS 4 Cyl.		
94.5" W.B.		
Panel Delivery	1200	1700

Model & Body Type	Wholesale Price	Retail Price
7 Passenger Wagon	1200	1700
9 Passenger Wagon	1200	1700
Wagon	1100	1600
Campmobile	1100	1600
1971		
VOLKSWAGEN 4 Cyl.		
95.3″ W.B. (Beetle)		
94.5″ W.B. (Others)		
2 Door Beetle Sedan	500	800
2 Door Super Beetle Sedan	600	900
Super Beetle Convertible	800	1100
Karmann Ghia Coupe	800	1100
Karmann Ghia Convertible	800	1100
2 Door Squareback Sedan	800	1100
Type 3 2 Door Sedan	900	1200
411 4 Cyl. 98.3″ W.B.		
3 Door Sedan	600	800
4 Door Sedan	600	800
STATION WAGONS 4 Cyl.		
94.5″ W.B.		
Panel Delivery	1000	1300
Station Wagon	1000	1300
Kombi Wagon	900	1200
Campmobile	900	1200
1970		
VOLKSWAGEN 4 Cyl.		
94.5″ W.B.		
2 Door Beetle Sedan	500	800
Beetle Convertible	700	1000
Karmann Ghia Coupe	700	1000
Karmann Ghia Convertible	600	900
2 Door Fastback	600	900
2 Door Squareback	800	1100
STATION WAGONS 4 Cyl.		
94.5″ W.B.		
Wagon	800	1100
7 Passenger Wagon	900	1200
9 Passenger Wagon	1000	1300

Audi

The Audi is another new Volkswagen model that has tarnished the rising VW star. Owners complain of major mechanical defects such as an exhaust system that self-destructs and premature brake wear around 10,000 miles. The motor often acts like an old-fashioned oil burner, and reports from Audi owners of major engine overhauls between 24,000 and 36,000 miles are not uncommon. The transmission may also malfunction because of defective internal gears. Much to its credit, Volkswagen has extended the warranty coverage on the exhaust system, motor, and transmission defects up to 36,000 miles.

Many Audi owners report that servicing is expensive and parts are constantly on back order. Consequently, many owners polled stated they would not buy another Audi.

Major Recall Campaigns
Audi, Incorporated

Make	Model	Model Year	Brief Description of Defect	Number of Pages on File	Number of Vehicles Recalled
Audi	100	1973	Possibility that electrical fan motor controlling temperature of engine cooling system may develop short. If condition occurs, it could result in electrical fire in lead wire to the motor.	3	16,000
Audi	100, 100LS & 100GL	1973	Possibility that chemical residue from thread rolling process was not entirely removed from brake caliper bolt threads. If condition exists,	3	12,500

Make	Model	Model Year	Brief Description of Defect	Number of Pages on File	Number of Vehicles Recalled
			residue may affect caliper bolts and cause bolt breakage.		
Audi	80 (Fox)	1973	Possibility that mounting bolts for rear wheel backing plates were extended by lateral force applied when rig was used to hoist vehicle for loading in ship.	10	13,500
Audi	100	1975	Possibility that securing nut which holds front exhaust pipe bracket to automatic transmission housing may come loose. If condition exists, bracket may vibrate and contact return fuel line resulting in damage to line.	2	2,000

USED CAR PRICES (APPROXIMATE)
Audi

Model & Body Type	Wholesale Price	Retail Price
1978		
FOX		
849 Sedan 2D	$5000	$5800
850 Sedan 2D	5100	5900
331 Wagon 4D	5300	6200
5000		
433 Sedan 4D	7200	8500

Model & Body Type	Wholesale Price	Retail Price
1977		
Sedan 4D	4000	4500
Sedan 2D	4000	4500
Audi Fox		
Sedan 4D	3800	4200
Sedan 2D	3700	4300
Wagon 4D	4100	4700
1976		
Audi		
4 Door Sedan	3500	4000
2 Door Sedan	3400	3900
Audi Fox		
4 Door Sedan	3400	3800
2 Door Sedan	3300	3700
4 Door Wagon	3600	4000
1975		
FOX 4 Cyl. 105.3″ W.B.		
2 Door Sedan	2600	3000
4 Door Sedan	2700	3100
4 Door Wagon	2700	3100
100 LS 4 Cyl. 97.2″ W.B.		
2 Door Sedan	3000	3400
4 Door Sedan	3000	3400
1974		
100 LS 4 Cyl. 105.3″ W.B.		
2 Door Sedan	2200	2600
4 Door Sedan	2300	2700
FOX 4 Cyl. 97.2″ W.B.		
2 Door Sedan	2000	2400
4 Door Sedan	2200	2600
1973		
FOX 4 Cyl. 105.3″ W.B.		
2 Door Sedan	1600	2100
4 Door Sedan	1700	2300
100 LS 4 Cyl. 105.3″ W.B.		
2 Door Sedan	1900	2400
100 GL 4 Cyl. 105.3″ W.B.		
2 Door Sedan (Auto. Trans.)	2300	2800
4 Door Sedan (Auto. Trans.)	2400	2900

Model & Body Type	Wholesale Price	Retail Price
1972		
SUPER 90 4 Cyl. 98″ W.B.		
2 Door Sedan	1000	1300
4 Door Sedan	1000	1300
Station Wagon	1100	1400
100 4 Cyl. 105.3″ W.B.		
2 Door Sedan	1300	1600
4 Door Sedan	1300	1600
100 LS 4 Cyl. 105.3″ W.B.		
2 Door Sedan	1500	1900
4 Door Sedan	1500	1900
100 GL 4 Cyl. 105.3″ W.B.		
2 Door Sedan (Auto. Trans.)	1600	2000
4 Door Sedan (Auto. Trans.)	1600	2000
1971		
SUPER 90 4 Cyl. 98″ W.B.		
2 Door Sedan	700	900
4 Door Sedan	800	1000
Station Wagon	900	1100
100 LS 4 Cyl. 105.3″ W.B.		
2 Door Sedan	1100	1400
4 Door Sedan	1100	1400
1970		
SUPER 90 4 Cyl. 98″ W.B.		
2 Door Sedan	400	600
4 Door Sedan	500	700
2 Door Station Wagon	500	700
100 LS 4 Cyl. 107.5″ W.B.		
2 Door Sedan	700	900
4 Door Sedan	800	1000

Porsche

The ideal medium-priced sports car. While giving excellent overall driving performance and fuel economy, Porsche also brings with it a strong dealer network and a good supply of replacement parts. Depreciation is less than average, helping to offset the initial high retail-sales price.

Porsche owners have complained that dealer servicing is expensive, so it may be a good idea to cut loose from the dealer servicing as soon as the warranty period is terminated.

The mid-engined 914 is a much better buy as a used-car investment than the rear-engined 911, because the 914 can be bought used for almost half the price of a used 911. The 914 is also a more forgiving car on the highway and does not require as much of the expert handling as the 911. Don't look for used-car bargains, though; Porsche owners are usually well informed about their car's value and will not sell below list price unless there are some costly mechanical repairs on the horizon.

Major Recall Campaigns
Porsche, Incorporated

Make	Model	Model Year	Brief Description of Defect (Manufacturer's Corrective Action)	Number of Pages on File	Number of Vehicles Recalled
Porsche	914 and 914/6	1970	Possibility that seat lock adjustment mechanism may, under extreme loading of seat, fail to hold seat in firm position. (Correct by replacing with improved lock mechanism.)	13	2,017
Porsche	914, 914/6	1970	Possibility that fuel line connection and fuel filter may have been improperly secured during assembly, which could cause small quantities of fuel to escape. Also, fuel lines of fuel injectors for right bank of cylinders may in some instances have become deteriorated as a	15	8,340

Make	Model	Model Year	Brief Description of Defect (Manufacturer's Corrective Action)	Number of Pages on File	Number of Vehicles Recalled
			result of electrolyte dripping from battery. (Correct by modifying as required.)		
			Possibility that retaining bolt for front axle sub-frame may have been overtightened during assembly. (Correct by replacing where necessary.)		
Porsche	911T & 911 equipped w/CIS	1973 1974	Possibility that fuel hose inner diameter exceeds specifications. Condition prevents proper connections, resulting in fuel leaks in engine compartment of underneath vehicle. Also, O-ring gasket at rear of cold start valve may have been improperly installed and could permit gasoline leakage. If conditions exist, they could result in fire hazard.	5	6,000

Model & Body Type	Wholesale Price	Retail Price
1978		
Porsche 924	$9600	$11300
Porsche 924, Automatic	9900	11700
911 SC Coupe	15200	18000
911 SC Targa	16000	19100
928 Coupe	21900	26000
Turbo Carrera Coupe	28700	34000
1977		
Coupe (924)	8500	9000
Coupe (911S)	13000	14000
Cpe. Targa (911S)	13900	15000
Coupe Turbo Carrera	22000	25000
1976		
Porsche		
914 Rdstr. 2.0	5600	6600
914 Rdstr. 2.0 w/App. Group	5900	6800
912E Cpe.	8300	9300
911lS Cpe.	10800	12000
911S Targa	11400	12600
Cpe. Turbo Carrera	20000	23000
1975		
914 4 Cyl. 96.8″ W.B.		
1.8 5 Speed Roadster	5000	5700
1.8 5 Speed Roadster w/App. Group	5200	5900
2.0 5 Speed Roadster	5400	6100
2.0 5 Speed Roadster w/App. Group	5600	6300
911 6 Cyl. 89.4″ W.B.		
S 4 Speed Coupe (Anniv. Ed.)	9500	10400
S 4 Speed Coupe	10500	11400
S 4 Speed Targa Coupe (Anniv. Ed.)	13400	14800

Model & Body Type	Wholesale Price	Retail Price
S 4 Speed Targa Coupe	11500	12500
Carrera 5 Speed Coupe	12500	13600
Carrera 5 Speed Targa Coupe	13500	14700
1974		
914 4 Cyl. 96.8" W.B.		
1.8 Roadster	3300	3700
1.8 Roadster w/App. Group	3400	3800
2.0 Roadster	3500	3900
2.0 Roadster w/App. Group	3800	4400
911 6 Cyl. 89.4" W.B.		
4 Speed Coupe	7000	8000
Targa 4 Speed Roadster	7200	8200
S 4 Speed Coupe	8200	9200
S Targa 4 Speed Roadster	9200	10200
Carrera 4 Speed Coupe	9900	10800
Carrera Targa 4 Speed Roadster	10900	11900
1973		
914 4 Cyl. 96.5" W.B.		
1.7 5 Speed Roadster	2800	3400
1.7 5 Speed Roadster w/App. Group	2900	3500
2.0 5 Speed Roadster	3100	3700
2.0 5 Speed Roadster w/App. Group	3200	3800
911 6 Cyl. 89.5" W.B.		
T 4 Speed Coupe	5700	6400
T Targa 4 Speed Roadster	6200	6900
E 4 Speed Coupe	6200	6900
E Targa 4 Speed Roadster	6400	7200
S 4 Speed Coupe	6500	7200
S Targa 4 Speed Roadster	6900	7900
1972		
914 4 Cyl. 96.5" W.B.		
2 Door 5 Speed Roadster	2000	2500
2 Door 5 Speed Roadster	2000	2500
2 Door 5 Speed Roadster w/App. Group	2100	2600
911 6 Cyl. 89.5" W.B.		
T 4 Speed Coupe	4400	5100
T Targa 4 Speed Roadster	5000	5800
E 4 Speed Coupe	5100	5900

Model & Body Type	Wholesale Price	Retail Price
E Targa 4 Speed Roadster	5400	6200
S 4 Speed Coupe	5500	6300
S Targa 4 Speed Roadster	6000	6900
1971		
911 6 Cyl. 89.5" W.B.		
T 4 Speed Coupe	3500	4200
T Targa 4 Speed Roadster	4000	4700
Add for 5 Speed		
Add for Auto. Trans.		
E 5 Speed Coupe	4100	4800
E Targa 5 Speed Roadster	4500	5200
S 5 Speed Coupe	4500	5200
S Special Ratio Coupe	4600	5300
S Targa 5 Speed Roadster	5100	5800
1970		
911 6 Cyl. 89.3" W.B.		
T 4 Speed Coupe	2500	3000
T Targa 4 Speed Roadster	2900	3400
E 5 Speed Coupe	3000	3500
E Targa 5 Speed Roadster	3400	3900
S 5 Speed Coupe	3500	4000
S Special Ratio Coupe	3600	4100
S Targa 5 Speed Roadster	3900	4400

ITALIAN IMPORTED CARS

Alfa Romeo

A fair-weather sports car. Highly recommended for mild weather zones like California, Florida, and other areas south of lattitude 40. The initial retail price is high and depreciation is low despite a small dealer network. The Berlina Sedan, Spider Veloce, and GTV 2 plus 2 Coupe are excellent used-car buys.

When buying a used Alfa, verify the true model year by checking the date-of-manufacture production plate affixed to the driver's side door frame. Alfa's also have a tendency to fall quickly into disrepair if periodic maintenance has not been done competently. Naturally, a complete mechanical examination, preferably by an Alfa specialist, is a prerequisite to the purchase of any used Alfa Romeo. With fuel injection, dual overhead cam, a two-liter engine, five-speed transmission and four-wheel disc brakes, the Alfa needs few options. A well-maintained Alfa Romeo is one used car offer that not even Don Corleone could refuse.

The 1971 to 1973 Berlina models have had severe starting problems which have been corrected by a free carburetor kit supplied by the manufacturer to Berlina owners requesting the kit.

Major Recall Campaigns
Alfa Romeo, Incorporated

Make	Model	Model Year	Brief Description of Defect	Number of Pages on File	Number of Vehicles Recalled
Alfa Romeo	Spider 105.62 G.T.V. 105.51 Berlina 105.71	1971	Possibility that during assembly of fuse holder spring cup, which is secured to fusebox by a hollow rivet, rivet was incorrectly installed. If condition exists, could result in total loss of electric power.	8	2,552

ALFA ROMEO
AREAS OF PREMATURE RUSTING

All Models (1971 to 1973)

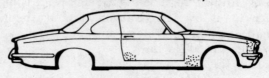

USED CAR PRICES (APPROXIMATE)
Alfa Romeo

Model & Body Type	Wholesale Price	Retail Price
1978		
EAST		
Alfetta 4-door Sports Sedan	$6500	$7700
Alfetta GT 2-door Coupe Sprint	7400	8700
2000 Spider Veloce Convertible	7800	9200
1977		
Sedan 4D Sports	5500	6400
Coupe Sprint Veloce	6500	7500
Conv. Spider Veloce	6400	7400
1976		
4 Door Sedan		
Alfetta Sports	4800	5700
GT Alfetta Coupe	5900	6900
Convertible		
Spider Veloce	5800	6800
1975		
4 Cyl. 88.6″ W.B. (Spid)		
98.8″ W.B. (Ber)		
94.5″ W.B. (GT)		
2000 Spider Veloce		
Convertible	4200	4700
Alfetta Berlina Sedan	4000	4500
GT Coupe	5000	5500

Model & Body Type	Wholesale Price	Retail Price
1974		
2000 4 Cyl.		
101.1″ W.B. (Ber)		
88.6″ W.B. (Spid)		
92.5″ W.B. (GT)		
4 Door Berlina	3000	3500
Spider Veloce	4000	4500
GT Veloce 2 + 2	3800	4300
1973		
2000 4 Cyl.		
92.5″ W.B. (Exc. Ber)		
101.1″ W.B. (Ber)		
4 Door Berlina	2200	2700
Spider Veloce	2700	3200
GT Veloce 2 + 2	2500	3000
1972		
2000 4 Cyl.		
92.5″ W.B. (Exc. Ber)		
101.1″ W.B. (Ber)		
4 Door Berlina	1600	2100
Spider Veloce	2100	2500
GT Veloce 2 + 2	1900	2400
1971		
2000 4 Cyl.		
92.5″ W.B. (Exc. Ber)		
101.1″ W.B. (Ber)		
4 Door Berlina	1200	1500
Spider Veloce	1600	2100
GT Veloce 2 + 2	1600	2100

Fiat

Fiats are freaky. They are well-built machines that have given millions of European motorists excellent fuel economy while providing sports-car performance on the highway. North American motorists should expect the same, but according to the hundreds of complaint letters pouring into North American auto consumer groups, such as the Washington Center for Auto Safety, Fiat imports take on a classic Dr. Jekyl and Mr. Hyde disposition as they cross the Atlantic.

Owners are most concerned over what they call inadequate servicing. Complaints regarding the high cost of parts replacement and periodic maintenance (some owners call it the "Italian Connection") abound. And because of the poor after-sales service by Fiat's weak dealer body, many Fiat owners state they would never buy another one. One disgruntled Fiat owner's frank evaluation of Fiat's North American service was, "It's not worth a—."

Reliability is another problem area reported by Fiat owners that could be traced back to poor service procedures. Although owners reported their cars gave excellent gas mileage, many complained of frequent stalling or surging that was difficult to correct at the dealer level. Cold-weather performance north of the 40th parallel also was said to be unacceptable.

By far the most angry responses from Fiat owners came from owners who were asked about Fiat's warranty performance. Owners complained that Fiat dealers would often overcharge for periodic inspections, charge for warranty work that was supposed to be free, or stall warranty work until the warranty period elapsed and then "discover" that the work was urgent. Just so Fiat will not feel this criticism is unfair, they are invited to read the numerous small-claims-court decisions on file, which back up each of the owner allegations published above. Fiat officials in the United States have promised to reform their warranty procedures. However, judging by the complaints still being received, this promise is not very convincing.

The major mechanical defects complained of by Fiat owners run the gamut of possible trouble spots. Nevertheless, most owners complained of defective motors, clutch assembly, and suspension system. One of the main reasons why Fiat cannot be considered a good buy, either as a new or used car, is because of severe corrosion reported by many owners of the 1971 to 1974 models. The premature corrosion affects particularly the 128 model, but complaints have been numerous on other models as well.

Best Models

Fiat sedan 1975

Worst Models

Fiat 850 1972–1973
Fiat sedan 124 1972–1974
Fiat coupe 124 1972–1975
Fiat 128 1972–1976
Fiat X1/9 1974–1976

FIAT
AREAS OF PREMATURE RUSTING

128 (1971 to 1974)

124 (1972 to 1974)

850 (1970 to 1972)

Major Recall Campaigns
Fiat Motor Company, Incorporated

Make	Model	Model Year	Brief Description of Defect (Manufacturer's Corrective Action)	Number of Pages on File	Number of Vehicles Recalled
Fiat	Spider 850 Spider 124	1970	Possibility that seat belts may not fit properly in all seat positions. (Correct by replacing fixed segment of belt with one of proper length, where necessary.)	7	15,104
Fiat	850 Spider 850 Spider	1970	Possibility that emission control hose may interfere with bracket which could cause hose to wear. Also, possibility that alternator fuse wire may interfere with hose clamp.	7	12,550
Fiat	All models	1974	Possibility that small metal shield was omitted during production. Shield is located between exhaust pipe and floor panel to prevent possible overheating of anti-rust protective substance sprayed under floor panel. If condition exists, anti-rust protective substance may overheat and cause fire.	3	Not Re-corded
Fiat	128 Sedan, station wagon & coupe	1971 1972 1973	Possibility that under carriage, particularly cross member where front suspension is attached, might become corroded	7	40,831

Make	Model	Model Year	Brief Description of Defect (Manufacturer's Corrective Action)	Number of Pages on File	Number of Vehicles Recalled
			from winter weather conditions where salt and/or sand are used to melt snow and ice. Corrosion can result in bending of frame where suspension control arm is attached. Condition could impair handling of vehicle.		
Fiat	XI/9	1974 1975	Possibility that accelerator cable was installed in manner which would cause accelerator assembly to function abnormally, causing breakage of accelerator cable. If condition exists, engine will idle and car will decelerate and danger of vehicle crash will exist.	7	25,000

USED CAR PRICES (APPROXIMATE)
Fiat

Model & Body Type	Wholesale Price	Retail Price
1978		
128		
2-Door Sedan	$2800	$3200
4-Door Sedan	3100	3600
Hatchback Coupe	3400	3900
X1/9	4500	5300
131		
2-Door Coupe	3800	4500
4-Door Sedan	3900	4700

Model & Body Type	Wholesale Price	Retail Price
Station Wagon	4200	5000
124 Spider	5400	6300
1977		
Fiat "128"		
Sedan 2D Standard	1900	2500
Sedan 4D Custom	2000	2600
Sedan 2D Custom	1900	2500
Station Wagon	2200	2800
Coupe 3D Custom	2300	2900
Convertible X1/9	3200	3900
Fiat "124"		
Convertible Spider	4200	4900
Fiat "131"		
Sedan 4D	2500	3000
Sedan 2D	2400	2900
Station Wagon	2700	3300
1976		
Fiat "128"		
2 Door Sedan	1700	2100
4D Custom Sedan	1800	2200
2D Custom Sedan	1800	2200
Station Wagon	1900	2400
Coupe	2000	2500
Convertible X1/9	3000	3500
Fiat "124"		
Convertible Spider	3500	4000
Fiat "131"		
4 Door Sedan	2200	2600
2 Door Sedan	2100	2500
Station Wagon	2400	2900
1975		
128 4 Cyl.		
96.4" W.B. (Sdn & Wgn)		
87.5" W.B. (Cpe)		
86.7" W.B. (X1/9)		
2 Door Sedan	1300	1800
4 Door Sedan	1400	1900
Station Wagon	1500	2000
SL Coupe	1600	2100
X 1/9 Coupe	2300	2800
131 4 Cyl. 98" W.B.		
2 Door Sedan	1900	2400
4 Door Sedan	2000	2500

Model & Body Type	Wholesale Price	Retail Price
Station Wagon	2200	2700
124 4 Cyl.		
95.3″ W.B. (Cpe)		
89.7″ W.B. (Spid)		
Sport Coupe	2300	2800
Spider	2800	3100
1974		
128 4 Cyl.		
96.4″ W.B. (Exc. Cpe)		
87.5″ W.B. (Cpe)		
2 Door Sedan	1100	1600
4 Door Sedan	1200	1700
3 Door Wagon	1300	1800
SL 2 Door Sport Coupe	1600	2100
124 4 Cyl.		
95.3″ W.B. (Exc. Rdstr)		
89.8″ W.B. (Rdstr)		
4 Door Sedan	1300	1800
4 Door Wagon	1400	1900
2 Door Sport Coupe	1700	2100
Sport Spider Roadster	1900	2400
1973		
128 4 Cyl.		
96.4″ W.B. (Exc. Cpe)		
87.5″ W.B. (Cpe)		
2 Door Sedan	700	1200
4 Door Sedan	750	1250
3 Door Wagon	1000	1500
SL 2 Door Sport Coupe	1200	1700
124 4 Cyl.		
95.3″ W.B. (Exc. Rdstr)		
89.9″ W.B. (Rdstr)		
4 Door Sedan	800	1300
4 Door Wagon	900	1400
2 Door Coupe	1500	2000
2 Door Spider Roadster	1700	2200
1972		
850 4 Cyl. 79″ W.B.		
2 Door Spider Roadster	600	900
128 4 Cyl. 96.4″ W.B.		
2 Door Sedan	400	600
4 Door Sedan	500	700
3 Door Wagon	600	900

Model & Body Type	Wholesale Price	Retail Price
124 4 Cyl.		
95.3″ W.B. (Exc. Rdstr)		
89.8″ W.B. (Rdstr)		
4 Door Special Sedan	600	800
4 Door Wagon	700	900
2 Door Sport Coupe	1200	1500
Spider Roadster	1300	1800
1971		
850 4 Cyl. 79″ W.B.		
2 Door Sedan	200	400
2 Door Sport Coupe	400	600
Spider Roadster	500	700
Spider Hardtop	600	800
Racer Coupe	700	1000
124 4 Cyl.		
95.3″ W.B. (Sdn & Wgn)		
89.8″ W.B. (Cpe & Spids)		
4 Door Special Sedan	500	700
Station Wagon	700	900
2 Door Sport Coupe	1000	1300
Spider Roadster	1100	1400
Spider Hardtop	1200	1500
1970		
850 4 Cyl. 79″ W.B.		
2 Door Sedan	100	300
2 Door Sport Coupe	300	400
Spider Roadster	400	600
Racer Coupe	500	700
124 4 Cyl.		
95.3″ W.B. (Sdn & Wgn)		
89.5″ W.B. (Cpe & Spids)		
4 Door Special Sedan	300	500
Station Wagon	400	600
2 Door Sport Coupe	600	900
Spider Roadster	800	1100
Spider Hardtop	900	1300

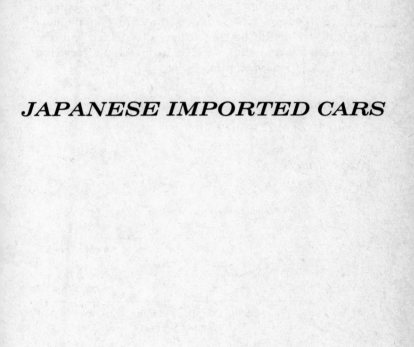

JAPANESE IMPORTED CARS

Colt/Arrow

Other Japanese auto makers could take lessons from the Colt's marketing staff on selling an economical "foreign" car to the American motoring public. (Chrysler markets the Colt, while Mitsubishi, Japan, manufactures the car, thank goodness.) Now with a five-speed overdrive transmission option and a 2000cc engine, this import is the best new or used subcompact buy. There are some negative reports from Colt owners concerning inadequate servicing by some Chrysler dealers dissatisfied with the low profit margin they receive from selling servicing Chrysler's Japanese import.

Best Models

Colt/Arrow 1973–1979

Worst Models

Colt/Cricket 1972

Major Recall Campaigns
Colt

Make	Model	Model Year	Brief Description of Defect	Number of Pages on File	Number of Vehicles Recalled
Chrysler	Colt and Arrow	1976	Engine vibration damper support bracket may fail.	N/A	718
Chrysler	Colt	1971	Carbon monoxide gas may leak into car interior.	N/A	N/A*

*N/A means not applicable.

Colt/Cricket (1972 to 1975)

USED CAR PRICES (APPROXIMATE)
Colt

Model & Body Type	Wholesale Price	Retail Price
1978		
COLT		
2 Door Coupe M/M (6M2)	$3100	$3400
2 Door Custom Coupe M/M (6H21)	3400	3800
4 Door Sedan M/M (6H41)	3500	3900
2 Seat Wagon (6H45)	4200	4800
1977	N/A	
1976	N/A	
1975		
COLT 4 Cyl. 95.3″ W.B.		
2 Door Coupe	1700	2200
4 Door Sedan	1700	2200
2 Seat Wagon	1800	2300
2 Door Hardtop	1800	2300
'GT' 2 Door Hardtop	1800	2300
1974		
4 Cyl. 95.3″ W.B.		
2 Door Coupe	1200	1400
2 Door Hardtop	1400	1600
4 Door Sedan	1400	1600
2 Door GT Hardtop	1500	1700
4 Door Wagon	1600	1800
4 Door Custom Wagon	1700	1900

Model & Body Type	Wholesale Price	Retail Price
1973		
4 Cyl. 95.3″ W.B.		
2 Door Coupe	800	1000
4 Door Sedan	1000	1200
2 Door Hardtop	1000	1200
2 Door GT Hardtop	1100	1300
4 Door Wagon	1100	1300
1972		
4 Cyl. 95.3″ W.B.		
2 Door Coupe	600	900
4 Door Sedan	700	1000
2 Door Hardtop	700	1000
4 Door Wagon	800	1100
1971		
4 Cyl. 95.3″ W.B.		
2 Door Coupe	400	700
4 Door Sedan	500	800
2 Door Hardtop	500	800
4 Door Wagon	700	1000

Datsun

After making its reputation with very economical and efficient small cars like the 510, Datsun has now contracted "Detroit fever" by adding on a lot of unnecessary gimmick options that price its cars out of many economy-minded motorists' reach. All of Datsun's 510 models, especially the 2-door 1973 model, are highly recommended, despite electrical and tire defects. Datsun's other models would be better left in Japan.

The 1971 and 1972 Datsun 240Z had very serious brake defects for which the vehicle was never recalled, but, as can be seen from the following confidential memorandum, these cars should have been recalled by the Department of Transport.

Rusting has been so bad on the 240Z, B210 and the 510 that Datsun has bought back, through its dealers, some vehicles where it was alleged that the premature rusting weakened the frame of suspension components, possibly making the car unsafe.

Datsun Confidential Brake Report

The 240Z front-brake situation is starting to get out of proportion, the customers are refusing to pay the expense for freeing-up the pads or the replacement of the pads (as well as disc refinishing in some cases).

The brake failures are occurring at mileage as low as 2,000 miles. In some cases, dealers absorbed the expenses when the customer definitely refused to pay, but dealers cannot anymore, due to the quantity of 240Z needing brake repairs.

We have to decide as soon as possible a solution before it gets in the hands of A.P.A. and Consumers' Affairs. Since the installation of the new modified caliper could definitely improve the situation the complaints will probably drop with the newly equipped model.

But for the previous one, those already on the road and probably those still in inventory, the situation will remain, if we decide to accept on warranty the repairs of the brake system providing it happened within the 12,000 miles, at that moment suggesting to dealers to remove a slight amount of material on the pad sides, we are aware that very little should be removed not to create any other problem, it is my opinion that the situation would be corrected, and would be quite less expensive than replacing the caliper assembly because being a security item of the first importance, the D.O.T. peoples, if they start to investigate, could probably insist on the replacement of calipers on all units.

Best Models

Datsun 1200 1971–1973
Datsun 510 1971–1973

Worst Models

Datsun B210 1974–1976
Datsun 610 1973
Datsun 240Z 1971–1972

NISSAN DATSUN
AREAS OF PREMATURE RUSTING

510 (1970 to 1973)

240Z (1971 to 1972)

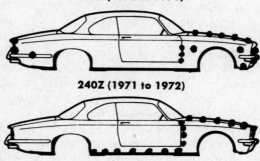

Major Recall Campaigns
Nissan Motor Corporation in U.S.A.

Make	Model	Model Year	Brief Description of Defect (Manufacturer's Corrective Action)	Number of Pages on File	Number of Vehicles Recalled
Datsun	PL510, WPL510 and HLS30	1968 1969 1970	Possibility that salts used in winter on highways will form mixture of salt water and mud which will accumulate on backs of sealed beam headlight units. When wet, the electrical circuit grounds through these deposits may set up an electrical corrosive action	14	118,976

Make	Model	Model Year	Brief Description of Defect (Manufacturer's Corrective Action)	Number of Pages on File	Number of Vehicles Recalled
			which could result in air entering sealed beam unit, causing failure. (Correct by installing rubber protectors.)		
Datsun	WPL 510 Station Wagon PL 521 Pickup Truck	1968 1969	Possibility that under extremely high temperatures, brake fluid may form chemical deposits on wheel cylinder wall. These deposits may slightly deform piston cup lip when it rides over them, resulting in leakage from loss of sealing. This condition could cause gradual loss of braking power and consequently is a driving hazard.	12	37,196
Datsun	PL510 Sedan WPL510 Station Wagon	Mfd. 8-9 1971 thru 3-15 1972	Possibility that under extreme cold weather and severe driving conditions, front brake hose, which is clamped to shock strut in a manner restricting its free movement, can crack at clamp, due to repeated bending of hose. Should crack occur, could result in loss of brake fluid, and loss of front brake function.	1	61,434

Make	Model	Model Year	Brief Description of Defect (Manufacturer's Corrective Action)	Number of Pages on File	Number of Vehicles Recalled
Datsun	LB110 Sedan KL110 Coupe	1971	Possibility of misalignment of secondary hood latch between hood and body, which could result in complete disengagement of hood latch, if primary hood latch has not been properly engaged and if vehicle is subject to strong wind pressure at high speeds.	2	86,429
Datsun	L520 & L521	Mfd. 4-65 thru 5-69	Possibility that accelerator pedal pad could lock under travel stop bolt head. If condition exists, depressed accelerator pedal would not return to closed position when released. (Correct by inspecting and installing bolt with larger head to preclude pedal pad from locking up.)	1	62,000
Datsun	240-Z	1973	Possibility that under some conditions, driver may experience difficulties in restarting engine when hot or engine may stall when making sharp right hand turn.	1	16,274

USED CAR PRICES (APPROXIMATE)
Datsun

Model & Body Type	Wholesale Price	Retail Price
1978		
B-210		
Two-Door Sedan Standard	$2900	$3300
Two-Door Sedan Deluxe	3200	3700
Four-Door Sedan Deluxe	3300	3900
Two-Door Hatchback	3500	4100
F-10		
Two-Door Hatchback (4-Speed)	4000	4300
Two-Door Hatchback (5-Speed)	3700	4400
Three-Door Wagon	3400	4000
200SX		
Two-Door Hardtop (5 Speed)	4200	5000
510		
Two-Door Sedan (4 speed)	3700	4300
Four-Door Sedan (4 speed)	3800	4500
Two-Door Hatchback (4 speed)	4000	4700
Five-Door Wagon (4 speed)	4200	4900
810		
Four-Door Sedan (4 sp.)	5200	6200
Five-Door Wagon (4 sp.)	5500	6500
620 PICKUP		
Short Bed (4 Speed)	3400	4000
Long Bed (4 Speed)	3500	4100
King Cab (4 Speed)	3800	4500
280Z		
Coupe	6600	8000
2 plus 2	7700	9300
1977		
Sdn. 2D Honeybee	2400	2800
Sedan 4D Dlx B210	2700	3100
Sedan 2D Dlx B210	2600	3000
Coupe 2D Dlx B210	2700	3100
Hatchback 2D F10	2800	3200
Wagon 3D F10	2900	3300
Sedan 4D 710	3000	3400
Sedan 2D 710	3000	3400
Coupe 2D HT 710	3200	3600
Wagon 4D 710	3400	3800
Cpe. 2D 200SX	3400	3800

Model & Body Type	Wholesale Price	Retail Price
Sedan 4D HLG810	3900	4300
Wagon 5D WHLD810	4200	4600
Coupe 2D 280Z	5500	6500
Coupe 2D (2+2) 280Z	6000	7000
Pickup (Short)	3100	3700
Pickup (Long)	3300	3900
1976		
KPLF10	2100	2500
WPLF10	2100	2500
HLB210 4D Sdn.	1900	2300
HLB210 2D Sdn.	2200	2600
HLB210 2D		
Honeybee Sdn.	1800	2100
HLB210 2D		
Hatchback	2000	2400
HL610 4D Sdn.	2200	2600
HL610 2D HT	2300	2700
HL610 St. Wgn. 4D	2400	2800
JHL710 4D Sdn.	2200	2600
JHL710 2D Sdn.	2200	2600
JKL710 2D HT	2400	2900
JHL710 St. Wgn. 4D	2500	3000
280Z 2D Cpe.	4200	5100
280Z Cpe. 2D (2+2)	4600	6500
HL620 Pickup (Short)	2300	2700
HLG620 Pickup (Long)	2400	2900
1975		
210 4 Cyl. 92.1" W.B.		
2 Door Sedan	1600	1900
4 Door Sedan	1300	1900
2 Door Coupe	1700	2000
620 LI'L HUSTLER 4 Cyl.		
100.1" W.B. (PU)		
110" W.B. (PU 7)		
Pickup	1700	2100
710 4 Cyl. 96.5" W.B.		
2 Door Sedan	1600	2000
4 Door Sedan	1600	2000
2 Door Hardtop	1700	2100
4 Door Station Wagon	1800	2200
610 4 Cyl. 98.4" W.B.		
4 Door Sedan	1800	2200
2 Door Hardtop	1900	2300

Model & Body Type	Wholesale Price	Retail Price
4 Door Station Wagon	2000	2400
280-Z 6 Cyl. 90.7″ W.B. (Cpe)		
102.6″ W.B. (2 + 2)		
2 Door Coupe	3800	4400
2 + 2 Coupe	4100	4700
1974		
B210 4 Cyl. 92.1″ W.B.		
2 Door Sedan	1200	1500
4 Door Sedan	1300	1600
2 Door Hatchback	1300	1600
610 4 Cyl. 98.4″ W.B.		
4 Door Sedan	1400	1800
2 Door Hardtop	1500	1900
4 Door Wagon	1500	1900
710 4 Cyl. 96.5″ W.B.		
2 Door Sedan	1200	1500
4 Door Sedan	1300	1600
2 Door Hardtop	1400	1700
260Z 6 Cyl. 90.7″ W.B.		
2 Door Coupe	3000	3500
2 Door 2 + 2 Coupe	3300	3800
LI'L HUSTLER 4 Cyl. 100.2″ W.B.		
2 Door Pickup	1400	1700
1973		
1200 4 Cyl. 90.6″ W.B.		
2 Door Sedan	900	1100
2 Door Coupe	1000	1200
510 4 Cyl. 95.3″ W.B.		
2 Door Sedan	1100	1300
610 4 Cyl. 98.4″ W.B.		
2 Door Hardtop	1200	1400
4 Door Sedan	1300	1500
4 Door Wagon	1200	1400
240Z 6 Cyl. 90.7″ W.B.		
2 Door Coupe	1500	3000
LI'L HUSTLER 4 Cyl. 100.1″ W.B.		
2 Door Pickup	1100	1300
1972		
1200 4 Cyl. 90.6″ W.B.		
2 Door Sedan	600	800
2 Door Coupe	700	900
510 4 Cyl. 95.3″ W.B.		
2 Door Sedan	700	900
4 Door Sedan	800	1100

Model & Body Type	Wholesale Price	Retail Price
4 Door Wagon	1100	1400
240Z 6 Cyl. 90.7" W.B.		
2 Door Coupe	2000	2500
521 4 Cyl. 99.6" W.B.		
2 Door ½ Ton Pickup	1200	1500
1971		
1200 4 Cyl. 90.6" W.B.		
2 Door Sedan	500	700
2 Door Coupe	600	800
510 4 Cyl. 95.3" W.B.		
2 Door Sedan	400	600
4 Door Sedan	500	700
4 Door Wagon	800	1100
240Z 6 Cyl. 90.7" W.B.		
2 Door Coupe	1600	2100
1970		
PL-510 4 Cyl. 95.3" W.B.		
2 Door Sedan	200	400
4 Door Sedan	300	500
4 Door Wagon	500	700
SPL-311 4 Cyl. 89.8" W.B.		
1600 Sport Roadster	700	1000
240Z 6 Cyl. 90.7" W.B.		
Sport Roadster	1400	1800

Honda

The Honda is the best import sold in North America. Parts supply is excellent, depreciation is slow, and Honda's initial retail sales prices for its new models are very reasonable.

The secret of Honda's success rests with its solid dealer network. Many of its dealers were first chosen when Honda penetrated the North American market with its popular motorcycles; they were then given the automobile franchises after submitting proof of their honesty, financial stability, and competency with the motorcycle trade.

Some Honda owners have complained of paint fading, premature brake wear, and excessive oil burning with some engines; however, Honda's customer-relations people have been very liberal in applying extended warranty coverage to these problems, even after the initial warranty period has elapsed. As with all subcompact cars, the Honda is principally an urban vehicle and should be used for city travel. Travel on fast expressways or rural highways can be dangerous because of the subcompact's small size. In fact, the Washington-based Insurance Institute for Highway Safety has determined that subcompact passengers in collisions have a mortality rate two and one-half times greater than passengers in intermediate sized cars.

Best Models

Honda Civic 1976–1979
Honda Accord 1976–1979

Worst Models

Honda Civic 1973–1975

HONDA
AREAS OF PREMATURE RUSTING

All Models (1974 to 1975)

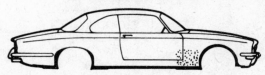

Make	Model	Model Year	Brief Description of Defect (Manufacturer's Corrective Action)	Number of Pages on File	Number of Vehicles Recalled
Honda	CL360	1974	Possibility that main wire harness may become chafed by forward edge of left front fuel tank mounting bracket. If condition exists, chafing may short circuit or sever wires within harness and cause electrical fuses to burn out. (Correct by inspecting and installing holder to prevent chafing of wire harness.)	3	66,856
Honda	Civic automobile	1974	Possibility that front seat left assemblies do not conform to requirements of Federal Motor Vehicle Safety Standard No. 209. (Correct by inspecting and modifying plastic boot to remove material which may cover buckle push-button release mechanism.)	2	66,109

Make	Model	Model Year	Brief Description of Defect (Manufacturer's Corrective Action)	Number of Pages on File	Number of Vehicles Recalled
Honda	CB360 & CB360G, CL360, CB360T, CL360K1	1974 1975	Possibility that if adjustment of cam chain tensioner is not properly maintained, or if cam chain tensioner slipper is broken, it is possible for chain to contact tensioner holder. If cam chain breakage occurs, there is possibility of engine and rear wheel lockup.	2	131,817

Used Car Prices (Approximate)
Honda

Model & Body Type	Wholesale Price	Retail Price
1978		
CIVIC 1200		
2-D Sedan 4-Speed	$2800	$3100
Hatchback 4-Speed	3000	3500
Hatchback Hondamatic	3100	3600
CVCC		
2-D Sedan 4-Speed	3100	3400
Hatchback 4-Speed	3300	3800
Hatchback Hondamatic	3400	3900
Hatchback 5-Speed	3600	4100
Wagon 4-Speed	3500	4000
Wagon Hondamatic	3600	4200
ACCORD		
Hatchback 2-D Sedan, 5-Speed	4100	4800
Hatchback Hondamatic	4200	5000
ACCORD LX		
Hatchback 2-D Sedan, 5-Speed	4800	5600
Hatchback Hondamatic	4900	5700

Model & Body Type	Wholesale Price	Retail Price
1977		
Sedan 2D CVCC	2200	2700
H'back 3D CVCC	2300	2800
H'back 3D CVCC (5 Speed)	2600	3100
Sta. Wgn. 5D CVCC	2500	3000
Sedan 2D Civic	2100	2600
H'back 3D Civic	2200	2700
H'back 3D Accord (5 Speed)	3400	4000
1976		
Honda		
Sdn. 2D CVCC	1800	2300
Sdn. H'bck. CVCC	1900	2400
Sta. Wgn. 5D CVCC	2100	2600
2D Civic Sdn.	1700	2200
Sdn. H'bk. 3D Civic	1800	2300
Accord 2D H'bk.	3000	3600
1975		
CIVIC 4 Cyl. 86.6" W.B.		
2 Door Sedan	1600	2000
Hatchback Sedan	1700	2100
Special 5 Spd. Hatchback Sedan	1800	2200
4 Door Station Wagon	1800	2200
1974		
CIVIC 4 Cyl. 86.6" W.B.		
2 Door Sedan	1200	1500
Hatchback Sedan	1200	1500
1973		
CIVIC 4 Cyl. 86.6" W.B.		
2 Door Sedan	900	1100
2 Door Sedan (Auto. Trans.)	1000	1200
Hatchback Sedan	1000	1200
Hatchback Sdn. (Auto. Trans.)	1100	1300
1972		
600 2 Cyl. 78.7" W.B.		
2 Door Sedan	400	600
2 Door Coupe	500	700

Mazda

Mazda is one of the worst Japanese imports found in North America. Parts are difficult to obtain, depreciation is rapid, the dealer network is constantly changing franchisers, after-sales service is atrocious, and many of its vehicles have fraudulently misrepresented the wrong model year (in Canada).

Mazda owners complain of defects affecting the motor (both conventional and rotary models), clutch, and braking performance. Mazda has extended the warranty to cover mechanical defects in the "O" rings of its rotary engines, which cause an excessive burning of oil due to improper internal sealing; however, many Mazda owners have complained that this warranty extension is not applied equitably to all rotary Mazda owners.

1972 and earlier Mazdas were particularly susceptible to failure of the rotor housing water "O" rings, and accompanying overheating. First symptoms are usually hard starting, rough idle for 10 to 20 seconds after start, white smoke in the exhaust, and coolant loss. In the latter stages, it may also lead to overheating. Should these symptoms occur, visit your local dealer to confirm the diagnosis. If confirmed, contact the Mazda Branch Service Representative for your area for information concerning Mazda's engine rebuilt/exchange program. All factory-rebuilt engines are equipped with an improved, Teflon-backed water "O" ring to reduce the chance of a second failure.

Mazda has recently been sued by the California Department of Consumer Affairs for allegedly not respecting the extended warranty on its rotary motors as it advertised it would.

Best Models

Mazda 808 1973

Worst Models

Mazda Rotary Engine 1973–1979

MAZDA
AREAS OF PREMATURE RUSTING

All Models (1971 to 1974)

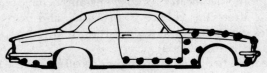

Major Recall Campaigns
Mazda

Make	Model	Model Year	Brief Description of Defect (Manufacturer's Corrective Action)	Number of Pages on File	Number of Vehicles Recalled
Mazda	RX-4 sedan, hard top & wagon	1974	Possibility that when engine is started, steering wheel will turn by itself, forcefully, in either direction due to improper tolerance within reaction sensing system. This could be caused by turning steering wheel without power steering pump in operation. (Correct by inspecting and replacing complete gear box assembly.)	12	2,218
Mazda	Pick-up trucks	1974	Possibility that exhaust pipe protector may be deformed, resulting from hitting projection on ground in vehicle off-road use. Should protector be	9	8,422

Make	Model	Model Year	Brief Description of Defect (Manufacturer's Corrective Action)	Number of Pages on File	Number of Vehicles Recalled
			crushed into exhaust pipe, shield surface temperature could rise to point where dry grass could smolder. This could occur only if vehicle is parked in tall dry grass and grass is in contact with protector. (Correct by installing additional protector underneath existing protector.)		

Used Car Prices (Approximate)
Mazda

Model & Body Type	Wholesale Price	Retail Price
1978		
GLC Sedan 3D	$2900	$3200
GLC Sedan 3D Deluxe	3100	3600
GLC 5D Deluxe	3300	3800
GLC Sport 5 Speed	3400	3900
RX4 Sedan 4D (5 Spd.)	5000	5900
RX4 Wagon (5 Spd.)	5100	6000
Cosmo Coupe 2D (5 Spd.)	5400	6400
RE Pickup (5 Spd.) (1977)	3500	4000
1977		
4 Cyl. INLINE		
Hatchback 3D (Std.)	2400	2700
Hatchback 3D (Dix)	2500	2800
Sedan 4D Mizer	2500	2800
Coupe 2D Mizer	2600	2900
St. Wgn. 4D Mizer	2800	3200
Sedan 4D	2600	2900

Model & Body Type	Wholesale Price	Retail Price
Coupe 2D	2600	2900
Station Wagon	2800	3200
Rotary Engine		
Sedan 4D	2900	3500
Station Wagon	3100	3700
Coupe 2D	2700	3100
Coupe Cosmo	3200	3800
1976		
Mazda 4 Cyl. INLINE		
4D Mizer Sedan	2000	2300
2D Mizer Cpe.	2100	2400
4D Mizer St. Wagon	2300	2600
4 Door Sedan	2200	2500
2 Door Coupe	2300	2600
4D St. Wgn.	2400	2700
Pickup	2300	2600
Mazda Rotary Engine		
4 Door Sedan	2500	2900
2 Door Hardtop	2600	3000
4D St. Wgn.	2700	3100
2 Door Coupe	2000	2400
4D St. Wgn.	2100	2500
2D Cosmo HT	2700	3300
Pickup	2200	2500
1975		
1800 4 Cyl. 104″ W.B.		
2 Door Pickup	1300	1700
808 4 Cyl. 91″ W.B.		
4 Door Sedan	1300	1700
2 Door Coupe	1300	1700
4 Door Wagon	1400	1800
ROTARY PICKUP Rotary 104″ W.B.		
2 Door Pickup	1600	1900
RX3 Rotary 91″ W.B.		
2 Door Coupe	1700	2000
4 Door Wagon	1800	2100
RX4 Rotary 99″ W.B.		
4 Door Sedan	2100	2400
2 Door Hardtop	2100	2400
4 Door Wagon	2200	2500

Model & Body Type	Wholesale Price	Retail Price
1974		
808 4 Cyl. 91″ W.B.		
Coupe	1000	1300
RX-3 Rotary 91″ W.B.		
2 Door Coupe	1400	1700
4 Door Wagon	1500	1800
RX-4 Rotary 99″ W.B.		
4 Door Sedan	1700	2000
2 Door Coupe	1700	2000
4 Door Wagon	1800	2100
1973		
RX-3 Rotary 91″ W.B.		
2 Door Coupe	1000	1200
4 Door Sedan	1000	1200
4 Door Wagon	1200	1400
RX-2 Rotary 97″ W.B.		
Sport Coupe	1300	1500
4 Door Sedan	1200	1400
808 4 Cyl. 91″ W.B.		
2 Door Coupe	700	900
4 Door Sedan	700	900
4 Door Wagon	900	1100
1800 4 Cyl. 104″ W.B.		
Truck	1000	1200
1972		
RX-2 Rotary 91″ W.B.		
2 Door Coupe	700	900
4 Door Sedan	700	900
4 Door Wagon	900	1100
RX-2 Rotary 97″ W.B.		
Sport Coupe		
4 Door Sedan	1000	1200
618 4 Cyl. 97″ W.B.		
2 Door Coupe	600	700
4 Door Sedan	600	700
808 4 Cyl. 91″ W.B.		
2 Door Coupe	300	400
4 Door Sedan	300	400
4 Door Wagon	500	600
1600 4 Cyl. 104″ W.B.		
Truck	600	800

Subaru

Considered by many motorists as the Japanese counter-part to the Volkswagen Beetle, Subaru has greatly improved since its early egg-shaped problem-prone pre-1972 models. Its early models were automotive freaks, with doors that opened into the wind and quality control defects that may have given Consumers Union nightmares.

Since those early experimental days, though, Subaru has become a new-car buy that is just one step behind Toyota and Datsun in overall driving performance and fuel economy. With front-wheel drive and a low sticker price, the Subaru rivals only the top-rated Honda in engineering excellence. Servicing, parts supply, and a rapid depreciation rate combine to place the Subaru fifth in the Japanese lineup of recommended new- and used-car buys. Only Mazda has a worse consumer-complaint record.

The most highly recommended model is the 1976 station wagon with four-wheel drive.

Best Models

Subaru Station Wagon 1975–1977

Worst Models

Subaru 1973–1975

**SUBARU
AREAS OF PREMATURE RUSTING**

All Models (1973 to 1974)

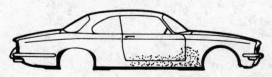

Make	Model	Model Year	Brief Description of Defect	Number of Pages on File	Number of Vehicles Recalled
Subaru	A23L, A22L Sedans and Coupe A62L, A63L Station Wagon	1972 1972	Possibility that retaining pin of head pin in coupler between brake master cylinder push rod and brake pedal may become dislodged. This could lead to brake impairment or no braking action at all.	16	9,841

Used Car Prices (Approximate)
Subaru

Model & Body Type	Wholesale Price	Retail Price
1978		
STANDARD SERIES (1600 cc)		
Sedan 2D (4-Spd.)	$3000	$3300
DL (1600 cc)		
Sedan 2D (4-Spd.)	3300	3800
Sedan 2D (Auto.)	3500	4000
Sedan 4D (4-Spd.)	3400	4000
Sedan 4D (5-Spd.)	3500	4000
Sedan 4D (Auto.)	3700	4200
Coupe 2D (5-Spd.)	3400	4000
Wagon 4D (4-Spd.)	3600	4200
Wagon 4D (5-Spd.)	3700	4300
Wagon 4D (Auto.)	3800	4400
Wagon 4WD (4-Spd.)	4000	4700
GF (1600 cc)		
Hardtop 2D (5-Spd.)	3700	4400
Hardtop 2D (Auto.)	3900	4500

Model & Body Type	Wholesale Price	Retail Price
ALL TERRAIN TRANSPORTER		
The Brat 4WD 2D	3800	4400
1977		
Sedan 2D	2100	2500
Sedan 4D	2300	2700
Sedan 4D (AT)	2400	2800
Sedan 2D	2200	2600
Sedan 2D (AT)	2300	2700
Coupe 2D	2400	2800
Station Wagon	2500	2900
Station Wagon (AT)	2600	3000
Station Wagon 4WD	2900	3300
Hardtop 2D	2800	3100
Hardtop 2D (AT)	2900	3300
1976		
DL 4D Sdn.	2200	2600
STD 2D Sdn.	2000	2400
DL 2D Sdn.	2100	2500
DL 2D Cpe.	2200	2600
GF 2D HT	2300	2700
DL St. Wgn.	2200	2600
DL St. Wgn. 4WD	2400	2800
1975		
Star 4 Cyl. 96.7″ W.B.		
Star Clipper 2 Door Sedan	1400	1800
Star Cruiser 4 Door Sedan	1500	1900
Shooting Star 2 Door Coupe	1600	2000
All Star 5 Door Station Wagon	1600	2000
Evening Star 2 Door Hardtop	1600	2000
Super Star 5 Door Station Wagon	1800	2200
1974		
1400 4 Cyl. 96.6″ W.B.		
DL 2 Door Sedan	1100	1400
DL 4 Door Sedan	1200	1500
DL 4 Door Wagon	1300	1600
GL 2 Door Coupe	1200	1500
1973		
1400 4 Cyl. 96.6″ W.B.		
DL 2 Door Sedan	800	1100
DL 4 Door Sedan	900	1200

Model & Body Type	Wholesale Price	Retail Price
DL 4 Door Wagon	1000	1300
GL 2 Door Coupe	900	1200
1972		
1300 4 Cyl. 95.3″ W.B.		
G 2 Door Sedan	500	700
G 4 Door Sedan	600	800
G 4 Door Wagon	700	900
1971		
Star 4 Cyl. 95.2″ W.B.		
1100 2 Door Sedan	300	400
1100 4 Door Sedan	400	500
1100 4 Door Wagon	500	600

Toyota

Datsun's bigger twin brother, Toyota has very few differences from Datsun except for a more liberal warranty, a larger dealer network, and a better-qualified staff. For these reasons, Toyota only trails Honda and the Mitsubishi (Chrysler) Colt in overall product quality and driving performance.

Toyota's rate of depreciation is average, although its new cars are priced a bit higher than competitive subcompacts. The major mechanical defects reported by Toyota over the past five years concern primarily the motor, carburetor, brakes, air conditioner, and chassis construction. Hundreds of consumers have reported that the engine head on their 1971 to 1973 Corolla 1600 has cracked as a result of faulty manufacture. Toyota also admitted liability for this mechanical defect by secretly extending the warranty up to five years for Corolla owners affected by this defect. See chapter on "Secret Warranty Extensions."

Best Models

Toyota Corolla 1975–1979

Worst Models

Toyota Corolla 1972–1973
Toyota Corona 1972–1973
Toyota Celica/Carina 1972–1973

TOYOTA
AREAS OF PREMATURE RUSTING

All Models (1970 to 1975)

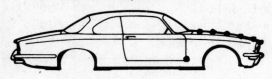

Major Recall Campaigns
Toyota Motor Company, Limited

Make	Model	Model Year	Brief Description of Defect • (Manufacturer's Corrective Action)	Number of Pages on File	Number of Vehicles Recalled
Toyota	Mark II	Produced for USA June 1969 to June 1970	Possibility that during cold weather brake fluid may not adequately flow between reservoir tank and master cylinder. This condition would permit gradual accumulation of air into master cylinder system, resulting in soft pedal during application of brakes. (Correct by installing improved master cylinder components.)	20	47,879

Make	Model	Model Year	Brief Description of Defect (Manufacturer's Corrective Action)	Number of Pages on File	Number of Vehicles Recalled
Toyota	Corona Corolla	1965 thru 1970 1971	Possibility that items placed in package tray under the right dash panel may inadvertently fall over protective partition and cause possible malfunction of accelerator linkage. (Correct by installing new partition.)	11	190,000
	Corolla-1200 Sedan Coupe Station Wagon	1971	Possibility that engine stall or engine hesitation may occur due to malfunctions in evaporative emission control system. Engine hesitation or stall may be hazardous in road driving due to lack of fuel or loss of power after prolonged high speed driving. (Correct by inspecting and modifying emission control system.)	13	110,614
	Corolla-1600 Sedan Coupe Station Wagon	1971			

Used Car Prices (Approximate)
Toyota

Model & Body Type	Wholesale Price	Retail Price
1978		
COROLLA—KE SERIES		
1401 Sedan 2D (N/A Calif.)	$2800	$3100
1405 Sedan 2D Cust. (5-Spd.) (N/A Cal.)	3000	3500
1407 Sedan 4D Cust. (5-Spd.) (N/A/ Cal.)	3200	3600
COROLLA—TE SERIES		
1501 Sedan 2D (Calif. Only)	2800	3100
1505 Sedan 2D Cust. (5-Sp.) (Calif. Only)	3100	3500
1507 Sedan 4D Cust. (5-Sp.) (Calif. Only)	3200	3600
1511 Sedan 2D Dlx	3200	3700
1512 Sedan 2D Dlx. (Auto)	3400	4000
1513 Sedan 4D Dlx	3300	3800
1514 Sedan 4D Dlx. (Auto)	3500	4100
1515 Sedan 2D Dlx (5-Sp.)	3300	3800
1517 Sedan 4D Dlx. (5-Sp.)	3300	3900
1553 Wagon 4D Dlx	3600	4100
1554 Wagon 4D Dlx. (Auto)	3800	4400
1557 Wagon 4D Dlx. (5-Sp.)	3600	4200
1575 Spt. Cpe. Dlx. (5-Sp.)	3500	4100
1572 Spt. Cpe. Dlx. (Auto)	3700	4300
1576 Spt. Cpe. SR5 (5-Sp.)	3900	4500
1585 Liftback 2D Dlx. (5-Sp.)	3600	4200
1582 Liftback 2D Dlx. (Auto)	3800	4400
1586 Liftback 2D SR5 (5-Sp.)	4000	4600
CORONA RT		
2201 Sedan 2D Cust	$3700	4300
2202 Sedan 2D Cust. (Auto)	4000	4500
2213 Sedan 4D Dlx.	3900	4600
2217 Sedan 4D Dlx. (5-Sp.)	4000	4700
2218 Sedan 4D Dlx. (Auto)	4200	4800
2253 St. Wgn. 4D Dlx.	4200	4900
2257 St. Wgn. 4D Dlx. (5-Sp.)	4300	5000
2258 St. Wgn. 4D Dlx. (Auto)	4400	5100
2217 St. Wgn. 4D Dlx. (5-Sp.)	4900	5800

Model & Body Type	Wholesale Price	Retail Price
CELICA RA		
2165 Coupe 2D ST (5-Sp.)	4200	4900
2162 Coupe 2D ST (Auto)	4400	5100
2175 Coupe 2D GT (5-Sp.)	4500	5300
2175 Coupe 2D (S.E.) (5-Sp.)	5000	6000
2192 Sedan 2D Liftback GT (Auto)	4900	5800
2195 Sedan 2D Liftback GT (5-Sp.)	4700	5500
2195 Sedan 2D Liftback GT (S.E.) (5-Sp.)	5200	6300
CRESSIDA MX		
3124 Sedan 4D (Auto)	5900	7000
3164 Wagon 4D (Auto)	6300	7500
PICKUP RN		
7061 Pickup 2D Std.	3400	4000
7062 Pickup 2D Dlx. (Auto)	3800	4400
7065 Pickup 2D SR5 (5-Sp.)	3800	4500
7067 Pickup 2D Dlx. (5-Sp.)	3600	4200
7361 Pickup 2D Std. Long Bed	3600	4100
7362 Pickup 2D Dlx. Long Bed (Auto)	3900	4500
7365 Pickup 2D SR5 Long Bed (5-Sp.)	3900	4600
7367 Pickup 2D Dlx. Long Bed (5-Sp.)	3700	4300
7663 Cab & Ch. 2D Camper	3500	4000
7681 Cab & Ch. 2D Commercial	3400	4000
LAND CRUISER FJ		
6181 Hard Top 2D (4-Sp.)	5500	6500
6153 St. Wgn. 4D (4-Sp.)	6400	7600
1977		
Corolla		
Sedan 2D	2200	2700
Sdn. 4D Cust. (5 Spd.)	2400	2900
Sedan 2D Deluxe	2500	3000
Sedan 4D Deluxe	2600	3100
HT 2D SR5	2800	3300

Model & Body Type	Wholesale Price	Retail Price
Sta. Wgn. 4D Dlx.	2800	3300
Spt. Coupe 2D Dlx.	2700	3000
Liftback 2D Dlx.	2800	3300
Sport Cpe. 2D SR5	2900	3400
Liftback 2D SR5	3000	3500
Corona		
Sedan 2D Cust.	2700	3200
Sedan 4D Dlx.	2800	3300
HT 2D Dlx. (5 Spd.)	2900	3400
Station Wagon 4D Dlx.	3000	3500
Celica		
Hardtop 2D ST	3300	3800
HT 2D GT (5 Spd.)	3400	3900
Lftbk 2D GT (5 Spd.)	3700	4200
Pickups		
Chassis & Cab	2500	3000
Pickup	2600	3100
Pickup (Long Bed)	2700	3200
Pickup SR5	2700	3300
Pkup SR5 (Long Bed)	2800	3400
Landcruiser		
Hardtop 2D	4100	5000
Station Wgn. 4D	4800	5700
1976		
Corolla		
2D Sdn.	1,900	2,300
2D Sdn. Dlx.	2,100	2,500
4D Sdn. Dlx.	2,100	2,500
2D HT Dlx.	2,300	2,700
2D HT Dlx. SR5	2,400	2,800
4D St. Wgn. Dlx.	2,300	2,700
2D Spt. Cpe. Dlx.	2,200	2,600
2D Liftback Dlx.	2,300	2,700
2D SR5 Spt. Coupe	2,400	2,800
2D Liftback SR5	2,400	2,800
Corona		
2 Door Sedan	2,400	2,700
4D Sdn. Dlx.	2,500	2,800
2D HT Dlx.	2,700	3,000
2D HT SR5	2,800	3,100
St. Wgn. Dlx.	2,800	3,100

Model & Body Type	Wholesale Price	Retail Price
Celica		
2D HT (ST)	2,500	3,000
2D HT (GT)	2,600	3,100
2D Liftback (GT)	3,000	3,500
Mark II		
4D Sdn. Dlx.	3,000	3,500
4D St. Wgn. Dlx.	3,100	3,600
Pickups		
Chassis & Cab	3,200	3,700
Pickup	3,300	3,800
PU Long Bed	3,300	3,800
PU SR5	3,400	3,900
PU SR5 (Long Bed)	3,400	3,900
Landcruiser		
2D HT	3,800	4,600
4D St. Wgn.	4,500	5,300
1975		
COROLLA 4 Cyl. 93.3″ W.B.		
2 Door Sedan	1500	1900
2 Door Deluxe Sedan	1500	1900
4 Door Deluxe Sedan	1600	2000
2 Door Hardtop	1700	2100
4 Door Station Wagon	1800	2200
SR-5 2 Dr HT (5 Spd Trans.)	1900	2300
CORONA 4 Cyl. 98.4″ W.B.		
2 Door Deluxe KD Sedan	1800	2200
4 Door Sedan	1300	2200
4 Door Station Wagon	1900	2300
2 Door Hardtop Automatic	2000	2400
SR-5 2 Door HT (5 Spd Trans.)	2000	2400
CELICA 4 Cyl. 95.5″ W.B.		
2 Door Coupe	1800	2200
ST Hardtop	1900	2300
GT Hardtop (5 Spd Trans.)	2000	2400
Mark II 6 Cyl. 101.7″ W.B.		
4 Door Sedan Automatic	2500	3000
2 Door Hardtop Automatic	2500	3000
4 Door Station Wagon Automatic	2700	3200
PICKUPS 4 Cyl.		
101.6″ W.B. (Exc. Longbed)		
110″ W.B. (Longbed)		

Model & Body Type	Wholesale Price	Retail Price
2 Door Pickup	1800	2100
2 Door Long-Bed Pickup	1900	2300
SR-5 Spt Truck (5 Spd Trans.)	2000	2400
LAND CRUISER 6 Cyl.		
90″ W.B. (Exc. Wgn)		
106.3″ W.B. (Wgn)		
Softtop	2300	2700
Hardtop	2400	2800
Station Wagon	2800	3300
1974		
COROLLA 4 Cyl. 91.9″ W.B.		
1200 2 Door Sedan	1300	1600
1600 2 Door Sedan	1500	1800
1600 4 Door Sedan	1600	1900
1600 2 Door Coupe	1700	2000
1600 2 Door Wagon	1700	2000
CORONA 4 Cyl.		
98.4″ W.B. (Exc. Mark II)		
101.8″ W.B. (Mark II)		
2 Door Sedan	1600	1900
4 Door Sedan	1200	2000
2 Door Hardtop	1700	2000
4 Door Wagon	1800	2100
Mark II 4 Door Sedan	1800	2100
Mark II 2 Door Hardtop	2000	2300
Mark II 4 Door Wagon	2100	2400
CELICA 4 Cyl. 95.5″ W.B.		
ST 2 Door Coupe	2000	2300
GT 2 Door Coupe	2100	2400
HI-LUX 4 Cyl. 101.7″ W.B.		
2 Door Pickup Truck	1700	2000
LAND CRUISER 6 Cyl.		
90″ W.B. (Exc. Wgn)		
106.3″ W.B. (Wgn)		
2 Door Softtop	2200	2500
2 Door Hardtop	2500	2800
4 Door Wagon	2800	3100

Model & Body Type	Wholesale Price	Retail Price
1973		
COROLLA 4 Cyl. 91.9" W.B.		
1200 2 Door Sedan	900	1200
1600 2 Door Sedan	1100	1400
1600 4 Door Sedan	1100	1400
1600 2 Door Coupe	1200	1500
1600 2 Door Wagon	1200	1500
CORONA 4 Cyl.		
95.7" W.B. (Sedn & Hdtp)		
101.8" W.B. (Mark II)		
4 Door Sedan	1200	1500
2 Door Hardtop	1300	1600
4 Door Wagon	1400	1700
Mark II 4 Door Sedan	1400	1700
Mark II 2 Door Hardtop	1500	1800
Mark II 4 Door Wagon	1600	1900
CELICA ST 4 Cyl. 95.5" W.B.		
2 Door Sport Coupe	1500	1800
HI-LUX 4 Cyl. 101.8" W.B.		
2 Door Pickup Truck	1300	1600
LAND CRUISER 6 Cyl.		
90" W.B. (Exc. Wgn)		
106.3" W.B. (Wgn)		
2 Door Softtop	2100	2600
2 Door Hardtop	2200	2800
4 Door Wagon	1600	3200
1972		
COROLLA 4 Cyl. 91.9" W.B.		
1200 2 Door Sedan	700	800
1600 2 Door Sedan	700	800
1600 4 Door Sedan	800	900
1600 2 Door Coupe	800	900
1600 2 Door Wagon	900	1200
CORONA 4 Cyl.		
95.7" W.B. (Exc. Mark II)		
98.8" W.B. (Mark II)		
4 Door Sedan	900	1000
2 Door Hardtop	1000	1100
Mark II 4 Door Sedan	1100	1200
Mark II 2 Door Hardtop	1100	1200
Mark II 4 Door Wagon	1200	1300

Model & Body Type	Wholesale Price	Retail Price
CELICA ST 4 Cyl. 95.5″ W.B.		
2 Door Sport Coupe	1200	1500
HI-LUX 4 Cyl. 99.8″ W.B.		
2 Door Pickup Truck	1200	1500
LAND CRUISER 6 Cyl.		
90″ W.B. (Exc. Wgn)		
106.3″ W.B. (Wgn)		
2 Door Softtop	1600	2100
2 Door Hardtop	1800	2300
4 Door Wagon	2200	2700
1971		
COROLLA 4 Cyl. 91.9″ W.B.		
2 Door Sedan	500	700
Sprinter Coupe	600	800
2 Door Wagon	600	800
1600 2 Door Sedan	600	800
1600 4 Door Sedan	600	800
1600 2 Door Coupe	600	800
1600 2 Door Wagon	700	900
CORONA 4 Cyl.		
95.7″ W.B. (Exc. Mark II)		
98.8″ W.B. (Mark II)		
4 Door Sedan	700	900
2 Door Hardtop	800	1000
Mark II 4 Door Sedan	700	900
Mark II 2 Door Hardtop	800	1000
Mark II 4 Door Wagon	900	1100
CROWN 6 Cyl. 105.9″ W.B.		
4 Door Sedan	1000	1200
4 Door Wagon	1200	1400
HI-LUX 4 Cyl. 98.8″ W.B.		
2 Door Pickup	900	1100
LAND CRUISER 6 Cyl.		
90″ W.B. (Exc. Wgn.)		
106.3″ W.B. (Wgn)		
2 Door Softtop	1200	1500
2 Door Hardtop	1500	1800
4 Door Wagon	1800	2100

Model & Body Type	Wholesale Price	Retail Price
1970		
COROLLA 4 Cyl. 90″ W.B.		
2 Door Sedan	300	500
Sprinter Coupe	400	600
2 Door Wagon	400	600
CORONA 4 Cyl.		
95.3″ W.B. (Exc. Mark II)		
98.8″ W.B. (Mark II)		
4 Door Sedan	500	700
2 Door Hardtop	600	800
Mark II 4 Door Sedan	600	800
Mark II 2 Door Hardtop	700	900
Mark II 4 Door Wagon	800	1000
LAND CRUISER 6 Cyl.		
90″ W.B. (Exc. Wgn)		
106.3″ W.B. (Wgn)		
2 Door Softtop	1100	1500
2 Door Hardtop	1300	1700
4 Door Wagon	1500	1900

SWEDISH IMPORTED CARS

Saab

Since 1961, Saab has been selling its Swedish economy car in the United States as a direct competitor to the highly publicized Volvo. Despite its early start, however, Saab has never been recognized by the North American motoring public as a credible alternative to the Volvo. In fact, some motoring magazines have characterized the early Saab owners as "intellectuals" and "misfits."

Actually, Saab is a much better car than the Volvo, especially in view of the rapid decline in Volvo quality since 1972. Gas mileage is excellent, and driving performance is everything one would expect in a European car. As with the Volvo, Saab has a rapid depreciation rate, but due to Saab's lower initial cost, the total financial loss is minimized.

Servicing is one major deficiency reported by Saab owners. Because of its small franchised dealer network, Saab of Sweden and its North American importers have been criticized by Saab owners for concentrating on the sale of new vehicles while used-vehicle servicing is neglected. The Washington-based Center for Auto Safety has been petitioned by one group of irate Saab owners for help in resolving what the owners' group collectively calls their "Saab story."

Saab has many of the same quality-control defects with its malfunctioning carburetor and electrical system as the Volvo. Owners report, though, that the manufacturer is very liberal in applying the warranty, even if the mileage or period of ownership warranty limitations have been exceeded.

The Saab has been criticized in this report by using the Volvo as a benchmark for comparison. This is unfair because the Saab must succeed or fail on its own merits. The Volvo comparison was unavoidable, though, because many motorists compare the two companies as a result of their common origin.

The Saab is a recommended new-car buy only for those motorists who plan to keep their vehicles five years or more. Anything less than that would be a losing proposition with Saab, as with most other European makes.

SAAB
AREAS OF PREMATURE RUSTING

All Models (1974 to 1975)

Major Recall Campaigns
Saab—Scania of America, Incorporated

Make	Model	Model Year	Brief Description of Defect (Manufacturer's Corrective Action)	Number of Pages on File	Number of Vehicles Recalled
Saab	95 and 96	1970	Possibility that fuel line to carburetor is improperly connected. This could allow fuel line to become unattached at carburetor causing fuel pump to push fuel onto hot engine manifold.	3	6,648
Saab	99	1971	Possibility that steering rack ball joints were improperly heat treated. Lack of treatment could cause loose steering after period of use. Excessive wear on rack ball joints could possibly result in loss of steering control.	4	1,221

Make	Model	Model Year	Brief Description of Defect (Manufacturer's Corrective Action)	Number of Pages on File	Number of Vehicles Recalled
Saab-Scania	95 and 96	1970 thru 1973	Possibility that under conditions of high ambient temperature, windshield could become separated from frame in high impact frontal collison. (Correct by installing windshield to withstand frontal collision to meet requirements of FVMSS No. 212.)	4	12,126
Saab	99E	1970 thru 1973	Possibility that pressurized fuel hoses and injector connecting hoses may be susceptible to deterioration after extended use, thus leading to fuel leakage and possibility of engine compartment fire. In some cases injectors have exhibited fuel leakage during cold start.	13	21,038
	99LE, EMS	1973			

Used Car Prices (Approximate)
Saab

Model & Body Type	Wholesale Price	Retail Price
1978		
2 Door (99 L2M)	$5400	$6000
2 Door (99 GL2M)	5700	6300
3 Door (99 GL3M)	6000	7000
3 Door AT/PS (99 GL3A)	6300	7400
5D Sedan (99 GL5M)	6300	7400
5D AT/PS (99 GL5A)	6700	7800
5D GLE Trim (99 GLEM)	6700	7800
5D GLE Trim AT/PS (99 GLEA)	7000	8200
3D EMS Trim (99 EMS)	6700	7900
Turbo	8500	10000
1977		
Sedan 2D	4500	5200
Sedan 4D	4700	5400
Sedan 3D	4800	5500
Sedan 5D	5000	5700
Sedan 2D	5000	5700
Sedan 4D	5500	6200
1976		
Saab		
2 Door Sedan	3600	4100
4 Door Sedan	3700	4200
3D Wgnback	4000	4500
2 Door Sedan EMS	4100	4600
1975		
99 4 Cyl. 97.75″ W.B.		
LE 2 Door Sedan	$2800	$3300
LE 4 Door Sedan	2900	3400
LE 3 Door Wagonback	3000	3500
EMS 2 Door Sedan	3000	3500
1974		
4 Cyl. 97.4″ W.B.		
99LE 2 Door Sedan	2100	2500
99LE 4 Door Sedan	2200	2600
99LE 3 Door Hatchback	2300	2700
99EMS 2 Door Sedan	2200	2600
97 Sonett III	2100	2500

Model & Body Type	Wholesale Price	Retail Price
1973		
4 Cyl. 98.3″ W.B.		
96 2 Door Sedan	1000	1300
95 2 Door Station Wagon	1200	1500
97 Sonett III	1800	2100
99 2 Door Sedan	1500	1800
99L 2 Door Sedan	1700	2000
99LE 2 Door Sedan	1800	2100
99L 4 Door Sedan	1700	2000
99LE 4 Door Sedan	1800	2100
99EMS 2 Door Sedan	2100	2400
1972		
4 Cyl. 98.3″ W.B.		
96 2 Door Sedan	700	1000
95 2 Door Station Wagon	900	1200
99 2 Door Sedan	1200	1500
99E 2 Door Sedan	1400	1700
99E 4 Door Sedan	1500	1800
97 Sonett	1500	1800
1971		
4 Cyl. 98.3″ W.B.		
96 2 Door Sedan	400	700
95 2 Door Wagon	600	900
99E 2 Door Sedan	900	1200
99E 4 Door Sedan	900	1200
97 Sonett III	1200	1500
1970		
4 Cyl. 98.3″ W.B. (95, 96)		
97.5″ W.B. (99)		
84.6″ W.B. (Sonett)		
96 2 Door Sedan	100	400
95 2 Door Wagon	300	600
99 2 Door Sedan	600	900
97 Sonett III	800	1100

Volvo

By directing much of its advertising to what it calls the "leisure class" and arrogantly boasting of its engineering refinements, Volvo provides potential customers with a preview of its attitude, which has turned many Volvo owners sour on Volvo.

Owners complain of repeated mechanical failures involving the carburetor (hard starting and excessive fuel consumption), electrical system (tune-ups are often a monthly affair), and a fuel-injection system by Bosch that leaks gasoline to such an extent that the National Highway Traffic Safety Administration has ordered that the problem be investigated to determine if a safety-related defect exists.

Up until 1971, Volvo had one of the best reputations in North America for providing its customers with well-built cars, and for providing a strong warranty to cover what small defects might have cropped up. But, time marches on, and Volvo's customer-relations policies and reputation have since changed dramatically. Owners complain that Volvo's warranty is no longer as liberal in practice as it once was, and what free warranty service is provided is handed out like food stamps to indigents.

Because of quality-control problems, Volvo has extended the guarantee on the fuel-injection assembly and carburetor for 36,000 miles without restriction to first owners. Some used Volvos, like the 140 series, may make excellent used-car buys as long as the pre-1971 models are chosen. Later models had serious problems with the brakes, clutch, chronic stalling, and a general lack of power.

Best Models

Volvo 122 1969–1970

Worst Models

Volvo 140 and 240 Series 1972–1976

VOLVO
AREAS OF PREMATURE RUSTING

All Sedans (1970 to 1973)

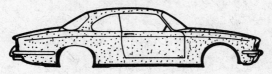

Major Recall Campaigns
Volvo of America Corporation

Make	Model	Model Year	Brief Description of Defect	Number of Pages on File	Number of Vehicles Recalled
Volvo	142, 144, 145 Fitted with evaporation	1970	Possibility that paper covered hot air hose used for evaporation system may catch on fire.	9	17,000
Volvo	142, 144 145, 164 182, 183	1968 thru 1972	Possibility that throttle control cable inner wire may become frayed and possibly cause throttle to become stuck in partially-open position. If condition exists, vehicle would become difficult to control.	7	39,943
Volvo	142, 144 145	1973 1974	Possibility that accelerator pedal lever could be of such design that rubber accessory floor mat or vehicle carpet could retard pedal's normal return to idle position.	11	17,523

Make	Model	Model Year	Brief Description of Defect	Number of Pages on File	Number of Vehicles Recalled
Volvo	242 244 245	1975	Possibility that insufficient torque was applied during assembly which could allow bolt to become separated from steering shaft coupling. Condition would result in reduction of steering precision and ultimately in loss of steering control.	5	10,000
Volvo	142, 144 & 145	1975	Possibility that fuel supply hose connecting fuel supply pipe to cold start valve (injector) on certain fuel injected models could have incorrect inside diameter which in turn could result in eventual fatigue and possible fuel leakage. If fuel leakage does occur, there is danger of fire starting in engine compartment.	2	12,000

Model & Body Type	Wholesale Price	Retail Price
1978		
*Does not include destination charges		
Sedan 2D 4-Sp. (242)	$5400	$6600
Sedan 2D Auto. & Power (242)	5900	7100
Sedan 2D Overdrive, Sunroof (242)	6100	7400
Sedan 2D GT Overdrive (242)	6600	8000
Sedan 2D Auto. & Power (Calif.) (242)	6800	8300
Sedan 4D (244)	5900	7100
Sedan 4D Auto. & Power (244)	6300	7600
Sedan 4D Overdrive, Sunroof (244)	6600	7900
Sedan 4D Auto., Sunroof & Power (244)	6600	7900
Wgn. 4D w/Power (245)	6200	7500
Wgn. 4D Auto. & Power (245)	6500	7800
Wgn. 4D Overdrive & Power (245)	6400	7700
Sedan 4D (264GLA)	8000	9800
Sdn. 2-D Auto. & Power (262)	11700	14700
Sdn. 4D Grand Luxe Auto. & Power (264)	8300	10200
Sdn. 4D Grand Luxe Auto. & Power (Sunroof) (264)	8600	10600
Wgn. 4D Grand Luxe Auto. & Power (265)	8500	10500
Sedan 4D (Sunroof) (264GLA)	8300	11200
Wagon 2D (265)	8100	10000
1977		
Volvo		
Sedan 4D 244	4900	5500
Sedan 2D 242	4700	5300
Station Wagon 4D 245	5500	6100
Sedan 4D 264GL	6000	7000
Sta. Wgn. 4D 265 GL	6100	7100
1976		
Volvo		
242 2D Sedan	3900	4500
244 4D Sedan	3700	4300
245 5D Wagon	4100	4700

Model & Body Type	Wholesale Price	Retail Price
262GL 2 Dr. Sedan	5800	6400
264 4D Sedan	5000	5600
264GL 4D Sedan	5300	5900
265 5D Station Wagon	5300	5900
1975		
242 4 Cyl. 104″ W.B.		
242 2 Door Sedan	2600	3100
244 4 Door Sedan	2700	3200
245 4 Door Station Wagon	2800	3300
164 6 Cyl. 107″ W.B.		
4 Door Sedan	3800	4300
1974		
142 SERIES 4 Cyl. 103″ W.B.		
142 2 Door Sedan	2000	2400
144 4 Door Sedan	2200	2600
145 5 Door Wagon	2200	2600
164E SERIES 6 Cyl. 107″ W.B.		
5 Door Wagon	2900	3400
1973		
142 & 1800 SERIES 4 Cyl.		
103″ W.B. (Exc. 1800)		
96.5″ W.B. (1800)		
142E 2 Door Sedan	1500	1800
144E 4 Door Sedan	1600	1900
145 4 Door Wagon	1700	2000
1800 ES Coupe (Auto. Trans.)	2500	3000
164E SERIES 6 Cyl. 107″ W.B.		
4 Door Sedan (Auto. Trans.)	2400	2700
1972		
142 & 1800 SERIES 4 Cyl.		
103.2″ W.B. (Exc. 1800)		
96.5″ W.B. (1800)		
142 2 Door Coupe	1200	1400
142E 2 Door Coupe	1300	1500
144 4 Door Sedan	1200	1400
145 4 Door Wagon	1400	1600
180E Coupe	2000	2300
1800 ES Wagon	2200	2500
164 SERIES 6 Cyl. 107.1″ W.B.		
4 Door Sedan	1900	2100
164E 4 Door Sedan	2100	2300

Model & Body Type	Wholesale Price	Retail Price
1971		
142 & 1800 SERIES 4 Cyl.		
102.4″ W.B. (Exc. 1800)		
103.1″ W.B. (1800)		
142 2 Door Sedan	900	1100
142E 2 Door Sedan	1000	1200
144 4 Door Sedan	900	1100
145 4 Door Wagon	1100	1300
1800 E Coupe	1600	2000
164 SERIES 6 Cyl. 106.3″ W.B.		
164 4 Door Sedan	1500	1800
1970		
142 & 1800 SERIES 4 Cyl.		
102.4″ W.B. (Exc. 1800)		
96.5″ W.B. (1800)		
142 2 Door Sedan	500	600
144 4 Door Sedan	500	600
145 4 Door Wagon	700	800
1800 E Coupe	1300	1700
122S 2 Door Sedan	500	700
164 SERIES 6 Cyl. 106.3″ W.B.		
164 4 Door Sedan	1000	1300

STANDARD EQUIPMENT: 240 Series: *Antenna, w/s mounted brakes, power assisted 4 wheel disc; Carpeting, full interior; Cigar lighter; Clock, quartz; Console, center; Defroster, elect. rear window; Engine: 4 cyl., 130″, 104 h.p. fuel injection; Glass, tinted; Glove box, locking; Ignition, solid state; Lights, warning; Mirror, day/nite R/V; Seats, reclining bucket frt.; Stereo speakers; Tires, steel belted radial CR14 WSW (Seds.), DR14 WSW (Wags.); Trim, cloth (Seds.), Vinyl (Wags.); Undercoating, two applications; Wipers, elect. rear window (Wagons).*

264 & 265 GL: *(In Addition to or in Place of 240 Equipment): Air conditioning; Carpeted trunk (Sed.); Engine: V6, 162″, 127 h.p. fuel injection; Lights, trunk & engine*